RICK CSIERNIK and
RACHEL BIRNBAUM

PRACTISING
SOCIAL WORK RESEARCH

Case Studies for Learning | Second Edition

Research skills are as critical to social work practitioners as skills in individual and group counselling, policy analysis, and community development. Adopting strategies similar to those used in direct practice courses, this book integrates research with social work practice, and in so doing promotes an understanding and appreciation of the research process.

This second edition of *Practising Social Work Research* comprises twenty-three case studies that illustrate different research approaches, including quantitative, qualitative, single-subject, and mixed methods. Six are new to this edition, and examine research with First Nations, organizing qualitative data, and statistics. Through these real-life examples, the authors demonstrate the processes of conceptualization, operationalization, sampling, data collection and processing, and implementation. Designed to help the student and practitioner become more comfortable with research procedures, *Practising Social Work Research* capitalizes on the strengths that social work students bring to assessment and problem solving.

RICK CSIERNIK is a professor in the King's University College School of Social Work at Western University.

RACHEL BIRNBAUM is a professor in the King's University College School of Social Work at the Western University.

RICK CSIERNIK and
RACHEL BIRNBAUM

PRACTISING SOCIAL WORK RESEARCH

Case Studies for Learning | Second Edition

UNIVERSITY OF TORONTO PRESS
Toronto Buffalo London

ISBN 978-1-4875-0226-3 (cloth)
ISBN 978-1-4875-2015-1 (paper)

∞ Printed on acid-free, 100% post-consumer recycled paper with vegetable-based inks.

Library and Archives Canada Cataloguing in Publication

Csiernik, Rick, author
Practising social work research : case studies for learning/Rick Csiernik and Rachel Birnbaum. –
Second edition.

Includes bibliographical references and index.
ISBN 978-1-4875-0226-3 (cloth). ISBN 978-1-4875-2015-1 (paper)

1. Social service – Research.   2. Social service – Case studies.   I. Birnbaum, Rachel, 1954–, author
II. Title.

HV11.C79 2017   361.3072   C2016-907699-7

University of Toronto Press acknowledges the financial assistance to its publishing program
of the Canada Council for the Arts and the Ontario Arts Council, an agency of the Government
of Ontario.

University of Toronto Press acknowledges the financial support of the Government of Canada
through the Canada Book Fund for its publishing activities.

**Canada Council
for the Arts** **Conseil des Arts
du Canada**

**ONTARIO ARTS COUNCIL
CONSEIL DES ARTS DE L'ONTARIO**
an Ontario government agency
un organisme du gouvernement de l'Ontario

Funded by the   Financé par le
Government gouvernement
of Canada   du Canada

Contents

List of Tables   ix

List of Figures   xi

Preface   xiii

Acknowledgments   xvii

About the Authors   xix

1. INTRODUCTION   3

The Case Study Method   3
The Research Process   7

2. PROBLEM SOLVING: BRIEF CASE STUDIES   17

Introduction: Steps in the Process of Research   17

Identifying the Problem

    CASE STUDY 1: Research and the Media: What Are You Being Told?   21

Ethics: Ensuring No Harm Comes to Participants

    CASE STUDY 2: A Question of Ethics: Willowbrook   33

    CASE STUDY 3: Another Question of Ethics: Studying HIV   47

    CASE STUDY 4: Ethical Issues of Obtaining Consent to Interview Children in
                      Post-Separation Disputes   57

    CASE STUDY 5: Respectful Ethical Research Practice: Working with
                      First Nations, Inuit, Innu, and Metis Peoples   68

Preparation: Conceptualizing, Operationalizing, and Sampling

CASE STUDY 6: Understanding Ideas and Counting Them   79

CASE STUDY 7: Implementing a Pilot Project: A Question of Sampling   88

CASE STUDY 8: Who Do You Ask? Sampling in a Qualitative Context   101

Research Methods

CASE STUDY 9: Criminal Justice Issues in Social Work Research: The Search for Causality   108

CASE STUDY 10: Psychometric Properties: How Should We Measure?   119

CASE STUDY 11: The Validity of Research   132

CASE STUDY 12: The Application of Quasi-experimental Design in Social Work Research   144

CASE STUDY 13: The Power of One: Single-Case Study Design   152

CASE STUDY 14: One More: Another Example of Single-Case Study Design   164

CASE STUDY 15: Asking Questions Properly: An Examination of Questionnaire Design   171

CASE STUDY 16: Asking Questions in Child Advocacy: Which Approach Is Best for Children?   196

CASE STUDY 17: What Does It All Mean? Qualitative Interviews with Children about Their Views and Experiences of Family Justice Professionals   209

CASE STUDY 18: Q & Q: Employing Both a Qualitative and a Quantitative Approach   222

CASE STUDY 19: On PAR: Engaging and Empowering Clients through Participatory Action Research   230

Data Collection and Statistical Analysis

CASE STUDY 20: Measuring Client Satisfaction: Do They Like Me?   248

CASE STUDY 21: Statistics: Adding Some Numbers   256

CASE STUDY 22: Descriptive Statistics: The First Step from Guessing to Knowing   265

CASE STUDY 23: Inferring What You Know: Selecting an Appropriate Statistical Test   274

3. CRITIQUING RESEARCH 285

Introduction 285
Critical Analysis of Qualitative Research 289
Critical Analysis of Quantitative Research 290

A Qualitative Design: Surviving the Tornado: Psychiatric Survivor Experiences
of Getting, Losing, and Keeping Housing 294
Cheryl Forchuk, Catherine Ward-Griffin, Rick Csiernik, and Katherine Turner

Critique 305
Rachel Birnbaum

A Quantitative Design: An Examination of Two Different Approaches to
Visitation-Based Disputes in Child Custody Matters 309
Rachel Birnbaum

Critique 332
Barbara Decker Pierce and Rick Csiernik

Index 339

List of Tables

1a	The Research Process	8
1b	Ethics and Research Role	14
2	Steps in the Research Process	17
2.3	Teleological versus Deontological Ethics	53
2.6a	Conceptualization and Operationalization	82
2.6b	Measurement Instruments	83
2.6c	Levels of Measurement	83
2.7a	School Social Work Staff – Academic Qualifications	95
2.7b	Comparison of Probability Sampling Approaches	96
2.8	Non-Probability Sampling Options	103
2.10	Approaches to Testing Validity	126
2.11	Threats to Validity	134
2.13	Violet's Data	156
2.14	Goal Attainment Scale for Play	167
2.17a	Codes Developed with Each Transcript	217
2.17b	Risks, Benefits, and Considerations for Children's Participation	218
2.18a	Comparing Quantitative and Qualitative Research	224
2.18b	Quantitative and Qualitative Research Equivalents	225
2.21a	Reported Poll Results: Percentage	260
2.21b	Actual Poll Results: Considering Standard Error	260
2.22a	Raw Data	267
2.22b	Descriptive Statistics Summary	271
2.23	Participant Characteristics	276
3a	Attrition in Child Behaviour Problems and Non-Responders and Responders by Type of Evaluation Intervention	319
3b	Attrition in Child Behaviour Problems by Type of Evaluation Intervention	320
3c	Positive Parent Comments Related to Each Evaluation Intervention	321
3d	Negative Parent Comments Related to Each Evaluation Intervention	321
3e	Children's Themes Related to Each Evaluation Intervention	322

List of Figures

2.2a	King's University College Ethics Protocol Submission Form	36
2.2b	Smith College School for Social Work Human Subjects Review Application	39
2.4a	Children's Participation in Separation and/or Divorce Processes: Information for Youth	61
2.4b	Children's Participation in Separation and/or Divorce Processes: Consent Form for Youth	62
2.4c	Children's Participation in Separation and/or Divorce Processes: Information for Parents	63
2.4d	Children's Participation in Separation and/or Divorce Processes: Consent Form for Parents	64
2.9a	Relationship between Variables – Confounding Variable	113
2.9b	Positive Relationship	114
2.9c	Negative (Inverse) Relationship	115
2.9d	Curvilinear Relationship	116
2.13a	Malcolm's School Attendance during Intervention	153
2.13b	Malcolm's School Attendance after Intervention	154
2.13c	Violet's Graph	157
2.13d	Violet's Chart – ABA Design	158
2.14	N'dina's Average Hourly Vocalizations	166
2.15a	A Questionnaire to Critique	172
2.15b	Fixed-Alternative Question	177
2.15c	A Problematic Question	177
2.15d	Open-Ended Question	178
2.15e	Possible Ambiguity	178
2.15f	The Good Agency	179
2.15g	Scale of Social Isolation	181
2.15h	Normalizing Questions	184
2.15i	Example of Matrix Format	184

2.15j	Contingency Question	185
2.15k	Consent Form	187
2.15l	Formal Questionnaire	188
2.17a	Children's Experiences with Family Justice Professionals	216
2.17b	Visual Representation of Coding	217
2.19	The Process of Participatory Action Research	235
2.20a	Example of a Custom-Designed Questionnaire	252
2.20b	CSQ – 8	252
2.21	Normal Distribution	258
2.23	Correlation	279
3	Three Overlapping Phases of Destruction within the Tornado of Mental Illness	297

Preface

Research is what we do in order to better understand our situation. There is a reciprocal relationship between research and practice. The primary purpose of research is the development of new knowledge and understanding to assist us in knowing something that was not previously known and to use this knowledge to inform practice.

Social work practitioner-researchers apply research knowledge, practice and skill to their social work practice. In turn, they incorporate research processes into their regular social work activities to improve their practice and enhance the assistance provided to clients and client systems. This inquiry may be in the form of systematic reflection, through following the progress of individual clients/groups/communities or through more formalized research processes such as evaluation or program designs. Being a social work practitioner-researcher also entails reading research studies and reports, reflecting about practice and research, being an informed consumer of research and becoming a critical thinker.

– Statement of Educational Philosophy, Master of Social Work Program, King's University College at Western University

In the spring of 2002, Barbara Decker Pierce and I (Rachel Birnbaum) had a conversation about the difficulties in teaching social work research methods to social work students. The texts used and the approach taken to teaching research methodology seemed unrelated to the real world of research and pedagogical approaches; as a result our students were feeling disconnected from the material and its application to practices with vulnerable, oppressed, and diverse populations in community, administration, and policy. The students had to take the course, as it was a requirement, but it was their least favourite at the undergraduate and graduate levels.

I brought to the conversation reflections on my past experience in which I had shared with my students the trials and tribulations of working on my dissertation in the real world. They laughed (my past tears) as I told them of government strikes at the time, families that would not complete forms, social workers who would not always follow clearly laid out protocols, and teachers who did not want to fill out questionnaires.

As I told them my story, I noticed that they began to grasp connections between the research design and the results and limitations of the study. While my reminiscences did make an amusing story, I noticed something more important: the students began asking questions, and engaging with the material, in a way that they had not previously. They talked about real clients, how organizations work and do not work, and about the policy implications of a particular piece of research. Using the dissertation as a case example spoke to them and, in turn, they were learning about research.

I raised the issue with Barbara about teaching research using case studies. Barbara was very much interested in this conversation, as she had a business management background and thought case studies as tool made perfect sense; she too had experienced similar frustrations in teaching research. In fact, she had already written and published several case-based studies in management, though not on social work. The more we talked the more we refined our ideas about a cased-based approach to teaching research methods. Next, we gave a presentation at the 2002 Social Sciences and Humanities Congress, receiving a positive response and encouragement to write an article about the topic. We then decided to try the approach out in a research class for undergraduate social work students in 2003. However, our initial results were mixed and we found little difference in student achievement, as measured by their grades, using a case-based approach versus the traditional teaching model, partly because the sample was very small. The irony of this, considering the topic, was not lost on us, but it gave us more fuel to keep talking about the idea and its application. Barbara then happened to mention to Rick Csiernik her thoughts about this approach and our pilot trial at King's University College.

Unknown to us, Rick had been using vignettes in teaching social work research for several years prior to joining the faculty at King's University College, drawing upon his experiences as a community-based social work researcher at both the Hamilton Social Planning and Research Council and the Addiction Research Foundation. He had also incorporated examples of research found in the popular press that had a social work orientation, research that discussed outcomes but did not relate how the findings were derived and thus resulted in an incomplete presentation of the research process. However, he had never developed an overarching theoretical foundation for his approach, but instead had based his teaching upon principles derived from community development and adult education. Upon joining the faculty at King's he had the opportunity to teach a variety of courses but not research. However, with the development of a new graduate studies program, the first to be offered by King's University College, he had begun to revisit his previous case studies in preparation for teaching the new MSW Practice Research course. He thought that the research that Barbara and I had been doing would be a natural fit: why not merge our ideas, experiences, and approaches into a book that took a novel approach to teaching research, an approach that would be more practice orientated and draw upon the strengths social work students brought to the academic environment? So our mutual interests in research, though evolved through quite different paths, began to come together over several years while we lived in three different cities but taught in the same School of Social Work. However, that story is for another book yet to be written.

After the first edition of the book was published it received a few favourable reviews and, like most research books, was purchased primarily by libraries and then languished on the back pages of the publisher's catalogue. But then a curious phenomenon occurred. A few years after its release book sales began slowly to increase and continued to increase, a rarity on any topic, let alone social work research. A few brave and bold professors had found the book; they noted that as promised on the back cover it was in fact a nontraditional approach and that students did find this process more engaging than traditional books, as the contents promised. This sequence of fortunate events led to the production of this second edition. Like the first edition, this book does not pronounce on whether there is a single truth or answer questions about the nature of reality, but it will demonstrate that what social workers do in their practice can be known and does, in all its many forms, constitute evidence. Every social work student who becomes a social work practitioner can also be a social work researcher and thus a knower who is capable of distinguishing between belief, assumption, and fact.

Some of the brief case studies that comprise Section 2 are based upon published articles or news stories, others are adaptations, amalgams, or variations of actual research involving several cases, and some are theoretical illustrations presented to illuminate a particular research issue, at times with tongue slightly in cheek. Six new case studies have been added to enhance the first edition, and now each case study is accompanied not only by a revised additional reading section but also by links to Internet sources to further support the theoretical ideas that underlie each case study. The two case inclusions in Section 3 are actual research products that have been selected to reflect different types of social work research. They illustrate the process of research while also indicating that the ultimate pursuit of research is not perfection, but rather the generation and sharing of knowledge. We hope that you will find this approach useful in acquiring knowledge of research methods and, more importantly, we hope that this text provides you with an enthusiasm for social work research and what it can be and can do, an enthusiasm that we feel and share.

Rick Csiernik, Hamilton, Ontario
Rachel Birnbaum, Toronto, Ontario
October 2016

Acknowledgments

Writing a research book for social workers is a daunting task, as there are so many varied thoughts on what social work research even is or should be and audiences that we wanted to speak to. We thank our reviewers of both editions for helping us to refine our own thinking, and especially our students, who patiently listened, tried out our vignettes and approaches, and provided invaluable feedback to us over the last few years. We also want to thank Virgil Duff for his patience and genuine interest in working with us on the first edition, Stephen Shapiro for shepherding us through production of the second, and Barbie Halaby, who provided excellent editing and proofreading; of course, any mistakes are our own. Many thanks to Marsha Kline Pruett for permission to print the Smith College School for Social Work Human Subjects Review Application. We are most grateful to King's University College for providing funding that assisted in the initial pilot study. We also wish to thank our families and friends, who listened with an attentive ear, despite the fact that they had to.

Finally, the first edition was painstakingly written, rewritten, revised, and revised again by three, not two, authors. Barbara Decker Pierce, past director of the School of Social Work, King's University College, and now professor emerita, was a core part of the conceptualization, development, and completion of the first edition. Without her ideas and talent a second edition would not have been possible, for there never would have been a first.

About the Authors

RICK CSIERNIK, BSc, BSW, MSW, PhD, RSW, CCAC, is Professor at the School of Social Work, King's University College at Western University. He has previously worked at the McMaster University Medical Centre, the Social Planning and Research Council of Hamilton, and the Addiction Research Foundation of Ontario (now the Centre on Addiction and Mental Health) and for the Ontario Ministry of Correctional Services. Rick has written and edited a dozen books, including *Just Say Know: A Counsellor's Guide to Psychoactive Drugs*; *Homeless, Housing and Mental Health*; *Substance Use and Abuse: Everything Matters*; and *Responding to the Oppression of Addiction*. He has authored over 150 peer-reviewed articles and book chapters and has presented at over 200 national and international conferences, workshops, and seminars. He has been part of research teams that have received over $3 million in funding and has been on the King's University College Honor Role of teaching 16 consecutive times. Rick was the co-developer of the McMaster University Addiction Studies Program, where he has taught for over 25 years, and was inaugural recipient of the McMaster University Instructor Appreciation Award.

RACHEL BIRNBAUM, PhD, RSW, LLM, is Professor cross-appointed in Childhood and Social Institutions (Interdisciplinary Studies) and Social Work at King's University College at Western University, London, Ontario. She has over 25 years of clinical practice experience working with children and families involved in separation and/or divorce. Her research focus is on interdisciplinary scholarship about children's participation post-separation, child legal representation, and access to justice in family law disputes. She has co-authored several books regarding children and post-separation and/or divorce: *Child Custody Assessments: A Resource Guide for Legal and Mental Health Professionals*; *Challenging Issues in Child Custody Disputes: A Guide for Legal and Mental Health Professionals*; and *Law for Social Workers* (with Thomson Reuters). She is the 2014 recipient of the Stanley Cohen Distinguished Research Award, the 2016 recipient of the Hugh Mellon Distinguished Research Award, and a member of the Royal Society of Canada, College of New Scholars, Artists, and Scientists. She was the president of the Ontario College of Social Workers and Social Service Workers for four years, the president of the Canadian Council of Social Work Regulators for two years, and the president of the Association of Family and Conciliation Courts–Ontario, 2015–16.

RICK CSIERNIK and
RACHEL BIRNBAUM

PRACTISING
SOCIAL WORK RESEARCH

Case Studies for Learning | Second Edition

CHAPTER ONE

Introduction

The Case Study Method

Research methodology is an essential pillar of social work practice knowledge. It is also a common area of knowledge to all helping professions and associated post-secondary learners. You will need to draw upon your knowledge and understanding of research in order to support a wide range of activities that comprise a contemporary social work career: direct practice, community work, program development, program evaluation, and policy analysis. Thus, while it is crucial that you take this opportunity to create a strong foundation, the reality is that research methodology has not been a favoured practice area for many social workers. There are several reasons for this. First, the material is often found to be daunting and the content is not taught from a social work orientation, but rather as a course that could be part of almost any related post-secondary discipline. Second, social work research is often associated with dry lectures and incomprehensible figures that do not tell us about the real-life structural barriers affecting our clients. Third, teaching a research course is antithetical to the teaching methodology generally employed in social work education, which engages students in examples and practical applications of theory to life situations.

This book is not intended as a traditional research methodology text suited to a traditional lecture-based course. We cover content similar to that found in traditional methods textbooks, but we adopt an alternative approach. Using this book, you will learn through a process that begins by introducing you to real-world research issues and, through case study descriptions, places you within the environment to resolve the problem and take the appropriate action. Case study analysis should not be done in isolation; rather, it is a mutual, collaborative process, as is an actual research process. Thus, you should use the opportunity to talk about the case you are studying and engage in constructive dialogue with other knowledge seekers. How would they approach the situation? What have they learned that can be helpful to others? Finally, the process, to be complete, requires that you take time to reflect on that process in order to consolidate and integrate the new learning. We believe that students who actively engage in this process of learning not only find research more enjoyable, but are better able to retain what they have learned and are more motivated to engage in actual research critique or activities when opportunities arise.

Why Case-Based Learning?

Those who have experience with case-based learning are impressed by the extent to which this approach alters the power dynamic in the classroom. Students engaged in case discussions become the focus of attention and contribute directly to their learning by participating in discussions that they direct and sustain. Case-based learning is discussion centred and professor facilitated, not instructor imposed; ideas flow from professor to student, from student to professor, and at its best from student to student. Students are empowered to take control of their own learning in a collaborative manner with others who share the same goal of learning new material. Power is more equally shared in the classroom when students have increased control over their role in the learning process. Case-based learning is much more in harmony with the social work profession's long-held values of empowerment and self-determination.

The process of learning with cases is also consistent with the interpretive perspective that knowledge is acquired through social construction, that is, in conversation and dialogue with others (Berger & Luckman, 1991; Corradi, Gherardi, & Verzelloni, 2010; Mulkay, 2014). Dialogue between students and the instructor establishes an appreciation of the situation and the issues facing the decision maker. The methodological concepts that are the focus of the discussion are imbedded in real-world situations and so are more likely to be remembered by students and integrated into their existing knowledge base.

In the commonly used lecture approach, research topics are presented in a customary pattern of methodological concept, followed by explanation, followed by examples, followed by the next concept, the next explanation, and new examples. While the examples are important in achieving student comprehension, they are often de-contextualized when they are presented. Students see little connection to real-world problems, and it is not surprising that they fail to see the relevance of social work research to other professional activities. Research skills are seen as a series of routine and, for many students, uninteresting processes engaged in by technicians: problem definition, literature review, research design, data collection and analysis, compilation of results, dissemination of new knowledge, and action. Those who engage in research practice understand that creating new knowledge involves a complex unfolding of interrelated and often iterative processes that take place within a particular context – that is, it involves connecting methodological knowledge to case situations that can be woven together and told as a story, rather than presented as a disembodied, unrelated set of activities. Telling stories in the form of case studies increases the relevance and meaning of what is being learned and allows participants to struggle with the real-world problems, engaging them more directly in their learning. Education in this manner is inherently interactive, as it occurs between teacher-learner as well as learner-teacher. Rather than memorizing definitions or repeating what the professor dictates, case-based learning establishes a process for interaction and opens a dialogue about learning. Since the fully developed case-study pedagogy provides opportunities for dialogue and reflection on real-world issues, it lends itself to the acquisition of knowledge in this manner. Thus using cases establishes an approach to learning that is equally consistent with constructivism; students are actively involved in the creation of new knowledge for themselves. Acquiring new knowledge in this fashion contributes to increased meaningfulness and enhanced retention of the material. The case-based approach satisfies the learning objectives of educators while at the same time enabling social work students to acquire basic methodological skills for use in any aspect of social work practice.

Using Cases for Learning Research Methodology

Case-based learning has been a key component of other professional education programs, particularly management, medicine, and teaching (Garvin, 2003; Harrington, 1991; Hitt, Ireland, & Hoskisson, 2012; Munn-Giddings & Winter, 2013). Learning from cases is also particularly appropriate when you are preparing to work in the uncertain and ambiguous context of professional social work practice (Austin & Packard, 2009; Jones, 2003).

The case studies prepared for this book are vignettes, centring upon the experience of actual social work researchers or amalgams of several scenarios used to illustrate a specific research issue or dilemma. You will be asked to place yourselves within each social worker's story and participate in resolving the dilemmas encountered in the course of both social work practice and social work research practice. As you make the leap of transferring your practice skills to the research case studies, you will expand your knowledge of research concepts and develop a foundation upon which to construct your own model of social work practice-research. As a vehicle for experiential learning, the case studies will allow you to tackle realistic and challenging issues in an environment where being imperfect is acceptable. Reading the case, thinking about a resolution, and developing a plan of action can provide you with the vicarious experience of being a social work researcher without feeling that you need to be the expert.

The Process of Case-Based Learning

Case-based learning begins with a period of individual student preparation followed by opportunities for guided discussion (Savery, 2015; Thistlethwaite et al., 2012). Start by reading the situation described in the case, identify pertinent information and key concepts, generate and evaluate options for action, and if possible, determine a preferred resolution to the problem. At the end of each case you are provided with a set of discussion questions and additional reading to assist in focusing your thinking and enriching the learning opportunity. After individual preparation you will be ready to share your analysis and engage in a group exploration of the issues, hopefully to learn through collective discourse and individual reflection. In our setting we allot 30 to 45 minutes of a three-hour class to small group discussion, which has been identified as being critical in enhancing student learning (Howe, 2004; Peterson & Miller, 2004). Talking about the case in a small group setting allows for an opportunity for both cooperative and collaborative learning, and it also provides the opportunity to voice your opinions in a setting that is less intimidating when you remain unsure of what you really do know.

The next stage of case-based learning involves a discussion of the case by the entire group. What distinguishes the case-study format from the traditional university research lecture is that the professor functions as a facilitator in order to guide, as occurs in most social work courses, and not to direct the case discussion. The most productive case discussion occurs when the class takes responsibility for building and sustaining the conversation. It should not turn into a Q&A session with the instructor generating the questions and the class looking for the "correct" answer. Instead of being the "expert" who continually lectures, the professor is managing a participative process that involves asking questions, providing encouragement, linking contributions and recording relevant points, managing the flow of the discussion, controlling time, and maintaining order. What results may not be much different from what would have been covered in a traditional lecture except that it is created by you and your classmates through your dialogue and discussion.

The final step in the case-study process is reflection to allow you to consolidate your learning. The tendency is for you as a student to leave the class and move on to your next activity. However, you won't make the best of the classroom experience without some conscious debriefing around the experience. This is a period of individual reflection that allows you to review your individual preparation, your small group session, and the class discussion to come to some conclusions about what transpired and what you learned from it. Review the new concepts that were covered in the class and think about ways to retain this information, to integrate it into your existing understandings of social work practice and the themes from your other courses. Reflection is a key component of adult education (Russell, 2005; Schön, 1983), as it allows learners to gain knowledge of their experiences in life from thinking about them.

The group-based case-study problem-solving approach that we advocate mirrors the research process in several ways. In both processes, you begin by identifying a problem and then generating several viable alternatives. These options are then evaluated; one is ultimately selected and implemented, with an extensive follow-up to assess what the outcome is in relation to the original problem. Depending upon the outcome, you might start all over again at the beginning or move forwards based upon your new knowledge and experience (Zastrow, 2011). As well, the small-group problem-solving process entails extensive brainstorming, which is an important skill for social work research and for both new and seasoned social work research practitioners. Consistently using small groups to examine case studies also serves as a form of social learning that can be used not only in studying research but in practising research both in school and ultimately in the field.

We hope that by providing vicarious experiences in the form of case studies we are preparing the ground for the reflection that is critical to learning. We also hope that the process involves you in active learning in a format more related to teaching methodologies employed in the mainstream social work curriculum. Finally, we hope this approach enables you to read the social work and other professional literature more critically and encourages you to undertake your own research with curiosity, confidence, and expertise.

The Research Process

Research is a process much like any journey that follows a set of steps – the map – guiding researchers – the travellers – to their destination (see Table 1a). While the path may appear quite orderly and direct, from time to time most travellers find themselves jumping ahead, retracing steps, and standing still to process new information and change course. However, when all is said and done, if they follow the path as prescribed they will have completed the journey and reached their goal: a contribution to knowledge to help guide practice and policy. Both quantitative (explaining) and qualitative (exploring) research patterns, despite their differences, go through related processes.

Having said this, context is everything. Social work is living a new reality: "do more with less." That is, see more clients, assist more people, put in more hours that you may not be paid for, and just keep the rhythm moving. One only needs to turn to cutbacks in any social services sector, be it hospitals, child welfare, family justice, or community

Table 1a   The Research Process

Question	Stage	Steps
What will I do?	Finding focus	Identify a purpose Establish the questions Search the literature Refine the questions
How will I do it?	Developing a Plan	Identify a sample Establish a design Develop a protocol
	Implementing the plan	Review the ethics Collect the data
What have I found out?	Drawing conclusions	Analyse the data Interpret the data
What will I do next?	Taking action	Communicate new knowledge Take action

organizations, and witness that social workers are experiencing tremendous pressures as governments are under tight fiscal restraints across North America. This means that social workers, in particular, have little time to process what is happening around them, let alone to think about best practices and to engage in dialogue about research or even to read the empirical literature to keep them abreast of their work.

In the final analysis, the research journey that we talk about requires reflection and time to explore. Enjoy the time you have now as a student to reflect on these cases and be aware that context is everything.

Identify a Purpose

Research has historically been identified as arising from the compelling need to know something; however, it can also arise in response to watching patterns emerge in practice, or through discussion with clients or in response to a social injustice and oppression. Regardless, it has some specific focus. The purpose of much of social work research is to solve problems that are causing concerns for others, though it can also be employed to learn something no one else knows, to respond to a newly identified need of a client that no one else has investigated, or to provide a distinctly social work perspective on an issue. However, it is unethical to carry out research on trivial issues or to use a client's or agency's time on topics that are not relevant. At the same time, it is not a good idea to identify a problem that is too large or is not amenable to research investigation. For example, issues of belief, while often important to explore as part of social work practice, are not typically good research topics. The ideal is to obtain information from the research endeavour that can contribute to the solution of the target problem or that provides a new way of thinking about the situation. Research conducted by social workers is normally applied research. Its purpose is to produce information that is needed to better understand the experience of our clients, to enhance practice or empower our communities, and to improve social policy.

Establish the Question

Once a problem has been identified, the next task is to continue to focus attention until you have identified the "just right" level of analysis. It's a bit like the three bears. You do not want a research project that is so large that it becomes unmanageable, but at the same time you do not want it so focused that it becomes irrelevant. Like Goldilocks, you are hoping to discover the one that's "just right." This comes with practice and through consultation with others, including agency staff and service consumers. The usual place to start is with some broad questions that come to you from your problem of interest. For example, let's say you are interested in the problem of marital dissatisfaction among the elderly. This is an important problem and one that could have increasing impact as the population ages. You could start your focusing activity with general questions such as: What are the characteristics of couples over the age of 75? What is the quality of marriages among elderly people? What does theory tell us about the developmental stage of aging and how this relates to social relationships? As a researcher, you may be starting with relatively little information about the problem that interests you. Looking for answers to these broad questions will help you to fill in your knowledge and may lead you to identify areas that are not well understood. The reality is that unless you target a relatively new problem, others will already be engaged in research in the area. Your task at this stage is it to immerse yourself in the literature to find out what is already known, though there are certainly questions on which little has been written, particularly by social workers. As your knowledge base increases, you can begin to focus more upon what the unanswered questions are and how your work can make a contribution. While reviewing the literature you may find that the nature of the problem changes as you learn more about it, or even that you no longer find the topic of interest. It is important to acknowledge waning enthusiasm if it happens, because the practice of research can become arduous and tiring at times, and the last thing you want is to be working on a topic for which you no longer have a passion.

Search the Literature

Above we used the term "immerse" when we introduced the idea of a literature review. This word was selected intentionally because that's often how you feel: floating in a sea of information and overwhelmed by it. Yet some researchers love it so much they cannot seem to stop, always seeking one more study or one more perspective. Neither situation is conducive to effective research practice. Too much confusion or too much devotion can drown the process. To avoid these potential dangers, we provide you with the following advice on how to manage the literature review process. To begin with, sometimes a researcher starts to look with too narrow a view and concludes that nothing is known about a particular problem. In most situations this is not the case. You need to be creative and open to fully appreciate the scope of the problem or topic. For example, researchers interested in the topic of intimate partner violence may be overwhelmed by the different definitions in the literature used to describe violence in relationships, the polarized discourse on the topic, and the need for more differentiation regarding violence. Yet all the literature in the different areas helps to inform an understanding of the topic. Start from the general and move to the more specific. This applies to the theoretical level as well. Understanding issues of power and control, for example, may help researchers interested in understanding the dynamics of violence, and this insight could be applied to intimate partner violence as well. If a literature review starts from the premise that there is nothing written about the problem, this usually means the researchers have taken too narrow a view.

Modern technology has produced great advances in our ability to identify and retrieve information. Gone are the days of book-based abstracts, library card catalogues, and journals read cover to cover to determine if there is an article related to your topic. Most literature reviews begin with database searches using pertinent keywords. It is common for university or college libraries to offer orientation sessions on how to be efficient in conducting searches. Librarians are keen on helping, since they are experts in this area and see helping students find information as an essential part of their role. There are search strategies you can use to make sure you are not overwhelmed by thousands of unhelpful references, making it difficult to find the few that will meet your information needs. For example, typing "poverty" and "women" into a keyword search on 23 January 2009 in Social Work Abstracts resulted in a listing of 361 references; in Scholar's Portal PsycINFO it produced 10,594 and in Google Scholar 789,000. However, by 23 May 2016 there were 445 Social Work Abstract articles listed for those two terms, 107,491 Scholar's Portal references (the database had expanded beyond only psychology-related journals), and 2,360,000 Google Scholar hits (found in 0.06 seconds). There is probably something of value in there, but finding it will be quite difficult. Knowing which databases to use, choosing strategies for efficient searching, and understanding how best to access the reports you need are key skills for social work researchers.

Searching the databases is a common start to your review, but sometimes it is better to start with more general information, particularly if you are not that familiar with a topic. Databases tend to contain journal article references that can be quite narrow or targeted. If you need a big-picture perspective it might be best to start with an encyclopedia or book that summarizes the area. Most library catalogue systems have a keyword search feature that will lead you to these types of texts. Another broad approach is to use an Internet search engine to seek out sites that address your topic. This is particularly helpful if you are looking for the most current information. It goes without saying, however, that this approach could easily lead again to information overload, and reports obtained from the Internet can be subject to error, unintended and in some cases intended. You need to use good critical judgment concerning what you choose to make note of or report. If you do plan to use information from an Internet site, you will need to record reference information such as the URL of the site and the date of retrieval, since information online is often time sensitive. It is also important to appreciate that Internet searches are only one way of obtaining information and do not always provide the best available evidence-informed information on a particular topic as it is rarely peer reviewed.

Conducting a literature review can be like creating a giant snowball. You start with something very small and build it to much larger proportions. Each activity leads to the next. Much of the literature you find will come from the references and citations of the articles and books that you read. That is why it is a good idea to look for the most current material first. By finding recent work you find a great deal of past information, because each author is building on the past. Sir Isaac Newton, the great seventeenth-century scientist, is famous for saying that "If I have seen farther it is by standing on the shoulders of giants."[1] You should likewise make use of the work of your precursors.

When researchers prepare their findings for publication they begin by writing a summary of what they found during their review of the literature. This section of their report sets the stage for the contributions of the current research. For the most part, the literature cited is derived from sources such as books, journal articles, research monographs, and dissertations. This does not mean that researchers do not derive insight or ideas from less traditional sources such as newspapers, magazines, television programs, documentaries, or conversations with other researchers, but these are not traditionally seen as credible sources for scientific work, particularly in quantitative research.

---

1 In a letter to Robert Hooke, dated 15 February 1676.

Once you have found an item of interest you next need a systematic way of keeping track of it. The key here is *systematic*. Eventually you will acquire a great deal of information, and if you want to be able to retrieve it quickly you will need to rely on a system. There are software packages that some students find helpful, particularly for preparing references. Others continue to rely on pre-technological approaches employing recipe cards or notebooks to record what they find as they progress through the literature. Whichever method you choose, it is vital to be able to connect a quote or idea with its author. If you plan to use a quote or an idea of someone else, you are in danger of committing plagiarism if you do not attribute it properly.

Finding and recording information are key activities of the literature review, but equally important is making critical judgments about what you find. You need to be cautious not only about information found online, but about everything you read. Just because something is written in a book or journal article does not mean it is true. The consumer of research, like all other consumers, needs to beware. Research is a messy process fraught with problems, complications, and limitations, as will be illustrated through the case studies in this book, and the sociology of science has a great influence on what is published and what is not. You need to make your own judgments about what to include and what to ignore, and more importantly to understand what from your standpoint is critical for yourself and for others to know. Do keep in mind that these judgments should be based upon the quality of the research, not on whether the findings agree with your preconceived preferences. It is not ethical to direct your literature review towards only the "truth" as you see it.

Refine the Question

At some point during the review process the researcher begins to obtain an appreciation of what specific questions should drive the research project. These questions are more focused than the ones that started the review, and hopefully will generate new knowledge to inform our understanding of a relevant social work issue. For example, Gladstone (1995) was interested in marital relationships among the elderly, the problem identified above. He decided to narrow his focus from all marital relationships among the elderly to just those of couples affected by institutionalization. From his literature review he concluded that "studies have made few comments on the nature of older marriages in the later stages of life when one or both spouses may be living in a care facility" (p. 52). Therefore, he conducted a study to try and answer the following three questions (p. 53): (1) How do older persons living or having a spouse living in a long-term-care institution perceive their marital relationship? (2) What is the perceived impact of institutional relocation on an older marriage? and (3) In what specific ways do spouses provide support to their husbands or wives when one or both are institutionalized?

Notice how he has narrowed his focus and targeted specific areas to investigate. His questions meet the "just right" criteria. They are not too large nor too trivial, and answering these questions will go far towards helping us understand the experience of spouses whose marriage is affected by institutionalization, a common event requiring social work intervention. When you have finished focusing your attention and have specific questions that need answering, you are ready to proceed to design a study that will help you answer those questions.

Social Workers and Research

An understanding of research methodology and the practice of research are fundamental skills of contemporary social workers. Many of the roles that social workers play require an understanding of research rules, procedures, and practices. According to Garvin (1981), there are three particular roles that encompass the scope of research activity within social work practice.

To begin with, all social workers are consumers of research. This is how they gather knowledge about important things, such as why certain individuals become dependent upon alcohol, what the needs are of women leaving prison, and which approach is best in helping children who are bullying. Much research has been conducted in social work and other social science disciplines to help us answer questions just like these. To build their knowledge base, social workers regularly read and evaluate research conducted by others. It is important to note that you must not only read the research but also critically evaluate the findings for yourself. Not all research published is applicable to your practice, and every study has limitations that need to be considered before accepting or incorporating the findings. You need to be able to identify what the limitations are and how these can influence the extent to which you accept the findings.

A second role for social workers to play is that of practitioner of research. One thing that social workers and the agencies that employ them want to know is whether their practice is effective. Do clients make progress towards achieving their goals and desired outcomes? To answer this question social workers draw upon their knowledge of research when they design and conduct practice or program evaluation. Scientifically measured outcomes of an intervention's effectiveness are stronger evidence than clinicians' beliefs about that effectiveness. Thus social workers conduct research in conjunction with their clients to answer important questions of effectiveness.

Table 1b   Ethics and Research Role

As social workers we have an ethical obligation to:	Role
… use interventions that are known to be effective – evidence-based practice.	Consumer of research
… continuously and rigorously evaluate our own practice.	Practitioner of research
… participate with others in the creation of new knowledge.	Participant in research

The final role for social workers is that of participant in research. A social worker may be part of a larger group investigating issues that affect their clients. It is quite common these days to see research conducted by groups of stakeholders who share a common interest in the wellness and concerns of the people they serve. Knowledge of research practices enables the social worker to play a valuable role in these research endeavours. It is highly likely that at some point in your career you will be approached to participate in such a project, and your ability to bring a social work perspective to the task and make a valuable contribution from the perspective of your profession depends upon your knowledge of and comfort with research.

Garvin's model is also helpful to reinforce the idea that not only is the conduct of research consistent with the role of social workers, but it is also an ethical obligation for those in our profession. Table 1b outlines this connection between ethical responsibilities and the research roles engaged in by social workers.

This discussion has led you through the steps to answer the first question of the research process, "What will I do?" The next section of the book will help you to explore the remaining steps of the process: "How will I do it?," "What have I found out?," and "What will I do next?"

Works Cited

Garvin, C.D. (1981). Research related roles for social workers. In R.M. Grinnell, Jr., & Y.A. Unrau (Eds.), *Social work research and evaluation*, pp. 547–52. Boston: Cengage Learning.

Gladstone, J. (1995). The marital perceptions of elderly persons living or having a spouse living in a long-term care institution in Canada. *Gerontologist*, *35*(1), 52–60. http://dx.doi.org/10.1093/geront/35.1.52

Additional Reading

Austin, M.J., & Packard, T. (2009). Case-based learning: Educating future human service managers. *Journal of Teaching in Social Work*, *29*(2), 216–36. http://dx.doi.org/10.1080/08841230802240993.

Berger, P.L., & Luckman, T. (1991). *The social construction of reality*. New York: Doubleday.

Corradi, G., Gherardi, S., & Verzelloni, L. (2010). Through the practice lens: Where is the bandwagon of practice-based studies heading? *Management Learning, 41*(3), 265–83. http://dx.doi.org/10.1177/1350507609356938.

Crosling, G., & Webb, G. (Eds.). (2002). *Supporting student learning: Case studies, experience and practice from higher education.* London: Kogan Page. http://dx.doi.org/10.4324/9780203417140.

Erskine, J.A., Leenders, M.R., & Mauffette-Leenders, L.A. (1998). *Teaching with cases.* London, ON: Ivey.

Garvin, D.A. (2003). *Making the case: Professional education for the world of practice. Harvard Magazine.* September/October.

Harrington, H. (1991). The case method. *Action in Teacher Education, 12*(4), 1–10. http://dx.doi.org/10.1080/01626620.1991.10463104.

Howe, C. (2004). All together now. *Psychologist, 17,* 199–201.

Hitt, M., Ireland, R.D., & Hoskisson, R. (2012). *Strategic management cases: Competitiveness and globalization.* Boston: Cengage Learning.

Jones, K. (2003). Making the case for the case method in graduate social work education. *Journal of Teaching in Social Work, 23*(1/2), 183–200. http://dx.doi.org/10.1300/J067v23n01_12.

Kassirer, J.P. (2010). Teaching clinical reasoning: Case-based and coached. *Academic Medicine, 85*(7), 1118–24. http://dx.doi.org/10.1097/ACM.0b013e3181d5dd0d.

Kim, S., Phillips, W.R., Pinsky, L., Brock, D., Phillips, K., & Keary, J. (2006). A conceptual framework for developing teaching cases: A review and synthesis of the literature across disciplines. *Medical Education, 40*(9), 867–76. http://dx.doi.org/10.1111/j.1365-2929.2006.02544.x.

Mulkay, M. (2014). *Science and the sociology of knowledge.* London: Routledge.

Munn-Giddings, C., & Winter, R. (2013). *A handbook for action research in health and social care.* London: Routledge.

Peterson, S.E., & Miller, J.A. (2004). Comparing the quality of students' experiences during cooperative learning and large group instruction. *Journal of Educational Research, 97*(3), 123–34. http://dx.doi.org/10.3200/JOER.97.3.123-134.

Russell, T. (2005). Can reflective practice be taught? *Reflective Practice, 6*(2), 199–204. http://dx.doi.org/10.1080/14623940500105833.

Savery, J.R. (2015). Overview of problem-based learning: Definitions and distinctions. In A. Walker, H. Leary, C. Hmelo-Silver, & P.A. Ertmer (Eds.), *Essential readings in problem-based learning: Exploring and extending the legacy of Howard S. Barrows* (pp. 5–15). West Lafayette, IN: Purdue University Press.

Schön, D.A. (1983). *The reflective practitioner: How professionals think in action.* New York: Basic Books.

Thistlethwaite, J.E., Davies, D., Ekeocha, S., Kidd, J.M., MacDougall, C., Matthews, P., . . ., & Clay, D. (2012). The effectiveness of case-based learning in health professional education. A BEME systematic review: BEME Guide No. 23. *Medical Teacher, 34*(6), e421–e444. http://dx.doi.org/10.3109/0142159X.2012.680939.

Williams, B. (2005). Case based learning – a review of the literature: Is there scope for this educational paradigm in prehospital education? *Emergency Medicine Journal, 22*(8), 577–81. http://dx.doi.org/10.1136/emj.2004.022707.

Zastrow, C. (2011). *Social work with groups: A comprehensive workbook* (7th ed.). Toronto: Thomson Brooks/Cole.

CHAPTER TWO

Problem Solving: Brief Case Studies

Introduction: Steps in the Process of Research

Just as in all other social work practice areas, there are distinct steps in the process of social work research. Typically, research courses teach these in a didactic manner that is not congruent with the practice of social work or how most social work practitioners process and apply new knowledge. Thus, in the following section we present 23 case studies to assist you in applying the theory needed to understand the distinct but inter-related and interdependent steps in the research process. Each case study applies to a critical aspect of research as outlined in Table 2; the case studies ultimately lead you to step nine, the ability to apply your knowledge and to analyse and critique the research of others as well as creating your own.

Table 2   Steps in the Research Process

Step	*Case Study*
1 Identify the problem	
Develop the research question	1. Research and the Media: What Are You Being Told?
2 Ethics: Ensure that no harm comes to participants through the process	2. A Question of Ethics: Willowbrook
	3. Another Question of Ethics: Studying HIV
	4. Ethical Issues of Obtaining Consent to Interview Children in Post Separation Disputes
	5. Respectful Ethical Research Practice: Working with First Nations, Inuit, Innu, and Metis Peoples
3 Conceptualize	6. Understanding Ideas and Counting Them
4 Operationalize	6. Understanding Ideas and Counting Them
5 Sample selection	
a. Probability sampling	7. Implementing a Pilot Project: A Question of Sampling

Table 2   (*continued*)

Step	Case Study
b. Non-probability sampling	8. Who Do You Ask? Sampling in a Qualitative Context
6 Research method	
a. Quantitative	
i. Causality	9. Criminal Justice Issues in Social Work Research: The Search for Causality
ii. Validity and reliability	10. Psychometric Properties: How Should We Measure?
iii. Internal and external validity	11. The Validity of Research
b. Quasi-experimental	12. The Application of Quasi-experimental Design in Social Work Research
c. Single subject	13. The Power of One: Single-Case Study Design
	14. One More: Another Example of Single-Case Study Design
d. Questionnaire design	15. Asking Questions Properly: An Examination of Questionnaire Design
e. Qualitative research	16. Asking Questions in Child Advocacy: Which Approach Is Best for Children?
	17. What Does It all Mean? Qualitative Interviewing with Children about their views and Experiences of Family Justice Professionals
f. Mixed methods	18. Q & Q: Employing Both a Qualitative and a Quantitative Approach
g. Participatory action research	19. On PAR: Engaging and Empowering Clients through Participatory Action Research
7 Collect data	20. Measuring Client Satisfaction: Do They Like Me?
8 Data processing (statistical analysis)	21. Statistics: Adding Some Numbers
	22. Descriptive Statistics: The First Step from Guessing to Knowing
	23. Inferring What You Know: Selecting an Appropriate Statistical Test
9 Implementing the plan	Case Studies 1–23
10 Application and action	When you have completed examining the 23 case studies you will have the knowledge to interpret research findings, critique the research of others, and take action using your own research as another critical component of your social work practice.

The beginning step in any research process is defining the problem or identifying the area of interest and linking it to theory or to various theories. What is it you want to know? What is the question you need to ask (Case Study 1)? The development of your research question in turn necessitates a formal review of the literature. Experienced qualitative researchers often directly explore the phenomenon of interest in greater depth before examining the literature, but new research practitioners will find understanding the material, or often lack thereof, on their topic of interest of value at the onset of the research process.

Critical in preparing to conduct research both as a research practitioner and as a social worker is that you always ensure that the interests of the individuals who you are working with are protected and that no harm comes to those participating in the study. Issues in ethics are explored in detail in Case Studies 2 through 5. Conceptualization follows the development of your question and draws from your review of the literature. This is the process where you develop and explicitly state in a clear and succinct manner the meaning of the ideas, concepts and, in quantitative research, variables that form the basis of your inquiry. Operationalization follows conceptualization and is the stage in the process of research where the social work research practitioner determines exactly how each idea in the study will be measured (Case Study 6).

The population you wish to know more about derives from the beginning stages of the research process and, of course, primarily from your original question, but you still need to determine whom you will be asking questions of or collecting data from within the population: the sample. The population is the group about whom you wish to know more or draw conclusions, while the sample is the group you actually study and around whom the research revolves. There are two distinct approaches to sampling, one pertaining to quantitative research (Case Study 7) and one to qualitative research (Case Study 8).

The how of the research process is the methodology. There are a broad range of options to select from, none of which is unique or exclusive to social work. However, the research method you select is governed to a significant degree by choices you have made in the previous stages of the research process. Your choice of research design is varied, including both quantitative and qualitative options along with combining the two into a mixed-methods approach or taking a more advocacy-orientated approach in conducting participatory action research. Issues pertaining to research methodology and design options are examined in depth in Case Studies 9 through 19.

Observation follows directly from the selection of your methodological approach. This is the stage where you collect the data that will become the focus of your analysis and interpretation (Case Study 20). Prior to analysis and interpretation, the observations must be transformed into information that can be analysed and interpreted. This is the data-processing stage, which can be quite simple or very complex depending upon the amount and nature of data you have collected. Analysis involves processing and interpreting the data and drawing conclusions that relate back to the original problem or idea (Case Studies 21–23). While many social workers are initially put off by quantitative research designs because of a fear of numbers, often qualitative analysis takes far more time and is just as complex due to the quantity and richness of the information collected. However, analysis is not the end of the social work research process. The final step is application and action, and this is of great importance for social work as a profession. It is fact-based knowledge that supports personal, community, and societal growth, development, and social change. How research is reported and is used to produce change is an integral component of the research process and allows us to be evidence-informed practitioners. Your goal after having examined and worked through the 23 case studies is to have both greater ability and greater confidence in appraising the work of others and working with them to complete research projects, and ultimately in pursuing your own research interests.

CASE STUDY 1
Research and the Media: What Are You Being Told?

1. Preamble

Why have you chosen to make social work your career? What is your standpoint? What is your world view and how have you come to determine what truth is and how you acquire it? What the general population considers truth is influenced by all forms of media. The following problem statement is based upon an actual newspaper recounting of a research initiative and provides you with no less but also no more than that day's readers of the newspaper would have learned and used to draw their conclusions. Words in quotation marks are direct quotes from that article. Read the following case study carefully, for you hold not only one standpoint but several: as a consumer of media information, as a social worker, and also as a beginning social work research practitioner.

2. The Problem

There are perceptions by members of the black community across Canada that the existing educational system is "racist and unresponsive." This was a perception that was also shared by members of the Alliance of Black Educators. One member of the Alliance was a social work researcher in Hamilton, a major Ontario urban centre. Among the researcher's stated beliefs are that "an enriched, appropriate curriculum in a Black school would help Black students develop a strong identity and respect for their Blackness."

3. The Process

As part of the research initiative a parents' advisory council was created, a standard practice in community-based and community-informed research. The "black parents group" evolved from the research and took on an advocacy function; the group not only made a formal request to the Hamilton Board of Education for the establishment of an alternative school to educate only black students, but also made a formal presentation to the

Ontario Royal Commission on Learning. The group's recommendations included that the alternative school be located in Hamilton and be staffed by black teachers and run by black administrators who would also serve as role models for the students. The parent group claimed that this was not segregationist, as attendance would be a choice for them and their children, much like having the option of being in either a gender-specific or co-educational class. The article also quoted a potential student who stated, "One of the things school teaches you is how to get along with other people, how to work in a group. In the workplace, or society, you're going to have to be with people of other races."

4. The Research

There are approximately ten thousand black families with children in Hamilton, more than enough to justify an alternative school for specialized programs. A sample of black children attending school in Hamilton and their parents was contacted by the researcher to learn of their educational experiences in the public school system. Parents reported in the study that their children felt alienated in the school system. They also felt that their children were singled out for disrespectful treatment, that this particular school board's race relations were "just window-dressing," and that parents have to solve problems themselves, as nobody from the school or the school board followed through. Another parent stated that [white] teachers had low expectations of black students and often channelled them into non-academic courses – "I find they really have preconceived notions about our ability to learn." The researcher was also quoted in the newspaper article as stating that the attitude towards black students was: "You can play basketball, but you cannot go into grade 12 advanced … We are all brawn and no brains."

Quantitative research conducted by the Toronto Board of Education (in a community one hour from Hamilton with a population of six million compared to Hamilton's half a million) was also quoted in support of the parent group's request, indicating that 9 per cent of its secondary school students were black, but blacks made up only 7 per cent of students in the advanced level. Black students were also reported to be over-represented in the lower academic streams (basic, 18 per cent, and general, 16 per cent) and at higher risk of dropping out.

5. Questions

1. *What are the underlying issues raised for you by reading the article?*
2. *What questions came to mind as you read this case study? Which were based upon the research and which upon the emotionality of the issue of race that the research investigates?*

3. *What are the strengths and limitations of the research and the manner in which it was reported?*
4. *Are you personally in support of the establishment of a school for black students only?*
5. *Based upon the presented research data, do you support the establishment of a school for black students?*
6. *Which lens did you read and analyse this case study through: consumer of media information, social worker, or social work research practitioner?*

6. Social Work Practice

Little remains as divisive in society as questions of diversity and minority rights, particularly around the issue of race. Reflect on how often you have seen a social work researcher quoted on the front page of a major newspaper; yet this is exactly what occurred with this controversial research issue. Thus, as social workers it is easy to become focused upon the issue of majority versus minority rights, disempowerment, role models, oppression, and funding priorities when reading this case. This case study is an example of why you must read all sections of a research article, including the methodology section, and why the popular press is called that rather than the empirical press. This type of knowledge source is also an indicator of why your social work practice should be informed by evidence, both quantitative and qualitative.

Social work practice is supported by a foundation of knowledge that includes such things as an understanding of client systems, theories about the nature and origins of social problems, and evidence as to the effectiveness of interventions. This type of knowledge informs decisions we make about what actions to take in our professional role. As a practising social worker you will need to build a strong foundation of knowledge to enhance your professional practice, but where will you obtain this knowledge? The answer to this question takes us into the realm of philosophy and the topic of epistemology. So we must begin by asking the most fundamental question: What constitutes knowledge?

The Philosophy of Knowledge

A paradigm is a world view that comprises a set of assumptions about the nature of reality and the nature of knowledge. While not explicitly stated, it still influences all aspects of the research process and what at times masquerades as research. An individual's paradigm is what helps shape the issues a person looks at, how they are looked at, and the methods used in approaching those issues. Likewise, a paradigm influences what we choose to exclude and thus what we choose not to consider in making an assessment. The process of research is also framed within larger issues, issues of ontology and epistemology. Ontology is the philosophy of reality, a branch of metaphysics relating to the nature and relations of being. Ontology involves the analysis of general and abstract concepts and the distinctions that underlie specific descriptions of any phenomenon in the world, such as time, space, process, and, most importantly for researchers, cause and effect.

The function of ontological analysis is to clarify the structure of knowledge and what can be known. Thus, ontology is the study of the nature of reality. Is there a single truth? Is it our task to make a discovery regarding a single truth? It pertains to the interpretation of realities and to the sharing of knowledge and is a description of concepts and relationships. It is the explicit specification of a conceptualization, the statement of a logical theory. Ontology refers to the study of what might exist.

Epistemology is the branch of philosophy concerned with the nature of knowledge. How do we know what we know? It is a set of assumptions about the nature of knowledge:

- When does knowledge count?
- What constitutes evidence?
- What types of knowledge are valued?
- What can be known?
- Who can know?

Sources of Knowledge

What is knowledge? This is a profound question of great complexity. For our purposes we will simplify things by looking at four commonly proposed sources of knowledge: (1) cultural traditions; (2) persons in authority; (3) experience; and (4) scientific research.

Each of us is raised in a cultural setting and through the process of socialization acquires knowledge of that culture's norms of behaviour and traditions. People raised in traditional Chinese culture know that the appropriate colour of a wedding dress is red and those raised in India accept that beef is not an appropriate source of human nutrition. While traditional knowledge is important and often relevant, it also has serious limitations. To begin with, it leads to the problem of cultural relativity. Different cultures "know" different things. Brides in Canada know that white is really the colour of a wedding dress just as diners in Argentina know that steak is a good choice for their evening meal. Which culture is correct? Which culture is wrong? Another problem with traditional knowledge is that often it comes in the form of folklore, which can be incorrect or misleading. Your mother may have told you not to go out with wet hair because if you do you are likely to catch a cold. Scientific evidence does not support this well-intentioned warning. This may seem like a relatively minor problem, but if our traditions tell us that members of other cultures or groups are to be feared or that certain members within our group are inferior to others, then traditional knowledge can lead to attribution errors and even more seriously to racism, sexism, ageism, ableism, classism, and other forms of stigmatization and oppression. These types of beliefs, which masquerade as forms of "knowledge," are annoyingly resistant to change, and we must be vigilant since they can lead to false assumptions and harmful actions.

Another source of our knowledge is from people in authority. Our parents, teachers, professors, religious leaders, and employers see passing on their knowledge as an important obligation to future generations. Again, while much of this knowledge is helpful and can speed up the acquisition process, it is also subject to error. Most importantly, people in authority may be out of date in their knowledge or it may also be tinged with belief that is not based in fact. New information is continually being generated, and it is not uncommon for new knowledge to update or even replace previous beliefs. There was a time when people in authority truly believed that the sun and planets orbited the earth, while one practice generation ago in social work there was no solution-focused or narrative therapy. In certain fields it is very difficult to keep up to date even if you make a concerted effort to be on the leading edge. When people in authority don't make this effort at all, it does not take long for their knowledge base to become seriously out of date and thus flawed.

A third and very common source of knowledge is our personal experience. I touch the stove and "know" that the stove is hot. While experience is a powerful teacher, it likewise can be subject to substantive problems. Sometimes instead of believing what we see, we see what we believe. Our interpretations of events that we experience are filtered through existing beliefs and biases. Even the simple act of seeing something happen is fraught with complications. Two people can observe the same event and attend to totally different aspects of it. We call this selective observation, and it explains, for example, why reports from witnesses at crime events are often incomplete or contradictory. Particularly troublesome is the problem of overgeneralization from our personal observations. We experience a negative event and draw conclusions from what we see, and then apply those conclusions to similar events in the future. All teenagers are disrespectful, all elderly people are slow and confused, and all professors are brilliant. Imagine what problems you could encounter if the preceding beliefs were part of your knowledge base.

Knowledge acquired from tradition, persons in authority, or personal experience is considered naturalistic knowledge. A large part of our existing knowledge base is naturalistic in nature. Scientific knowledge is the alternative to naturalistic knowing. This knowledge is the outcome of a process called the scientific method, which has a number of well-accepted attributes. To begin with, science is empirical. This means that it is based upon direct observation. Much of our personal experiential knowledge is also based upon observation, but scientific observation is directed by a strict set of rules, procedures, and techniques. The rules that govern scientific observation were developed by scientists to try to counteract the problems introduced by a researcher's existing beliefs and biases. The goal of following scientific methodology is to produce results that are as objective as possible. It is generally accepted that total objectivity is an unattainable ideal, but much can be done to reduce blatant bias and selective observation.

Another important characteristic of scientific knowledge is that it is provisional. Science does not prove things to be true. All knowledge is temporary and can be replaced by new knowledge if our original ideas are demonstrated to be incomplete or even false. That is what the scientist is trying to do through the research process: trying to accumulate evidence that our theories and understandings of the world are incorrect. To scientists all knowledge is probabilistic and provisional. The scientist says, "Given our understanding to date this idea is probably correct, but if at any time in the future if it can be shown to be false then it will be replaced by a new probable knowledge." From this perspective, if someone tells you that something is the truth they are not following scientific convention.

Finally, science is carried out in a public way and is open to critical review. Scientists publish and disseminate their research widely and follow standard prescriptions about the kind of information they need to convey in support of their conclusions. One of the purposes of this book is to provide you the tools that you will need to play your role as an informed consumer of research, one who can critically assess supporting information.

Of the four sources of knowledge described above, scientific research is the preferred option. Whenever possible, social workers are ethically obligated to seek out and use scientifically based knowledge. This is one of the major forces leading to and supporting the call for evidence-informed social work practice. In this approach to practice social workers make decisions about practice interventions informed by their understanding of evidence that the interventions they choose are helpful. Evidence comes from the findings of empirical research, not from the beliefs of those in authority or personal experience alone.

When working with a client system, the social worker takes into account the individual characteristics of that system, the values and preferences of the clients in the system, and evidence that what they decide to do will have beneficial outcomes.

Misuse of Knowledge

Knowledge of research rules, procedures, and practices is fundamental to the development of social work competency. Drawing on this knowledge contributes to the quality of the work we do as professional helpers and allows us to continually learn and grow as we progress through our professional life. Research is not something done by a select breed of academic eccentrics, but is intricately intertwined with the day-to-day performance of the professional social work role. However, there are also a variety of misuses of research of which you should be cognizant. As a social worker, when you initiate a project or are invited to participate you should assess whether the initiative can be completed, that the resources exist to do the research, and that the project is not simply using research as a political exercise or strategy or as a management tool. As you conduct the research ensure again that, along with ethical procedures, the instrument, sampling frame, and methodology are all appropriate and not designed with an inherent bias or selected with the intent to produce a predetermined result.

Abuses of research occur in its provision when the researcher or research team already knows what the answer is before beginning, and thus does not see or report the actual results, or when all results and data are not considered equal in value, or when false causalities are drawn. Research abuses can still occur after the successful completion of a research project, in what actually occurs with the findings. Organizations can disregard the results if they are not what was wanted or call for action in such a way that is too difficult to implement and thus does not occur. The research results can be shelved or new researchers hired until the results the organization wants are produced. Equally problematic is selecting only pieces of the research to respond to or to use in justifying an action or plan. However, what you must always be on guard for is the hogwash – when the researcher, regardless of discipline, attempts to present the research as though it and they were totally objective and there was no bias, standpoint, or subjective component to the process.

Distinguishing between Philosophical Concepts

In closing, we offer three questions to distinguish between ontology, epistemology, and methodology. The ontological question is:

What is the form and nature of reality and, therefore, what is there that can be known about?

The epistemological question is:

What is the nature of the relationship between knower and those that wish to know and what can be known?

The methodological question this leads to for the researcher is:

What process does the would-be knower use to find out what it is that can be known?

As we move forwards in the twenty-first century, social work epistemology, knowledge, and theory are being influenced by large forces, including increasing economic globalization and inequality, social exclusion and dislocation, advances in information and communication technologies, and continued trends towards devolution, privatization, and profitability in the human service sector. So how will you come to know what you know?

7. Responding to the Case

This case study raises several issues, of what knowledge is, what research is, and how research should be reported. The most significant research issue in the newspaper article above pertains to a controversial topic: How exactly will "black" be determined? Research questions you should have asked are: How will that construct be determined, and how "black" would a student have to be to qualify to go to this specific school if it were to be funded? If you consider this problematic, unethical, or perhaps simply impossible to resolve rationally, then reflect upon the fact that a process and criteria do exist in the Canadian education system, where this issue was raised, for determining who is French enough to qualify to attend a French-language school.

The second component of the research relates to the numbers, and how knowledgeable and comfortable you are with numbers and the theory of numbers. Hopefully, you were aware that using numbers obtained from one school board, Toronto, and applying them to the school board the parents' group was lobbying, Hamilton, was a research error. You cannot simply take numbers from one population and state that they apply equally to another. Also pertaining to that part of the newspaper report is that 7 per cent versus 9 per cent may or may not be a significant finding, but from what you read you cannot be sure. It could be relevant if your $n = 10,000$, but not if $n = 100$. Likewise, reporting that blacks were "over-represented in the lower academic streams (basic, 18 per cent, and general, 16 per cent) and at higher risk of dropping out" without providing comparative percentages and the actual numbers is misleading if not irrelevant. None of these percentages have any merit in isolation without some numeric baseline so that actual values can be ascertained. As well, it is important to know by what criteria students were labelled as black so that any future comparative quantitative analysis conducted in another school board could operationalize the variable in the same way.

These last points also relate to the reporting of research. A newspaper, television program, or Internet website's primary intent is typically not to provide you with an in-depth summary of the research but rather highlights of the interesting part of the story. There is typically little if any mention of methodology. Thus, to be an informed consumer of social work research and of research and knowledge in general requires the ability to be a critical observer of what is presented and what is omitted.

Finally, this case study should highlight that research is not value neutral, but rather can be extremely value laden and a political process in all aspects, from how the problem is asked to its conceptualization and operationalization, how the data are analysed, and, of course, how they are eventually presented by you or someone interpreting on your behalf.

Read wisely.

8. Research Insight

There are a number of different ways to categorize research. One is to determine whether it is basic research or applied research. Basic research focuses primarily upon the development and testing of theory. While social workers have made contributions to this type of research, it is typically the domain of social scientists such as psychologists, anthropologists, and sociologists. Social workers are more likely to engage in applied research, which is not necessarily driven by theory. The purpose of this type of research is to solve practical problems. When social workers are engaged in research such as needs assessments or program or practice evaluation, they are engaged in applied research. Applied research is a more common research activity for non-academic social workers practising in the community.

There is a further categorization of research into exploratory, descriptive, or explanatory. Exploratory research takes place when the researcher is just beginning to look at a problem or phenomenon of interest, particularly if there is little known about it. The purpose here is to add information to our understanding to enable us to move on to more sophisticated and rigorous research approaches. Descriptive research studies are intended to identify characteristics, qualities, or circumstances of entities of interest. In a needs assessment we might conduct a descriptive study to identify important characteristics of the people living in a community of interest. We engage in activities such as surveys, censuses, and interviews to determine frequencies, averages, and variation of these characteristics or variables of interest. The final purpose of research is explanatory. In this type of research our purpose is to explain the things we are interested in.

This of course brings us back to theoretical research. We conduct experiments to determine if variables are causally related, to help explain why weak social support might be related to parenting capacity. Not surprisingly, the distinctions among these types of research are often fluid, but the researcher should have an overall understanding of her or his purpose before engaging in the research activity: Is the intention to explore a problem, describe a problem, or explain a problem?

9. Further Reflections

1. *What is your underlying ontology? How did this affect how you first perceived the case study?*
2. *Did examining the case in depth change your standpoint? If so, how and why?*
3. *Are there any misuses of knowledge in the case?*
4. *How important are research findings in the development of your views on social work issues?*

10. Additional Reading

Aymer, C., & Okitikpi, T. (2000). *Epistemology, ontology and methodology: What's that got to do with social work?* London: Taylor & Francis.

Bartels, N. (2003). How teachers and researchers read academic articles. *Teaching and Teacher Education, 19*(7), 737–53. http://dx.doi.org/10.1016/j.tate.2003.06.001.

Bronson, D.E., & Davis, T.S. (2011). *Finding and evaluating evidence: Systematic reviews and evidence-based practice.* New York: Oxford University Press. http://dx.doi.org/10.1093/acprof:oso/9780195337365.001.0001.

Carey, S.S. (2011). *A beginner's guide to the scientific method.* 4th ed. Toronto: Thompson/Nelson Canada.

Cox, C. (1995, May 3). Blacks struggle over issue of education. *Spectator (London, England)*, A1–A2.

Chu, W.C., & Tsui, M.S. (2008). The nature of practice wisdom in social work revisited. *International Social Work, 51*(1), 47–54. http://dx.doi.org/10.1177/0020872807083915.

Davidov, E., Schmidt, P., & Billiet, J. (2011). *Cross-cultural analysis: Methods and applications.* New York: Routledge.

Fisher, M. (2011). Practice literate research: Turning the tables. *Social Work & Society, 9*(1), 20–8.

Hall, J.C. (2008). A practitioner's application and deconstruction of evidence-based practice. *Families in Society, 89*(3), 385–93. http://dx.doi.org/10.1606/1044-3894.3764.

Hardwick, L., & Worsley, A. (2011). The invisibility of practitioner research. *Practice, 23*(3), 135–46. http://dx.doi.org/10.1080/09503153.2011.569971.

Howard, M.O., McMillen, C.J., & Pollio, D.E. (2003). Teaching evidence-based practice: Toward a new paradigm for social work education. *Research on Social Work Practice, 13*(2), 234–59. http://dx.doi.org/10.1177/1049731502250404.

Hudson, C.G. (2009). Decision making in evidence-based practice: Science and art. *Smith College Studies in Social Work*, *79*(2), 155–74. http://dx.doi.org/10.1080/00377310902832334.

Karger, H.J. (1999). The politics of social work research. *Research on Social Work Practice*, *9*(1), 96–9. http://dx.doi.org/10.1177/104973159900900109.

Kirk, S.A., & Reid, W.J. (2002). *Science and social work: A critical appraisal.* New York: Columbia University Press. http://dx.doi.org/10.7312/kirk11824.

Stanfield, J. (2011). *Rethinking race and ethnicity in research methods.* Walnut Creek, CA: Left Coast Press.

Zeira, A., & Rosen, A. (2000). Unraveling "tacit knowledge": What social workers do and why they do it. *Social Service Review*, *74*(1), 103–23. http://dx.doi.org/10.1086/514459.

11. Internet Resources

How to Read Academic Research

Western University Libraries, "How to Read a Scholarly Article":
   https://www.youtube.com/watch?v=3SmOq6gENPM
Dr. Russell James, "How to Read Academic Research":
   https://www.youtube.com/watch?v=XvnUojPCftk
Kishwaukee College Library, "How to Read a Scholarly Journal Article":
   https://www.youtube.com/watch?v=EEVftUdfKtQ

Designing a Research Question

Resources for Behavioural Science Researchers, "The Relationship between the Research Question, Hypotheses, Specific Aims, and Long-Term Goals of the Project":
   http://www.theresearchassistant.com/tutorial/2-1.asp
Research Rundowns, "Writing Research Questions":
   https://researchrundowns.wordpress.com/intro/writing-research-questions/
Stride Project, "Designing a Research Question":
   https://www.youtube.com/watch?v=KEuzeL06IwM
Laurier Library, "Developing a Research Question":
   https://www.youtube.com/watch?v=Ga7w-czB7lo

Evaluating Sources

Western University, "Evaluating Sources":
   https://www.youtube.com/watch?v=EyMT08mD7Ds
Libncsu, "Evaluating Sources for Credibility":
   https://www.youtube.com/watch?v=PLTOVoHbH5c
Dnews, "Is Wikipedia a Credible Source?":
   https://www.youtube.com/watch?v=jHrGsxSpM5E

Paradigms and Epistemology

Dr. Arwen Raddon, "Early Stage Research Training: Epistemology & Ontology in Social Science Research":
http://www2.le.ac.uk/colleges/ssah/documents/research-training-presentations/EpistFeb10.pdf

Nurse Killam, "Complex Research Terminology Simplified: Paradigms, Ontology, Epistemology and Methodology":
https://www.youtube.com/watch?v=8xvpxBVCo0c

Kent Löfgren, "What Is Epistemology? Introduction to the Word and the Concept":
https://www.youtube.com/watch?v=lI9-YgSzsEQ

Kent Löfgren, "What Is Ontology? Introduction to the Word and the Concept":
https://www.youtube.com/watch?v=XTsaZWzVJ4c

Politics of Research

Brian Martin, Information Liberation (London: Freedom Press, 1998), chapter 7, "The Politics of Research":
https://www.uow.edu.au/~bmartin/pubs/98il/il07.pdf

CASE STUDY 2
A Question of Ethics: Willowbrook

1. Preamble

There are in fact two things, science and opinion; the former begets knowledge, the latter ignorance.

– Hippocrates

Human rights are inseparable from social work theory, values, ethics and practice.

– United Nations Centre for Human Rights

2. The Problem

Willowbrook was a traditional residential institution for the care of developmentally delayed[1] children opened early in the first half of the twentieth century in Staten Island, New York. Nearly three-quarters of the residents had a reported IQ of less than 60 and were voluntarily placed in care by their parents or legal guardians. Infectious diseases were more prevalent in the North American population after World War II than they are today, and even more prevalent at Willowbrook. The question was asked, and funding provided to determine, whether there was any form of immunization that could be created to minimize the risk to Willowbrook's residents and to the general population from some of these potentially fatal infectious diseases.

3. The Process

In 1954 Dr. Saul Krugman was appointed consultant in pediatrics and infectious disease at Willowbrook State Hospital. Two years after his appointment Dr. Krugman and two colleagues, both physicians, began to study one of these infectious diseases, hepatitis A.

---

1 In 1954 the term "mentally retarded" would have been used.

The research protocol entailed injecting serum to produce hepatitis in the patients/ subjects. The research was approved and funded by the Armed Forces Epidemiological Board, the Committee on Human Experimentation of New York University, and the New York State Department of Mental Hygiene.

The purpose of the research was to gain a better understanding of hepatitis and to develop methods of immunizing against the disease. The rationale for exposing the children to strains of hepatitis was that:

- they were bound to be exposed to the same strains under the natural conditions existing within Willowbrook;
- they would be admitted to a special, well-equipped and well-staffed unit where they would be isolated from exposure to the other infectious diseases that were prevalent in the institution, including parasitic and respiratory infections; and
- thus they would be at least risk for multiple infections during their time as research subjects.

4. The Research

Four times per year from 1956 until 1970 the medical researchers selected 12 to 15 children at Willowbrook to participate in their longitudinal study, providing them a sample of over 700 children. Only those children whose parents or guardians provided informed consent to participate in the study were included. Parents were briefed about the risks and benefits of the research and the potential outcomes, both positive and negative, for their children. During the course of the 14 years of this study some of the children died from the disease, though most lived and those that became ill during the trials did receive additional care as outlined in and promised by the research protocol. The participation of these children in this research provided the basis for the vaccines we use today and that you, your family, or your clients may have taken to prevent or combat hepatitis A. Thus, you may have already directly or indirectly benefited from the research you are about to critique or may benefit from it in the future.

5. Questions

1. *As the social worker on the external multidisciplinary research ethics committee, what questions or issues would you have asked before approving the research study?*
2. *What are your thoughts on the research protocol itself?*
3. *What are the ethical implications of the research?*

6. Social Work Practice

Defining Ethics

Ethics is the branch of moral philosophy concerned with human conduct and moral decision making, with being a good person and doing the right thing. An ethic is a statement of the most fundamental principle of conduct. It is an attempt to answer the question of what is right and what is wrong in a systemic manner. Ethics is a discipline examining our values, beliefs, moral principles, and the justification of these. It is in essence the actual values and rules of conduct by which we live our lives. When we think about ethics the question typically arises: How should we think and thus how should we act?

Key elements underlying ethical decision making include:

- What we perceive to be right and wrong
- Our sense of social responsibility
- Societal values
- The criminal justice system and its laws.

Behaviour considered unethical from a social work standpoint includes:

- Violation of confidentiality
- Exceeding one's level of professional competence
- Negligent practice
- Claiming expertise one does not possess
- Imposing one's values on a client
- Creating dependency in a client
- Conflict of interest
- Questionable financial arrangements
- Sexual activity with a client.

In essence, any activity that leads to exploitation, insensitivity, incompetence, irresponsibility, and abandonment is unethical behaviour, but how is this connected to ethical behaviour in research practice?

Research Ethics Guidelines

Just as there are formal ethical guidelines to govern social work practice, so are there specific policies to govern the practice of research. Contemporary academic, medical, and government organizations all have standard ethical protocols that are publicly stated and enforced by a research ethics review committee (RERC), though smaller, community-based agencies may not have formal processes in place. Before beginning a research project it is common for the researcher to prepare and submit an ethics submission for review by this committee, sometimes called an Institutional Review Board (IRB). A typical research ethics submission should address:

- Foreseeable harms and risks to subjects, including deception
- How free and informed consent will be sought
- Potential conflicts of interest involving the researcher, participant, or sponsor
- The extent to which the privacy of participants and the confidentiality of the data will be protected
- Safeguards for vulnerable persons, including student participants.

Guidelines of the Canadian Social Sciences and Humanities Research Council (1981), written decades ago but only 11 years after the conclusion of the Willowbrook study, stated that

> greater consideration must be given to the risks of physical, psychological, humane, proprietary and cultural values than to the potential contribution of the research to knowledge although the latter should always be borne in mind. (p. 4)

Figure 2.2a is the checklist that accompanies an ethics submission by student social work researchers at King's University College in London, Ontario. This checklist is based on one designed by the Canadian Institutes of Health Research, the Natural Sciences and Engineering Research Council of Canada, and the Social Sciences and Humanities Research Council of Canada (2010). Note the level of detail and supporting information that is reviewed by the committee before ethics approval is provided.

Figure 2.2a   King's University College Ethics Protocol Submission Form

1. All the investigator(s) signed and dated the Application Form	YES ___ NO ___
2. The Supervisor, where applicable, signed and dated the Application Form	N/A___ YES ___ NO ___
3. The following documents are appended:	
a) The Research Protocol;	YES ___ NO ___
b) Information sheet for participants (even if consent is not sought)	YES ___ NO ___
c) The Consent Form (or justification for no need of written consent)	YES ___ NO ___

4. The following components of the Ethics Protocol Submission Form
are present and satisfactory:

    a) Brief description of the Research Project;   YES ____ NO ____

    b) Description of foreseeable harms and risks;   YES ____ NO ____

    c) Explanation of how free and informed consent will be sought;   YES ____ NO ____

    d) Statement of whether there any foreseeable conflicts of interest   YES ____ NO ____
          involving the researcher, participants or sponsors;

    e) Explanation of the extent to which privacy of research participants   YES ____ NO ____
          and confidentiality of the research data will be protected;

    f) Statement of whether particular safeguards for student participants   YES ____ NO ____
          and vulnerable persons are needed;

    g) Statement of whether continuing ethics review of research is needed   YES ____ NO ____

RESEARCH PROTOCOL

5. The Research Protocol contains a satisfactory description of:

    a) The goal and purpose of the research;   YES ____ NO ____

    b) The procedures (including recruitment and debriefing)   YES ____ NO ____
          in the research.

6. The content of the Research Protocol is consistent with the answers   YES ____ NO ____
given in the Ethics Protocol Submission Form.

INFORMATION SHEET AND CONSENT FORM (if needed)

7. The information sheet clearly identifies:

    a) The name of the investigator(s);   YES ____ NO ____

        The name of the supervisor, where applicable;   N/A ____ YES ____ NO ____

        The affiliation of the investigator(s);   YES ____ NO ____

        The phone number of the investigator(s);   YES ____ NO ____

    b) The sponsor(s) of the research, if any.   N/A ____ YES ____ NO ____

8. The information sheet clearly explains:

    a) that the proposed procedure or intervention is for research;   YES ____ NO ____

    b) that participation is voluntary and can be withdrawn at any time;   YES ____ NO ____

    c) that the participant will keep the information sheet and one copy   YES ____ NO ____
       of the signed consent form;

    d) the purpose of the research;   YES ____ NO ____

    e) whether participants will be randomly assigned   N/A ____ YES ____ NO ____

    f) that the participants will have access to standard practice   N/A ____ YES ____ NO ____

    g) the likely time needed for each involvement of the participant;   YES ____ NO ____

    h) the nature of foreseeable inconveniences and harms associated   YES ____ NO ____
       with the research and the likelihood of their occurrence;

    i) potential benefits to the participant or to others associated   YES ____ NO ____
       with the research and the likelihood of their occurrence;

    j) the alternative(s) to research participation;   N/A ____ YES ____ NO ____

k) how anonymity and confidentiality will be protected if necessary   YES ___ NO ___
(Who will have access to the data; how it will be stored;
if participants will be identified in publications);

l) the details regarding reimbursement, if any;   N/A___ YES ___ NO ___

m) possible conflict of interest or commercialization of the findings;   N/A___ YES ___ NO ___
if any;

n) contact information for questions (the investigator) and   YES ___ NO ___
complaints (normally the Department Chair/Director of the School
of Social Work/Coordinator of the interdisciplinary program);

o) that the participants keep the information sheet and a copy of the   YES ___ NO ___
consent form

9. The consent form does not include:

a) a statement releasing the researcher(s), sponsor(s), institutions(s),   YES ___ NO ___
or agents(s) from liability for negligence;

b) a statement or description of the research that pressures or unduly   YES ___ NO ___
sways people to participate.

10. The consent form is written:

a) in the prospective participant's or participant's parent/guardian's   YES ___ NO ___
preferred language;

b) at an appropriate level, taking into consideration the type   YES ___ NO ___
of participant (e.g., child or adult or special needs);

c) with simple explanations of all complex terms.   YES ___ NO ___

11. The consent form:

a) Includes a space for the signature of the participant (or parent or   YES ___ NO ___
guardian), of the investigator(s) (and of a witness if the research
involves high risks) and date;

b) There is consistency between the consent form content and the   YES ___ NO ___
information sheet content.

12. The researcher needs to inform subjects that original material will be   YES ___ NO ___
retained for five years.

In 2009, after seven years of review and multiple rounds of consultation across Canada, the Tri-Council Policy Statement on Ethical Conduct for Research Involving Humans (TCPS) that serves as the standard guidelines used by research ethics boards at Canadian universities was modified to better meet the needs of qualitative researchers. The original policy statement was primarily written to meet the needs of biomedical research, which is quite distinct from what most social workers will be engaged in. Alterations applying to qualitative research include:

1. Under specified circumstances written consent will not be required.
2. Informed consent will be inferred by the participant's agreement to interact with the researcher, and no further verification or documentation will be required.
3. Research ethics approval will not be required for observing people in public places, nor for conducting web-based research that uses only publicly available information.
4. Subjects who wish to be identified for their contribution can be named in a document or presentation.

Other countries have similar processes, as illustrated by Figure 2.2b, a Human Subjects Review Application from Smith College in Northampton, Massachusetts.

Figure 2.2b   Smith College School for Social Work Human Subjects Review Application

Project title: _____

Name of researcher: _____

Check one: _____ MSW _____ PhD

Home phone: _____   Email: _____

Research advisor: _____

The signature below testifies that I, as the researcher, pledge to conform to the following: As one engaged in research using human subjects, I acknowledge the rights and welfare of the participants involved. I acknowledge my responsibility as a researcher to secure the informed consent of the participants by explaining the procedures and by describing the risks and benefits of the study. I assure the Committee that all procedures performed under the study will be conducted in accordance with those federal regulations and Smith School for Social Work policies that govern research involving human subjects.

Any deviation from the study (e.g.: change in researcher, research methodology, participant recruitment procedures, data collection procedures, etc.) will be submitted to the Committee by submitting a Protocol Change Form for which you MUST receive approval *prior* to implementation. I agree to report all deviations to the study protocol or adverse events IMMEDIATELY to the Committee.

Researcher:

_____
(Typed name)   (Signature)   (Date)
Research Advisor/Committee Chair

_____
(Typed name)   (Signature)   (Date)

Review status: ___ **Exempt** ___ **Expedited**   ___ **Full**   ___ **Not Approved**

This study protocol has been reviewed and approved by the Smith College School for Social Work Human Subjects Review Committee (HSRC).

_____

Chair, Smith College SSW HSRC Date

IN THE SECTIONS BELOW WHERE DESCRIPTIONS ARE REQUESTED, BE SURE TO PRO-VIDE SUFFICIENT DETAIL TO ENABLE THE COMMITTEE TO EVALUATE YOUR PROCEDURES AND RESPONSES.

1. DESCRIPTION OF RESEARCH PROJECT INVOLVING HUMAN PARTICIPANTS

Briefly summarize the purpose of the study, the over-arching research question, the specific research design you will use and why you have chosen it for this study, and the planned use of human partici-pants, and a brief synopsis of relevant literature that points to need for further study (NO MORE THAN A HANDFUL OF ARTICLES) with sufficient detail and in clear, concise language *(space will expand in all sections as you enter your information)*:
(enter information here…)

2. PARTICIPANTS: if you are only observing public behaviour, skip to question d in this section.
   a) How many participants will be involved in the study?
      ___12–15   ___ ≥ 50   ___ Other (how many do you anticipate)
   b) List specific eligibility requirements for participants (or describe screening procedures), includ-ing exclusionary and inclusionary criteria. For example, if including only male participants, say so, and *explain why*. If using data from a secondary de-identified source, skip to question e in this section.
   c) Describe how participants will be recruited. ***Be specific: give step-by-step description***. (*Attach all flyers, letters, announcement, email messages etc. that will be used to recruit.* **Include the following statement on any/all recruitment materials/emails/postings, etc.**: This study protocol has been reviewed and approved by the Smith College School for Social Work Human Subjects Review Committee (HSRC).)
   d) Is there any relationship between you as the researcher and the participants (e.g. teacher/stu-dent, superintendent/principal/teacher; supervisor/clinician; clinician/client, etc.) that might lead to the appearance of coercion? If so, what steps will you take to avoid this situation. For example: "I will not interview individuals who have been direct clients."
   e) Are the study *target subjects* members of any of the following federally defined vulnerable popu-lations? (ONLY check if the study focus area is SPECIFICALLY based on any of the listed groups. For instance, if your study is about how persons who are economically disadvantaged access ser-vices, you DO check "Economically disadvantaged" category below. DO NOT CHECK IF SOME OF THESE FOLKS MAY BY CHANCE BE IN A MIXED SAMPLE – EXCEPT IF THERE ARE CHILDREN/UNDER 18 YEAR OLDS. Thus: if you are asking about how individuals who live in inner city locations get to services, you DO NOT check any of the categories below, because there is a range of types of people who live in these environments who may wish to participate, and you do not define the population as "economically disadvantaged.)

Be aware that checking "yes" *automatically requires the HSR Full Review*.

_____Yes   _____No

If "Yes," check the group(s) all that apply in your study:

___ minors (under 18 years of age) Please indicate the approximate age range of minors to be involved. Participants under age 18 require participant assent AND written consent from the parent/legal guardian. Please use related forms.

___ prisoners

___ pregnant women

___ persons with physical disabilities

___ persons with diagnosed mental disabilities

___ economically disadvantaged

___ educationally disadvantaged

3. RESEARCH METHODS:

(Check which applies)

___ Interview, focus group, non-anonymous questionnaire

___ Anonymous questionnaire/survey

___ Observation of public behaviour

___ Analysis of de-identified data collected elsewhere ("secondary data")

Where did these data come from originally?

_____

_____

Did this original research get IRB approval? ___ Yes   ___ No

(Skip to BENEFITS section)

___ Other (describe) _____

_____

Describe the nature of the interaction between you and the participants. In addition, if applicable, include a description of the ways in which different subjects or groups of participants will receive different treatment (e.g., control group vs comparison group, etc.).

a) Please describe, with sufficient detail, the procedure/plan/research methodology to be followed in your research (e.g. this is a quantitative, survey based study; tell us what participants will do; etc.).

b) How many times will you meet/interact with participants? (*If you are only observing public behaviour, SKIP to question d in this section.)*

c) How much total time will be required of each participant?

d) Where will the data collection occur (please provide sufficient detail)?

e) If you are conducting surveys, attach a copy of the survey instrument to this application. If you are conducting individual interviews or focus groups, including ethnographies or oral histories, attach a list of the interview questions as an "Attachment." Label attachments alphabetically, with descriptive titles (e.g.: *Attachment A: Interview Questions*).

4. INFORMED CONSENT: (*If you are only observing public behaviour, SKIP to next section*)

    a) What categories of consent documentation will you be obtaining from your participants? (Check all that apply)

        ___ written participant consent

        ___ written parent/guardian consent

        ___ Child assent 14–17

        ___ Child assent, assent 6–13

        ___ Adult with guardian consent

    b) Attach original consent documents. *note: be advised that electronic signatures and faxed, signed consents ARE allowed. Please describe how you will gain consent.

5. COLLECTION/RETENTION OF INFORMATION:

    a) With sufficient detail, describe the method(s) of recording participant responses (e.g., audiotape, videotape, written notes, surveys, etc.).

    b) Include the following statement to describe where and for how long will these materials will be stored and the precautions being taken to ensure the security and safety of the materials.

        All research materials including recordings, transcriptions, analyses and consent/assent documents will be stored in a secure location for three years according to federal regulations. In the event that materials are needed beyond this period, they will be kept secured until no longer needed, and then destroyed. All electronically stored data will be password protected during the storage period.

    c) Will the recordings of participant responses be coded for subsequent analysis? ***If you are only observing public behaviour, SKIP to next section***.

        ___ Yes

        ___ No

6. CONFIDENTIALITY:

    a) What assurances about maintaining privacy will be given to participants about the information collected?

        ___ 1. Anonymity is assured (data cannot be linked to participant identities)

        ___ 2. Confidentiality is assured (names and identifying information are protected, i.e., stored separately from data)

        ___ 3. Neither anonymity nor confidentiality is assured

    b) If you checked (2) above, describe methods to protect confidentiality with sufficient detail. Describe how you will maintain privacy of the participant as well as the data.

    c) If you checked (3) above, explain, with sufficient detail, why confidentiality is not assured.

    d) If you checked (3) above, provide sufficient detail that describes measures you will take to assure participants understand how their information will be used. Describe and attach any permissions/releases that will be requested from participants.

7. RISKS:

    a) Could participation in this study cause participants to feel uncomfortable or distressed?

        ___ Yes

        ___ No

    If yes, provide a detailed description of *what steps* you will take to protect them.

b) Are there any other risks associated with participation (e.g. financial, social, legal, etc.)?
   ___ Yes
   ___ No
   If yes, provide a detailed description of the measures you will take to mitigate these additional risks.

8. COMPENSATION: (*If you are only observing public behaviour, SKIP to the next section*)

Describe any cash or "gifts" (e.g.: coffee shop gift card) that participants will receive for participating in this research (see guidance about payment/gift compensation in the Smith School for Social Work Human Subjects Review Guideline, at the HSR site in the SSW website).

9. BENEFITS:

   a) Describe the potential benefits for you, the researcher, in conducting this study.
   b) Describe the potential benefits for individuals who participate as subjects, EXCLUDING payment/gift compensations.
   c) Describe the potential benefits to the field of clinical social work from this research.

10. Final application elements:

   a. Include the following statement to describe the intended uses of the data:
      The data collected from this study will be used to complete **[*include which is applicable: my Master's in Social Work (MSW) Thesis; my Doctoral degree*].** The results of the study may also be used in publications and presentations.
   b. If there are Co-Researchers, cooperating departments, and/or cooperating institutions, follow the following instructions:
      If you are working with/conducting your research with a researcher working at another institution or organization, include a letter of approval from that institution's IRB or agency administrator. If there are multiple researchers, indicate only one person on the Documentation of Review and Approval as the researcher; others should be designated as "Co-Researcher(s)" here.
   c. TRAINING: Include the following statement to describe training:
      I have completed the Collaborative Institutional Training Initiative (CITI) on line training course prior to HSR approval. The certificate of completion is on file at the SSW and was completed within the past four years.

7. Responding to the Case

As the social work member of the research ethics review committee, there is little you could have commented upon even if you did have concerns. As noted in the case study, the research was approved by the original Institutional Review Board and for valid reasons. There was no overt deception, and the risks of the research, along with the research benefits, were clearly laid out, including the possibility of death. Free and informed consent was given by those who had legal authority to do so, and the sponsors of the research were known and explicitly stated. While you may have raised additional concerns about conflicts of interest, the relationship between the researcher and the sponsoring group was disclosed and was in fact more overt than even some contemporary research is. Finally, not only were there safeguards for vulnerable persons, but participants in fact received more and better medical care than non-participants, as promised, which in and of itself could be considered another ethical issue.

The research design was of high quality. It was longitudinal, comparative with a homogeneous population in a regulated environment to account for confounding (extraneous) variables. From a methodological perspective this was a much better approach than many social work researchers are able to apply even today, due often in part to ethical constraints.

However, despite the fact it was good technical research, that it passed ethical scrutiny, and that the research may well have directly assisted you, as it has the authors of this book, you may still have an underlying unease. The question you may still be struggling with is: When is informed consent not informed consent but rather coercion?

From a twenty-first-century lens we can observe that these children were not valued as members of society, and thus parents and guardians may not have been as vigilant regarding the risks inherent in the experiment's parameters. The children's participation in this study may have allowed their guardians to believe that their "mentally retarded" children were making "some type of meaningful contribution" to society and perhaps even benefitting their able siblings, and likewise the researchers may very well have believed that using this vulnerable population in this manner was acceptable. However, research can pass all the prescribed tests yet still fail our personal practice ethics – which is never a bad thing.

8. Research Insight

Willowbrook was not the first example nor anywhere near the worst of questionable ethical practices. This dubious distinction was made evidently obvious during the Nuremburg Trials after World War II which exposed the inhumane experiments the Nazis undertook in concentration camps during the war. However, we in North America also have several infamous examples. Between 1942 and 1952, some of Canada's leading nutrition experts, in cooperation with the federal government, conducted controlled experiments without informed consent on malnourished Indigenous groups in Northern Manitoba and in various residential schools, purposefully withholding food to observe the effects of starvation-level diets.

In the United States the most infamous is the Tuskegee syphilis experiment that was conducted under the guidance of the Public Health Service from 1932 until 1972. Two groups of economically disadvantaged African American men from rural Alabama were involved – 400 men who had contracted syphilis and 200 who had not. While all received free medical care, none of those with syphilis were ever informed they had the disease or were treated for it so that the natural progression of syphilis could be longitudinally studied. This is despite the fact that by the end of the 1940s penicillin had become a standard for treatment. The researchers not only knowingly failed to treat the men for over 25 years, they prevented them from accessing other programs that would have informed and treated them. It was only when knowledge of the experiment was leaked to the media that it was halted. The outcomes included not only men who died prematurely from the disease but also their wives who contracted the disease, some of whom did so while pregnant and gave birth to children with congenital syphilis. This study was a major reason for the establishment of the Office for Human Research Protection in the United States and the establishment of IRBs and RERCs in post-secondary institutions and medical facilities.

9. Further Reflections

1. *In the preamble to this case study Hippocrates states: "There are in fact two things, science and opinion; the former begets knowledge, the latter ignorance." Do you agree?*
2. *When is informed consent not informed consent but rather coercion?*
3. *What recourse do we have as social workers if we are ever faced with a situation like Willowbrook?*

10. Additional Reading

Banks, S. (2005). *Ethics, accountability and the social professions*. New York: Palgrave Macmillan.

Baumrind, D. (1985). Research using intentional deception: Ethical issues revisited. *American Psychologist, 40*, 165–74.

Bogolub, E.B., & Thomas, N. (2005). Parental consent and the ethics of research with foster children: Beginning a cross-cultural dialogue. *Families in Society, 86*(4), 511–19.

Buckle, J., Dwyer, S., & Jackson, M. (2010). Qualitative bereavement research: Incongruity between the perspectives of participants and research ethics boards. *International Journal of Social Research Methodology, 13*(2), 111–25.

Canadian Institutes of Health Research, Natural Sciences and Engineering Research Council of Canada, & Social Sciences and Humanities Research Council of Canada (2010). *Tri-council policy statement: Ethical conduct for research involving humans*. http://www.pre.ethics.gc.ca/pdf/eng/tcps2/TCPS_2_FINAL_Web.pdf

Farley, A. (2009). The challenges of implementing evidence based practice: Ethical considerations in practice, education, policy, and research. *Social Work & Society, 7*(2), 246–59.

King's University College (2015). *Checklist for ethical assessment of research protocols.* http://www
.kings.uwo.ca/research/research-resources-committees/research-ethics-review-committee/

Morrow, V., & Richards, M. (2007). The ethics of social research with children: An overview.
Children & Society, 10(2), 90–105.

Mosby, I. (2013). Administering colonial science: Nutrition research and human biomedical experimentation in Aboriginal communities and residential schools, 1942–1952. *Histoire Sociale, 46*(1),
145–72.

Pyer, M., & Campbell, J. (2013). The "other participant" in the room: The effect of significant adults
in research with children. *Research Ethics, 9*(4), 153–65.

Reverby, S. (2009). *Examining Tuskegee: The infamous syphilis study and its legacy.* Chapel Hill:
University of North Carolina Press.

Simpson, C. (2003). Children and research participants: Who makes what decisions? *Health Law
Review, 2,* 20–9.

Thomas, N., & O'Kane, C. (2006). The ethics of participatory research with children. *Children
& Society, 12*(5), 336–48.

United Nations Centre for Human Rights. (1994). *Human rights and social work: A manual for
schools of social work and the social work profession.* New York: United Nations.

11. Internet Resources

Government of Canada, "Tutorial Course on Research Ethics (CORE)":
http://www.pre.ethics.gc.ca/eng/education/tutorial-didacticiel/

Government of Canada, "Tri-Agency Framework: Responsible Conduct of Research":
http://www.rcr.ethics.gc.ca/eng/policy-politique/framework-cadre/

Chris Flipp, "Research Ethics":
https://www.youtube.com/watch?v=Zbi7nIbAuMQ

CASE STUDY 3
Another Question of Ethics: Studying HIV

1. Preamble

Overheard in the waiting room of a social service agency:

> CLIENT 1: The first rule of social work is to do no harm to your client.
> CLIENT 2: It worries me that they need a rule to know that.

2. The Problem

There has been a decades-long struggle to provide alternative interventions for injection drug users (IDUs) in both Canada and the United States as part of the larger public health campaign to minimize the risk and spread of HIV. During that time social workers, along with nurses and other health professionals, have staffed clinics in Europe providing free needles and a safe and hygienic place for IDUs to use. As well, counselling is provided to respond to issues of daily living and to provide support to those contemplating a move to reducing or stopping their drug use.

Another treatment option is methadone maintenance, though it is no less controversial. Methadone is a long-acting synthetic opioid analgesic with properties similar to those of morphine, first synthesized by the Germans in preparation for World War II as an alternative to opium-based analgesics. It was later discovered to be effective as a harm-reduction option for individuals dependent upon other opioids, as it produces morphine-like actions and cross-tolerance but does not produce a psychoactive effect when given orally. Unlike morphine and heroin, methadone is not administered by injection, is highly effective in alleviating both physical and psychological cravings for other opioid use when administered orally, and is excreted slowly. A single dose is effective for up to 24 hours, and as it is orally administered, methadone eliminates the risk of transferring blood-borne diseases though needle sharing.

3. The Process

In an attempt to determine if a centre for IDUs should be opened in Vancouver and to provide an empirical foundation for a highly emotional debate, a team of researchers applied for $900,000 in funding to examine the long-term impact of injection drug use on HIV and AIDS. To obtain funding they were required to receive approval from the multidisciplinary research ethics review committee at the University of British Columbia. To do so they needed to demonstrate not only that their research design was sound and would likely generate new knowledge, but that in its completion the research would do no harm.

4. The Research

The Vancouver Injection Drug Use Study proposed to follow 1,200 injection drug users over three years. Part of the $900,000 requested was targeted as an inducement to encourage participation over the course of a longitudinal study of a transient and hard-to-reach population. As part of the study's methodology, all 1,200 participants were to be interviewed seven times and receive $25.00 for each interview they completed; however, no additional social or health supports were to be offered. The total amount to be paid to participants equaled one-quarter of the grant's total financial allocation. It should also be noted that at the time of the study, $25.00 was the approximate cost of one street buy of heroin. Another important issue was that a significant minority of the population to be studied were of Indigenous ancestry, and this traditionally marginalized population also did not receive any additional supports so as not to bias the research protocol.

All of those who participated in the study would also be regularly tested for HIV and tuberculosis as well as having access to counselling from social workers at any time during their participation in the study. However, methadone maintenance, a clinically proven method of harm reduction, was not included as a treatment option, as it would have necessitated the establishment of a clinic to administer the drug when the intent of this research was to assess what type of clinic was needed and would be most beneficial.

5. Questions

In your role as one member of the research ethics review committee, discuss:

1. *What ethical issues are raised by this proposal?*
2. *What additional questions would you ask of the researchers?*

3. *What are the implications of the fact that a significant minority of the participants were of Indigenous heritage?*
4. *Are there any modifications to the research that you would like to suggest?*
5. *Do you approve this study?*

6. Social Work Practice

Voluntary Participation and Coercion

As we noted in the previous case study, any social work activity that leads to exploitation, insensitivity, incompetence, irresponsibility, or abandonment is deemed to be unethical behaviour, but how is this connected to ethical behaviour in research practice? There are key research practices that have their foundation in the ethics of our profession. For example, because we believe in individual self-determination, we do not force people to participate in research projects. They have free will, which means they can refuse to take part or withdraw from involvement at any time. This is called voluntary participation. While as a principle this appears fairly clear at first, social work researchers must be sure that participants are not unintentionally coerced into participation. For example, consider an agency that asks its clients to participate in a program evaluation, telling them that their participation is totally voluntary. Some clients will accept this on face value, but other clients may be less convinced it is so. They may not want to participate but voluntarily agree to do so because they are afraid that if they say no they will experience negative consequences such as delayed or even no service. Thus, provision of service must never be tied in any way to participation in the evaluation or in any type of research, and those who choose not to participate should be treated exactly the same as those who agree to take part in the research.

Another common example of unintended coercion occurs when people are offered an incentive, in the form of money or special privileges, if they agree to participate in a study. Researchers employ this strategy to increase the number of people in their samples. While in most cases the incentive is considered a token offer by the researcher intended to offset the cost and inconvenience of participation, it may have much greater value to the person who receives it. If a person would rather not take part in the research project but is doing so for the money, a free meal, or some valued privilege, then that would be considered coercive and unethical. In particularly, in studies involving substance-using participants concerns have been raised that monetary incentives may lead to increased substance use and increased coercion (Finch, Kuksis, & DiProspero, 2015).

Before the research begins the researcher must fully inform potential participants of a number of factors that could influence their decision to participate voluntarily. They need to be told:

- the purpose of the research, with deception only allowed in rare situations where the research design requires less than full disclosure;
- what they will be required to do;
- the time it will take;
- any potential benefits to them from participation; and
- any potential harm that could come to them as a result of participation.

"Harm" in this context is understood quite broadly. Obviously, if what participants are being asked to do could cause pain or discomfort they should be warned, but harm extends to emotional and social aspects of participation as well. The researcher has to be aware that asking a person to answer personal questions regarding their sexuality identity or to recall traumatic events in their lives could result in feelings such as sadness, anxiety, or fear or might even re-traumatize the participant. If there is any potential for harmful affect as an outcome of participation, research subjects need to be warned of this and offered support or counselling if they agree to participate and then do suffer troubling emotions as an outcome of the study. As well, participation in a research initiative may expose an individual to social consequences such as stigmatization, isolation, or ridicule. While researchers endeavour to "do no harm," they must look at many aspects of harm to ensure they have achieved their goal.

Informed Consent

Information regarding the risks of the research should be provided to potential participants in written form so that they can review it before agreeing to participate. After they have looked over the information on the form, the standard procedure is to ask those who agree to participate to sign it to signify their consent. Informed consent is a requirement of all ethical research and can become quite challenging if the intended participants are illiterate or speak a different language. The written material must be in a language and written in a style that people can truly understand. There are additional challenges if intended participants are children or if they lack the intellectual capacity to understand what they are being asked to do. In situations like these the researcher usually tries to obtain substitute consent from a parent or person who has legal authority to represent the person. If this is the case, the researcher should also make every effort to determine what the potential participant understands about what they are being asked to do and, to the extent possible, attempt to obtain the participant's consent as well. For example, if you are doing research with adolescents it would be ethical practice to obtain legal informed consent from a parent as well as consent from the child, but if the child is an infant this would not be possible.

The consent form should also contain information such as:

- the name(s) and contact information of the researcher(s);
- the sponsor (funder) of the research; and
- how the person's privacy will be protected.

Depending upon the research design it may be possible to collect anonymous information. This means that no one, not even the researcher, can connect a participant with the information he or she provided. In other cases this is not possible, so the researcher must assure the individual that the information she or he provides will be kept confidential. "Confidential" means that the researcher knows who provided what information but promises not to tell anyone else. Confidentiality is another ethical value of our profession. To make sure that confidentiality is maintained, the researcher must also assure the participant that reasonable care will be taken to keep others from obtaining access to the information collected. In some research each participant is assigned a number, and data are collected and stored according to numbers, not names. This is actually good practice because it means that casual observers cannot determine who provided the data, but it does not mean the data are anonymous. Somewhere there is a list that shows the names and corresponding numbers, allowing data to be connected to persons. If you are taking this approach, then participants need to be advised that the information will be confidential. By definition, anonymous information is confidential, so it's not necessary to tell participants that the information is both anonymous and confidential.

Significance of the Research

Additional considerations in assessing whether a proposed research project is ethical include whether the purpose is significant enough to ask people to participate; frivolous research is unethical, as is research that is not well designed and thought out. Finally, having an ethically sound proposal is important, but it is not enough to ensure an ethical research endeavour. During the implementation and analysis phases the researcher must continue to act in an ethical manner. It is not ethical to demean or ridicule research participants, to falsify research findings, or to hide disconfirming results.

Ethical Decision Making

Most competent social work researchers, practitioners, and research practitioners easily avoid ethical problems. However, from time to time individuals will disagree as to what constitutes ethical behaviour or a situation will arise where two or more ethical standards conflict. In this situation you need to consider what actions you can take to make a final decision. It is these ethical dilemmas that create problems – the "lose-lose" situation where, regardless of which course of action is taken, there will be some negative repercussions.

There are two fundamental approaches to guide you in resolving ethical dilemmas: teleological and deontological. Teleological decision making is goal directed and consequentialistic in its approach. Its focus is on the anticipated beneficial outcome of a given situation or action. The outcome that is important here is overall consequences rather than the outcome for an individual. Teleological ethics draws its name from the Greek term *telos*, which referred to an archery target. A teleological approach is one that orients each action or activity towards a goal or a target that is deemed to be good. A teleological ethic orients actions to ends and chooses those means that lead to a desired outcome that has been identified with "the good." Thus, actions taken under this type of ethical decision making framework are good by virtue of the consequences they produce. We should act in a certain manner because it will produce the most positive result. Teleological ethical approaches, being consequentialist in nature, focus upon expected outcomes of our actions leading to cost/benefit and cost/effectiveness-based courses of action. This is a model that has been regularly followed by the social work professional in fostering benevolence for clients.

In contrast, deontological ethical decision making is concerned with the balancing of rights and duties and tends to reject purely outcome-orientated considerations as mistaken. While not ignoring outcomes entirely, this philosophical approach states that certain types of actions are inherently correct and thus good, or wrong and thus bad. It enjoins us to take the correct action because it is in fact the right thing to do. The right thing to do can then be identified by appeal to some form of external authority such as the Ten Commandments or a code of practice of a professional body such as social work, psychology, or addiction counselling. *Deontological* is derived from the Greek word for "duty," and thus this approach is orientated less to benefits or harms produced by action than to fundamental restrictions on how we may act. A deontological perspective is centred on the conviction that consequences of an action do not in themselves determine whether the action is morally correct or wrong. Rather, this perspective maintains that whether an action is ethical depends upon whether it is in accordance

Table 2.3 Teleological versus Deontological Ethics

Teleological	*Deontological*
Goal directed	Certain kinds of actions are inherently right or good
Actions are good by virtue of their consequences	Actions are good because they are the right thing to do
We should do the right thing because it will produce the most positive results	We do the right thing because it is right
Anchored to some non-moral purpose	Actions based upon an external authority
Utilitarian	Rule driven

with and is performed out of respect for certain absolute and universal principles such as respect for others. A comparison of these alternative approaches is presented in Table 2.3.

Few of us are purely teleological or deontological ethical decision makers, but rather follow both paths at different times and in different situations. What is critical to know is which philosophical approach we are using and why, and to be able to document and explain the process of our decision making.

7. Responding to the Case

Reflect upon your thoughts and discussions regarding the case and consider: Did you approach the scenario from a teleological or from a deontological perspective?

Depending upon your approach, you would have discussed some or all of the following key issues:

1. What are the ethics of not providing a treatment alternative that has been previously demonstrated to have value in reducing suffering and disease, especially when one is working with and studying a vulnerable population?
2. Is the potential benefit of empirically demonstrating a need for a controversial and socially unpopular treatment that may help many in the future balanced by the potential risk to current study members, who may become ill and even die during the study period? Underscoring this question is the consideration that the greater the number of participants who become ill or die, the more likely you are to be funded for your controversial and socially unpopular program.
3. At what value does an inducement unduly bias voluntary participation?

4. Is there an inherent conflict of interest between the study and social work ethics?
5. Is there an inherent conflict of interest between the study and the specific social work code of ethics you are mandated to follow?
6. Was this a coercive study?
7. Are there any other implications when working with a highly marginalized population?

The study was ultimately funded for its full amount, but not without its critics. There was an ongoing debate regarding the amount of the inducement, with claims that it was simply too great both in terms of the entire allocation of funds and that it allowed if not encouraged participants to obtain additional illicit substances upon completion of each interview.

Despite being approved by both a hospital and a university research ethics review committee, the study was dogged by claims that it was unethical because it did not include a methadone component. The researchers contended that since funds for methadone treatment and physicians willing to supply it were in short supply, and since the purpose of the research was not to develop a new program but to study a social issue, they should not be mandated to include methadone treatment. Again, both research ethics review committees agreed, though not without some public consternation, including the chair of one committee stating publicly that while the study passed all the ethical criteria there were still moral issues with it. Ultimately, it was deemed not to be the researchers' responsibility to include an intervention in their study that was not readily available, even if the entire sample contracted HIV during the course of the research.

At the time of writing Vancouver has established and is operating a safer injection site (SIS) for intravenous drug users, the only one in North America, though its funding remained tenuous for years, highlighted by the Harper government's repeated attempts to shutter it. This program, which has been empirically demonstrated to save client lives every year it has operated, arose because of this research. As well, methadone maintenance has become a more established intervention option not only in British Columbia but also across much of Canada. So as with Willowbrook this research that placed participants at risk has benefited thousands because of that risk.

8. Research Insight

Another Canadian example of an ethical dilemma arising from a research study involved Dr. Nancy Olivieri, who was working at the Hospital for Sick Children in Toronto, Ontario. Dr. Olivieri was the principal investigator of a research study that indicated negative outcomes for an experimental drug to combat thalassemia, a rare blood disorder. When she attempted to publish her findings the sponsoring pharmaceutical company, Apotex, tried to suppress her results and have her removed from the hospital. This forced Dr. Olivieri to sue the hospital and the pharmaceutical company under the dictum of academic freedom in order to maintain her livelihood and, more importantly in research, her reputation. Thus, when conducting research you need to be very clear on who ultimately has ownership of the outcome and how the owner may implement the research findings, as your outcomes can often have unintended consequences affecting an array of people.

9. Further Reflections

1. *Was no harm done here?*
2. *Are there any situations where a research study could receive ethics board approval and yet not meet the standards of ethical social work practice?*
3. *If you were chair of the committee, would you have resigned based upon the decision the group arrived at? Why or why not?*

10. Additional Reading

Antle, B., Regehr, C., & Mishna, F. (2004). Qualitative research ethics: Thriving within tensions. In A.R. Roberts & K.R. Yeager (Eds.), *Evidence Based Practice Manual* (pp. 126–36). New York: Oxford University Press.

Bell, K., & Salmon, A. (2012). Good intentions and dangerous assumptions: Research ethics committees and illicit drug use research. *Research Ethics*, 8(4), 191–99.

Butler, I. (2002). A code of ethics for social work and social care research. *British Journal of Social Work*, 32(2), 239–48.

Canadian Association of Social Workers. (2005). *Code of ethics*. Ottawa: Canadian Association of Social Workers.

Cottrell, R.C. (2014). Scientific integrity and the market for lemons. *Research Ethics*, 10(1), 17–28.

Davison, J. (2004). Dilemmas in research: Issues of vulnerability and disempowerment for the social worker/researcher. *Journal of Social Work Practice*, 18(3), 379–93.

DuVal, G., & Salmon, C. (2004). Research note: Ethics of drug treatment research with court-supervised subjects. *Journal of Drug Issues*, 34(4), 991–1006.

Finch, S., Kuksis, M., & DiProspero, C. (2015). Creation of a miniature black market with use of gift cards for research participants in an addicted population. *Canadian Journal of Addiction*, 6(3), 27.

Hardina, D. (2004). Guidelines for ethical practice in community organization. *Social Work*, 49(4), 595–604.

Johnsson, L., Eriksson, S., Helgesson, G., & Hansson, M.G. (2014). Making researchers moral: Why trustworthiness requires more than ethics guidelines and review. *Research Ethics*, *10*(1), 29–46.

Mertens, D., & Ginsberg, P. (2009). *The handbook of social research ethics*. Thousand Oaks, CA: Sage.

Peled, E., & Leichtentritt, R. (2002). The ethics of qualitative social work research. *Qualitative Social Work: Research and Practice*, *1*(2), 145–69.

Reamer, F. (1998). The evolution of social work ethics. *Social Work*, *43*(6), 488–500.

Reamer, F. (2013). *Social work values and ethics* (4th ed.). New York: Columbia University Press.

Shuchman, M. (2005). *The drug trial: Nancy Olivieri and the science scandal that rocked the Hospital for Sick Children*. Toronto: Random House.

11. Internet Resources

Articles

Candice Vallantin, "The Ethics of Addiction Studies":
   http://thetyee.ca/News/2012/05/23/Addiction-Studies-Ethics/
American Psychological Association, "Five Principles for Research Ethics":
   http://www.apa.org/monitor/jan03/principles.aspx
Resources for Research Ethics Education, "What Is Research Ethics?":
   http://research-ethics.net/introduction/what/#research-ethics

Videos

Dr. Sam Fiala, "Research Ethics":
   https://www.youtube.com/watch?v=Ir3VvYNzHeM
Case Western Reserve University, "Ethics Workshop Part 1 – Overview of Moral Reasoning and Ethical Theory":
   https://www.youtube.com/watch?v=TwKryWlGCT0

Website

Resources for Research Ethics Education:
   http://research-ethics.net/

CASE STUDY 4
Ethical Issues of Obtaining Consent to Interview Children in Post-Separation Disputes

1. Preamble

The movement towards the inclusion of children in the decision making process following separation or the divorce process is emerging as an important area of practice, policy, and research. The *UN Convention on the Rights of the Child* creates an obligation for governments to ensure that children are provided with an opportunity to express their views about decisions affecting their well-being, consistent with their age, capacity, and desire to participate. The *Convention* has been a significant underlying factor in the growing concern for and commitment to allowing children more say in decisions that affect their future well-being. What is clear from the legal framework of the *Convention* and research is that children have a right to be heard and are interested in being heard.

2. The Problem

Despite these protections, certain controversies and tensions continue to exist with respect to children's participation in parental decision making post-separation. These tensions are a result of attempts to balance the vulnerability of children and their need for protection given their age and developmental level, on the one hand, with their rights as individuals on the other. In addition, parents, lawyers, mental health practitioners, and judges all express concerns regarding appropriately involving children in their parents' dispute. Moreover, obtaining ethics approval from an institutional research ethics board to interview children and provide them with a token of appreciation for their time is an equally daunting and exhaustive process.

3. The Process

Funding was obtained to hear directly from children about their views and experiences of their parents' separation process and how they felt being involved with family justice professionals in the process. Names of children were obtained through reviewing closed custody and access files in three court sites in Ontario (two in Toronto and one in

London) from 2005 to 2008. However, ethics approval was still required in order to allow the children to be interviewed even by telephone to learn what they actually had to say about their experiences interacting with judges, mental health professionals, and lawyers. Telephone calls and follow-up letters also needed to be sent to the parents, some of whom were no longer directly communicating because of the nature of the divorce, advising them of the study and requesting them to ask their children to participate in the study and for the parents to give their permission for their children to participate.

Given that the study involved separation and divorce it was vital to have both parents be aware of the study, regardless of the disposition of their separation/divorce proceedings, and for both to sign consent forms irrespective of sole or joint custody. If both parents were involved in mediation or other alternative dispute resolution (ADR) processes, it was more likely that they would be open to being involved and be cooperative. However, if either parent refused to sign the consent forms then the youth would not be eligible to participate in the study even if she or he wished to. Likewise, if both parents consented but the youth did not, the youth would not be eligible to be part of the study.

4. The Research

The goal of the study was to conduct qualitative interviews with:

(1) 30 children between the ages of 7 and 17 years;[2]
(2) youths who were involved in their parents' separation and/or divorce;
(3) youths who come from a mix of rural and urban areas;
(4) youths who are from different cultural and ethnic backgrounds; and
(5) youths who could read and speak English.

Each parent had to be contacted individually and advised that the research was being conducted so they could explain and discuss it with their child and be able to answer any questions their child might have regarding what the study entailed and what they would be asked to discuss during the interview. Each parent and child received either a mailed or a faxed Information Form and Consent Form outlining the nature of the study and requesting the child's involvement. Both parents and youth needed to be

---

2 These ages were chosen as they possess the cognitive abilities developmentally to participate fully in the interview process. In addition, it is important that they also sign consent for their individual participation. Both written and oral consent is reflected in the Child & Family Services Act, where children age 7+ need to provide written consent to be adopted and children age 10+ must provide written consent to release their medical records. In addition, signing consent to participate validates and makes the whole process transparent for the youth's participation in the study.

aware that participation in the study was voluntary but that for participating each young person would receive a $25.00 honorarium to compensate them for their time. No identifying information would be released about them before, during, or after the study and only those parents and youths who signed consent forms *before* the interviews began could part of the study.

Also important to consider in preparing for the interviews is that during the course of answering questions the youths might have feelings of the separation and/or divorce process rekindled.

Following is the interview guide that was developed:

1. What do you remember about your parents' separation? What was it like for you (emotionally/academically/behaviourally)?
2. How did you find out about the plans that were made for your care (i.e., did parents, your lawyer/social worker, the judge tell you)? What do you think would be the best way for children to learn about the arrangements for your care?
3. How were you involved in decisions your parents made about living apart? What do you think would be the best way to be involved or not?
4. Did plans for your care change over time? How were you involved in decision making about the changes?
5. What can you tell me about your participation in the process? (Did you feel heard/understood, were your wishes put forward, who told you about the final decision?)
6. What did you find helpful about (legal, legal/social work, judicial interview, child custody assessment) being involved in the process? What was not helpful?
7. What advice would you give to lawyers/social workers/judges who work with youths to help others in similar circumstances?

5. Question

Develop the necessary consent forms to carry out the research that will be acceptable to your university's Research Ethics Review Committee (RERC).

6. Social Work Practice

While approval of research ethics was given for the study, it was not without additional questions from the RERC. For example, committee members wanted to know if it was problematic to provide children with an honorarium as it could be viewed as an inducement to be interviewed rather than compensation for their time. They wanted to know why the honorarium was $25.00 and if it had to be that amount. The researchers were asked how they would know that the young person was getting the honorarium and it was not being kept by one of the parents. The committee asked how the researchers would know that the young person was alone and talking in a safe, confidential environment. They asked what would happen if the young person had been involved in some form of abuse themselves by a guardian or had witnessed some form of abuse against their guardian and this information was shared during the interview. These were all valid questions and required thoughtful and respectful dialogue between the researcher and the committee. This discussion demonstrates the importance of providing the RERC with as much background and contextual information as possible so they can understand the research better, given that many on the committee may not be in the social sciences or involved in applied research.

In addition, interviewing children for research purposes is different from clinical interviewing, though you must be just as attuned to the child's feelings and issues. Parents may often consent on behalf of their child as they (the parent) believe the child will say what they (the parent) want told. More often than not in this type of research when there is high conflict, children may refuse consent because they do not wish to be put back in the middle of the dispute between their parents or wish to talk to anyone else about the situation yet again. Despite the importance of the research, the child's wishes must be respected above the parental consent and no child should be interviewed who does not want to be. Children need to know that they can say no, answer some questions, or respond to none at all throughout the research process. Having said this, many children who did participate in the interviews reported that they were grateful someone asked them about their views and experiences. As has often been said, they want "a voice and a choice."

7. Responding to the Case

To successfully meet the requirements of the RERC you need to complete four distinct documents:

i)   information form for youth
ii) information form for parents
iii) consent form for youth
iv) consent form for parents.

The actual forms are presented here to allow you to compare your documents to what was used in completing this study.

Figure 2.4a   Children's Participation in Separation and/or Divorce Processes

INFORMATION FOR YOUTH

INTRODUCTION

Dr. Rachel Birnbaum, School of Social Work, King's University College at Western University, is exploring the different ways the voice of the child is being heard as a result of their parents' separation and/or divorce.

The purpose of the study is to explore how you experienced being part of that process by having a lawyer, a lawyer and social worker, an interview with the judge, or being part of a child custody and access assessment. It is important to hear what you have to say about your experience with one of these services at that time and to have your thoughts and views known. In addition, this research *may* offer important insights to hearing the voice of other youths during these times.

We would greatly appreciate your expertise and consent to be interviewed in this process. You will receive a $25.00 honorarium for your valuable time.

If you have any questions or concerns please feel free to contact me at 1-800-265-4406, ext. 4431.

PRIVACY AND CONFIDENTIALITY

All information collected will be used for research purposes and will be kept confidential. However, any information that suggests abuse or neglect will result in a report to a Children's Aid Society. Codes will be used in place of real names for all information and all information that will identify you or your family will be kept separate and held by Dr. Birnbaum in a locked cabinet.

VOLUNTARY PARTICIPATION

Your participation in this research project is completely voluntary and you may answer some or none of the questions and you will still receive a $25.00 honorarium for your valuable time.

THANK YOU

This research project may be helpful in servicing children and families who are presently involved in separation and divorce related matters. Your assistance in being part of this research project is greatly appreciated. Please feel free to contact Rachel Birnbaum for aggregate reporting of the results when the study is completed.

Dr. Rachel Birnbaum, Ph.D., RSW, LL.M.
Professor
King's University College at Western University

Figure 2.4b   Children's Participation in Separation and/or Divorce Processes

> ## CONSENT FORM FOR YOUTH
>
> The Project has been explained to me. I understand that the information gathered about me will be kept confidential. I have been told of the possible risks (any information that suggests abuse or neglect will result in a report to a Children's Aid Society) and benefits of the Project and that this information may help in understanding what services are more or less helpful to children during times of separation and/or divorce. I have been assured of privacy and confidentiality, and that no information that discloses my identity will be released or printed without my prior verbal and written permission.
>
> 1) The information is used only by Rachel Birnbaum.
> 2) All information obtained will be kept in a secure locked filing cabinet in Rachel's office. The information will be destroyed by [place a date here].
> 3) Codes are used in place of real names for all information and all information that identifies me will be kept confidential.
> 4) I will receive a $25.00 honorarium for my participation.
> 5) I will receive a copy of both the Information for Youth and this Consent Form.
> 6) I may contact Rachel Birnbaum to obtain the results when the study is completed and that all information is presented anonymously.
>
> I understand that my participation in this Project is completely voluntary and it has been explained to me that I can withdraw at any time. My signature below signifies my written permission to participate in this Project.
>
> _____   _____
> Print your name   Your signature
>
> _____   _____
> Witness   Witness signature
>
> If you have any questions or comments, please call Rachel Birnbaum toll-free at: 1-800-265-4406, ext. 4431, King's University College at Western University.

Figure 2.4c   Children's Participation in Separation and/or Divorce Processes

INFORMATION FOR PARENT/S

INTRODUCTION

Dr. Rachel Birnbaum, School of Social Work, King's University College at Western University, is exploring the different ways the voice of the child is being heard as a result of their parents' separation and/or divorce.

The purpose of the study is to explore how your child experienced being part of the process by having a lawyer represent them, a lawyer and social worker, an interview with the judge, or being part of a child custody and access assessment. It is important to hear what your son/daughter had to say about their experience with the service that was being provided to them at that time. In addition, this research *may* offer important insights about hearing the voice of the child during times of parental separation and about what works and what does not for children.

We would greatly appreciate your consent to interview your son/daughter. Your son/daughter will receive a $25.00 honorarium for their participation.

This information is being sent to you to advise you of this study and request your permission to have your son/daughter interviewed by Dr. Birnbaum.

PRIVACY AND CONFIDENTIALITY

All information collected will be used for research purposes and will be kept confidential. However, any information that suggests abuse or neglect of your child will result in a report to a Children's Aid Society. Codes will be used in place of real names for all information and all information that will identify you or your son/daughter will be kept separate and held by Dr. Birnbaum in a locked cabinet in her office.

VOLUNTARY PARTICIPATION

Your participation and your son/daughter's participation in this research project is completely voluntary.

THANK YOU

This research project may be helpful in servicing children and families who are presently involved in separation and/or divorce related matters. Your assistance in discussing this research project with your son/daughter is greatly appreciated. Please feel free to contact Dr. Birnbaum for aggregate reporting of the results when the study is completed.

Dr. Rachel Birnbaum, Ph.D., RSW, LL.M.
Professor
King's University College at Western University

Figure 2.4d Children's Participation in Separation and/or Divorce Processes

CONSENT FORM FOR PARENT/S

I, _____ of _____

  (please print name)   (address)

acknowledge that I am a/the parent/guardian with _____ legal responsibility

                                  (sole/joint)

for _____ .

    (print child's full name)

I have read and understood the information sheet provided to me. Based on this document and my discussions with Dr. Rachel Birnbaum, I feel that I understand the purpose of this project and am willing to have my son/daughter participate. I understand that I will receive a copy of both the Information for Parents and this Consent Form.

I understand that any information gathered about me and my son/daughter will be kept confidential and private and destroyed by [place a date here]. Personal information will not be used to contact myself or my child after this project is complete.

A final report will be produced and may be made public, but will not contain any identifying information on myself or my son/daughter. Information collected will be reported as aggregate or in themes from the data collected – any individual comments or quotes will be kept anonymous – with only age and gender of children identified. The information obtained is being used only by the research team (Professor Birnbaum) and only for the purposes of reporting on findings of this research.

I have been told of the possible risks (e.g.: any information that suggests abuse or neglect will result in a report to a Children's Aid Society) and benefits of the project (e.g.: this information may benefit in understanding how children's voices are heard and whether it was helpful or not). I understand that information on local family justice services and other resources will be available to me if I require assistance. I further understand that if my child requires assistance during or after the interview session, Dr. Birnbaum will be available to him/her to provide information on available resources.

By signing this consent form (please circle applicable box):

(a) I confirm that I am the sole custodian of the child and have sole decision making regarding my son/daughter and have the legal right to provide consent for him/her to participate in this project;

(b) I confirm that I share decision making regarding our child and will provide permission to have our child's other parent contacted to sign consent for participation in this project that is required.

I understand that my son/daughter's participation in this Project is completely voluntary and it has been explained to me that he/she can withdraw at any time. I also confirm that I am not presently involved in any family litigation.

My signature below signifies my written permission for my son/daughter to participate in this Project.

I understand that when the research is completed I may contact Dr. Birnbaum regarding the results in aggregate form that may be published.

_____	_____	_____
Print your name	Your signature	Date
_____	_____	_____
Witness	Witness signature	Date

If you have any questions or concerns, please feel free to contact Dr. Rachel Birnbaum toll-free at: 1-800-265-4406, ext. 4431, at King's University College at Western University.

8. Research Insight

Given the potential effect on a child as an outcome of participating, each youth and his/her parent(s) were also given a resource list for their community in case there was a need to seek additional assistance or counselling.

9. Further Reflections

The following was the initial screening process employed to obtain participants for the study.

Screening Decisions (Initial Telephone Call)

Do you have a youth aged 7–17 who lives full-time with you or for whom you have shared physical custody? Would you be interested in hearing more about this project and answering some questions that will help us determine if your son/daughter would be interested in an interview? If your child does fit the criteria, we will make sure we have consent from both you and your child before he/she participates in any group. Any youth who participates in this project will be provided with a $25.00 honorarium for their time and expertise.

I do need to ask you a few questions before we start.

(Screening Questions)

1) I would like to talk to your child/youth about their participation in the separation and/or divorce process.
2) I would like to talk to your child/youth who had been involved with (name the service they had obtained). What is the situation regarding your son/daughter?
   (a) the child lives with both legal guardians;
   (b) the child lives with you and you have full decision making responsibility (go to question 4);
   (c) the child lives with you (at least 50 per cent of the time) and you have joint decision making responsibility (go to question 5);
   (d) you have access to your son/daughter as well as joint decision making responsibility (go to question 5);
   (e) you have access to your son/daughter but you do not have decision making responsibility (may not be eligible; ask to contact other parent for information).

3) Would you be willing to share contact information for the other parent so we can contact them to determine if they would consent to your son/daughter participating in this study? (if response is no, not eligible)

4) Are there any active court cases or proceedings involving custody and/or access or decision making responsibilities between you and your son/daughter's other parent? (referring to target youth in question only)

5) Is there any reason why your son/daughter could not participate? (Prompt: looking for reading/writing/hearing issues)

Version One: If Parent Agrees

Thank you for taking the time to talk to me. How may I contact your son/daughter? Which telephone number is the best one to reach you at? Which time of day is the best for me to contact him/her?

Version Two: If Parent and/or Child Is Not Included in Study

Thank you for taking the time to talk to me. Unfortunately the information that you provided does not meet the criteria for the interview.

Prompt: one or more of the answers must have been in the **exclusion** criteria:

Inclusion/Exclusion Criteria:

(i)   there is a youth between 7 and 17 living in the household (e.g., full-time or at least 50 per cent of the time);

(ii) the youth and parent(s) have the ability to speak/read English;

(iv) the youth's parent(s) are not presently in litigation regarding custody and/or access or decision making responsibilities of that youth;

(v)   the youth is willing to participate in a confidential interview and signs the consent form; and

(vi) the parent(s) contacted has sole decision making responsibility or joint decision making with a willingness to contact the youth's other parent to obtain permission for their child to participate.

10. Additional Reading

Birnbaum, R., Bala, N., & Cyr, F. (2011). Children's experiences with family justice professionals and judges in Ontario and Ohio. *International Journal of Law, Policy and the Family*, *25*(3), 398–422.

Campbell, A. (2013). I wish the views were clearer: Children's wishes and views in Australian Family Law. *Children Australia*, *38*(4), 184–91.

Carroll-Lind, J., Chapman, J., Gregory, J., & Maxwell, G. (2006). The key to the gatekeepers: Passive consent and other ethical issues surrounding the rights of children to speak on issues that concern them. *Child Abuse & Neglect, 30*, 979–89.

Cashmore, J. (2006). Ethical issues concerning consent in obtaining children's reports on their experience of violence. *Child Abuse & Neglect, 30*, 969–77.

Coyne, I. (2010). Research with children and young people: The issue of parental (proxy) consent. *Children & Society, 24*, 227–37.

McLaughlin, H. (2006). Involving young service users as co-researchers: Possibilities, benefits, and costs. *British Journal of Social Work, 36*, 1395–410.

Simpson, C. (2003). Children and research participation: Who makes what decisions. *Health Law Review, 11*(2), 20–9.

Williamson, E., Kent, J., & Ashcroft, R. (2005). Conducting research with children: The limits of confidentiality and child protection protocols. *Children & Society, 19*, 397–409.

11. Internet Resources

Ethics of Social Research and Children

Ethical Research Involving Children:
http://childethics.com/

Virginia Morrow, "The Ethics of Research with Children and Families in Young Lives: Practical Experiences":
http://www.younglives.org.uk/sites/www.younglives.org.uk/files/YL-WP53-Morrow-EthicsOfResearchWithChildren.pdf

Tri-Council Research Ethics Training website:
http://tcps2core.ca/welcome

CASE STUDY 5
Respectful Ethical Research Practice: Working with First Nations, Inuit, Innu, and Metis Peoples

1. Preamble

Throughout the residential school era in Canada children living in the institutions endured unimaginable physical, mental, and sexual duress. They were also subject to unauthorized tests and often bizarre experiments. In the midst of World War II, Foster (1943), an American, undertook extrasensory perception (ESP) experiments at the Brandon Manitoba Indian Residential School without the students' or their parents' consent. Fortunately, in this instance no recorded harm occurred as this was a rudimentary ESP study where children were asked to guess what symbol or sign was on hidden cards using their ESP. Foster found that "Indian" children produced better outcomes than "American" children, though this entire area of inquiry (not surprisingly) has been deemed unscientific. However, other authorized studies that also did not obtain student or parent permission were less eccentric and benign and far more insidious. Federally sponsored and supported research ranged from withholding vitamins and inducing starvation to better understand the science of nutrition to inoculating children with an experimental tuberculosis vaccine which produced permanent hearing loss in some of the children.

Prior to the 1980s, the term *Indian* was in common use in Canada to refer to the dominant Indigenous group. In 1980, hundreds of chiefs met in Ottawa and used the collective noun First Nations in their document, *Declaration of the First Nations*. In 1982, the National Indian Brotherhood became the Assembly of First Nations, the political voice for First Nations people in Canada. Symbolically, the term elevated First Nations to the status of "first among equals" alongside the English and French as founding nations of Canada. It is also reflective of the sovereign nature of many communities and the ongoing quest for self-determination and self-government. The Canadian Constitution (1982) declared that aboriginal peoples in Canada include Indian (First Nations), Inuit, and Metis peoples. First Nations is a uniquely Canadian concept and one not in use among Indigenous peoples outside of Canada.

Inuit refers to a group of culturally related Indigenous peoples inhabiting the Arctic regions of Canada (Northwest Territories, Nunatsiavut, Nunavik, Nunavut, Nunatukavut), the United States (Alaska), Denmark (Greenland), and Russia (Siberia). *Inuit* means "the people" in the Inuktitut language and is written Δ ᓄΔᶜ in traditional script. An individual member of this group is referred to as an Inuk (Δ ᓄᵇ). The Inuit homeland is known as Inuit Nunangat (Δ ᓄΔᶜ ᓄᓇᵇᒪᶜ), which refers to the land, water, and ice contained in the Arctic region. In Canada (ᖃᐊᓇᔾᐋᐋ) the Inuit are recognized as a distinct group under the Constitution (ᖃᐸᕐᐸᑎᔪᑎᐸᐸ).

The word *Innu* means "human being" in the Innu language of Innuaimun. Innu inhabit the eastern subarctic regions of northern Labrador and Quebec. Neither they nor the Inuit were included in Canada's Indian Act as regular contact had not yet been established when that law was enacted and these peoples were not yet in the way of intended expansion. "Eskimo" (a derogatory term which means "eater of raw meat") relocation initiatives did not begin until the mid-1930s but then were carried out throughout much of the remainder of the twentieth century, with devastating cultural effects. In 1967, the year of Canada's centennial as a nation, large groups of Innu were relocated to make room for an air force base, which began the Davis Inlet tragedy. In 2006, the Innu of Labrador, who represent only a portion of this group as the majority live in Quebec, were formally recognized under the Indian Act of Canada.

Metis are people of mixed European and Indigenous ancestry, and one of the three recognized native peoples to Canada. They originated largely in Western Canada and emerged as a political force in the nineteenth century, radiating outwards from the Red River Settlement. While the Canadian government politically marginalized Metis after 1885, Metis have since been recognized as an Indigenous culture with rights enshrined in the Canadian Constitution. The Metis homeland consists of the three Prairie provinces (Manitoba, Saskatchewan, and Alberta) along with parts of Ontario, British Columbia, the Northwest Territories, and the northern United States. The Metis have a common culture, history, and political tradition and are connected through an extensive network of interpersonal and social relationships.

2. The Problem

First Nations, Inuit, Innu, and Metis peoples have slowly begun to regain their rights and their voice in Canada, though it has literally been a battle. This historic oppression, a direct result of official government policy, has also led to outright violence climaxing with the shooting death of Dudley George by the Ontario Provincial Police in 1995 at Ipperwash Provincial Park over land rights claims (Hedican, 2008). Caledonia, Ontario, is the setting for one of the longest and most bitter land reclamations. Underlying issues of oppression and racism that arose from the process led to violent altercations involving both sides in this dispute.

As with all violence, unintended consequences arise. Children living on the Six Nations of the Grand River Territory reserve attend school on the reserve until grade 8 but then are bussed to high schools in neighbouring Caledonia, Cayuga, Hagersville, and Brantford. First Nations, Inuit, Innu, and Metis youth have historically attained lower levels of education than the general Canadian population in part due to residential schools but also due to larger structural factors. The tension between the Six Nations/Caledonia communities and the overt antagonism towards First Nations children attending high school off reserve made the likelihood of successful school completion of even greater concern. In 2006, in an attempt to address the needs of Six Nations students and also as a response to the tensions related to the land claims/rights issues, Suzie Miller, a First Nations grade 3 teacher from Six Nations, initiated the innovative and culturally groundbreaking "Pen Pal Project."

3. The Process

The Pen Pal Project involved Ms. Miller's class writing to another grade 3 class of children off the reserve who lived in and attended primary school in Caledonia. At the end of the school year the two classes, who knew each other only through correspondence, met to share in a cultural exchange and fun activities. Over the course of the next five years the Pen Pal Project grew so much that in the 2011–12 academic year 1,000 First Nations children from Six Nations of the Grand River Territory were involved with 1,000 non–First Nations children. Although the project was a cultural and community development success, the project initiator and supporters in both the Six Nations and the Caledonia (Grand Erie) School Boards wanted to know more specifically what impact it had on the children and the community. If what they had observed could be verified their goal was to export the initiative to other communities who, like Caledonia, had developed antagonistic relationships between Indigenous and non-Indigenous children to benefit both groups.

A research project was conceived involving members of the Grand Erie District School Board and community members of Six Nations, who requested assistance developing a participatory action research project (see also Case Study 19) to review the effects of the Pen Pal Project on the children and families involved. The goal of this initial exploratory research inquiry was to gather qualitative information from both the youth who participated during the inaugural year (who were now in their first year of high school) and from their parents about how being involved in the Pen Pal Project affected their understanding of their pen pals' culture and how it aided in their transition to high school. This is particularly important for Six Nations children, who in grade 9 move from a small rural school environment where they are the majority to a large high school where they immediately become a visible minority. Thus, the typical issues associated with the life cycle transition from elementary to high school are further intensified by being transported out of their home community into a larger setting that is unfamiliar and primarily populated by a distinct dominant cultural group.

4. The Research

The population for the study consisted of First Nations and non–First Nations students in grade 9 in Caledonia, Ontario, who had participated in the inaugural year of the Pen Pal Project. Eligible participants would have written letters to members of the other group when they were in grades 3 and 4 and would have participated in the year-end cultural events. These individuals would be interviewed individually while their parents would be invited to participate in one of four focus groups. The goal of the process was to ascertain if and how being involved in the Pen Pal Project affected their understanding of their pen pals' culture and if the process assisted them in their transition to high school.

5. Question

What steps would you take in designing the research protocol to be both ethical and respectful of the participants given the history they bring to the Pen Pal Project?

6. Social Work Practice

Research involving Indigenous peoples in Canada has been defined and carried out primarily by non-Indigenous researchers. The approaches used have not generally reflected Indigenous world views, and the research has not necessarily benefited those of First Nations, Inuit, Innu, and Metis heritage or their communities. As a result, Indigenous peoples continue to regard research, particularly research originating outside their communities, with a certain measure of mistrust, which is certainly justifiable.

Beginning in 2004 the Canadian Institutes of Health Research (CIHR), the Social Sciences and Humanities Research Council (SSHRC), and the Natural Sciences and Engineering Research Council (NSERC) began revising their research guidelines and policies in order to achieve a greater sensitivity to Indigenous knowledge and the rights of Indigenous communities. One major presentation to the commission was made by the Indigenous Peoples' Health Research Centre. They presented their recommendations to the panel based upon an extensive literature review, practice wisdom, and the cultural foundations and traditions of the research team. While the recommendations were specifically made for the Interagency Advisory Panel on Research Ethics, the principles should extend to any researcher working with this population. They indicated that:

- The jurisdiction of Indigenous peoples over their culture, heritage, knowledge, and political and intellectual domains must be explicitly recognized.
- Further conceptual development is needed in regard to an ethical space as the appropriate venue for the expression of an ethical research order that contemplates crossing cultural borders. The conceptual development of the ethical space requires principles that cement practices of dialogue, negotiation, and research agreements with Indigenous authorities in any research involving Indigenous peoples.
- In recognition of Indigenous jurisdiction, research agreements need to be negotiated and formalized with authorities of various Indigenous jurisdictions before any research is conducted with their people.
- Empowerment and benefits must become central features of any research entertained and conducted with respect to Indigenous peoples.
- Protection and recognition of Indigenous peoples' intellectual and cultural property rights by researchers and institutions must be part of any funding.
- Indigenous peoples must exercise control over all research conducted within their territories, or which uses their peoples as subjects of study. This includes the ownership, control, access, and possession of all data and information obtained from research involving Indigenous peoples.
- Understanding Indigenous social structures and systems, and the role of education in the process of knowledge and cultural transmission, is a vital necessity in coming to terms with research involving Indigenous peoples. Education in these respects must be supported with appropriate funding and resources.
- Steps must be taken to immediately implement policy that will ameliorate inherent conflicts between research ethics board policies and Indigenous ethical requirements, the primary example being the barriers to meaningful negotiation of consent and research parameters on the part of community participants prior to the receipt of formal approval from institutional research ethics boards.

The outcome of the initiative by the three national funding bodies has been to place a greater emphasis on appropriate community engagement. This is a process that establishes the interaction between a researcher and the community. The intent going forward is to develop collaborative relationships. These may take the form of review and approval from formal leadership to conduct research in the community, joint planning with a responsible agency, commitment to a partnership formalized in a research agreement, or dialogue with an advisory group expert in the customs governing the knowledge being sought. The engagement may range from information sharing to active participation and collaboration, to empowerment and shared leadership of the research project. Also important to the process is the right of the community to allow a research process but to choose not to engage in part of the project, or to outright reject the proposal. What must always be at the forefront of the research process is recognition of the importance of the ongoing relationships, the need for mutuality in terms of benefits of participating, and the sometimes not straightforward process of determining who the key people are in an Indigenous community.

Core ethical principles of contemporary research involving human participants are respect for the persons in the study, concern for the welfare of the persons involved in the study, and justice. These take on even greater importance when working with Indigenous peoples given the historic exploitation that has occurred. This research process, as all others, must begin with ensuring the free, informed, and ongoing consent of all participants. The concerns of First Nations, Inuit, Innu, and Metis for their continuity as peoples with distinctive cultures and identities must be demonstrated in the research, and research practice must be conducted in keeping with these world views. Codes of research practice with Indigenous populations go beyond the scope of ethical protections for individual participants, extend to the interconnection between humans and the natural world, and include obligations to maintain (and pass on to future generations) knowledge received from ancestors as well as that developed in the ongoing research initiatives.

Concern for welfare goes even further, requiring consideration of participants and prospective participants in their physical, social, economic, and cultural environments, along with concern for the community to which participants belong. This acknowledges the important role of Indigenous peoples in promoting their collective rights, interests, and responsibilities and not only taking into account the welfare of individual research participants. The emphasis is on ensuring that the research enhances the capacity of Indigenous groups to maintain their cultures, languages, and identities.

The third principle, justice, speaks to the inherent imbalance of power that exists between researchers and participants. Harms that arise from research are seldom intentional but still can occur with substantive repercussions. In the case of First Nations, Inuit, Innu, and Metis peoples, abuses stemming from research have included misappropriation of sacred songs, stories, and artefacts; devaluing of their knowledge as primitive or superstitious; violation of community norms regarding the use of human tissue and remains; failure to share data and resulting benefits; and presentation of information that has misrepresented or stigmatized entire communities.

Where the social, cultural, or linguistic distance between the community and researchers from outside the community is significant, the potential for misunderstanding is likewise ever-present (see Etienne & Brownbill, 2017). Engagement between the community involved and researchers, initiated prior to recruiting participants and maintained over the course of the research, can enhance ethical practice and the quality of research. Further, investigators can enhance the process by involving community representatives in the interpretation of the data and the review of research findings before the completion of the final report and before finalizing all relevant publications resulting from the research. Taking time to establish a relationship can promote mutual trust and communication, identify mutually beneficial research goals, define appropriate research collaborations or partnerships, and ensure that the conduct of research adheres to the core principles of respect for persons, concern for welfare of both individuals and the collective, and justice (Government of Canada, 2015).

7. Responding to the Case

In this project, the researchers who were not from Six Nations had an advantage over most other forms of inquiry conducted with First Nations, Inuit, Innu, and Metis peoples in that they did not have to start fresh in gaining the trust of the community or determining who key and secondary decision makers were. Because of past interactions supporting the Pen Pal Project as allies, the research team was invited in to be part of the research process from its onset. Thus the important but often lengthy process of community engagement and trust building that is essential when a non-Indigenous researcher works with an Indigenous population was not required. This process of trust building can take longer than an actual research project in some instances.

As this was exploratory research, two qualitative approaches were selected: key information interviews and focus groups (see Case Study 16). Important decisions were made reflecting the unique nature of the study. First both Indigenous and non-Indigenous research assistants needed to be hired. Every interview would be conducted by a team consisting of both an Indigenous and a non-Indigenous research assistant to ensure that at least one member has knowledge or experience of the culture of the community. As well, no member of the core research team or initiator of the Pen Pal Project would be directly involved in data collection so that not only would there be no coercion, but there would also be no appearance of coercion to participate. Interviews would be held at the school where the children first participated, either in Caledonia or in Ohsweken, which is part of the Six Nations territory. The research assistants would look for information regarding the lived experience of the youth, how being involved in the Pen Pal Project affected their cultural understanding of their peer group, and, for First Nations students, how it aided their transition to high school.

Participation by all youth would be allowed only with the permission of their parents; once parental permission was obtained the youths themselves would be asked if they would voluntarily agree to be individually interviewed (a similar protocol as discussed in Case Study 4). Parents would also be invited to participate but they would participate in focus groups rather than individual interviews. Four focus groups were initially planned, two to be held in Six Nations at the local elementary school and two to be held in Caledonia at the local high school. Here too the interviewer team would consist of one Indigenous and one non-Indigenous researcher.

The credibility of the project would be reinforced as the Pen Pal Project initiator, Suzie Miller, would not only be the lead in contacting all youth and their families to inform them of the research project but would also be part of the research team. This further establishes ownership of the research and the outcomes not with the outside research experts but within the community that directly experienced outcomes of the Pen Pal Project.

8. Research Insight

When working with any group but particularly First Nations, Inuit, Innu, and Metis peoples, the research document outlining the goals and the process of the inquiry should be formally agreed upon. This would include how participants are to be recruited, how data is to be collected, who will have access to the information collected, and how the findings would be disseminated and to whom. At a minimum, the agreement should address the ethical protections that would apply to securing individual consent for a comparable project and should specify any commitments regarding collective community participation, decision making, and sharing of benefits. When possible, as with the Pen Pal Project, members of the Indigenous community should be part of the entire research process, from data collection to analysis and dissemination. In addition when working with this group it is important to acknowledge the knowledge holders. Building relationships, clarifying the goals of a project, and negotiating agreements require a significant investment of time from the community, and any funding obtained for research with these groups should account for appropriate financial compensation for this time. Finally, researchers should be aware of the first language of Indigenous participants and translation of the results should be made available as part of the research process as required to meet language needs (Government of Canada, 2015).

What the legacy of research with First Nations, Inuit, Innu, and Metis peoples teaches us is that regardless of whom we work with, relationship is essential in ethical research practice. Ownership is key. Who has the knowledge? Who owns this knowledge? How is it to be gathered, examined, and shared? All are vital questions in framing your research practice. As ethical social work practitioners we do *with*, not *to* or *for*. We do likewise as ethical social work researchers, regardless of with whom we are engaged. Research, as are all aspects of social work practice, is a joint, mutually respectful process.

9. Further Reflections

Some American colleagues indicated that while they found this example interesting and relevant, they did not understand the language we used to describe the Indigenous peoples of Canada. In some jurisdictions in the United States the term *Indian* is still used. This is of course not only politically but also geographically incorrect. If you recall your colonialized grade school history you would have been incorrectly taught that Columbus discovered the land mass called North America, which of course had existed for billions of years before being "discovered." After centuries of oppression, in the twentieth century Indigenous Canadians began to slowly reclaim their rights and with this a proper conceptualization of who they are as a people. In the United States *Native American* has become the commonly used moniker. In Canada the federal government department responsible for this group is now called Aboriginal Affairs, though the first tab of their website in 2015 was still "Indian status," which does not reflect who these peoples are. Some members do not like the term *aboriginal* as it is reminiscent of the term *abnormal* and reflects their treatment since soon after first contact as well as the residential school experience. *Indigenous*, the term used in this case study, is a collective term, though it does fully not reflect the diversity of the population. First Nations, Inuit, Innu, and Metis peoples is quite cumbersome both to say and to type, but then sometimes respect entails just a little bit of effort. Etiquette advises to reference people by the term they prefer.

10. Additional Reading

Aboriginal Healing Foundation. (2007). *Addictive behaviours among aboriginal people in Canada.* Ottawa: Aboriginal Healing Foundation.

Assembly of First Nations (n.d.). First Nations ethics guide on research and Aboriginal traditional knowledge. http://www.afn.ca/uploads/files/fn_ethics_guide_on_research_and_atk.pdf

Burnette, C.E., Sanders, S., Butcher, H.K., & Rand, J.T. (2014). A toolkit for ethical and culturally sensitive research: An application with Indigenous communities. *Ethics & Social Welfare*, *8*(4), 364–82.

Caine, V., Davis, C., Jacobs, T., & Letendre, A. (2004). Ethics in the context of research and Indigenous peoples: A bibliography. *Pimatziwin*, *2*(1), 91–120.

Ermine, W., Sinclair, R., & Jeffery, B. (2004). *The ethics of research involving Indigenous Peoples. Report of the Indigenous Peoples. Health Research Centre to the Interagency Advisory Panel on Research Ethics.* Saskatoon: Indigenous Peoples' Health Research Centre.

Etienne, M., & Brownbill, K. (2017). Understanding the ultimate oppression: Alcohol and drug use in Native Land. In R. Csiernik & W.S. Rowe (Eds.), *Responding to the oppression of addiction* (3rd ed., pp. 295–315). Toronto: Canadian Scholars' Press.

First Nations Centre. (2006). *First Nations conceptual frameworks and applied models on ethics, privacy and consent in health research and information. Summary report.* Ottawa, ON: National Aboriginal Health Organization.

Foster, A.A. (1943). ESP tests with American Indian children. *Journal of Parapsychology*, *7*, 94–103.

Government of Canada (2015). *Research involving the First Nations, Inuit and Metis peoples of Canada.* http://www.pre.ethics.gc.ca/eng/policy-politique/initiatives/tcps2-eptc2/chapter9-chapitre9/

Hedican, E. (2008). The Ipperwash Inquiry and the tragic death of Dudley George. *Canadian Journal of Native Studies*, *28*(1), 159–73.

Jackson, K.F. (2010). Ethical considerations in social work research with multiracial individuals. *Journal of Social Work Values and Ethics*, *7*(1). Retrieved from http://www.jswvearchives.com/spring2010/5ethicalconsiderations.pdf

Kanatami, I.T. (2007). Negotiating research relationships with Inuit communities. http://cnnro.ca/wp-content/uploads/2015/03/Negotiating-Research-Relationships-Researcher-Guide-2007.pdf

Kovach, M.E. (2010). *Indigenous methodologies: Characteristics, conversations, and contexts.* Toronto: University of Toronto Press.

Lavallee, L.F. (2009). Practical application of an Indigenous research framework and two qualitative Indigenous research methods: Sharing circles and Anishnaabe symbol-based reflection. *International Journal of Qualitative Methods*, *8*(1), 21–40.

Martin, K.L. (2008). *Please knock before you enter: Aboriginal regulation of outsiders and the implications for researchers.* Brisbane, AU: Post Pressed.

Smith, L. (2010). *Decolonizing methodologies: Research and Indigenous peoples.* New York: Zed Books.

11. Internet Resources

Pen Pal Project:
   http://www.penpalproject.ca/
Assembly of First Nations:
   http://www.afn.ca/index.php/en
Inuit Tapiriit Kanatami (ITK):
   https://www.itk.ca/
Innu Nation:
   http://www.innu.ca/

Metis Nation:
    http://www.metisnation.ca/
Indigenous and Northern Affairs Canada:
    http://www.aadnc-aandc.gc.ca/eng/1307458586498/1307458751962
Truth and Reconciliation Commission of Canada:
    http://www.trc.ca/websites/trcinstitution/index.php?p=3
The National, Truth and Reconciliation report released:
    https://www.youtube.com/watch?v=rlKiltMeK-8
UCO Observer, "Reconciling to a Hard Truth":
    https://www.youtube.com/watch?v=Z1h9djZOgGc

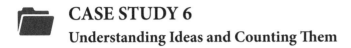

CASE STUDY 6
Understanding Ideas and Counting Them

1. Preamble

Of all the skills we have and acquire en route to becoming social workers, our primary tool remains language. It is integral in every aspect of the social work process. Likewise, language is integral in every aspect of the research process. Therefore, social work researchers must be precise in their use of language, for what appear to be simple ideas or words such as "effective," "successful," and "wellness" do not mean the same thing to everyone who reads your work. Thus the meaning of your words, your language, must always be carefully explained.

2. The Problem

The importance of work and its role in satisfying needs is a natural union. However, this endeavour that meets both our basic and higher-order needs also leads us to premature disability and death. The workplace gives us our livelihood, gives us individual and collective meaning, and is a foundation of society, but sometimes these things come at a high cost to our wellness. Those working as occupational social workers routinely face the stress associated with work and the problems that work brings to employees' home lives. One attempt to intervene positively has been occupational assistance in the form of Employee Assistance Programs (EAPs), but critics of this approach claim that EAPs are nothing more than mechanisms of social control. As a social work researcher who believes in positive intervention in the occupational sector, you propose a study to investigate the "conceptual, analytical, research, and historical issues required to develop a model of occupational assistance that would enhance both employee and organizational wellness and would not be considered a means of social control."

3. The Process

You have conducted an extensive review of the literature using Social Work Abstracts, Social Service Abstracts, SCOPUS, PsychINFO, ProQuest Psychology Journals, ERIC Plus Text, PubMed, Social Science Citations, and Google Scholar, and in developing your idea you have arrived at a crucial point. The entire research process hinges upon one core concept: understanding what exactly wellness is and how you could measure this construct in the workplace context.

4. The Research

In conducting your literature review you discover that the contemporary definition of wellness developed out of the World Health Organization's (1946) definition of health, which states that health is a state of complete physical, mental, and social well-being and not merely the absence of disease or infirmity. Dunn (1961) added that well-being involved the mind, the body, the environment, the family, community life, and a compatible work interest. Ardell (1977) stated that wellness constituted more than merely a state of being not ill, or being "unsick." He believed that even prevention was an inadequate goal, as prevention could be viewed as being mostly a reactive, defensive response. For Ardell, the state of wellness not only consisted of the physical but also involved a person's self-image, vocation, and relationships along with the person's social environment. *A New Perspective on the Health of Canadians* (Health and Welfare Canada, 1974) was the first government document to suggest that biological factors along with environmental hazards and lifestyle issues such as alcohol, tobacco, and other drug misuse and abuse, fitness, recreation, and nutrition were all determinants both of sickness and of health. Discussions in the literature on what constitutes wellness have also included the ability to maintain relative control over emotional states in response to life events and have referred to stress management and how one responds to emotional crises. Adams & Csiernik (2001) wrote about wellness relating to spirituality, including Maslow's concept of self-actualization, while Schafer (1992) considered the ability to engage in clear thinking and to think independently as critical to achieving a state of wellness. Other authors suggested important factors are having healthy social systems such as family, work, school, and religious affiliations, as well as the ability to interact effectively with others, including the development of appropriate relationships among friends, families, co-workers, and communities (Green & Shellenberger, 1991; Perry & Jessor, 1985; Schafer, 1992; Sefton et al., 1992).

Clearly, before you can proceed any further you must sort through all of this information and develop your own understanding of this complex term. You need to develop a conceptual framework that allows you to fully conceptualize and operationalize wellness as it relates to work.

5. Questions

1. *What is your conceptual definition of wellness? How would you define the idea of wellness so that there is a common understanding of the term among anyone that reads your research study?*
2. *How would you operationalize this conceptualization? In what ways will you measure or count the ideas expressed in the definition of wellness that you have proposed to determine if your intervention has produced any positive change?*

6. Social Work Practice

Conceptualization

Conceptualizing is the refining and specifying of abstract concepts. In the research process it is the stage in which you provide a definition of your ideas so that they can be readily measured, thus providing a specific understanding of the concept in the context of your research question. This definition is referred to as a nominal definition, and it should be provided in any reports or articles written about the research. It will allow the reader to understand your definition of important terms and concepts. Conceptualized definitions are typically derived through your review of literature on your topic.

Operationalization

Operationalization is how you measure your conceptualized variables. It is the translation of an idea into a measurable construct, and it is the step that sets the stage for data collection. Through thorough and detailed conceptualization and operationalization of ideas, you increase the likelihood that the research can be properly replicated by others or yourself in the future or be used in a comparative analysis of other research. Table 2.6a compares these two important processes.

Table 2.6a   Conceptualization and Operationalization

Conceptualization	Operationalization
• The refining and specifying of abstract concepts	• The way you will measure your concepts
• Providing a definition that can then be measured	• The translation of an idea into a measurable construct distinct from dictionary definitions
• Providing a comparative definition	• Provides the context for data collection
• Defining the term within the context of the research study	• Needs to be a reliable and valid process that can be replicated by yourself and others

7. Responding to the Case

Conceptualization

The critical variable that needs defining is "wellness." "Wellness," however, is quite a common term as well as quite an overused and often incorrectly used term. As such it has a range of possible interpretations and thus potentially multiple conceptualizations. By thinking about what the term means to you and by talking about it with your classmates, you may have developed a valid nominal definition. This particular study conceptualized wellness along five distinct dimensions:

- *physical health:* fitness, nutrition, adequate rest and sleep, medical self-care including psychoactive drug use along with the absence of disease;
- *psychological health:* the ability to maintain relative control over emotional states in response to life events. Psychological health is associated with stress management and responses to emotional crises and is the subjective sense of well-being, including personality, stress management, life goals, perceptions, and feelings along with health-inducing and illness-preventing behaviours;
- *spiritual health:* love, charity, purpose, inner peace, caring for others, prayer, belief in a higher power, and meditation;
- *intellectual health:* education, achievement, role fulfilment, and career development, including professional development seminars or returning to school to obtain further education and additional certificates, diplomas, or graduate education; and
- *social health:* family, work, and school relationships; religious affiliation; social values, customs, and supports and the ability to interact effectively with others, including the development of appropriate relationships among friends, families, co-workers, and communities.

Table 2.6b   Measurement Instruments

Physical Health	• General Health Questionnaire (Goldberg, 1978)
Psychological Health	• Affect Balance Scale (Bradburn, 1969) • Centre for Epidemiologic Studies Depression Scale (Radloff, 1977) • Rosenberg Self-Esteem Scale (Rosenberg, 1965)
Social Health	• Family Environmental Scale (Moos & Moos, 1994) • Social Stability Scale (Skinner, 1981)
Spiritual Health	• JAREL Scale (Hungelmann et al., 1987)
Intellectual Health	• Self-report Likert Scale

Operationalization

Once you have defined your idea, or in quantitative research, your variable, you still need to determine how to operationalize it. Simply put, how are you going to count this concept known as wellness? Taking the conceptualized terms individually allowed for a series of specific valid and reliable instruments (see Case Study 10) to be selected to measure the conceptualized term, along with one self-report Likert scale (Table 2.6b). If an abstract term such as wellness can be concretized in this manner, any variable you are interested in quantifying can be if you follow a similar process.

8. Research Insight: Levels of Measurement

Quantitative research requires numerical data for analysis. These data vary in precision, and the precision of data has important implications when conducting statistical analysis. The type of statistical analysis that is possible depends upon the precision of the data available for analysis: the more precise the data, the more powerful the statistical analysis. Data are grouped into four categories of precision (Table 2.6c).

These categories are referred to as the levels of measurement. The first and least precise level is called *nominal*. Nominal data are in the form of categories. If you ask a person whether he or she is a full-time student (measuring intellectual health), there are two possible answers, yes and no. This allows us to categorize respondents into two groups, those who are attending full time and those who are not. Assigning codes to the answers, in this case either "1" or "2," is convenient for data recording, but the numbers

Table 2.6c   Levels of Measurement

Lowest Level of Precision	Nominal
	Ordinal
	Interval
Highest Level of Precision	Ratio

assigned to the answers are not values, only codes – short forms for "yes" and "no." They don't actually convey the idea of more or less. While the number 2 is higher than the number 1, this does not mean that people who are in school are in some way better than people who are not. All we can tell is that they are different.

The level of precision of the data increases at the next level of measurement, *ordinal* data. For example, if you ask respondents how often they attend a religious service (a traditional measure of spiritual health) and give them four categories from which to choose – (1) seldom, (2) occasionally, (3) regularly, or (4) frequently – the data you receive are considered at the ordinal level. At this level you can group the respondents into categories, as is the case with nominal data, but in addition you can rank the categories in some way. The codes assigned to the answers now also convey rank as well as difference. Someone in category 4 (frequently) attends meetings more regularly than someone in category 2 (occasionally). However, these numbers are still codes and not actual values, because while 4 is more than 2, in this case you can't say that someone in category 4 attends twice as often as someone in category 2. A great deal of information collected in social work research is at this level of precision.

Greater precision can be gained by asking the person how many services they attend in a month. Here you do not provide the respondent with categories. They are asked to provide the actual number. This level of precision is called the *ratio* level, and with it the numbers can be used for arithmetic calculations. Someone who states that they attend synagogue four times a month does indeed attend twice as often as someone who attends only twice a month. Ratio level data are at the highest level of precision. There are a few common ratio level variables of interest, such as age, income, number of children, number of marriages, and years of education. Any question that can be answered by an actual numerical value is considered ratio level data.

There is another level of measurement that in terms of precision falls between ordinal and ratio level. It's called *interval* level. Levels of measurement were first developed in the physical sciences, and the most common example of interval level data is temperature. Temperature is reported as a number, but scales commonly used to measure it have no absolute zero; you can have no children but you cannot have no temperature. Temperature scales do have a zero measure, but this does not designate the total absence of temperature (unless of course you are measuring in degrees Kelvin, but if you are doing this you should be studying physics and not social work). Researchers have developed a large number of multi-item scales that measure an array of psychosocial variables of interest to social workers, characteristics such as depression, happiness, self-esteem, and anxiety. The data (scores) derived from these types of scales are considered interval data if the scales are used widely and have gone through a rigorous process called standardization.

In general, when you are determining your measures it is best to try to obtain the highest level of precision possible. Higher levels of precision can always be transformed into lower levels, but the opposite is not possible. If you have asked a person how old they are you can always put them in an age category such as "senior." However, if a person has indicated they fall in the senior age category you do not know the exact age: is it 75, 85, or 95?

9. Further Reflections

1. *What are the implications of two different groups of researchers studying the same phenomenon using different conceptualizations and operationalizations?*
2. *As a consumer of research, how do you assess which study to base your practice upon if the two groups come to different and even contradictory conclusions and recommendations?*
3. *Social work research necessitates the ongoing conceptualization and operationalization of abstract concepts such as self-esteem, hope, and wellness. There are multiple databases which you can search to help you define your concepts, including (but not limited to) Social Work Abstracts, Social Service Abstracts, SCOPUS, PsychINFO, ProQuest Psychology Journals, ERIC Plus Text, PubMed, Social Science Citations, and Google Scholar. Typically, as a student you will not search more than one or two of these for any given paper you have to write. What are the implications of this process in terms of how you develop your own understanding of abstract concepts that serve as the tools for your profession?*

10. Additional Reading

Adams, D.W., & Csiernik, R. (2001). A beginning examination of the spirituality of health care practitioners. In R. Gilbert (Ed.), *Health care and spirituality: Listening, assessing, caring*, pp. 34–50. Amityville: Baywood.

Ardell, D. (1977). *High level wellness*. Emmasus, PA: Rodale.

Bhui, K., Mohamud, S., Warfa, N., Craig, T.J., & Stansfeld, S.A. (2003). Cultural adaptation of mental health measures: Improving the quality of clinical practice and research. *British Journal of Psychiatry*, 183(3), 184–6.

Bradburn, N. (1969). *The structure of psychological well-being*. Chicago: Aldine.

Busseri, M.A., & Sadava, S.W. (2011). A review of the tripartite structure of subjective well-being: Implications for conceptualization, operationalization, analysis, and synthesis. *Personality and Social Psychology Review 15*(3): 290–314. http://dx.doi.org/10.1177/ 1088868310391271

Csiernik, R. (2014). *Workplace wellness: Issues and responses*. Toronto: Canadian Scholars' Press.

Daigneault, P.M., & Jacob, S. (2009). Towards accurate measurement of participation: Rethinking the conceptualization and operationalization of participatory evaluation. *American Journal of Evaluation, 30*(3), 330–48.

Dunn, H. (1961). *High level wellness.* Arlington: R.W. Beatty.

Fischer, J., & Corcoran, K. (2013a). Measures for clinical practice and research: A sourcebook (Vol. 1). *Couples, families, and children.* New York: Oxford University Press.

Fischer, J., & Corcoran, K. (2013b). Measures for clinical practice and research: A sourcebook (Vol. 2). *Adults.* New York: Oxford University Press.

Göb, R., McCollin, C., & Ramalhoto, M.F. (2007). Ordinal methodology in the analysis of Likert scales. *Quality & Quantity, 41*(5), 601–26.

Goldberg, D. (1978). *Manual for the General Health Questionnaire.* Windsor: National Foundation for Educational Research.

Green, J., & Shellenberger, R. (1991). *The dynamics of health and wellness: A biopsychosocial approach.* Toronto: Holt, Rinehart and Winston.

Health and Welfare Canada. (1974). *A new perspective on the health of Canadians.* Ottawa: Health and Welfare Canada.

Glomb, T.M., & Tews, M.J. (2004). Emotional labour: A conceptualization and scale development. *Journal of Vocational Behavior, 64*(1), 1–23.

Heinemann, A.W. (2010). Measurement of participation in rehabilitation research. *Archives of Physical Medicine and Rehabilitation, 91*(9), S1–S4.

Hodge, D.R., & Sand, R. (2002). Conceptualizing spirituality in social work: How the metaphysical beliefs of social workers may foster bias towards theistic consumers. *Social Thought, 21*(1), 39–61.

Hungelmann, J., Kenkel-Rossi, E., Klassen, L., & Stollenwerk, R. (1987). *JAREL Spirituality Well-Being Scale.* Milwaukee: Marquette University College of Nursing.

McHugh, M.L., & Villarruel, A.M. (2003). Descriptive statistics, part I: level of measurement. *Journal for Specialists in Pediatric Nursing, 8*(1), 35–7.

Mooney, P., Epstein, M.H., Ryser, G., & Pierce, C.D. (2005). Reliability and validity of the Behavioural and Emotional Rating Scale: Parent Rating Scale. *Children & Schools, 27*(3), 147–55.

Moos, R., & Moos, B. (1994). *Manual for the Family Environmental Scale* (2nd ed.). Palo Alto, CA: Consulting Psychology Press.

Moscou, S. (2008). The conceptualization and operationalization of race and ethnicity by health services researchers. *Nursing Inquiry, 15*(2), 94–105.

Ogle, R.S., & Batton, C. (2009). Revisiting patriarchy: Its conceptualization and operationalization in criminology. *Critical Criminology, 17*(3), 159–82.

Perry, C.L., & Jessor, R. (1985). The concept of health promotion and the prevention of adolescent drug use. *Health Education Quarterly, 12*(2), 169–84.

Radloff, L. (1977). CES-D scale: A self-report depression scale for research in the general population. *Applied Psychological Measurement, 1*, 385–401.

Rosenberg, M. (1965). *Society and the adolescent self-image.* Princeton, NJ: Princeton University Press.

Schafer, W. (1992). *Stress management and wellness.* Toronto: Harcourt Bruce Jovanovich.

Sefton, J., Wankel, L., Quinney, H., Webber, J., Marshall, J., & Horne, T. (1992, March 12–13). Working towards well-being in Alberta. Paper presented at National Recreation and Wellness Conference, Coburg, Australia.

Skinner, H. (1981). Assessment of alcohol problems: Basic principles, critical issues and future trends. In Y. Israel, F. Glaser, H. Kalant, R. Popham, W. Schmidt, & R. Smart (Eds.), *Research advances in alcohol and drug problems* (Vol. 6, pp. 319–69). New York: Plenum Press.

Ward, C., & Kus, L. (2012). Back to and beyond Berry's basics: The conceptualization, operationalization and classification of acculturation. *International Journal of Intercultural Relations, 36*(4), 472–85.

World Health Organization. (1946). *Constitution.* New York: WHO.

11. Internet Resources

Types of Data: Nominal, Ordinal, Interval, Ratio

Graphpad, "What is the difference between ordinal, interval and ratio variables? Why should I care?":
    http://www.graphpad.com/support/faqid/1089/
Web Centre for Social Research Methods, "Levels of Measurement":
    http://www.socialresearchmethods.net/kb/measlevl.php
Nurse Killam, "Nominal, Ordinal, Interval and Ratio Data: How to Remember the Differences":
    https://www.youtube.com/watch?v=LPHYPXBK_ks
Statistics Learning Centre, "Types of Data: Nominal, Ordinal, Interval/Ratio – Statistics Help":
    https://www.youtube.com/watch?v=hZxnzfnt5v8
how2stats, "Nominal Ordinal Interval Ratio – Explained":
    https://www.youtube.com/watch?v=u90XkFRcdDU
Joel Schneider, "Measurement Scales and Variables":
    https://www.youtube.com/watch?v=YyAwRGP2TZk

Conceptualization and Operationalization

Cengage, "Conceptualization and Operationalization":
    http://www.cengage.com/resource_uploads/downloads/0534507786_28792.ppt
Qingwen Dong, "Conceptualization and Operationalization":
    https://www.youtube.com/watch?v=3m430elqoLc
comresearch 224, "Conceptualization, Operationalization, Units of Analysis, Levels of Measurement":
    https://www.youtube.com/watch?v=uaqUzUFHgUg

CASE STUDY 7
Implementing a Pilot Project: A Question of Sampling

1. Preamble

Who is counted and how the counting occurs is an integral part of the research process. However, this important process is one that we too often do not examine closely enough.

2. The Problem

There is a significantly high level of homelessness in Canada, particularly considering this nation's wealth. This is a structural problem that exists nationally for a host of reasons. The cabinet of Manitoba's provincial government decides that, to show national leadership, some innovative but applied program should be adopted in attempting to address this chronic issue prior to the next provincial election, to be held in the next 18 months. Funding is provided for the development of a pilot project to address this issue, with a preliminary report expected within one year.

3. The Process

Staff of the Ministry of Youth Services are charged with conducting a literature review on behalf of the Manitoba government. One recurrent theme in the literature is that younger persons have a difficult time obtaining housing due to a lack of adequate income, which is in turn linked to having insufficient job-specific skills. A group of job placement workers and housing coordinators from across the province meet to develop a specific, effective training program. After a review of the literature, key stakeholder interviews, and four focus groups held in Winnipeg, a two-month program is developed, including a literacy component, computer basics, job interviewing tactics, personal presentation skills, telephone etiquette, housing search strategies, and interpersonal problem solving.

4. The Research

Participants for the study are recruited by sending an email to all those registered with the Youth Employment Centres in Dauphin, Norway House, and Brandon from

1 November to 15 January. As well, any walk-in client that requests assistance with housing is invited to participate in the pilot project. A comparison group for the study consists of randomly selected individuals from the provincial homelessness registry. There were 151 persons in each group.

Program effectiveness was determined by recording the number of days of homelessness for those in both groups from 1 March until 1 September. During the data-collection period the comparison group members averaged 12 days of homelessness, while those in the control group averaged 52. The study team believes that this significant statistical difference indicates that their pilot project was successful and should be implemented province wide.

5. Questions

1. *What feedback do you have for the study team regarding the sampling they used in conducting the pilot project?*
2. *What suggestions can you offer to improve the sampling approach of the research?*

6. Social Work Practice

Unit of Analysis

All research begins with the element of interest. What is the thing that we want to know something about? In most social work research the element of interest is a person, as usually the thing we are trying to understand is human behaviour. When we conduct research directed towards the study of the person our unit of analysis is the individual. However, the individual unit of analysis does not always mean an individual person. For example, if we are reviewing individual newspaper editorials to determine the extent of gender bias our unit of analysis is the individual, but in this case the individual element is an editorial, not a person. The unit of analysis can also be at higher levels of aggregation. Our unit of analysis can be groups, families, communities, organizations, or even social artefacts such as funerals or riots. The unit of analysis is the entity that has the characteristic we wish to study. This can lead to confusion, because sometimes in order to measure the characteristic in a higher level of aggregation we need to measure something about the individual elements that make up the aggregation. The important criterion is to determine the unit that has the characteristic of interest. For example, imagine we are interested in studying work groups (the work group is the unit of analysis) and want to determine if group cohesion (the target characteristic) is related to work performance. To measure the cohesion of the group we might ask individual members to complete a group cohesion measurement scale. Even though we collect the information from individual members to determine the group's level of cohesion, our unit of analysis is the group, not the individual. Similarly, we might be interested in understanding the influence of marital happiness on child adjustment. The unit of analysis in this case is the couple, since marital happiness is a characteristic of the couple. However, to measure couple happiness we would need to ask each individual partner to complete a measure of marital happiness. This does not change the unit of analysis; it is still the couple. The unit of analysis does not depend upon from whom or what the data are collected, but is determined by the entity that has the characteristic of interest.

It is important to clearly identify the unit of analysis before you address sampling because understanding the unit of analysis will determine the appropriate universe of elements. The universe contains all the elements that share the characteristic you are targeting: all people, all families, or even all funerals. It is virtually impossible to work at the level of the universe. We cannot study all people or all families in the world, or all the funerals that have ever taken place. Thus the universe is narrowed down to a more manageable level, the population. The population is the set of elements from which you could realistically select a sample: all people in Canada, all families in Nova Scotia, all funerals in Yellowknife since the year 2000. While these are more manageable groupings, they are still very large, and other than for census surveys we do not usually study an entire population. As a rule, researchers select a subgroup of elements from the population for study. This subgroup is called a sample, and the element is called a case. Each level contains fewer elements than the one before. The case is one element, the sample a group of elements, the population is all elements within a reasonable limiting frame, and the universe is all possible elements.

Sampling in Quantitative Research

In quantitative research we measure something about the case (the unit of analysis) and take the same measurement of every case in the sample. When we are done we know something about the cases in our sample, but it is usually more important to be able to say something about the cases in the population. We want to be able to generalize our findings from the sample to the population. We can do this if our sample is representative of the population. For example, we determine the age of the cases in our sample and find out that the average age is 37. If our sample is representative of the population, then the average age of the population will also be 37. However, whenever we select a sample there is likely to be some measure of error. While it is not likely that the average

age is exactly the same in the sample as it is in the population, if the sample is representative of the population then the average age of the population will be close to 37. The measurement of the characteristic in the sample is referred to as the sample statistic. The measurement of the same characteristic in the population is called the population parameter. Researchers fully acknowledge that they cannot eliminate sampling error, but they do everything they can to try to reduce it. The ideal is a sample statistic that is as close to the population parameter as possible. There are accepted approaches to reducing the amount of sampling error, that is, to increasing the extent to which the sample is representative of the population. The first approach concerns the way in which sample cases are selected from the population. Random case selection increases the likelihood that the sample will be similar to the population. It will not guarantee that the sample is representative; there is still a possibility that the sample is not similar to the population, but that possibility is reduced by random selection. The amount of sampling error is also reduced if the sample size is large. For example, if you have a population of 1,000 elements and you randomly select one case to be in your sample, what is the probability that that one case will be representative of the 1,000? It is probably not very large. However, if the sample included 999 cases it is very likely that the sample would be representative. This example is just theoretical because you would not select just one case for your sample, nor would you select 999: in the latter case you might as well measure the entire population. However, it does illustrate the influence of sample size on representativeness.

What would happen if every element of the population was the same age? In this case, selecting one element would result in a representative sample with respect to age. Again, this is not very likely, but it illustrates another way to reduce sampling error, by increasing the homogeneity of the population. While this is usually not under the control of the researcher, it is true that there is less sampling error in populations that have a small range of values for the characteristic of interest. If you know that a population is relatively homogeneous with respect to a particular characteristic, you can be more certain that a randomly selected sample will have a small amount of error with respect to that characteristic.

Sample error can affect the generalizability of results, and so can sample bias. Sample bias occurs when selection of the cases for a sample distorts its representativeness. This distortion can occur intentionally or unintentionally. For example, a social worker is asked to select a sample from her caseload to receive an agency satisfaction questionnaire. If the social worker selects only cases that she thinks will offer a favourable review, the sample would be considered biased. This is because it is not representative of the population of all her cases since it does not contain any clients that would present a more negative perspective. This example illustrates an instance of intentional biasing, which is clearly unethical, but bias can be introduced unintentionally as well. For instance, an agency decides to survey client satisfaction and provides a questionnaire to the first 15 clients that come in for their appointment after the start of the survey. With this approach the sample may only include clients who came to the agency for weekday appointments, that is, the first 15 clients who came for an appointment on the Monday the survey began. If this is the case, they may not be representative of the entire population of clients. The agency's sample would not include clients who attended during evenings, on weekends, or other days of the week. This means that the opinions expressed by their sample cases may not reflect the opinions of the others not surveyed and cannot be considered representative of the population of all agency clients. The clearest way to avoid biasing a sample is to randomly select cases for the sample from the population of interest.

Probability Samples

Probability samples are constructed using some form of random selection process, and because of this the researcher can actually calculate the probability that a particular element will be selected. This does not necessarily mean that every case has the same probability of being selected, although this is often the case, but it does mean that the probability can be calculated. To construct a probability sample the researcher needs to have access to a list of all elements in the population. This list is called a sampling frame. It is often difficult or impossible to acquire a sampling frame, but unless you have one you cannot construct a probability sample. Lack of a sampling frame is the most common reason a researcher chooses the alternative non-probability approach. For the sampling frame to be useful, it is also important that it be accurate and up to date. Approaches to probability sampling include:

Simple random sampling: With this approach each element in the population does have an equal chance of being selected for the study. If the population is quite small, the easiest way to randomly select the sample is to write the name of each element on a piece of paper and place the papers in a bin, bag, or even hat. Then select names until you have the number you need for your sample, making sure to replace each name after it has been selected to ensure that all names still have an equal probability of being selected. If a name already selected gets selected a second time, replace it and draw again. For larger populations the elements can be numbered starting with the number 0. Then, using a table of random numbers, a subset of numbers is selected from the table. Cases corresponding to the numbers in the subset become the elements in the sample. Alternatively, computer software programs that analyse data can be used to identify a random sample. They use the same approach as the table of random numbers but save the researcher steps in numbering and matching.

Systematic random sampling: Elements of the population are listed and, after randomly establishing a starting point, every "*k*th" element (e.g., every fifth case or every tenth case) from the list is chosen for inclusion in the sample. To determine "*k*," the size of the population is divided by the size of the sample. For example, if the population includes 1,500 elements and you want 100 cases in your sample, then $k = 1500/100 = 150$. To select the sample you pick a random location to start on the list and then select every 150th case to include in your sample.

Proportional stratified random sampling: Rather than selecting at random from your entire population, you divide your population into various categories, determine what percentage of the population each category represents, and then randomly select elements from each category until your sample includes the same percentage of elements from each of the categories as is found in the entire population. This method is used if you have information that allows you to separate the population into subgroups. It is preferred because it artificially creates greater homogeneity of the population, which leads to a reduction in the amount of sampling error. For example, if your population is the children who have received service at your daycare centre you will have the information you need to separate the population into categories based upon age. You know that 20 per cent of the children are aged two, 30 per cent are aged three, 40 per cent are aged four, and 10 per cent are aged five. You decide to sample 20 children for your research. If you want the age distribution of children in the sample to be the same as that in the population, you will need to select four (20 per cent x 20) aged two, six (30 per cent x 20) aged three, eight (40 per cent x 20) aged four, and two (10 per cent x 20) aged five. The sampling frame now gets divided into the four age-based subgroups and then either a simple random or systematic random approach is used to select the appropriate number of cases from each age group. If you have a large population and the information you need about each element of the population to create groups, you can use this to stratify on more than one dimension.

Non-proportional stratified random sampling: Rather than having the sample reflect the actual population proportions, here you select the sample so that the proportional representation of the categories is not the same as that found in the population. As with stratified random sampling, though, the selection within each category is random. This approach is sometimes taken when there is a small subgroup within the population whose perspective you want to include in your data but, given the smallness of the group, a representative case may not get selected using a simple random selection approach. If this approach is adopted, care must be taken to make sure that the data are adjusted appropriately to reflect the over-representation of selected groups before analysis takes place.

Cluster sampling: This method of sampling begins by dividing the population into large groups, known as clusters or units, and then from each cluster randomly selecting smaller and smaller clusters, ensuring that at each level the subunits are still randomly selected. The primary distinguishing feature is that the process entails the selection of elements in the groups, the clusters, rather than of individuals, such as selecting school boards from a province and then schools from within the school board and then social workers responsible for working with different grades within each of the schools selected. Cluster sampling is used when it is impractical or even impossible to compile an exhaustive list of the elements composing the target population. It is in essence simple random sampling where each sampling unit is a collection, or a cluster of elements.

Differences between the various approaches to probability sampling are illustrated in Table 2.7b based upon the population of 100 staff working in school social work departments in Ontario illustrated in Table 2.7a.

7. Responding to the Case

While there are numerous sampling issues that should be noted from this case study, the most significant is that the participants in the study constitute a non-probability sample. This is problematic, since the intent of the research was to demonstrate that the outcomes for the study participants could be generalized to the entire population. To make a strong case for this, the researchers should have tried to construct a probability sample. Not one of the methods discussed above was employed. In fact, the sample was recruited in a manner that biases the sample in a number of ways:

- Using email to recruit potential participants, while decreasing costs and targeting younger persons, does not allow for equal probability for all potential participants to be eligible for the study.
- Likewise, the randomness essential in probability sampling was skewed by including those in the pilot study who asked for specific programming.
- Members of the experimental group were volunteers while members of the control group were randomly selected from a registry. There is an inherent difference in motivation between individuals who volunteer and those in a random sample of any population.

Table 2.7a   School Social Work Staff – Academic Qualifications*

00	BSW	20	BSW	40	SSW	60	BSW	80	MSW
01	BSW	21	BSW	41	BSW	61	MSW	81	SSW
02	MSW	22	SSW	42	BSW	62	SSW	82	MSW
03	SSW	23	BSW	43	MSW	63	SSW	83	MSW
04	PHD	24	MSW	44	BSW	64	BSW	84	MSW
05	SSW	25	BSW	45	MSW	65	BSW	85	BSW
06	SSW	26	BSW	46	BSW	66	BSW	86	MSW
07	SSW	27	BSW	47	BSW	67	MSW	87	SSW
08	BSW	28	MSW	48	BSW	68	MSW	88	BSW
09	MSW	29	MSW	49	SSW	69	SSW	89	MSW
10	BSW	30	BSW	50	SSW	70	MSW	90	MSW
11	BSW	31	BSW	51	MSW	71	PHD	91	BSW
12	BSW	32	MSW	52	BSW	72	MSW	92	BSW
13	SSW	33	BSW	53	BSW	73	BSW	93	MSW
14	BSW	34	MSW	54	MSW	74	SSW	94	MSW
15	BSW	35	PHD	55	MSW	75	MSW	95	SSW
16	SSW	36	MSW	56	BSW	76	MSW	96	MSW
17	BSW	37	BSW	57	BSW	77	MSW	97	MSW
18	BSW	38	SSW	58	MSW	78	MSW	98	SSW
19	PHD	39	MSW	59	SSW	79	MSW	99	BSW

* Sampling frame

- The location of the pilot, Dauphin, Norway House, and Brandon, while representing different parts of the province of Manitoba, may not be representative of the entire province. At a minimum, these more rural communities are distinct from the main population centre in the large city of Winnipeg.
- The source of the experimental group (targeted communities) sample and the source of the control group (province-wide registry) sample are not related; thus the groups are not comparable.

Table 2.7b   Comparison of Probability Sampling Approaches

Simple Random Sampling	20 numbers selected at random:		
	2, 61, 65, 29, 98, 73, 13, 41, 37, 55, 72, 11, 39, 51, 62, 94, 49, 93, 28, 68		
$n = 20$	*Category*	*Sample*	*Total Population*
	SSW	4	20
	BSW	6	40
	MSW	10	36
	PhD	0	4
$n = 16$	16 numbers selected at random:		
	8, 74, 99, 2, 43, 33, 81, 7, 23, 24, 41, 43, 25, 62, 67, 0		
	Category	*Sample*	*Total Population*
	SSW	4	20
	BSW	7	40
	MSW	5	36
	PhD	0	4
Systematic Random	kth = 5 beginning at number 56		
	select numbers:		
$n = 20$	56, 61, 66, 71, 76, 81, 86, 91, 96, 01, 06, 11, 16, 21, 26, 31, 36, 41, 46, 51		
	Category	*Sample*	*Total Population*
	SSW	3	20
	BSW	10	40
	MSW	6	36
	PhD	1	4
$n = 16$	kth = 6 beginning at number 11		
	select numbers:		
	11, 17, 23, 29, 34, 41, 47, 53, 59, 65, 71, 77, 83, 89, 95, 01		
	Category	*Sample*	*Total Population*
	SSW	1	20
	BSW	8	40
	MSW	5	36
	PhD	2	4

Table 2.7b (*continued*)

Stratified Random – Proportional	Category	% of population	sample size
n = 20	SSW	20	4
	BSW	40	8
	MSW	36	7
	PhD	4	1
n = 16	Category	% of population	sample size
	SSW	20	3
	BSW	40	6
	MSW	36	6
	PhD	4	1
Stratified Random – Non-Proportional	Category	% of population	sample size
n = 20	SSW	34	5
	BSW	40	5
	MSW	36	5
	PhD	4	4
n = 16	Category	% of population	sample size
	SSW	24	4
	BSW	40	4
	MSW	36	4
	PhD	4	4

Cluster

1. Randomly Select Province: Ontario

2. Randomly Select School Boards:

Algoma, Halton, Hamilton, Kingston, Moosonee, Nippising, St. Catharines

3. Randomly Select Schools

Algoma – Mountain View

Halton – St. John

Hamilton – Norwood Park

Kingston – Saint Michael

Table 2.7b (*continued*)

Moosonee – Moosonee Public
Nippissing – Silver Birches
St. Catharines – Briardale
4. Randomly Select Grades: 6 and 8
5. Sample is social workers who provide services to grade 6 and 8 students at the seven selected schools.

8. Research Insight

A simple way to enhance the research design would have been to add an additional observation period prior to commencing data collection. The initial design was a comparison group post-test:

Experimental Group	X	O
Comparison Group		O

Legend: X = intervention; O = observation

An improved design would have been a comparison group pre-test and post-test:

Experimental Group	O	X	O
Comparison Group	O		O

Using this design, even given the several flaws with the comparison group, the data would still have been able to indicate if there was a change in days of homelessness pre- and post-intervention for the experimental group. Another revised design, a one-group pretest–post-test:

Experimental Group	O	X	O

is not as strong a design, but the data would have been of more value than what the project team had at the conclusion of the pilot project.

Also, congratulations if you discussed the point that there is no indication in the brief case study why, given the original problem focus, the project team focused their training only upon younger persons. The idea of any form of random sampling was disregarded through the entire process, leading to findings of no value.

9. Further Reflections

1. *After reviewing the options presented in the Social Work Practice section, which approach to sampling would you recommend in light of the project's goals?*
2. *In your position as a social work practicum intern, how would you raise concerns you had with a research project given your status and authority within the agency?*
3a. *Considering the ethical standpoint of social work, who is it that we should be counting when practising social work research?*
3b. *Are there any groups whose views are structurally missed that need to be better represented through the practice of social work research?*
3c. *Which other often-invisible populations should have been considered for inclusion in this study?*

10. Additional Reading

Barnett, V. (2009). *Sample survey: Principles and methods.* New York: Oxford University Press.

Bowen, A., Williams, M., & Horvath, K. (2004). Using the Internet to recruit rural MSM for HIV risk assessment: Sampling issues. *AIDS and Behavior, 8,* 311–19.

Cochran, W.G. (2007). *Sampling techniques* (3rd ed.). New York: Wiley.

Field, L., Pruchno, R., Bewley, J., Lemay, E., Jr., & Levinsky, N. (2006). Using probability vs. non-probability sampling to identify hard-to-access participants for health-related research. *Journal of Aging and Health, 18*(4), 565–83.

Lohr, S. (2009). *Sampling: design and analysis.* Boston: Cengage Learning.

Miller, D.R., Skinner, K.M., & Kazis, L.E. (2004). Study design and sampling in the veteran's health study. *Journal of Ambulatory Care Management, 27,* 166–79.

Miller, P.G., Johnston, J., Dunn, M., Fry, C.L., & Degenhardt, L. (2010). Comparing probability and non-probability sampling methods in ecstasy research: Implications for the Internet as a research tool. *Substance Use & Misuse, 45*(3), 437–50.

Onwuegbuzie, A., & Collins, K. (2007). A typology of mixed methods sampling designs in social science research. *Qualitative Report, 12*(2), 281–316.

Thompson, S. (2012). *Sampling* (3rd ed.). Hoboken, NJ: Wiley.

Uprichard, E. (2013). Sampling: Bridging probability and non-probability designs. *International Journal of Social Research Methodology, 16*(1), 1–11.

11. Internet Resources

Sampling

Chris Flipp, "Quantitative Sampling":
https://www.youtube.com/watch?v=WKUAop1Pre0

TOURO COLLEGE LIBRARY

Statistics Learning Centre, "Sampling: Simple Random, Convenience, Systematic, Cluster, Stratified – Statistics Help":
   https://www.youtube.com/watch?v=be9e-Q-jC-0

Simple Random Sampling

Explorable, "Simple Random Sampling":
   https://explorable.com/simple-random-sampling
Chris Stanley, "Simple Random Sample":
   https://www.youtube.com/watch?v=htWpMtLJmKg
Steve Mays, "Simple Random Sampling":
   https://www.youtube.com/watch?v=yx5KZi5QArQ
Shawn Burke, "Simple Random Sampling":
   https://www.youtube.com/watch?v=jUBtNBVy42M

Stratified Random Sampling

Explorable, "Stratified Sampling Method":
   https://explorable.com/stratified-sampling
Steve Mays, "Stratified Sampling":
   https://www.youtube.com/watch?v=sYRUYJYOpG0
apethan, "Sampling: Stratified Random Sampling":
   https://www.youtube.com/watch?v=lJqV1vrxtHc
R. Backman, "Stratified Random Samples":
   https://www.youtube.com/watch?v=4zJADWl5Hj0

Cluster Sampling

Explorable, "Cluster Sampling":
   https://explorable.com/cluster-sampling
Chris Stanley, "Cluster Sampling":
   https://www.youtube.com/watch?v=35AG-cykxg4
Rahul Patwari, "Cluster Sampling":
   https://www.youtube.com/watch?v=pV3FAVr086s

1. Preamble

Each individual step in your research process is important if you are to obtain relevant data to analyse and interpret. Thus, who is asked is just as important to your research as who is counted.

2. The Problem

In preparing a research grant in which you hope to qualitatively examine the myth that community-based mental health consumer survivors tend to be more violent than the general population, you conduct a broad-based literature review and focus in on those who have impulse control disorders. Understanding the cause of a mental health issue and the best way to intervene is an issue in all the helping professions, not only social work. Unfortunately, historically social workers have not been as active in research as other disciplines such as psychology, psychiatry, and nursing, and thus social workers often rely on the work of other professions to assist us in developing our theoretical paradigms and frameworks.

3. The Process

During the course of gaining insight into this area of practice you come across hundreds of references on the topic of impulse control disorders, though very few that take a qualitative approach. As you sort through and compartmentalize the articles you find one reference a number of times that informs the opinions of many subsequent articles. Edwards and her colleagues, a group of psychologists, wrote this article in 1943, and it was among the first to qualitatively examine the issues now commonly collapsed into the nebulous categorization that is impulse control disorder, from a purely clinical perspective. However, the reported findings challenge your perspective upon this issue. As a good researcher, you don't ignore the article and hope that the grant review panel has never heard of Edwards; neither do you merely accept the interpretation of Edwards's research by others. Rather, you go back to the original source from 1943 even though it is not available online and you cannot download it. The pursuit of a well-researched grant proposal forces you to venture forth into the university library's archives, find the original journal, and photocopy the pages manually.

4. The Research

In examining the original article you discover that Edwards was not a university-based behaviourist well versed in community research, but rather a psychodynamic psychologist with a private practice in San Francisco, California. She conducted the research for her paper by mailing questionnaires to alumni from her university using alumni letterhead. She asked her former classmates to complete five open-ended questionnaires each on individuals who had been diagnosed as having an impulse control disorder or significant signs of impulsivity. If the psychologist did not have five such patients, Edwards asked that they consider any patient they had who was diagnosed as having any issue resulting in difficulty in controlling their behaviour or any variant of obsessive compulsive disorder.

5. Questions

1. *What issues do you have with Edwards's sampling strategy?*
2. *How would you have improved the sampling process?*
3. *Explain why Edwards's findings may contradict your working hypothesis.*

6. Social Work Practice

Non-probability Sampling

There are two types of sampling procedures, probability and non-probability. Non-probability samples are descriptive while probability samples allow for inferences to be made to the entire population of interest. Non-probability samples are used when a researcher does not know the size of the entire population or is not able to obtain access to the entire population. In non-probability sampling those in the study do not necessarily represent the entire population of interest. Non-probability sampling is also typically less complicated and less costly to conduct than is probability sampling and is most useful in exploratory, descriptive, and qualitative research studies.

That researchers engage in qualitative research, however, does not mean that their methods are less rigorous. In fact, qualitative social work researchers often need to be even more precise than quantitative social work researchers because they collect so

Table 2.8   Non-Probability Sampling Options

Purposive Sampling	Interview all school social workers in your community who are MSW and have been in their current jobs for 10 years or more.
Convenience Sample	Select school social workers who are field practice instructors and who will be attending a professional development workshop sponsored by your School of Social Work.
Quota Sample	Discover from the director of social work for the school board that it employs five SSWs, five BSWs, and 10 MSWs. Ask the director to give a survey to one each of their SSW and BSW staff and two to MSWs.
Snowball Sample	Ask the field placement coordinator if she knows any school social workers who serve as field supervisors and ask the field coordinator to introduce you. Use that school social worker as a contact to other school social workers.

much data. Just as there are specific sampling methods for collecting data from subjects in experimental and quasi-experimental research approaches, there are specific methods for conducting non-probability sampling, which is typically though not always employed in qualitative studies (Table 2.8).

Elements in non-probability samples are not selected by using a random process, and therefore we do not know the probability of any particular element of the population being selected for the sample. Approaches to non-probability sampling include the following.

Purposive sampling, also referred to as a judgment sample, involves the researcher selecting a sample based upon her/his own knowledge of the population, or basically upon his/her own judgment. In purposive sampling the researcher purposely seeks out predetermined individuals for inclusion in the sample. This is common when conducting key informant interviews or when trying to obtain a broad range of views on an issue. A purposive sample is also useful when you specifically wish to select atypical clients or subjects for your research.

Convenience sampling occurs when the researcher selects the sample based upon its resemblance to the population of interest and its availability. The researcher selects cases on the basis of ease of access. University-based research where students are interviewed in a classroom is a classic example of convenience sampling. Stopping shoppers in a busy mall to ask them questions is another common instance of convenience or accidental sampling. The key issue here, as in all aspects of non-probability sampling, is that there is no random selection and thus no ability to generalize the findings to a larger population.

Quota samples are constructed by the researcher to ensure that the sample reflects the population of interest on one or more predetermined dimensions. For example, if a population of social work students contains 30 per cent undergraduate and 70 per cent graduate students a researcher might select the first three BSW students that enter a meeting and the last seven MSW students, so that the ratio between known subgroups in the sample and the population is similar. Their selection is made on the basis of convenience, but there are additional criteria that have to be met before the case is included in the sample.

Snowball sampling is typically employed when working with an unknown, hard-to-find, or invisible population. It is most commonly used in qualitative field exploration when it is difficult to find potential respondents, such as transgendered sex workers who are willing to be interviewed for a study on safe injection drug sites. Once you identify one member of the population you wish to study, you ask the respondent to refer you to others of the same group. You use these contacts to find further members of the population and, like a snowball rolling down a hill, you eventually build up enough momentum to create a sizable sample.

Sample Size

Another important decision for the researcher to make is sample size. How many cases should be included in the sample? To a certain extent the answer to this question depends on the purpose and design of the research. It is not uncommon for qualitative studies to include only a few cases, whereas a quantitative survey may involve hundreds of respondents. Since generalizability is not usually an issue in qualitative research, the more important criterion for qualitative samples is that cases included represent the full range of the phenomenon under investigation. The researcher is seeking maximum variation among the cases considered. For the purposes of determining the trustworthiness of the analysis, it is also suggested that the researcher try to include negative case examples, that is, cases that do not appear to conform to emerging interpretations. For example, a qualitative researcher who is interested in the experience of single-parent fathers finds that the fathers she has interviewed so far are in part-time or poorly compensated positions, and so looks for a father who is regularly employed in a well-paying job. Often the researcher will establish a method of identifying cases, for example the snowball approach, and continue to include cases until the addition of more case examples no longer adds to their understanding. This endpoint is referred to as the point of data saturation. Using this approach, the qualitative researcher's sample grows over time. This means that it may not be possible to determine the exact size of the sample in advance.

Note: A more in depth examination of sample size is provided in the final segment of the case study section: Data Collection and Statistical Analysis.

7. Responding to the Case

The intent of this case study, along with introducing the various forms of non-probability sampling procedures (none of which were used in this study), is to illustrate the importance of using original sources. It may seem convenient to refer to an article without reading it in its entirety or, as in this case, by understanding it only through other people's interpretations, but doing so does much to explain why contradictory explanations for a phenomenon may arise – the processes were very different. The reported study by Edwards and her colleagues is a fictitious example of a poor sampling frame, but many procedures that are just as flawed end up in the literature and, worse, quoted by others.

Among Edwards's many errors, the most prominent include:

- The lack of any systemic approach to the sampling
- The bias in who was included in the original sample
- The bias of those who completed the survey
- The bias in determining which patients were to be included in the survey
- The lack of any systemic approach to the research
- The lack of awareness that you cannot generalize beyond the sampling frame regardless of the demographics of samples from one study to the next.

8. Research Insight

If you are conducting descriptive research, there are methods of calculating the number of cases required to get reasonably accurate estimates of population parameters (see http://www.surveysystem.com/sscalc.htm for a tool to help determine sample size). You need to know what the acceptable level of accuracy is (usually 95 or 99 per cent) and the size of the population (see also Case Study 23).

9. Further Reflections

1. After reviewing the options presented in the Social Work Practice section, which approach to sampling would you recommend in light of the original project's goals?
2a. What are the social work research implications of not going back and reviewing the original sources?
2b. What are the social work practice implications of not going back and reviewing the original sources?
3. Are qualitative sampling techniques any less rigorous than quantitative sampling approaches?

10. Additional Reading

Baker, R., Brick, J.M., Bates, N.A., Battaglia, M., Couper, M.P., Dever, J.A., . . ., & Tourangeau, R. (2013). Summary report of the AAPOR task force on non-probability sampling. *Journal of Survey Statistics and Methodology, 1*(2), 90–143. doi:10.1093/jssam/smt008.

Baltar, F., & Brunet, I. (2012). Social research 2.0: Virtual snowball sampling method using Facebook. *Internet Research, 22*(1), 57–74.

Bhutta, C.B. (2012). Not by the book: Facebook as a sampling frame. *Sociological Methods & Research 41*(1): 57–88. http://dx.doi.org/10.1177/0049124112440795

Bornstein, M.H., Jager, J., & Putnick, D.L. (2013). Sampling in developmental science: Situations, shortcomings, solutions, and standards. *Developmental Review, 33*(4), 357–70.

Cochran, W.G. (2007). *Sampling techniques* (3rd ed.). New York: Wiley.

Faugier, J., & Sargeant, M. (1997). Sampling hard to reach populations. *Journal of Advanced Nursing, 26*(4), 790–7.

Griffiths, P., Gossop, M., Powis, B., & Strang, J. (1993). Reaching hidden populations of drug users by privileged access interviewers: Methodological and practical issues. *Addiction (Abingdon, England), 88*(12), 1617–26.

Groger, L., Mayberry, P., & Straker, J. (1999). What we didn't learn because of who would not talk to us. *Qualitative Health Research, 9*(6), 829–35.

Im, E.O., & Chee, W. (2011). Quota sampling in Internet research: Practical issues. *Computers, Informatics, Nursing, 29*(7), 381–5.

Magnani, R., Sabin, K., Saidel, T., & Heckathorn, D. (2005). Review of sampling hard-to-reach and hidden populations for HIV surveillance. *AIDS (London, England), 19*, S67–S72.

Onwuegbuzie, A.J., & Leech, N.L. (2005). The role of sampling in qualitative research. *Academic Exchange, 9*, 280–4.

Pernod, J., Preston, D.B., Cain, R.E., & Starks, M.T. (2003). A discussion of chain referral as a method of sampling hard to reach populations. *Journal of Transcultural Nursing, 14*, 100–7.

Palys, T. (2008). Purposive sampling. In L.M. Given (Ed.), *The Sage encyclopedia of qualitative research methods* (Vol. 2, pp. 697–8). Thousand Oaks, CA: Sage.

Sadler, G.R., Lee, H.C., Lim, R.S.H., & Fullerton, J. (2010). Recruitment of hard-to-reach population subgroups via adaptations of the snowball sampling strategy. *Nursing & Health Sciences, 12*(3), 369–74.

Sibona, C., & Walczak, S. (2012, January). Purposive sampling on Twitter: A case study. In *45th Hawaii International Conference on System Sciences (HICSS)*, pp. 3510–19. http://dx.doi.org/10.1109/HICSS.2012.493

Teddlie, C., & Yu, F. (2007). Mixed methods sampling. *Journal of Mixed Methods Research, 1*(1), 77–100.

11. Internet Resources

Non-Probability Sampling

Nikki Hozack, "Sampling: Non-Probability Sampling":
   https://www.youtube.com/watch?v=4VO_xHHD180
Chris Flipp, "Qualitative Sampling":
   https://www.youtube.com/watch?v=-Dn4u9DPmDs
Rahul Patwari, "Non-Probability Sampling":
   https://www.youtube.com/watch?v=-kwdXEXC7yE

Purposive Sampling

T. Palys, "Purposive Sampling," in Given (Ed.), *The Sage Encyclopedia of Qualitative Research Methods*, vol. 2:
   http://www.sfu.ca/~palys/Purposive%20sampling.pdf
ACAPS Project, "Purposive Sampling":
   https://www.youtube.com/watch?v=FuzE3Lrw2t0

Quota Sample

R. Backman, "Quota Sampling":
   https://www.youtube.com/watch?v=NW2RPAYfq4g

Snowball Sampling

Explorable, "Snowball Sampling":
   https://explorable.com/snowball-sampling
bethie1988, "Snowball Sampling: Seattle Grace":
   https://www.youtube.com/watch?v=BIEteh4nryM

CASE STUDY 9
Criminal Justice Issues in Social Work Research: The Search for Causality

1. Preamble

One of the most contentious areas of research and statistical reporting remains the criminal justice area, as crime data are really the end result of a process and the result of decisions about how you count. Does a decrease in crime mean there was less criminality, or simply that fewer police officers were on the street or fewer individuals were brought to trial in a given year? When researching any contentious social issue, one must always incorporate a macro examination of the data along with a detailed examination of the issue being presented to arrive at an accurate and just conclusion about causation.

2. The Problem

Poverty disenfranchises individuals in many ways, including its association with inadequate access to legal services and supports. Individuals who are apprehended and charged with a criminal offence are placed in detention, and must remain in detention awaiting trial unless they have the financial ability to post bail. Individuals are also detained without access to bail if they are deemed to be of ongoing danger to the general population or at risk of flight from authorities. It is believed that there is a disproportionate likelihood of an individual's being convicted and incarcerated for two or more years if he or she was detained prior to trial rather than being released into the community to await trial. Thus, civil rights advocates hypothesize that those with the least amount of financial resources are incarcerated disproportionately because of their financial situation rather than the seriousness of their offence, further oppressing them because of their poverty.

3. The Process

The New Brunswick provincial government, on a trial basis, sets up a special community project as part of its legal aid process. The two-year pilot project will provide bail to low-income individuals charged with non-violent crimes. The funds are to be administered by a community board that must provide a formal written report on the outcome of the project to the government prior to the call of the next provincial election. The community board, many of whom are selected because of their affiliation to and financial support of the current sitting government, must assess whether this controversial pilot project helped to make the criminal justice system fairer for low-income people charged with committing an offence.

4. The Research

In the five years prior to the commencement of the pilot project, 52 per cent of those charged with an offence were held in detention until their trial commenced. This was the highest rate for any province in Canada. Those detained were 2.8 times as likely to be convicted as those released when family background and type of crime (violent versus non-violent) were controlled for. This was the impetus that inspired social work civil rights advocates to press the provincial justice minister to move forwards with the pilot project.

During the course of the two-year pilot project a randomized controlled experiment was initiated for persons committing non-violent crimes. In a randomized design each participant has the same chance of being placed in either the group which will receive the intervention (experimental group) or a group that is used to ascertain if the intervention produced a change (control group). Of those detained who could not post bail, 504 individuals were selected for inclusion in the study. The experimental group consisted of 252 randomly selected persons for whom the community group posted bail with the individual's consent and 252 individuals who constituted the control group and who unfortunately remained incarcerated awaiting trial. Of the experimental group, 103 (40.9 per cent) were found innocent when they went to trial, while 38 (15.1 per cent) of the control group were found innocent.

5. Questions

1. *What is your appraisal of the research design that was the impetus for the pilot project?*
2a. *As a member of the community board, what do you recommend to the government?*
2b. *What is your rationale for the recommendation?*

6. Social Work Practice

Developing Theory

Understanding the human condition is a complex undertaking, but trying to learn as much as we can about human behaviour, the regularities of social interaction, and the influences of context on human agency are all essential to effective social work practice. The social science disciplines of psychology, anthropology, and sociology, for example, study the regularities or patterns of the human experience to help us add to our understanding. They do this by developing theory. A theory consists of a description of one of these patterns along with an explanation as to why it should occur. For example, delinquency is an all-too-common pattern of adolescent behaviour. Research has established that delinquent behaviour in young people is associated with low levels of attachment, commitment, and belief in the values of the dominant society. These are all important dimensions of social control. To explain this pattern, control theories of delinquency (Hirschi, 1977) begin by asserting that all individuals experience unfulfilled needs or desires for items such as money, sex, excitement, and revenge. Social control serves as a restraint on non-normative approaches to meeting these needs. Individuals with weak levels of social control are not restrained and can therefore meet these needs in the easiest and fastest manner; often this means by committing delinquent acts. Having a theory enables us to make better predictions as to future behaviour. If we encounter an individual with weak levels of attachment, commitment, and belief in the values of society, and if our theory is correct, we could predict that the person will probably engage in delinquent acts. The word "probably" is very important here. Primarily because of the complexity of human nature, theory cannot predict anything with certainty. Not every adolescent with low levels of social control will engage in delinquent behaviour. There is a strong possibility that will be the case, but the outcome is not certain for any given youth. That is why we refer to theory as "probabilistic." Also keep in mind that all theory is open to refinement or even replacement if a theory is developed that better reflects the complexity of this type of behaviour.

It is also important to emphasize that theory is only one part of developing our understanding of human behaviour. Theory describes a pattern of human behaviour and provides an explanation of why that pattern might exist. Obviously it needs to make logical sense, but making sense is not enough. To include a theory into our understanding of the world, we need to have empirical evidence to support it. "Empirical" means that we have actually observed the relationships described in the theory using the methodology of scientific investigation. In the 1980s in the United States popular theories of delinquent behaviour led to the development of the Scared Straight program. Children at risk of committing delinquent acts were taken to an adult prison faculty to see what life was like for those doing "hard time." The logic was that once they saw the harsh realities of prison life they would be less inclined to commit criminal acts in the future. However, empirical research did not support this predicted outcome. In fact, studies showed that youth who participated in the program were more likely to engage in delinquent behaviours than those for whom absolutely nothing was done. In this case the theory made logical sense to many but the evidence did not support it, and the approach has been abandoned, except of course in "reality" television.

Hypotheses and Variables

Theory development must be accompanied by theory testing. These complementary processes develop through a cycle that starts with the observation of patterns of behaviour. These patterns are described as generalizations, which are then explained in a theory. Once a theory has been proposed, hypotheses can be developed to test the accuracy of the theory, and the cycle then returns to observation as the researcher watches to see if the hypothesized relationships occur as predicted. If they do, there is empirical evidence to support the theory; if not, new observations may lead to revised generalizations, beginning the cycle again. In terms of the above example of adolescent delinquency, a researcher observed a particular group of adolescents engaged in delinquent behaviour and noticed that this appeared to be associated with weak levels of social control. The researcher generalized this to all adolescents and suggested that delinquency is the result of low social control, and then developed a theory to explain why this might be true. From this theory hypotheses were developed that suggested adolescents with weak social controls were more likely than adolescents with strong social controls to engage in delinquent behaviour, and studies were conducted that supported the associations predicted in the hypotheses. The process in the first part of the cycle, from observation to theory, is referred to as induction or theory development; the process in the second part, from theory to observation, is called deduction or theory testing.

Hypotheses are statements derived from theory that predict a relationship between variables of interest. Useable hypotheses are conceptually clear; specific, with terms clearly conceptualized and operationalized (see Case Study 6); related to existing theory; and presented in a manner that allows them to be researchable – for what ought to be investigated and what can be investigated are not always the same thing.

Variables are simply concepts that vary, that change when influenced by something else. A variable is an element that can have more than one value. A variable represents a concept that can be categorized into two or more exhaustive and mutually exclusive categories. To be exhaustive implies that every object can be placed into a category; there is a place for all. To be mutually exclusive means that each object can be placed into one and only one specific category. If a characteristic does not vary it is considered a constant and not appropriate for inclusion in a hypothesis. Hypotheses are not questions or statements of belief. They are predictions, such as "Youth with weak parental attachment are more likely to have committed delinquent acts than youth with high levels of attachment." The subject of analysis is youth, the variables of interest are attachment and delinquency, and the relationship predicted is one of association. Low levels of attachment will be associated with youth who exhibit delinquent behaviour, whereas high levels of attachment will not. Another way of stating the hypothesis is "Youth who have committed delinquent acts will have a lower level of parental attachment than youth who have not committed delinquent acts." This is a hypothesis of difference. A third approach would be to state the hypothesis as "The higher the number of delinquent acts committed, the lower the level of parental attachment." In this case we would have a hypothesis of correlation. This last approach is a special form of association that can only be determined if we can measure the two variables of interest at a high level of precision. Regardless of how the hypothesis is worded, we would be able to gather data to test whether the outcome is as predicted. If it is, then we can say we have empirical support for our theory. However, it is important to understand that even if our observations are consistent with our hypotheses, we cannot say we have proven that it is the weak social controls that cause delinquency. Given that most research is conducted on samples or subgroups of populations and not an entire population, one instance of a positive outcome cannot be considered proof of our theory. There is always the possibility that the group selected for study is different from the population, and so the results of our study would not be the same if we observed the entire population. However, if our observations do not support our hypotheses then our theory is put into question. We may need to replicate the study to make sure the negative outcome was not an artefact of poor implementation, or change the design in some way to compensate for study limitations, or rethink our theory on the basis of these new observed outcomes.

Independent, Dependent, and Confounding/Extraneous Variables

The variables in a hypothesis play specific roles, and these roles are designated by naming the variables. The independent variable is the variable that is postulated to explain another variable. The dependent variable is the variable being explained. It varies or responds to changes in the independent variable if the two are related in some way. It is the effect being examined; it is the relationship we are interested in knowing more about. If we hypothesize that weak parental attachment causes delinquent behaviour, then parental attachment is assuming the independent variable role and delinquency the dependent variable role. If instead we propose that delinquency leads to poor parental attachment, then the roles are reversed; the independent variable in this case is delinquency and the dependent variable is parental attachment. Whether a variable is independent or dependent depends on the direction of causality, not on the variable itself. For example, consider the following two hypotheses:

i)   Anxiety causes sleeplessness.
ii) Sleeplessness causes irritability.

In the first hypothesis sleeplessness is the dependent variable, and in the second it is the independent variable.

There is always the possibility that a hypothesized relationship between the independent and dependent variables is actually being produced by a third variable. We call this either a confounding or an extraneous variable. This type of variable represents alternative explanations for any observed relationships and is what researchers need to continually be aware of in drawing conclusions or making inferences. The relationship between extraneous or confounding variables and dependent and independent variables is illustrated in Figure 2.9a.

Figure 2.9a   Relationship between Variables – Confounding Variable

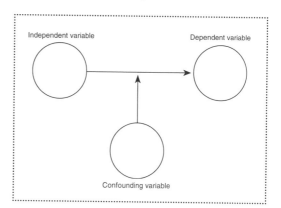

Variable Relationships

There are three types of hypothetical relationships between variables: a positive relationship, a negative relationship, or a curvilinear relationship. Variables are positively related if a change in the independent variable leads to a similar change in the dependent variable. For example, the hypothesis that an increase in the number of hours you study will cause an increase in the grade you achieve suggests a positive relationship between hours studied and grade achieved. Figure 2.9b provides a graph that illustrates this hypothesized positive relationship. A change in the independent variable (studying) creates a change in the dependent variable (grade) in the same direction: as studying increases, the grade increases (see also Case Study 23).

A negative or inverse relationship occurs when a change in the independent variable produces a change in the dependent variable, but in this case the change is in the opposite direction. For example, the hypothesis that studying is negatively related to test anxiety suggests that as studying increases, test anxiety decreases. Figure 2.9c illustrates the negative relationship. A change in the independent variable (studying) creates a change in the dependent variable (test anxiety) in the opposite direction: as the number of hours of study increases, the level of test anxiety decreases.

The third type of relationship is called a curvilinear relationship. In this case, a change in the independent variable causes a change in the dependent variable in the same direction up to a particular value of the independent variable, at which point further changes in the independent variable will cause an opposite change in the dependent variable. If we look at the relationship between studying and grade, we might

Figure 2.9b   Positive Relationship

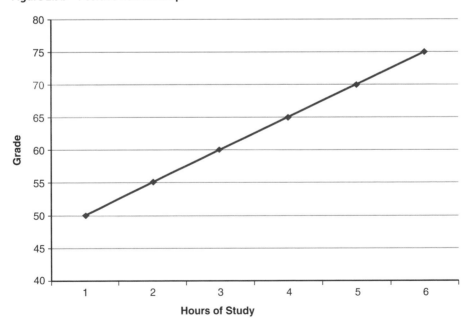

Figure 2.9c   Negative (Inverse) Relationship

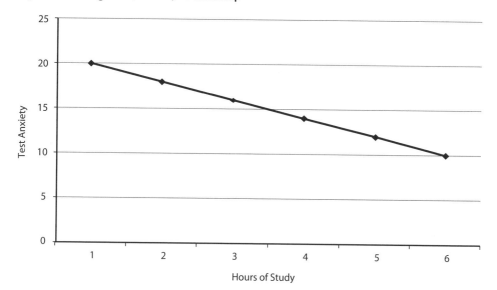

better represent it as a curvilinear relationship: studying does help up to a point, but after that additional studying does not help increase grade and can even contribute to a decline in grade. Figure 2.9d illustrates this curvilinear relationship. From this graph it would appear that up to the six-hour point an increase in time spent studying produces an increase.

The Search for Causation

What did the social worker or the social work intervention actually have to do with the outcome? Did the change in the independent variable, the factor that you have some control over and that is often your intervention as a social worker, produce a change in the dependent variable, the item that you are observing? In determining causation you must look for three factors to be present:

1. *Co-variation:* As the independent variable changes, so does the dependent variable.
2. *Temporal Ordering:* The change in the dependent variable is preceded by the change in the independent variable.
3. *Elimination of Alternative Explanations:* This ensures that it is the dependent variable that is causing the independent variable to change, and not some third confounding factor.

Figure 2.9d Curvilinear Relationship

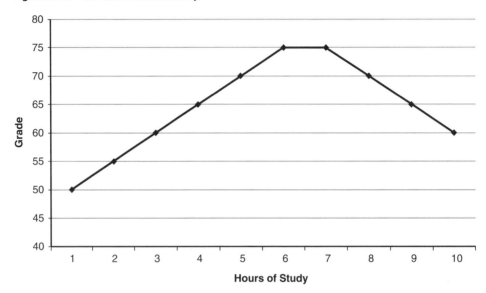

7. Responding to the Case

The theory that formed the basis for social work advocates was far from conclusive, and thus the pilot study was a wise process in which to engage before committing permanent funding. While poverty and oppression could very well be the reason for the difference, there remained alternative explanations, such as that those who could afford bail could also afford better legal representation. However, after a rudimentary examination of the pilot study's findings, even without conducting a formal statistical analysis, the results appear clear. As a member of the community board, you should have no hesitation in stating that the pilot project demonstrated that poverty was leading to unfair conviction of individuals who otherwise might not have been convicted, and that the pilot project should be extended. While a majority of subjects in both the experimental and control groups were found guilty, the likelihood of conviction if the accused was detained rather than coming to trial as a free man or woman was 2.7 times greater, nearly identical to the observations that led to the controlled study. As your research also used a randomized controlled experiment, the concerns of internal validity (see Case Study 11) were addressed by the nature of your research design, and the three criteria of causality are met. The action arising from the research will be to address a long-standing injustice to a marginalized population, a significant reason all social workers should engage in research as part of their practice.

8. Further Reflections

1. *Why is causality such a critically important quantitative research concept?*
2. *Is social work research that searches for causal relationships of greater utility than other forms of research that do not?*
3. *When making programming and policy decisions, how much emphasis should be placed upon the empirical results? What other factors are typically considered, and what weight is given to these? What are the implications of this balancing of factors?*

9. Additional Reading

Bachman, R., & Schutt, R. (2013). *The practice of research in criminology and criminal justice.* Thousand Oaks, CA: Pine Forge Press.

Bronson, D.E., & Davis, T.S. (2011). *Finding and evaluating evidence: Systematic reviews and evidence-based practice.* New York: Oxford University Press.

Davies, P., Francis, P., & Jupp, V. (2011). *Doing criminological research.* Thousand Oaks, CA: Sage.

Gibbs, L.E. (1991). *Scientific reasoning for social workers: Bridging the gap between research and practice.* New York: Macmillan.

Hirschi, T. (1977). Causes and prevention of juvenile delinquency. *Sociological Inquiry, 47,* 322–41.

Howell, J.C. (2003). *Preventing and reducing juvenile delinquency: A comprehensive framework.* Thousand Oaks, CA: Sage.

King, R., & Wincup, E. (2007). *Doing research on crime and justice.* New York: Oxford University Press.

Lohman, M.C. (2001). Deductive and inductive on-the-job training strategies. *Advances in Developing Human Resources, 3*(4), 435–41.

Sheppard, M., & Ryan, K. (2003). Practitioners as rule using analysts: A further development of process knowledge in social work. *British Journal of Social Work, 33*(2), 157–76.

Tsang, A. (2000). Bridging the gap between clinical practice and research: An integrated practice-oriented model. *Journal of Social Service Research, 26*(4), 69–90.

Walters, K. (1990). Critical thinking, rationality and the Vulcanization of students. *Journal of Higher Education, 61*(4), 448–67.

Westerfelt, A., & Dietz, T. (2009). *Planning and conducting agency-based research: A workbook for social work students in field placements.* Don Mills, ON: Longman.

Wilks, S.E., & Spivey, C.A. (2010). Resilience in undergraduate social work students: Social support and adjustment to academic stress. *Social Work Education, 29*(3), 276–88.

Zeira, A., & Rosen, A. (2000). Unraveling "tacit knowledge": What social workers do and why they do it. *Social Service Review, 74*(1), 103–23.

10. Internet Resources

Hypothesis Testing

Ron Wallace, "Research Questions, Hypothesis and Variables":
    https://www.youtube.com/watch?v=_BmjujlZExQ
MsLemmonsClass, "Research Questions and Hypothesis":
    https://www.youtube.com/watch?v=6PgQuDjnq64
Sparkling Psychology Star, "How to Write Hypotheses":
    https://www.youtube.com/watch?v=9NCbNgnIhH8

Variables

Nurse Killam, "Independent, Dependent and Confounding Variables in Quantitative Research":
    https://www.youtube.com/watch?v=mFIvsqVir48
Sparkling Psychology Star, "Variables IV, DV, Extraneous Variables":
    https://www.youtube.com/watch?v=sQlgPwCSIMM
Elizabeth Lynch, "Confounding":
    https://www.youtube.com/watch?v=1Cn1smM3kbQ

Causation

TEDx Talks, "The Danger of Mixing Up Causality and Correlation: Ionica Smeets at TEDxDelft":
    https://www.youtube.com/watch?v=8B271L3NtAw
trustmetrics, "Correlation vs. Causation: How to Tell the Difference":
    https://www.youtube.com/watch?v=rEksYS9ZNU4
Joseph Cohen, "Causality":
    https://www.youtube.com/watch?v=IOUWP4n7gds

CASE STUDY 10
Psychometric Properties: How Should We Measure?

1. Preamble

One of the most important decisions to make when you are designing a summative program evaluation, an evaluation that is outcome focused, is to determine how you are going to measure the dependent variable. This is the process of operationalization discussed in Case Study 6. The reason this is an important step is that if you select or design a poor measure you will end up with bad data. Every statistician knows that "garbage in means garbage out." Thus, even the most sophisticated and accurate data analysis will not fix the problem of poor input data. Good measures must have strong psychometric properties that are both reliable and valid.

2. The Problem

A group of four experienced practitioners formed a social work research committee at the active treatment hospital where they were employed in Quebec. Ginette, Laurette, Jean, and Marie represented three of the busiest services in their large metropolitan hospital: neurology, cardiology, and nephrology. Patients came from a large, bilingual, and ethnically diverse geographic area and were quite ill by the time they reached inpatient status. As a group, the social workers were supportive of evidence-informed practice, as this was the standard of care for all the health care professions represented in their multidisciplinary teams. Recently Ginette had been reading some interesting research on the association between anxiety and healthy recovery. It appeared as if patients who experienced high levels of anxiety preoperatively had worse health outcomes than those whose anxiety was more moderate. The group wondered if ameliorating high levels of anxiety could contribute to more positive health outcomes for patients.

3. The Process

The social work research team decided to begin by conducting a literature review to ascertain results from other studies that looked at various social work interventions intended to reduce anxiety. Drawing upon their clinical experience and the social work literature in this area, they developed a new, brief service protocol to guide their work with anxious patients. The four social workers decided to use this new protocol to address situational anxiety among both Anglophone and Francophone inpatients waiting for surgery or others undergoing medical procedures in hospital. As conscientious and principled social workers, they wished to demonstrate that their new intervention had the positive effects that a logic model[3] suggested it should. Thus, they became the first social workers to apply for an internal hospital research grant in order to design a study to test the efficacy of their new approach, with the goal of publishing their results.

4. The Research

The social work research team's design involved measuring a patient's anxiety before providing the intervention and then measuring the same patient's anxiety after the intervention was completed. The four hoped to show that the patient's level of anxiety would decrease after service to establish that the intervention had had a positive effect. One of their first tasks was to determine how they would measure anxiety. Laurette wanted to ask the patient to rate his/her level of anxiety on a scale from 1 to 10. If the intervention was helpful the person's score should be less after treatment than before. Jean wasn't so sure that was the best way to go: "I remember from my research methods course at school that anxiety is a very complex construct, and as such we should use a multi-item scale to measure it." She thought that asking one broad question might not provide a good measure of the person's level of anxiety. Marie agreed, but pointed out that the development of multi-item scales was a complicated and time-consuming task and she doubted they had the expertise to develop a good scale: "A multi-item scale might be better, but we haven't got the time or talent to develop one."

5. Questions

1. *What would be the characteristics of a good measure of anxiety for this setting?*
2. *What items would you include in the measure?*
3. *How should the social work research team proceed?*
4. *What are the additional implications arising from working in a bilingual setting?*

---

3   A logic model is a depiction of the processes to be used to produce the results desired by an organization or a specific program. It typically consists of inputs, activities, outputs, and outcomes or impacts.

6. Social Work Practice

Rating Scales

Many of the human characteristics that social workers are interested in are complex and multidimensional. When we measure a characteristic or construct, we want to make sure we are covering all its dimensions. This is why a multi-item rating scale is considered superior to a single-item measure. Compare asking a person to rate her level of anxiety on a scale of 1 to 10 versus asking her to respond to a number of questions each of which addresses a certain dimension of anxiety. The latter approach is more likely to give you a true indication of the person's level of anxiety.

A great deal of research time and attention has been directed towards the development of useful rating scales for common psychosocial constructs. Appropriate measures can be identified when you are conducting your literature review. Look to see what scales other researchers have used. Standardized rating scales are also published in compendiums of commonly used psychological tests, and many scales are now available on the Internet (e.g., http://www.walmyr.com). If you are fortunate, there is a commonly used measure that you can employ so that you do not have to develop your own. There is no need to reinvent the wheel if a suitable measure is available. For anxiety a recognized scale that can be used at no cost is the Hamilton Anxiety Rating Scale (HAM-A) (http://dcf.psychiatry.ufl.edu/files/2011/05/HAMILTON-ANXIETY.pdf), but how do you know that this well-known scale is actually appropriate to use?

Issues in Collecting Data

Regardless of where you find it, before you adopt someone else's measure you need to be convinced that it has strong psychometric properties. Will the rating scale give you consistent results – that is, is it reliable – and does it measure the construct you are interested in investigating – that is, is it valid?

Every time you take a measurement there is the possibility that there is some error in the result. Sometimes this error is the result of random events that may or may not influence the outcome each time you use a measure. What we would like is a measure that produces the same results each time it is used, a measure that produces consistent results. If this is the case, then we say we have a reliable measure. Error that is due to random events is, by its very nature, difficult to avoid. There could be some amount of random error in every measurement taken. There are ways, however, that the researcher can try to keep random error to a minimum. Some of these address the way in which the data are collected; others address the respondents themselves. In terms of the data collection, when you are taking a measurement make sure that the environmental conditions are accommodating. For example, if you are using a self-administered questionnaire to collect data and the room is noisy, hot, or being used for other activities, respondents can easily become distracted and make mistakes in completing the questionnaire. Sometimes events occur that the researcher does not anticipate; for example, the fire alarm goes off, tragic world events occur just before the survey is administered, or someone in a group of respondents experiences an epileptic seizure. If such distracting events occur, the researcher needs to consider their possible effect on the reliability of the data.

The design of questionnaires can also affect a measure's reliability. If the language of some of the questions cannot be understood by respondents or is ambiguous, the data could be unreliable. For example, if you ask a respondent if they drink, with responses "yes" or "no," you are most likely to get unreliable data, since the word "drink" may have a different meaning to different respondents. Random error may also be introduced if you ask a person to answer a question about things they are unlikely to remember. For example, if you ask someone how many kilometers they have driven in the past month, it's unlikely you will get a consistent answer depending upon when in the month the person is asked. People cannot usually recall this kind of detail, and their answers will contain varying amounts of error. If the questionnaire itself is long or uninteresting, people answering it may at some stage just switch off and go through the motions of answering, again producing unreliable information. One of the most critical considerations when designing a questionnaire is the extent to which the design and question development maximize reliability (see also Case Study 15).

There may also be characteristics of the respondents that affect the reliability of the information collected. There are some people who do not like to admit they don't know the answer to a question. This means that they will go as far as guessing or even manufacturing an answer instead of saying they don't know. Others do not take answering questionnaires seriously or for whatever reason are not paying attention to what they are doing. They may not see answering the questionnaire as important. As well, they may be ill or having difficulty paying attention due to personal worries or distractions. Any condition of the individual or external environment that reduces a respondent's ability or willingness to concentrate on the task at hand will likely affect the reliability of the data.

Reliability

There are ways to actually assess the reliability of some measures. The most basic is called test-retest reliability. You apply your measure and then, after the passage of a set period of time, apply it again. If the measure is reliable you will likely get the same answer on both occasions. If you do this across a large number of respondents you can calculate the correlation between the two testing events. If the measure is reliable, the test-retest correlation should be a high positive number. The accepted standard is usually .60 or higher (1.0 being a perfect score). This works best if the characteristic being measured is fairly stable and the period of time between test and retest is not too long. This approach will also only capture unreliability that is related to the actual measure, not the many external factors that could on any given occasion reduce a measure's reliability.

How can you determine if a multi-item scale is reliable? Most standardized tests come with a description of the scale and how to use it. One of the items covered in the description is the result of reliability testing conducted during the test construction. The most common measure of reliability for multi-item scales is called a Cronbach alpha. This is a measure of the rating scale's internal consistency. It is based on the idea that if all the items in a scale are measuring the same characteristic then there should be consistency in a person's responses. If a person indicates a high rating on one item he or she should rate all the others high as well. The Cronbach alpha is calculated by first correlating each item with every other item. If all items on a scale are measuring the same thing, you would expect to derive high positive inter-item correlations. The Cronbach alpha is the average of the inter-item correlations. A high positive Cronbach alpha means that the rating scale has a high degree of consistency. By convention, researchers consider a Cronbach alpha of .80 or greater to be the necessary level for strong internal consistency. This level can be relaxed to .70 if the scale is exploratory. So before you use someone else's rating scale make sure that the Cronbach alpha is greater than .80. On occasion the authors of a standardized rating scale will also provide a test-retest indication of reliability. This means that they administered the test to the same group of respondents under similar conditions on two separate occasions. If the test is reliable, scores on the first test should be similar to scores on the second test. The degree of similarity is quantified by calculating a correlation coefficient. A high test-retest correlation also means a high level of consistency.

As well, keep in mind that using a reliable scale does not necessarily mean you will receive reliable data from your administration of the scale. Since reliability is affected by random error, there is always the chance that external factors will interfere with your testing and result in a reduction in reliability. Therefore, it is best to test and report on the Cronbach alpha of your administration of the scale.

Validity

While some error introduced into our measures is due to random events, there is another type of error that results from systemic distortion. This means that the error occurs every time the measure is used. Think of a measuring tape that has been incorrectly calibrated or has a worn edge. It is supposed to measure height, but the data it provides are incorrect, and incorrect every time the faulty measure is used. Since the tape is supposed to measure height but does not, we would say that it is not a valid measure of height. Validity addresses the accuracy of the measure: does it actually measure the concept it says it measures? Is a measure of depression actually measuring depression, or is it measuring frustration or anxiety instead? A researcher needs to establish as clearly as possible that the measures being used are valid representations of the concepts of interest. It is important to keep in mind that in order for a measure to be considered valid, it must first be reliable. Reliability is a necessary but not sufficient condition for validity. Alternatively, that a measure is reliable does not mean it is valid. The poorly calibrated tape measure described above may consistently produce the same measurement result of my height and so is considered reliable, but it is not an accurate measure of my height. It is reliable but not valid.

How can you determine a measure's validity? Again, the description of the measure should report the results of validity testing conducted during the scale development. There are two main approaches to determining validity, each of which has various ways of establishing validity. Ideally both approaches are addressed by a scale's authors. Keep in mind that while in this section we are talking about multi-item measures, these methods of establishing validity can be applied to single-item measures as well.

The first approach we call *non-empirical*, since it uses judgment. There are two non-empirical approaches to establishing validity. In the first, those constructing the scale send a copy of it to a group of "experts" who are asked two questions. The first is: Do the items in this scale look like they measure the construct? If so, the scale is said to have face validity. A scale that allegedly measures anxiety should contain items that look like they are determining anxiety. For example, items such as "I am afraid of being left alone," "I worry all the time," and "I feel pressure in my chest when I have to do something new" appear to be measuring anxiety, while an item such as "I never get my own way" does not. The second question asked of the experts is: Do the items appear to cover all dimensions of the construct? If so, the scale is said to have content validity. For example, if I design a test that attempts to measure your knowledge of research methodology and I only include questions about experimental design, my test would not have content validity. By excluding questions on topics such as sampling, questionnaire design, and psychometrics, I fail to cover all dimensions of the construct "knowledge of research methodology." Since determinations of face and content validity depend upon the judgments of other people, it is important to know who these people are and why the test's authors believe they are qualified to make these judgments before you decide whether the construct has been properly operationalized.

However, expert judgment is a relatively weak basis for claims of validity. A stronger claim is established by the authors having conducted some form of *empirical investigation* of a scale's validity. There are many ways to do this, but all fall into one of two broad categories: criterion-related validity and construct validity.

Approaches to criterion-related validity take the results from an administration of the scale and compare these to some external criterion that is also an indicator of the construct under consideration. One type of criterion-related validity is called concurrent validity: to test a scale's concurrent validity authors compare the results from their scale to some other measure of the same construct that is already agreed to be reliable and valid. If there is a high correlation between these two then the new scale is considered to have high concurrent validity. Usually the alternative to which the new scale is compared uses a different approach to measuring the same variable. For example, if the new rating scale was to measure aggression, the results from the scale could be compared to behavioural observation of aggression. People who are judged on the basis of observation to be aggressive should score high on the paper-and-pencil rating scale for aggression. If the rating scale is a valid measure of aggression, there should be a high correlation between the two approaches.

Another criterion-related approach to determine validity is called predictive validity. The idea behind this approach is that if the rating scale is a good measure of the construct the results should be helpful in predicting some future event or outcome. For example, a scale to measure marital satisfaction should be able to reliably predict marital breakdown. Couples who scored high on the scale should experience lower rates of marital breakdown than couples who scored low. Hence, the authors of a new scale administer the scale to a group of couples and then follow the group for a predetermined period of time. At the end of that period, if the scale is a valid measure of marital satisfaction there should be an association between score on the scale and the incidence of marital breakdown. If this is the case, then the scale is said to have predictive validity.

The final type of criterion-related validity is called known-groups validity. The idea here is that if the scale is a valid measure of the construct we should be able to use the results of the scale to separate respondents into distinct groups based on their scores on the measure. To test this, respondents are selected who vary on some predetermined characteristic that the scale is supposed to measure. Let's say they are adolescents who have had multiple school suspensions and criminal justice involvement for drug use or children who have never been in trouble at school or with the law. If a scale developed to measure the likelihood of developing addiction is valid, it should be able to reliably differentiate to which group a particular respondent belongs. If it can correctly do this a high percentage of times it is said to have known-groups validity.

The second approach to empirically determined validity is construct validity, and it is divided into two subgroups: convergent validity and discriminant validity. These approaches start with the idea that many social science theories address the relationship among psychosocial variables. If the variable we are interested in measuring is part of a well-supported theory, we can use this theory to test the construct validity of our measure of the variable. For example, suppose a theory tells us that there is a positive relationship between anger and depression. If we are developing a measure of depression, and it is a valid measure, there should be a positive correlation between the scores from our measure of depression and the scores on a psychometrically strong measure for anger. If this is the case then we say that our measure has construct validity. Discriminant validity suggests the opposite, that if there is no theoretical reason for two constructs to be related then there should be no correlation between them. If, for example, previous research has not been able to show a relationship between depression and intelligence, and if our scale is a valid measure for depression, there should be no correlation between scores of depression using our scale and scores for IQ. The terminology here is a bit confusing because some people refer to known-groups validity as discriminant validity. (What we are addressing here is *discriminant construct* validity.) Due to this confusion, some researchers refer to this type of validity as divergent construct validity. A summary of these approaches to establishing the validity of scales is provided in Table 2.10.

Table 2.10   **Approaches to Testing Validity**

Non-Empirical Approaches – based on judgment

    – face validity

    – content validity

Empirical Approaches – based on statistical analysis

• Criterion-related validity

    – concurrent validity

    – predictive validity

    – known-groups validity

• Construct validity

    – convergent validity

    – discriminant validity

Choosing the Correct Scale

Now that you have identified a scale with strong psychometric properties, you need to consider whether it is appropriate to use the scale to measure a construct in the population you will be studying. A measure for anger developed for use with adults, even if it has demonstrated reliability and validity, would not be appropriate for use with children. Nor would it be a good idea to use a rating scale for marital satisfaction developed for use on middle-class North American couples in your study of marital satisfaction among Iraqi immigrants or Syrian refugees. A concept such as marital satisfaction is very culturally bound, so measurement of it needs to take into consideration cultural differences. Another issue you need to consider is the language of the scale. Since most scale development has taken place in North America, English is the predominant language of scales. If the intended respondents are not English speaking, some researchers choose to translate the scale, but purists would say that this will compromise its reliability and validity. If you do translate you should follow a procedure referred to as "back translation": the English scale is translated into the other language by one translator, then translated back into English by a second translator, and then the two English translations are compared to ensure the meaning has not changed due to translation. Because multicultural research is increasing, it is possible to find scales in a variety of languages. Extending your literature review to non-English-language publications may help you to find language-appropriate scales.

Logic Models

Logic models are tools used to both develop and evaluate programs in a systemic manner (Alter & Murty, 1997). They are visual depictions outlining resources required, services to be delivered, the target groups that may be surveyed or interviewed, and the intended outcomes a program proposes to achieve in both the short term and the long term (Cooksy, Gill, & Kelly, 2001; Knowlton & Phillips, 2009; Renger & Titcomb, 2002; Savaya & Waysman, 2005). The intent of a logic model is to identify an issue and present a proposed program or service to address that issue while supporting the development of an evaluation framework through which to measure the program outcome. A logic model facilitates understanding for evaluators, program creators, funders, and front-line staff regarding how a service is delivered and what it hopes to achieve as well as what is needed in order to offer the service. A properly designed logic model offers a clear pathway on how to evaluate what a program was intended to address.

7. Responding to the Case

Jean is correct in stating that it is probably best to look for an existing measure of anxiety. Since anxiety is a much-studied construct, it is likely that a rating scale already exists. There are psychometric, administrative, and ethical concerns involved in deciding which rating scale to use. The scale should have demonstrated reliability with a Cronbach alpha in excess of .80. In the team's judgment the scale should have face validity and content validity. It should look like the items measure anxiety, and those items should cover the full dimension of the construct. The team should also look for a scale that has empirical evidence of its validity. Reports of criterion-related or construct validity would increase the team's confidence that the scale is actually measuring anxiety. It would also be helpful if they had examples of where the scale they select has been used to measure anxiety in a hospital or health care setting.

The scale should be short and easy to administer. The participants in their research are people in distress to begin with. They may not feel well enough to complete an extensive instrument or may tire during administration. Both of these could reduce the reliability of the data collected.

There are also ethical concerns to take into account. Again, the intended participants are already vulnerable and could be emotionally fragile. It is important that the act of completing the scale not cause subjects, who are patients in the hospital, additional emotional strain or harm. The items in a scale should be reviewed with this in mind before that particular scale is selected.

Since the patients are likely to speak both French and English, it would be best to use language-appropriate scales and have them administered by researchers who speak the language of the participant. The best approach would be to use a rating scale that has both English and French versions, but if this is not possible the researchers may have to back-translate either a French-language or English-language scale. As well, it would be worthwhile to build into their research design an opportunity to pre-test the administration of the scale to make sure that it works as intended in this complex environment.

8. Further Reflections

1. *What additional vigilance is necessary when conducting research with a multilingual or non-literate population?*
2. *What is the utility of discussing a Cronbach alpha in your research results?*

3a. *Find several scales (see additional readings and Internet resources below). Of those you found, which would be most appropriate for the population being examined in this case study?*

3b. *What was its Cronbach alpha?*

3c. *Was there a French translation?*

4. *How could you apply a logic model to this process?*

9. Additional Reading

Adcock, R. (2001). Measurement validity: A shared standard for qualitative and quantitative research. *American Political Science Review*, *95*(3), 529–46.

Alter, C., & Murty, S. (1997). Logic modeling: A tool for teaching practice evaluation. *Journal of Social Work Education*, *33*(1), 103–18.

Baer, D.M., Harrison, R., Fradenburg, L., Petersen, D., & Milla, S. (2005). Some pragmatics in the valid and reliable recording of directly observed behaviour. *Research on Social Work Practice*, *15*(6), 440–51.

Coakley, T.M., & Orme, J.G. (2006). A psychometric evaluation of the Cultural Receptivity in Fostering Scale. *Research on Social Work Practice*, *16*(5), 520–33.

Cook, D.A., & Beckman, T.J. (2006). Current concepts in validity and reliability for psychometric instruments: Theory and application. *American Journal of Medicine*, *119*(2), 166.e7–166.e16.

Cooksy, L., Gill, P., & Kelly, P. (2001). The program logic model as in integrative framework for a multi-method evaluation. *Evaluation and Program Planning*, *24*(2), 119–28.

DeVon, H.A., Block, M.E., Moyle-Wright, P., Ernst, D.M., Hayden, S.J., Lazzara, D.J., . . ., & Kostas-Polston, E. (2007). A psychometric toolbox for testing validity and reliability. *Journal of Nursing Scholarship*, *39*, 155–64.

Fischer, J., & Corcoran, K. (2013a). Measures for clinical practice and research: A sourcebook (Vol. 1). *Couples, families, and children*. New York: Oxford University Press.

Fischer, J., & Corcoran, K. (2013b). Measures for clinical practice and research: A sourcebook (Vol. 2). *Adults*. New York: Oxford University Press.

Golafshani, N. (2003). Understanding reliability and validity in qualitative research. *Qualitative Report*, *8*(4), 597–606.

Hamilton, M. (1959). The assessment of anxiety states by rating. *British Journal of Medical Psychology*, *32*(1), 50–5.

Healy, M., & Perry, C. (2000). Comprehensive criteria to judge validity and reliability of qualitative research within the realism paradigm. *Qualitative Market Research*, *3*(3), 118–26.

Kellogg Foundation. (2001). *Logic model development guide*. Battlefield Creek, MI: Kellogg Foundation.

Kilpatrick, K.L. (2005). The Parental Empathy Measure: A new approach to assessing child maltreatment risk. *American Journal of Orthopsychiatry*, *75*(4), 608–20.

Knowlton, L., & Phillips, C. (2009). *The logic model guidebook: Better strategies for great results*. Los Angeles: Sage.

Krieger, N., Smith, K., Naishadham, D., Hartman, C., & Barbeau, E.M. (2005). Experiences of discrimination: Validity and reliability of a self-report measure for population health research on racism and health. *Social Science & Medicine*, *61*(7), 1576–96.

McMillan, J.D., & Abell, N. (2006). Validating the Level of Stability Index for Children. *Research on Social Work Practice*, *16*(3), 326–37.

Mooney, P., Epstein, M.H., Ryser, G., & Pierce, C.D. (2005). Reliability and validity of the Behavioural and Emotional Rating Scale: Parent rating scale. *Children & Schools*, *27*(3), 147–55.

Renger, R., & Titcomb, A. (2002). The three-step approach to teaching logic models. *American Journal of Evaluation*, *23*(4), 493–503.

Riege, A.M. (2003). Validity and reliability tests in case study research: A literature review with "hands-on" applications for each research phase. *Qualitative Market Research*, *6*(2), 75–86.

Savaya, R., & Waysman, M. (2005). The logic model. *Administration in Social Work*, *29*(2), 85–103.

Smith, D.C., Huber, D.L., & Hall, J.A. (2005). Psychometric evaluation of the Structured Clinical Interview for DSM-IV Childhood Diagnoses (KID-SCID). *Journal of Human Behavior in the Social Environment*, *11*(3/4), 1–21.

Spielberger, C.D. (2010). *State-Trait anxiety inventory*. New York: John Wiley & Sons.

Van Emmerik, A.A., Schoorl, M., Emmelkamp, P.M., & Kamphuis, J.H. (2006). Psychometric evaluation of the Dutch version of the post-traumatic cognitions inventory (PTCI). *Behaviour Research and Therapy*, *44*(7), 1053–65.

Zalaquett, C. & Wood, R. (Eds.). (1998). *Evaluating stress: A book of resources*. Lanham, MD: Scarecrow Education.

10. Internet Resources

Rating Scales

Walmyr Publishing, "Assessment Scales":
　　http://www.walmyr.com/scales.html
Graham R. Gibbs, "Ratings & Scales," Part 3 of 3 on Questionnaire Design:
　　https://www.youtube.com/watch?v=_aOhcGf8EcY
Tobii Dynavox, "Rating Scale":
　　https://www.youtube.com/watch?v=YHQfamdj810

Reliability and Validity

Web Centre for Social Research Methods:
　　http://www.socialresearchmethods.net/kb/relandval.php
Donna Gregory, "Reliability and Validity":
　　https://www.youtube.com/watch?v=fnF2hrLZHoA

Anxiety Measures

R.L. Spitzer, K. Kroenke, J.B.W. Williams, and B. Lowe, "A Brief Measure for Assessing Generalized Anxiety Disorder":
http://www.integration.samhsa.gov/clinical-practice/GAD708.19.08Cartwright.pdf

Shelina Bhamani, "Social Anxiety in University Students: Measurement Instrument Database for the Social Science":
http://www.midss.org/sites/default/files/social_anxiety1.pdf

Per Bech, "Measuring States of Anxiety with Clinician-Rated and Patient-Rated Scales":
http://cdn.intechopen.com/pdfs-wm/19365.pdf

Logic Model

Community Tool Box, "Developing a Logic Model or Theory of Change":
http://ctb.ku.edu/en/table-of-contents/overview/models-for-community-health-and-development/logic-model-development/main

PACE MySPH, "A Simple Logic Model":
https://www.youtube.com/watch?v=ny7dwU3HpHc

Pell Institute, "How to Create a Logic Model":
http://toolkit.pellinstitute.org/evaluation-guide/plan-budget/use-a-logic-model-in-evaluation/

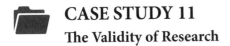

CASE STUDY 11
The Validity of Research

1. Preamble

In conducting research you not only have to focus on what is being asked and what you are doing, but also on how you actually carry out the initiative.

2. The Problem

The Saskatchewan government, in its ongoing priority of saving money on social services, has decided to change your residential addiction facility's funding from a maximum of 28 days per person to 21 days as the minister sees it as a way to save 25 per cent of the budget. In an effort to demonstrate that your programming should remain 28 days long, your board of directors asks your executive director, who is not a social worker, to empirically determine if there is a difference in client outcome between the 28-day program and a 21-day program.

3. The Process

Your agency, Humblewood, is a multidisciplinary organization providing a holistic range of treatment methods. The majority of your clients are police officers, fire fighters, loggers, and retired military personnel. The facility is located 24 kilometers southeast of Moose Jaw (which ironically was where members of Al Capone's criminal organization, including Capone himself, hid from American authorities for a time during American Prohibition) in a peaceful rural valley bordering a large wooded ravine. As the executive director will be overseeing the project, you are left in charge of administering Humblewood while he personally directs this groundbreaking research initiative. Before beginning your programming assignment, you inform the executive director, based upon your formal training as an ethical social work research practitioner, that all clients should be asked if they wish to participate in the study and that no client should in any way be coerced into participating.

4. The Research

The executive director follows your recommendation and asks for volunteers through each step of the study. Of the September clients, 12 males and 16 females volunteer for the experimental group. Of the November group, 3 males, 8 females, and 2 transgender clients volunteer. You group the remaining 4 males, 44 females, and 1 transgender client into your control group. Then a staff member requests a leave due to family emergency and a maternity leave begins three months early. You are now forced to make staffing changes between the two groups so that the November group has two male clinicians while the September group has six staff working with them during the course of their program. As a result, you must draw upon several self-help groups to present during the evening sessions that would typically be covered by professional staff. This is to ensure both continuity of care and that the two groups receive the same number of program hours as mandated by your accreditation requirements.

To ensure that good results are obtained, on each day for two weeks prior to admission the executive director has the clients complete the measurement instruments so that while they are in treatment it will not take them as long to complete the necessary forms. The clients do the same for two weeks after treatment cessation. The executive director chooses two valid and reliable research instruments, the Beck depression scale and BASIS-32 outcome measurement, but then, to save on the cost of obtaining the rights, chooses to use the brand-new public domain Relaxation and Prevention (RAP) scale to measure all five distinct elements of wellness. This, of course, is only for the experimental group, as the control group will not have to complete any forms, since they have chosen not to participate.

The September client participants complete the form weekly, and results vary, but the executive director reports in his monthly staff meeting that there is general improvement. A minor fire caused by smoking in a non-smoking area in the third week forces one-third of your group to move off-site, and thus you are not able to complete the entire process of evaluation with them. In November, because you are short staffed and the first-week results are very encouraging, supporting your September findings, the executive director conducts only one measurement. As well, you discover that the control and experimental groups are discussing the test results during group work time, but the group worker tells you this is a good thing as it is enhancing the differentiation phase of the group's development. However, during the one group session you regularly co-facilitate, you find it difficult to distinguish who is in the experimental and who is in the control group based upon their statements. You report this to the executive director, and he concurs with your belief that further testing might be compromised, since everyone was aware who was in the experimental group and who was not. He switches to a more qualitative mode and personally selects four clients to interview in depth, all of whom unfortunately drop out of treatment before it concludes.

The executive director prepares his report and asks for your comments. The report provides an extensive analysis highlighted by statistically significant findings indicating that clients in a 28-day program showed significant improvements on the Beck, the BASIS-32, and the RAP scales as well as providing positive feedback during the qualitative interviews. The executive director is so excited that he states in his conclusion that this study proves not only that your agency should continue to provide a 28-day residential program, but that all facilities across Saskatchewan if not Canada should retain a 28-day programming cycle.

5. Question

What issues should you raise with your director about the research he has conducted before he forwards the report to the board?

6. Social Work Practice

Internal Validity

Validity in terms of research instruments and scales refers to the extent to which a measure really measures what it is intended to measure.

However, when we consider causation, there is a second and very different use of the term "validity." Internal validity is the confidence we have that the results of the study accurately identify the independent variable as the cause of changes in the dependent variable. Are there equally plausible explanations for the results we observed? External validity is the extent to which we can generalize findings of our study to its intended population. There are a variety of threats to internal and external validity that every social work researcher must be aware of so that she or he does not come to a false conclusion regarding cause and effect (Table 2.11). Issues of

Table 2.11 Threats to Validity

Internal	External
• Time-order ambiguity	• Selection-treatment interaction
• Selection bias	
• History	• Setting-treatment interaction
• Instrumentation	
• Testing	• History-treatment interaction
• Maturation	
• Statistical regression	
• Mortality	
• Diffusion of treatments	

internal and external validity are of particular importance to examine in quantitative research when randomization is not possible.

Time-order ambiguity. Also known as causal time order, this is a concern whenever there is uncertainty regarding the timing or sequencing of the independent variable and the dependent variable. In the experimental design it must be clear that the program/intervention comes before the measurement of possible change in the dependent variable.

Selection bias. Comparisons have little meaning if the groups being investigated are not comparable. Randomly assigning subjects to groups increases the probability that the groups will be similar, especially if the number of subjects is large. It also counters any argument that the researcher purposely biased the groups in some way to manipulate the outcome.

History. History refers to some external event or extraneous variable occurring during the course of the study that might interfere with the findings or be a confounding variable. For example, you deliver a support group program to increase the morale of a group of seniors living in a retirement residence, and after the program the morale of the group has increased. However, one week before the program ended the home installed a big-screen television and the Blue Jays went on a 10-game winning streak. The morale increase may have been a result of the program, but it could also be attributed to the television and the Jays (history). If your design had included a control group you could have tested the alternative explanation. If the morale of the control group did not change then you could argue that the television was not responsible for the rise in morale in the experimental group. Both groups were exposed to the television but only one group was exposed to the social work program; and since only the group that was exposed to the program had an increase in morale, you have a good argument that it was the program and not the television (and the Blue Jays' winning streak) that caused the change.

Instrumentation. This refers to the actual measures used in the research. If the researcher changes the measurement tool between the pre-test and the post-test, changes in scores may be the result of differences in the instrument used, not changes in the participant. For example, a teacher provides a special tutoring program to her students. She measures their knowledge before the program using one test and measures their performance after the program using a different test. If her students have better grades after the program, she could claim her tutoring caused the increase; however, someone else could argue that the test after the program was easier than the one given before, and this was why the students had higher scores. Using a control group provides her with information to determine whether hers or the alternative is a better explanation. If the test is indeed easier, then the control group grades would increase as well. To argue that it was her program that made the difference, she would have to show that the grades of the control group did not increase.

Testing or initial measurement effect. By simply being given a research instrument to review or by doing the test over and over again, a research subject can become better at it and achieve a higher score, or become bored by it and produce a poorer score because they no longer pay attention to the task or questions. As with instrumentation, having a control group will allow you to determine if changes that occur within your experimental group are merely an artefact of the testing experience and not a measure of program-produced improvement.

Maturation. Some dependent variables are subject to change as the result of developmental maturation or the passage of time. For example, a social worker provides a three-month program to reduce depression in people who have recently lost a partner to cancer. She shows that after the program there has been a decline in the group's level of sadness; however, someone could argue that the decrease in depression was simply due to the passage of time since the death. If she had used a control group she could determine if this was the case: if the reduction in depression was due to time alone, people in the control group would also have experienced a reduction in sadness.

Statistical regression. Regression to the mean refers to the tendency of those who initially post extreme scores to provide responses closer to the population mean on subsequent measurements. If you are a student who typically scores around 75 per cent and you happen to get 90 per cent on one test, it is likely that you will score closer to 75 per cent on the next. Your reversion to a lower score does not happen because you have become a poorer student, but more likely because the high score was unusual for you. This becomes a problem if a researcher decides to include only clients with a very high or very low initial score in a study. Changes in results after the intervention may occur simply because initial scores of the subjects were an extreme measure for them and not reflective of their normal scores. Having a control group will allow the researcher to see if regression to the mean is a better explanation of change.

Using a control group allows the researcher to counter arguments that changes in experimental group scores were due to history, instrumentation, testing, maturation, or statistical regression, because if any of these had occurred they would have affected the scores of those in the control group as well. If scores for the experimental group are different, then this difference cannot be attributed to these threats, and there is a strong argument that since only those in the experimental group received the intervention, the intervention caused the change.

However, there is one threat to the internal validity of a research design that cannot be controlled for by using a control group, and it is very common:

Mortality. While this threat to internal validity can refer to the actual death of subjects during the study, it more commonly is used to refer to those who drop out of the study prior to its conclusion. This threat to internal validity is also known as attrition. It can influence your findings when those that drop out of a program differ in some relevant way from those who remain and that difference is reflected in the outcome measure. If, for example, in the morale-boosting program referred to above residents who were sad or depressed dropped out of the program, their scores would not be included in the post-test measurement. Since you would only be measuring the morale of happier people, it would be no surprise that the score of the group increased, but in this case it wasn't because of the program – it was because the sad people dropped out. While you cannot control for this in the design of the evaluation, you can build in incentives for people to finish the program and make sure contact is maintained throughout to reduce the problem of drop-outs.

Finally, there is a threat to internal validity that actually occurs specifically because you use a control group:

Diffusion of treatment. This occurs when subjects in the experimental group discuss with those in the control group what occurred during the intervention. In essence, they contaminate the control group by exposing them to the intervention. Again, this needs to be addressed when considering your research protocols. It is important to reduce the possibility that subjects in one group come in contact with subjects in the other.

Control and Comparison Groups

While an experiment provides many controls and has the strongest internal validity, it is not often possible to create a true control group in social work research. To begin with, there are serious ethical and fairness concerns. By definition, a control group receives no intervention, and when you are working with individuals or communities with expressed needs it is not ethical to ignore their concerns just for the purposes of research. The issue of randomly determining who receives treatment and who does not is also problematic. Most agencies have waiting lists for services, and while it may make sense from a research perspective to take the first 20 people on the list and randomly assign them to an experimental and control group, it probably does not make sense to the person who was first on the list but who, due to the randomness of the selection process, is relegated to the non-treatment control condition. This issue of non-intervention for some is especially true if you plan to make observations for a long period of time after the intervention concludes. To respond to these problems, a researcher will sometimes construct a comparison group rather than a control group.

There are still two groups and the design of the experiment is similar, but membership in the groups is not randomly assigned. For example, the researcher will take the first 10 people on the waiting list and consider them the experimental group, and then take the next 10 on the list and designate them the comparison group. This change has implications in terms of threats to internal validity. To begin with, you no longer have a strong argument against selection bias: it is the researcher who determines who goes in which group, so the possibility of bias exists. Also, the researcher can no longer count on random assignment to increase the probability that the two groups are the same (random assignment is when each person has the same chance of being assigned to the treatment – experimental – group as to the non-treatment group). As a result of this, it is usual practice with comparison groups to determine how similar the groups really are. They are compared on a number of demographic variables so consumers of the evaluation can make judgments about similarity. Comparison is particularly important in terms of the dependent variables. The two groups need to have very similar pre-test scores on the outcome variables as well. To increase similarity, the researcher can go as far as purposely creating matched pairs of subjects. In the waiting list example above, the evaluator can take the first 10 clients from the waiting list and then review the remainder of the waiting list to find 10 clients with similar characteristics to the first 10 for the control group, thus creating matched pairs. As there is a weaker level of internal control, designs that employ comparison rather than control groups are called quasi-experimental (see Case Study 12). Below is an example of the classic quasi-experimental design, commonly referred to as a non-equivalent control group design, which features a comparison group.

$$O_1 \quad X \quad O_2$$
$$O_1 \qquad O_2 \qquad \qquad O = \text{Observation} \qquad X = \text{Intervention}$$

When an "R" is added to the nomenclature it indicates that participants were randomly assigned, and the design becomes the classic research design the pre-test–post-test control, which means that there was an experimental group and a control group. This design, by definition, entails that most of the issues of internal validity discussed above have been controlled for.

$$R\ O_1 \quad X \quad O_2$$
$$R\ O_1 \qquad O_2$$

External Validity

If we conduct a program evaluation with strong internal validity and demonstrate that the program had a positive outcome, we also want to be able to argue that if we offered this program to a different group of participants we would experience similar outcomes. We want to be able to generalize our findings from our research participants to all people like these participants. This is the issue of generalizability. External validity is the extent to which we can generalize findings of our study to its intended population. As with internal validity, there are several common threats to external validity.

Selection-treatment interaction. This refers to how representative the sample is of the population to which the conclusions are being applied. Will the program work as well with people from different cultural or ethnic groups, with people at different life stages, with people of different educational qualifications or levels of income? This is why it is so important to start with a sample that is as representative of the intended target population as possible. Volunteering to be part of a study can also introduce bias and thus threaten external validity. People who volunteer may be very different from people who do not, even if they share similar characteristics such as age, gender, income, ethnicity, and race.

Setting-treatment interaction. Any research project conducted with a specific group of individuals in a certain setting may not be generalizable beyond the parameters of that setting. From a systems perspective, environment is an important component of human agency. Will your program work in different physical locations? This is a particularly common argument against the generalizability of results obtained in a university laboratory setting: will the outcome be the same in the real world?

History-treatment interaction. On occasion an experiment could take place at a time that coincides with a significant event external to the research, such as 9/11. The results of this experiment thus cannot be generalized because of the impact of history on the intervention. On a smaller scale history-treatment interaction could also come into play when the program is delivered at a specific time of year. Does the temporal context have any effect on the treatment? For example, does the fact that you deliver a program in summer become a factor in the success of the intervention?

7. Responding to the Case

The following were the very distinct threats to internal validity that occurred in the course of conducting the research:

Selection bias. As we said above, comparisons have little meaning if the groups being investigated are not comparable. In this case the two experimental groups consisted of 15 male, 24 female, and 2 transgender volunteers while the control group, which in reality was a comparison group (see the discussion above), had 4 male, 44 female, and 1 transgender non-volunteers. Both the voluntary versus non-voluntary nature of the groups and the sex imbalance speak to a selection bias.

History. The fire that forced one-third of the group to move off-site is an example of an incident that might have accounted for or influenced the study's outcomes.

Testing (initial measurement effect). In this case this effect could have occurred when the executive director had the subjects practise taking the tests every day for two weeks prior to their admission to the program.

Mortality. The only four subject/clients to be part of the qualitative component of the study all dropped out not only of the study but of the treatment program, negating the value of that component of the research.

Diffusion of treatment. If there had not already been an expectation of a positive outcome among staff of the agency with the executive director overseeing the study, the briefing at the monthly staff meeting about the initial successes could have led to a bias among those working with the clients during the course of the study. Likewise, that clients in the experimental and control groups discussed the research study with each other during their group work time could have led to diffusion of treatment.

There were also of course several threats to the external validity of this research that make any attempts to generalize the results problematic.

Selection-treatment interaction. In this case the population being sampled consisted of police officers, fire fighters, loggers, and retired military personnel. While this is an important population to serve, it is hardly indicative of the general addiction treatment population. Volunteering to be part of a study can also be a factor causing bias and thus threatening external validity.

Setting-treatment interaction. There is little question that the results from this study would be difficult to generalize beyond the population studied, let alone to the rest of Saskatchewan or to Quebec or Prince Edward Island.

You should also have pointed out to the executive director that his use of the term "control group" was incorrect. A control group by definition implies random assignment and lack of difference between those receiving the treatment or intervention and those not. In this case the control group was in reality a comparison group; while they did attend the same treatment program at the same time as the experimental group, by their choice not to volunteer they are in at least one significant way different from the experimental group. As well, there was a distinct sex difference between the experimental group and the comparison group, which may not have occurred if there had been random assignment to the two groups.

Finally, you should also have picked up that at no time was there any actual comparison between a 28-day and a 21-day program, the original question. All the research was done within the parameters of one residential program, making the study even more irrelevant, regardless of how significant the statistics presented were.

8. Research Insight

Once an evaluation has been designed it is important to give serious consideration to who should carry it out. Assigning the task to an existing staff member has a number of advantages. Internal evaluators are likely more familiar with the programs, staff, and clients of the agency. They can come up to speed much more quickly than an external evaluator. It is also likely that they have already developed a level of trust that is helpful when conducting an evaluation. They have existing relationships with the people involved, so it can be easier for them to get the cooperation of others. From an administrative perspective, it can be less expensive to use an existing staff member, particularly if they add the evaluation task to an existing workload. However, not many social service agencies possess the necessary resources to have a full-time evaluator on staff. If funds are tight it may be possible to partner with another agency, an academic researcher, or a community-based research group such as a local social planning council to conduct evaluations. As well, assigning the work to an existing staff member may be more affordable and convenient, but this approach can also cause problems, particularly if the person does not have appropriate research training or cannot find the time to conduct a high-quality evaluation. An agency employee charged with the task of evaluation may be put in a difficult position if he/she has to convey bad news to colleagues. When the results of the evaluation are not as expected, there is a tendency to "shoot the messenger" or consider him or her incompetent at the task. Neither situation is likely to contribute to a very positive performance evaluation. Probably one of the most difficult things for an insider to do is to convey an appropriate level of objectivity. People will assume that the results reflect a certain amount of subjectivity or self-interest. To avoid claims of bias, an agency is best off in hiring an external evaluator who has the necessary time and knowledge for the task. There are organizations or consultants that specialize in program evaluation, and for a (usually significant) price they can be contracted to conduct the evaluation. However, in reality external evaluation is not a choice for many agencies that do not have the money in their budgets to hire expert help. Nor do they feel that an outsider can ever truly appreciate the complexities of the human service programs that they run. It is usually a combination of resources and politics that determines who, internal or external, carries out an evaluation.

9. Further Reflections

1a. Which questions of validity are of greatest concern for social work researchers?

1b. Which issues of validity are most difficult to address when conducting agency or community-based research?

2a. Considering all the possible sources of error and bias in any research project, what is the utility of conducting agency-based research knowing it will be flawed and inaccurate on at least one dimension, if not more?

2b. How would you justify the time and money necessary to conduct methodologically strong social work research, knowing that the outcomes will still more than likely have several limitations?

10. Additional Reading

Botsford, A.L., & Rule, D. (2004). Evaluation of a group intervention to assist aging parents with permanency planning for an adult offspring with special needs. *Social Work, 49*(3), 423–31.

Eldridge, S., Ashby, D., Bennett, C., Wakelin, M., & Feder, G. (2008). Internal and external validity of cluster randomised trials: Systematic review of recent trials. *BMJ (Clinical Research Ed.), 336*(7649), 876–80.

Gibbert, M., Ruigrok, W., & Wicki, B. (2008). Research notes and commentaries: What passes as a rigorous case study? *Strategic Management Journal, 29*(13), 1465–74.

Hertel, J. (2010). Keep it simple: Study design nomenclature in research article abstracts. *Journal of Athletic Training, 45*(3), 213–14.

Juni, P., Altman, D., & Egger, M. (2001). Systematic reviews in health care: Assessing the quality of controlled clinical trials. *British Medical Journal, 323*(7303), 42–6.

Lecavalier, L., Gadow, K.D., DeVincent, C.J., Houts, C., & Edwards, M.C. (2009). Deconstructing the PDD clinical phenotype: Internal validity of the DSM-IV. *Journal of Child Psychology and Psychiatry, and Allied Disciplines, 50*(10), 1246–54.

McDermott, R. (2011). Internal and external validity. In J.N. Druckman, D.P. Green, J.H. Kuklinski, & A. Lupia (Eds.), *Cambridge handbook of experimental political science* (pp. 27–40). Cambridge: Cambridge University Press.

Steckler, A., & McLeroy, K.R. (2008). The importance of external validity. *American Journal of Public Health, 98*(1), 9–10.

Stith, S.M., Rosen, K.H., McCollum, E.E., & Thomsen, C.J. (2004). Treating intimate partner violence within intact couple relationships: Outcomes of multi-couple versus individual couple therapy. *Journal of Marital and Family Therapy, 30*(3), 305–18.

Sue, S. (1999). Science, ethnicity and bias: Where have we gone wrong? *American Psychologist*, *54*(12), 1070–7.

Troller, J., Csiernik, R., & Didham, S. (2006). An examination of individual and group outcomes of male and female community treatment clients. *Journal of Groups in Addiction & Recovery*, *1*(3/4), 17–29.

Weisz, A., & Black, B.M. (2001). Evaluating a sexual assault and dating violence prevention program for urban youths. *Social Work Research*, *25*(2), 89–100.

Winter, G. (2000). A comparative discussion of the notion of "validity" in qualitative and quantitative research. *Qualitative Report*, *4*(3/4).

11. Internet Resources

Internal Validity

Dr. Sam Fiala, "9–Threats to Internal Validity":
https://www.youtube.com/watch?v=F7kjR30tEAc
Prof. Nikki Hozack, "Internal Validity":
https://www.youtube.com/watch?v=_UPUtlHDM0A&list=PL9UclLWgCU1U-PzPQNXFNyv6TlasE9IK2
morgankenneth12, "Internal Validity":
https://www.youtube.com/watch?v=MYtsuA4GRj8

External Validity

SDC Sport Eastbourne, "BTEC Research Methods: External Validity":
https://www.youtube.com/watch?v=OIs7kRVjhvE
Study.com, "Threats to External Validity: Sample Characteristics, Stimulus Characteristics & Experimental Arrangements":
http://study.com/academy/lesson/threats-to-external-validity-i-sample-characteristics-stimulus-characteristics-experimental-arrangements.html
Study.com, "Methods for Increasing External Validity":
http://study.com/academy/lesson/methods-for-increasing-external-validity.html

Comparison Groups

Coalition for Evidence Based Policy, "Which Comparison-Group ('Quasi-Experimental') Study Designs Are Most Likely to Produce Valid Estimates of a Program's Impact?":
http://coalition4evidence.org/wp-content/uploads/2014/01/Validity-of-comparison-group-designs-updated-January-2014.pdf

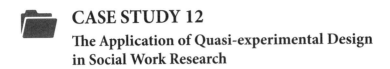

CASE STUDY 12
The Application of Quasi-experimental Design in Social Work Research

1. Preamble

In the field of research the universally acknowledged gold standard is the true experimental design. In this form of research, a sample of the population of interest is randomly divided into two groups – a control group that does not receive the treatment intervention and an experimental group that does receive the intervention – for the purpose of examining what differences, if any, there are between the two approaches. The standard notation for this is:

$$R\ O_1 \quad X \quad O_2$$
$$R\ O_1 \quad\quad O_2$$

However, in social work our ethics do not allow us to deprive people of treatment in any form. So how do you conduct research? Fortunately, there are designs that allow us to examine different counselling options while still providing assistance to those who request it. These designs are called quasi-experimental because they allow us to provide for both a comparison group and a treatment group while not breaching our ethical principles.

2. The Problem

For your field placement you have been assigned to a community mental health agency that has an extensive waiting list. You have chosen to work on the child and adolescent unit because the existing waiting list will provide you with an excellent opportunity for client contact and to develop expertise in an area of clinical interviewing with which you have had little experience.

After reviewing the case files of the clients who have been assessed and accepted for treatment but placed on a waiting list due to insufficient agency resources, you discover that a significant number of children have been referred because of concerns around refusing to attend school. This is an area in which your field supervisor has limited knowledge and experience and that the agency has not pursued in the past. Thus, both your professor and your field supervisor encourage you to take on an active role in addressing the concern.

3. The Process

As part of your learning contract, your professor has suggested that you conduct a research study as one component of your placement experience under the inquiry section. As well, your professor has asked that every member of your seminar group learn about one contemporary social work intervention and how it applies directly to each student's individual field setting. Being an astute student, you decide to combine the two requirements into one project while simultaneously addressing the needs of the clients on your agency's waiting list.

4. The Research

You begin the research process by conducting a literature review examining school refusal and discover that while cognitive behavioural therapy has been highly recommended as applicable and effective for this problem, little actual applied community-based research has been conducted. In consultation with your field instructor, you determine that you will easily be able to open at least six new files per month over the course of five months of your practicum before you have to begin to consider termination. You will need to decide which families to select for treatment and which families to use for comparison.

5. Questions

1. *How would you design your study to meet the expectations of your professor as well as the needs of your practicum agency and those of your clients? Consider this in light of the fact that you ethically and practically cannot use the gold standard for research.*
2. *What are potential threats to both internal and external validity posed by your suggested design?*

6. Social Work Practice

Contrasting Experimental and Quasi-experimental Designs

In social work practice it is difficult if not impossible to not provide treatment to any client. Most institutional review boards and university ethics committees would be hard pressed to pass an ethics review based upon a denial of service to some participants, your control group, if you were to use an experimental design. Thus, you need to be creative, responsive, and adaptive and of course always ethical in serving your clients' needs first while conducting your research to gain new knowledge and enhance your practice.

The key difference between quasi-experimental design and experimental design relates to those not receiving the intervention or treatment. In a true experimental design those not receiving intervention are referred to as a control group, while in quasi-experimental design these research participants are called a comparison group. Comparison groups are chosen for convenience rather than through randomization, the critical attribute of an experimental group.

Experimental Design

To describe the various design options scientist have developed a system of notation or nomenclature. In this system exposure to the independent variable is noted as X. Measurement of the dependent variable is noted as O. For example, the design described as "$O_1 X O_2$" means that for each subject in the sample the researcher began by measuring the dependent variable at one point in time (O_1). This is referred to as the pre-test measurement event. Next, subjects were exposed to the independent variable (X). Finally, after exposure to the independent variable the dependent variable was measured again (O_2). This is the post-test measurement event. In evaluation research the program or intervention is considered the independent variable – it is the element that is hopefully causing the change, and a desired program outcome is the dependent variable. Let's say we are offering a group program with the goal of reducing anxiety. The independent variable is the intervention and the dependent variable is anxiety. If we used the example design above we would first measure a subject's level of anxiety (O_1), deliver the program (X), and measure participants' level of anxiety again after the program was over (O_2). If the anxiety level went down – the desired outcome – we could argue that the program had been a success; however, our argument would not be particularly strong. Although we can demonstrate that the cause came before the effect and that there is an association between program participation and the positive outcome, this design does not provide any protection from third-criterion arguments. The change could be attributed to the program, but it could also be the result of a number of other things happening in the person's life. Using this design does not provide strong enough evidence that the program alone caused the reduction in anxiety; there are many alternative explanations of why we observed that reduction. To counter these alternative explanations, we need to strengthen the design. When scientists want to establish causality, they design an experiment in which subjects are randomly assigned to one of two groups: an experimental group who will be exposed to the independent variable and a control group who will not. The standard notation for this design is:

$$R\ O_1 \qquad X \qquad O_2$$
$$R\ O_1 \qquad\qquad\quad O_2$$

This design is referred to as the classic experimental design or the pre-test–post-test control group design. In this case there are two groups being observed. The first group is considered the experimental group and the second group is the control group. "R" means that membership in the groups was determined by using a random process of assignment. Ideally the two groups are exactly the same, the only difference being that the experimental group is exposed to the independent variable (X) and the control group is not. When all the measurements have been taken the researcher compares the outcomes. If the value of the dependent variable for the experimental group has changed but the value for the control group stays the same, then the researcher has a strong argument that the independent variable was the cause of the change. This is because the only difference between the two groups is that one was exposed to the independent variable and the other was not.

In evaluations using an experimental design, called a randomized control trial (RCT), the experimental group experiences the program and the control group does not. The evaluator compares the groups after the intervention to see if the experimental group did better than the control group. A slight variation on this design occurs in evaluations when decision makers want to determine if the effect of the program persists over time. The experiment will indicate if there is a change immediately after the intervention, but usually we want to know if the change lasts. To answer this question the researcher adds subsequent measurement events to the design. For example, if the researcher decides to repeat the measurement of the dependent variable 3 months and 12 months after the program, the design would look like this:

$$R\ O_1 \qquad X \qquad O_2 \qquad O_3 \qquad O_4$$
$$R\ O_1 \qquad\qquad\quad O_2 \qquad O_3 \qquad O_4$$

This experimental design has strong internal validity as discussed in Case Study 11.

Quasi-experimental Design

There are two fundamental quasi-experimental designs from which you may build variations. The first is the comparison group pre-test–post-test design:

$$O_1 \qquad X \qquad O_2$$
$$O_1 \qquad\qquad\quad O_2$$

In this design you collect data from both the group receiving intervention and the group not receiving intervention (O_1), intervene (X), and then collect a second set of data (O_2). This design is also referred to as a non-equivalent comparison group. The second type of quasi-experimental design is the time series design:

$$O_1 \, O_2 \, O_3 \, O_4 \, O_5 \, X \, O_6 \, O_7 \, O_8 \, O_9 \, O_{10}$$

In this design there is no comparison group; rather, you collect data at several set intervals prior to intervening ($O_1 \, O_2 \, O_3 \, O_4 \, O_5$), then you intervene (X), and then you again collect data at several set intervals after the intervention is complete ($O_6 \, O_7 \, O_8 \, O_9 \, O_{10}$). However, all quasi-experimental designs contain distinct threats to both internal and external validity, as the groups are not randomized, as occurs with a true experimental design.

7. Responding to the Case

In this case study, you wish to test whether the cognitive behavioural treatment intervention actually assists your population in returning to school. The appropriate quasi-experimental design to select would be the comparison group pre-test–post-test design.

$$O_1 \qquad X \qquad O_2$$
$$O_1 \qquad\qquad\quad O_2$$

Thus, after you have gone through ethics approval and discussed the design with both your field supervisor and professor, your research design would entail gathering data from the family files on 60 families in total, 30 for your treatment group and 30 for your comparison group. Each family would receive a questionnaire designed to obtain demographic information, while in the treatment group of 30 children you would also hand out two questionnaires before and after the intervention pertaining to the cognitive behavioural therapy. Those on the waiting list whom you could not see during your practicum would serve as the comparison group. You would gather both pre- and post-test information as you did with the experimental group, the only difference being that you did not provide a cognitive approach in the control group, as this is what your research question is all about.

After you have completed the study and are discussing the results, you also must discuss the various threats to internal and external validity that arose due to the need to employ a quasi-experimental design with a comparison group rather than an experimental design with its corresponding control group.

Threats to Internal Validity:

Time-order ambiguity	No, because the assignment to groups and data collection proceeded the intervention
Selection bias	Potentially for while both groups had applied to the program for assistance with their child's behaviour there was no random assignment to groups
History	No, because both groups experienced the same current events
Instrumentation	No, because both groups filled out the same questionnaires
Testing	No, because both groups completed instruments
Maturation	No, because both groups experienced the same developmental processes
Statistical regression	No, because the members of both groups belonged to low-income families
Mortality	Potentially, as some children (because of behavioural problems) might not show up for the post-test
Diffusion of treatment	None observed

Threats to External Validity:

Selection-treatment interaction	No, because the research subjects were selected from a common waiting list from one agency
Setting-treatment interaction	Possible, as all participants came from one agency in one community
History-treatment interaction	Possible, as the research followed the timelines of an academic year

Thus, while there are some limits to the research, the results could be of value to several stakeholder groups, including the student, the practicum class, the agency, and the agency's clients.

8. Further Reflections

1. *Using a quasi-experimental approach, design a research study for your placement agency.*
2. *What ethical issues must be considered and addressed in selecting your methodology?*

3a. *Which threats to internal and external validity are you most likely to face in designing the research for your practicum environment?*

3b. *How would you address these?*

9. Additional Reading

Behi, R., & Nolan, M. (1996). Quasi-experimental research design. *British Journal of Nursing (Mark Allen Publishing)*, 5(17), 1079–81.

Campbell, D., & Stanley, J. (1963). *Experimental and quasi-experimental designs*. Chicago: Rand McNally.

Ciaranello, A., Molitor, F., Leamon, M., Kuenneth, C., Tancredi, D., Diamant, A., & Kravitz, R. (2006). Providing health care services to the formerly homeless: A quasi-experimental evaluation. *Journal of Health Care for the Poor and Underserved*, 17(2), 441–61.

Cook, T., & Campbell, D. (1979). *Quasi-experimental design*. Toronto: Rand McNally.

Grinnell, R.M., & Unrau, Y.A. (2011). *Social work research and evaluation: Foundations of evidence-based practice* (9th ed.). Oxford: Oxford University Press.

Hisle-Gorman, E. (2006). Teaching social work research: A comparison of web-based and in-class lecture methods. *Journal of Technology in Human Services*, 24(4), 77–92.

Reid, W., Kenaley, B., & Colvin, J. (2004). Do some interventions work better than others? A review of comparative social work experiments. *Social Work Research*, 28(2), 71–81.

Rudd, A., & Johnson, R. (2008). Lessons learned from the use of randomized and quasi-experimental field designs for the evaluation of educational programs. *Studies in Educational Evaluation*, 34(3), 180–8.

Vincent, C., Reinharz, D., Deaudelin, I., Garceau, M., & Talbot, L. (2006). Public telesurveillance service for frail elderly living at home, outcomes and cost evolution: A quasi experimental design with two follow-ups. *Health and Quality of Life Outcomes*, 4, 41. http://dx.doi.org/10.1186/1477-7525-4-41

10. Internet Resources

Quasi-experimental Design

Brooke Miller, "Quasi-experimental Designs":
   https://www.youtube.com/watch?v=baVmE3pY5mE

EPIC Principles of Program Evaluation, "Quasi-experimental":
   https://www.youtube.com/watch?v=ZcFrmJKbCh4

Study.com, "Quasi-experimental Designs: Definition, Characteristics, Types & Examples":
   http://study.com/academy/lesson/quasi-experimental-designs-definition-characteristics-types-examples.html

UNICEF, "Quasi-Experimental Design and Methods":
   https://www.unicef-irc.org/publications/pdf/brief_8_quasi-experimental%20design_eng.pdf

Threats to Internal and External Validity

Robert S. Michael, "Threats to Internal & External Validity":
   http://www.indiana.edu/~educy520/sec5982/week_9/520in_ex_validity.pdf
Rodsazon, "Threats to Internal and External Validity":
   http://www.slideshare.net/rodsazon/threats-to-internal-and-external-validity

Threats to External Validity

zapohd1965, "Threats to External Validity":
   https://www.youtube.com/watch?v=dfZ_FjLD7JM
Gavin Shafron, "Threats to External Validity Lecture":
   https://www.youtube.com/watch?v=eXXFN6NaFMM
Laerd, "Threats to External Validity":
   http://dissertation.laerd.com/external-validity-p3.php

CASE STUDY 13
The Power of One: Single-Case Study Design

1. Preamble

There is a common perception that research entails months of preparation and dozens if not hundreds of subjects. This perception can be correct; however, there are instances when an individual client can be not only the focus of our clinical time but also the sole focus of our research.

2. The Problem

Malcolm, an only child, has just entered middle school, and his parents have recently separated and apparently will soon be divorced and living in different cities. Unsurprisingly, his distress is manifesting itself at his new school, where his marks have begun to drop and he is starting to miss class on a regular basis. As a newly graduated social worker in a new city yourself, you have been assigned responsibility for the high school's feeder schools in the community, giving you a caseload significantly larger than you had during your field placements. You received only a brief orientation to the school system and your new position, as the other social workers are just as busy as you are. However, you were given the mandate to be creative and use any new theories or practices from your education that you deemed appropriate, as you are the first new social worker on staff in 10 years. Professionally, you are still establishing your primary theoretical orientation and are unsure which method of intervention to try with Malcolm.

3. The Process

You will have an initial assessment session with Malcolm, but it will be at least one month before you can begin working with him on a regular basis. Using this opportunity, you decide to combine the assessment with an individual research design to better inform your practice as a new school social worker. During your assessment you learn that Malcolm's favourite activity is swimming, but now that he lives with his father on weekends it is difficult to get to the pool due to distance and to the other tasks that need to be done on Saturdays and Sundays. His mother works three nights a week, which also limits his opportunity to swim.

4. The Research

Part 1

You have the office staff forward you Malcolm's attendance record for the previous four weeks prior to beginning your work with him. You use this attendance data to establish a baseline. In the interim your caseload continues to grow, and you decide that at this time you do not have time to engage in extensive loss and grief counselling with Malcolm, and instead you will attempt a brief intervention to produce a positive change in Malcolm's system. Thus, during your initial post-assessment meeting you decide to be creative in when and how you work with him. You contract with Malcolm that you will meet with him for 45 minutes at the end of the school day once every week for six weeks on one of the days his mother has to work late. During each week you are scheduled to meet, if he misses two or more days of school you will spend the time talking; if he misses one day he can go swimming for 20 minutes and you and he will talk for the rest of the time; but if he has perfect attendance the entire time will be spent swimming. The overall goal of the contract is to increase school attendance. Malcolm agrees and signs the contract, as do both his mother and father and your supervisor, who commends you on your innovative idea. Figure 2.13a illustrates the outcome of his attendance pattern as a result of your intervention.

Figure 2.13a   Malcolm's School Attendance during Intervention

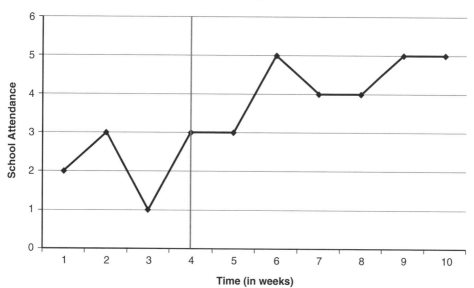

5. Questions (Part 1)

1. *What conclusions can you draw from this study?*
2. *What are your choices for action as Malcolm's social worker?*
3. *Identify the strengths and weaknesses of this single-subject design methodology.*
4. *What are the barriers to implementing single-subject research in social work practice?*
5. *What are the benefits?*

Part 2

Your conclusion, based upon your intervention and your data, is that Malcolm is adjusting well and that there is no longer a need to continue to meet with him. However, recalling the weaknesses of the AB single-subject research design (see below), you continue to have Malcolm's home school monitor his attendance and forward you his attendance pattern. The data at the end of the month are illustrated in Figure 2.13b.

Figure 2.13b   Malcolm's School Attendance after Intervention

5. Questions (Part 2)

1. *What conclusions can you draw from this study?*
2. *What are your choices for action as Malcolm's social worker?*
3. *What are the strengths and weaknesses of this single-subject design methodology?*

6. Social Work Practice

Single-Subject Design

Single-subject methodology is a fundamentally different way to approach research, and in some ways is as distinct from quantitative research as qualitative designs are. In single-subject design the client is his or her own control, which allows a social worker to actively and easily integrate clinical practice with research practice. Single-case designs allow for the researcher to examine the effects of intervention on an individual client and to directly examine the outcome of theory on practice.

Single-subject research is idiographic. It is sometimes referred to as single-case study or as research with an "n of 1" ($n = 1$). Information about one client is, of course, not generalizable. However, a case for causality can be built through replication. If the same intervention approach is employed over a range of individual clients and the outcome is always positive, there is an argument that the intervention is making a contribution to the outcome.

Single-subject research begins with the identification of a problem and target behaviours that represent manifestations of the problem. Together the client and social worker agree on an intervention to change the client's behaviour in an agreed-upon direction. If the client consents, she or he participates in the evaluation of the intervention's effectiveness by recording incidents of targeted behaviour for analysis. Different aspects of the behaviour can be measured, such as its frequency, duration, or intensity or by measuring the interval between instances of the behaviour. For example, increasing the frequency of social contact with friends, reducing the duration of arguments between spouses, or lessening the intensity of anxiety experienced by a new mother could all indicate progress towards problem resolution.

AB Design

Single-subject research uses the time series experimental design. Using standard notation, it can be represented as:

$$O_1 \, O_2 \, O_3 \, O_4 \, X \, O_5 \, O_6 \, O_7 \, O_8$$

The target behaviour is considered the dependent variable and the intervention is considered the independent variable. In its general form the design involves taking a number of observations of target behaviour prior to implementing the intervention (X), and then taking repeated measurements of the same behaviour once the intervention has begun.

The set of observations taken prior to introduction of the intervention is called the baseline phase and is labelled "A." In the illustration above the baseline phase consisted of four measurements, but the actual number is determined by the client's behaviour and by the social work research practitioner. Baseline measurements are taken until the client's target behaviour has reached a reasonably stable level. What constitutes "a reasonably stable level" is up to the social worker to determine. The baseline phase is intended to document what would be considered normal behaviour on the part of the client. Measurements are taken after the commencement of the intervention and used to determine if there is a change in the normal pattern. This set of measurements is referred to as the intervention phase and assigned a capital letter for labelling purposes. For example, Violet wants to stop smoking. She enrolls in a six-week "Smoke No More" class where the practitioner uses single-subject research to document change. She is asked to record her smoking behaviour for the two weeks prior to the course and then during the course. Table 2.13 provides a chart of her data.

While it is possible to use statistical analysis on this data, it is more common to take the data and construct a line graph that illustrates the pattern of behaviour over time. Analysis consists of interpreting the graph, that is, describing the pattern. Figure 2.13c presents a graph of Violet's data.

Since Violet was a smoker, the baseline phase was very short, because smoking every day was her normal behaviour. When the course started (week 3) her smoking behaviour began to change, and by the end of the course she had stopped smoking altogether.

While this graph illustrates that change has taken place, we cannot argue that it was the course that caused the change. History is the most common threat to the internal validity of this design. There is no way to defend against the alternative explanation that something else happened at the same time as the course commenced and was the real

Table 2.13   Violet's Data

Phase	Week	Smoke-Free Days
Baseline phase A	1	0
	2	0
Intervention phase B	3	4
	4	6
	5	7
	6	7
	7	7
	8	7

Figure 2.13c   Violet's Graph

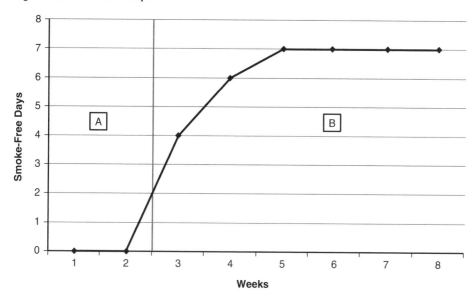

cause of Violet's quitting. However, what are the chances of this external event coinciding with the start of the program? The data are supportive of the course's effectiveness, but are not proof that it works. That's why replication is helpful in building a stronger case. If the course is offered seven times, and each time the graph of all participants looks similar to Violet's, what are the chances that history could explain the outcome? They are probably quite low, but only probably.

ABA Design

The AB design is the most rudimentary form of single-subject research, and with its use comes some ethical concerns because it requires delay of the intervention until the baseline data stabilize.

This can be avoided if there are secondary data available that contain the behavioural information required. For example, school records could be used to determine attendance data for students or telephone records from the school to the parents indicating that a child was not in class. It may also be possible to ask the client to provide retrospective data from their memory. However, the reliability of recall data may be suspect. In some cases practitioners choose to eliminate the baseline phase altogether. This type of research becomes a "B-Only" design. There are many concerns about this approach

Figure 2.13d Violet's Chart – ABA Design

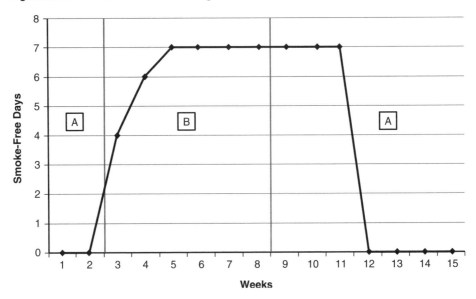

because there is no documentation concerning the normal level of behaviour prior to the intervention. In essence, it is a variant of the X O pre-experimental design and is subject to a number of threats to internal validity. However, it does provide information about the level of behaviour during the intervention and can be followed by an A phase to document persistence. This would require continued observations of the target behaviour after the intervention has terminated. Data from a subsequent A phase would allow the researcher to address the persistence of the intervention effect. Did the behaviour attain a new normal level that continued after the intervention was withdrawn, or did it return to previous levels? Using an ABA design as illustrated in Figure 2.13d would help answer this question.

This figure shows that the effect lasted for three weeks following the end of the program (week 8), but that Violet returned to smoking after week 11. Persistence of the effect for a short time after the termination of the intervention followed by a return to former levels of the behaviour is called a honeymoon effect.

The ABA design also helps identify a delayed positive reaction. This occurs when the full impact of the intervention is not felt until sometime after the intervention's end. If researchers only use an AB design, they would not be able to identify an effect from the intervention and might conclude that it was unsuccessful. The ABA design would enable monitoring behaviour to determine if the effect is indeed delayed. The ABA design permits analysis to extend beyond the termination of the intervention. However, there is a practical difficulty in employing this design: once an intervention is terminated the client may lose contact with the agency or worker, and it can be difficult to obtain needed data. Once service has ended, clients are less interested in collecting data.

Additional Single-Subject Design Options

While the AB and ABA designs are the most common, it is possible to design other approaches to answer questions about client behavioural change. For example, the ABAB (the withdrawal or reversal) design can answer whether or not the desired behaviour change is evident only while the client is engaged in the intervention. The baseline (A) is established, following which the intervention is initiated (B). Then the intervention is removed for a period of time (A), and after that time is reintroduced (B). If the behaviour is dependent upon the client's being engaged in treatment, the chart will reflect this: the desired behaviour will only be manifest during the intervention phases, the "B" periods. Keep in mind, however, that there may be ethical concerns about the withdrawal of a service that is providing positive gains for a client, especially if the reason for the withdrawal is research, not clinical practice.

If additional interventions are added to the client experience, these are assigned different letters. For example, the ABC design consists of the baseline phase followed by intervention B, which is stopped after a period of time to be followed immediately by intervention C. This will illustrate the cumulative effect of interventions B and C. It is important to note that if the behaviour does not change during intervention B and then moves in the desired direction after the start of intervention C, this does not mean that intervention B is ineffective. There may be something occurring during intervention B that makes intervention C more effective. To test this out, the social work research practitioner may choose to compare the outcome of a client receiving the ABC design to one receiving just the AB or the AC.

An "A BC" design indicates that the baseline period is followed by the client receiving interventions B and C concurrently. An ABAC design means that there is a period of no involvement with the client between the termination of intervention B and the start of intervention C. This would establish the stabilization of a new normal level of behaviour prior to the initiation of the second intervention. As you can see, designing single-subject research can get quite complicated, but regardless of the design chosen, the process is exactly the same. It begins by establishing a target behaviour. Repeated measurements of some dimension of this behaviour are then taken over a period of time and data are graphed for visual interpretation. What is being interpreted is the pattern of behaviour, and what the social work research practitioner is looking for are changes in patterns that reflect the client experience with the intervention.

When to Use Single-Subject Research

Single-subject research is most appropriate when the client's goals specify a change in behaviour and the measurement of that behaviour is clear and straightforward. The measurement selected should also be reasonably sensitive to change over a practical time period. It would not be helpful to use "inviting one's mother for Mother's Day dinner" as the behaviour that indicates attainment of the goal of an enhanced relationship with one's mother.

In most cases it is the client who is recording the measurements. An added benefit of this approach is that the client can feel empowered by taking control of the measurement process. By engaging the client in the research activity, you involve that client more directly in his or her own change process. However, it is important that the measurement task be acceptable to the client, that is, easy to do and non-intrusive. For example, it is probably more effective to ask a depressed client to count how many times a day they break out into tears than to ask them to complete a two-page depression questionnaire daily. This approach becomes moot, however, if the client forgets or neglects to collect the data or doesn't take the data collection task seriously. Determining the best way to measure target behaviours is an important activity, even though it may require a certain amount of creativity on the part of the social worker and the client.

As with all activities of practice, the needs, preferences, and best interests of the client system must come first. It is important not to let the demands of the research activity interfere with these ethical obligations. Research should not take precedence over service. Despite its obvious shortcomings, single-system research is one of the simplest ways for practitioners to include research in their regular activities, to use actual evidence in day-to-day practice, and to further involve clients in their own change.

7. Responding to the Case

Part 1

There are three possible conclusions that you can draw from your study:

- Your intervention worked and is responsible for the change in Malcolm's attendance.

- Your intervention in conjunction with other life events led to a positive change in Malcolm's school attendance.
- Your intervention had nothing to do with Malcolm's being in school more often.

This triad of possibilities underscores both the strength and weakness of the AB single-subject design. The important finding is that positive change did occur, and you are able to readily demonstrate this to all the parties concerned about Malcolm. You now have become a knower in regard to your practice as a social worker, and you have rather easily and simply integrated research into your practice, which is the first step to becoming an evidenced-informed social worker. However, the results obtained from this design do not allow you as a social work research practitioner to definitively state that your intervention led to the change or that the change will be permanent.

Unfortunately, the six weeks you initially contracted for with the client and his system have concluded and your goal, regardless of why it was achieved, has been met; you have no reason as a social work practitioner to continue to see Malcolm. As well, your budget for swim passes has been depleted. This, however, is where also being a social work research practitioner becomes an asset. As part of your ongoing single-subject design you know that you can add another baseline (A) observation period onto the end of an AB single-subject design, making it an ABA design, to monitor whether the change produced is maintained. Thus, your choices as Malcolm's social worker can be extended beyond direct clinical practice.

Part 2

Adding the second baseline observation period (A) will make a rudimentary AB design a more informative ABA design. Through this process, which would have taken you only a few minutes over the course of a month, you are able to observe that while the change was initially maintained, Malcolm's previous pattern of poor school attendance re-emerged. Again you are not able to conclude exactly why this happened, though in this case, when you are integrating research and practice, you do know that your client needs additional support. In this instance, as the social worker, you are fortunate in that the relationship is still strong enough, and that all parties have agreed, to allow you to re-enter the system and try your second intervention option. As you had two hypotheses when you began your work with Malcolm, you may now test the second and switch to more intensive counselling regarding loss and the grief produced by his parents' impending divorce. Of course, you will continue to collect data, now evolving your research design to an A B1 A B2 design and assessing if this second intervention is helping to achieve the goal of improving Malcolm's school attendance. The limitations of the AB design still apply here, but you know that when you complete your counselling sessions you will add yet another A phase to continue to monitor whether your work has achieved a lasting change with the client. The ABAB design also has the potential to demonstrate a causal relationship by demonstrating that the problematic behaviour varies according to the presence or absence of the social work intervention.

8. Further Reflections

1. *Based upon your current or past social work practicum setting or, alternatively, a current or previous volunteer setting, design a single-subject study that would assist in determining the outcome of a social work intervention with a client.*
2. *What barriers exist/existed in that setting that prevent social workers from integrating single-subject design into their daily practice? How could these be overcome?*

9. Additional Reading

Barlow, D.H., & Hersen, M. (1984). *Single-case experimental designs: Strategies for studying behaviour change* (2nd ed.). Elmsford, NY: Pergamon.

Bradshaw, W. (2003). Use of single-system research to evaluate the effectiveness of cognitive-behavioural treatment of schizophrenia. *British Journal of Social Work, 33*(7), 885–99.

Collins, P.M., Kayser, K., & Platt, S. (1994). Conjoint marital therapy: A practitioner's approach to single system evaluation. *Families in Society, 75*(3), 131–41.

Early, B.P. (1995). Decelerating self-stimulating and self-injurious behaviours of a student with autism: Behavioural intervention in the classroom. *Social Work in Education, 17*(4), 245–55.

Foster, L.H. (2010). A best kept secret: Single-subject research design in counseling. *Counseling Outcome Research and Evaluation, 1*(2), 30–9.

Kratochwill, T. & Levin, J. (Eds.). (1992). *Single-case research design and analysis: New directions for psychology and education.* Hillside, NJ: Lawrence Erlbaum.

Lowe, M.R., Bunnell, D.W., Neeren, A.M., Chernyak, Y., & Greberman, L. (2011). Evaluating the real-world effectiveness of cognitive-behaviour therapy efficacy research on eating disorders: A case study from a community-based clinical setting. *International Journal of Eating Disorders, 44*(1), 9–18.

Mattaini, M.A. (1996). The abuse and neglect of single-case designs. *Research on Social Work Practice, 6,* 83–90.

Richards, S., Taylor, R., Ramasany, R., & Richards, R. (1999). *Single-subject research: Applications in educational and clinical settings.* San Diego: Singular Publishing Group.

Slonim, N.V. (1997). Evaluating practice: The dual roles of clinician and evaluator. *Families in Society, 78*(3), 228–39.

Teall, B. (2000). Using solution-oriented interventions in an ecological frame: A case illustration. *Social Work in Education, 22*(1), 54–61.

10. Internet Resources

John B. Wasson, "Single Subject Design":
    http://www.practicalpress.net/updatenov05/SingleSubject.html
Bill Miller, "Single Subject Research Design (SSRD)":
    http://www.vchri.ca/i/pdf/SingleSubjectResearch.pdf
B.J. Byiers, J. Reichle, and F.J. Symons, "Single-Subject Experimental Design for Evidence-based Practice":
    http://www.ncbi.nlm.nih.gov/pmc/articles/PMC3992321/

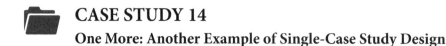

CASE STUDY 14
One More: Another Example of Single-Case Study Design

1. Preamble

What would you do if you knew you couldn't fail?

It's never too late to begin integrating research into your practice. It is not always necessary to begin with an observation phase; there are several research designs that allow you to begin collecting data at the same time you begin working with your client.

2. The Problem

N'dina is a bright seven-year-old who is cute and precocious with very good grades but who will no longer talk to anyone at school. She does her homework, listens to her teachers, and raises her hand when she has to go to the washroom, but will not talk when spoken to in the large classroom environment, small groups, or one-on-one. N'dina is selectively mute. Needless to say, her parents, who are Somali refugees, are equally frustrated with and concerned about her behaviour, and come to your community agency looking for assistance.

3. The Process

At the beginning of your first session you introduce yourself to N'dina. She acknowledges you with a large smile and a small sound somewhat like hello but does not appear anxious to engage you in dialogue, though neither does she appear upset about being in your office. As part of your assessment, you discover that when she comes home from school she will talk with her mother and father, though she tends to ignore her younger sister, who is two. N'dina will talk with friends who are on her hockey team, both boys and girls, though Alex and Ben are her best friends; but she will not always talk with them and will never do so at school, not even with Alex or Ben. N'dina enjoys playing hockey very much, and her parents tell you that there was quite a scene at home when they told her she could not play if she did not start talking at school. It was this incident that led them to schedule an appointment with you. N'dina's parents would like her to talk at school even if it is only once or twice a day, but they fear any intervention that might lead to a decrease in communication in other parts of her life. Her parents report that both N'dina's teacher and principal are willing to assist in any way possible.

You recommend an eight-week behaviour-modification-based intervention with a three-week break in the middle to accommodate the December school holidays. As well, in order to monitor that increases in communication at school are not negatively offset by changes in communication at home or with friends, you enlist N'dina's mother, father, and teacher along with the school social work practicum student as co-researchers. (The title "research assistant" is important, as the school is not able to allocate additional counselling resources to N'dina because it cannot be demonstrated that her mutism is affecting her academic performance, but designation as a research project allows further resources to be allocated.)

4. The Research

You believe that there is no time to begin collecting preliminary baseline data, and that holding off any intervention would not only be unethical but would also not be in the best interests of N'dina. Nonetheless, you are not certain that your intervention will work, as literature on selective mutism is rare, particularly when the child is otherwise doing well. As you begin your work with N'dina, you have her parents observe her for one hour a night and collect data on the number of times she speaks, either to initiate a conversation, ask a question, or respond verbally using more than a single word. They are also asked to do the same when N'dina goes to a hockey practice or game, which is two or three times per week. Likewise, the social work intern will enter the class for one hour a day to observe if the behaviour modification program the teacher is trying with N'dina is having any effect on verbal behaviour. You obtain the results shown in Figure 2.14.

5. Questions

1. *What conclusions can you draw from this study?*
2. *What do you do next in terms of treatment and research?*
3. *How much time should you spend attempting to determine what the underlying reason is for N'dina's selective mutism?*

Figure 2.14 N'dina's Average Hourly Vocalizations

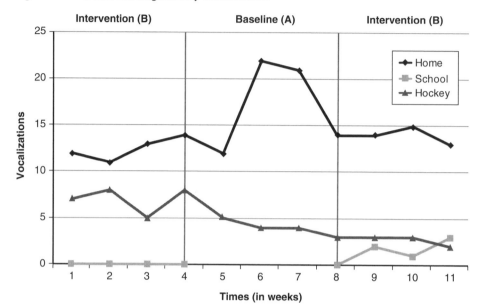

6. Social Work Practice

Goal Attainment Scaling

Effective social workers are keenly interested in understanding the impact of their work. They want to be able to evaluate their practice. Is the client system they are help-ing experiencing improvement? Do their actions make a difference? "Did my work with Ms. Jiffar reduce her sadness over the death of her mother?" Being able to answer such questions provides feedback about the usefulness of the intervention approach and the effectiveness of the worker in applying it. Practice evaluation methods can as-sist in identifying progress or lack of progress towards client-established goals. It is a source of information that can inform practice on a case-by-case basis. To enhance single-subject design another data collection approach can be added: goal attainment scaling (GAS). These two approaches are inexpensive, are easy to employ, take little time, and provide immediate feedback to the practitioner and client system. They both employ research methodologies to measure outcomes one client at a time. However, the data they produce cannot be generalized. We refer to this type of research as ideo-graphic: having to do with the single, the one. Its purpose is to document change, but on its own it cannot be used to argue for causality. Using these approaches, we can determine that Ms. Jiffar is not as sad as she was before we started working with her, but we cannot attribute the change to our intervention or our skills as a practitioner. More importantly, however, if we document that change has not taken place or that change is in the opposite direction to what we expect, we can determine that the intervention is not having a positive effect and make adjustments.

The Process of GAS

Goal attainment scaling allows the social worker to determine the extent to which a client has achieved predetermined goals. It is a useful evaluation method for those who use goal setting as an intervention approach. GAS also has the added advantage of serving as part of the intervention method as well as the evaluation tool. There are four steps in the process. To begin with, the client and the social worker identify a problem that the client would like to work on and establish behaviours that would indicate change in the problem area. They then work together to establish behavioural indicators that reflect a range of outcomes, from what would be considered the most unfavourable outcome to what would be the most favourable. These outcomes are described and arranged on a five-point scale ranging from −2 to +2, with the expected level of performance being allocated the "0" value. Table 2.14 is an example of a GAS for improving the interactive play behaviour of a child with autism spectrum disorder. Scaling in this manner accepts the possibility that the target behaviour might not improve and in fact may become more problematic. It doesn't bias the scale towards success. And these are not standardized scales: each scale is constructed for a particular individual based on his or her current level of behaviour and expectations for success. In practice

Table 2.14 Goal Attainment Scale for Play

Level	Outcome	Description
−2	Most unfavourable outcome thought likely	Isolated play – would not separate from parent, would not enter playroom, total dependence on parent.
−1	Present level of performance	Parallel play – plays in group but does not interact with adults or children.
0	Expected level of success	Interactive play – plays in group, interacts with children or adults less than 50% of the time.
+1	More than expected level of success	Interacts through adult structuring with other children 80% of the time.
+2	Most favourable expected level of success	Interacts with peers cooperatively – imitates activities.

it is common for the social worker and client to identify a number of behaviours to target. From a strengths perspective it is better to identify positive behaviour as targets, with the hope that the intervention will increase the occurrence of positive actions rather than contribute to the removal or reduction of negative behaviours.

GAS can be an excellent approach to monitoring success, but it has been criticized because of the subjectivity involved in rating. If the social worker conducts the rating there is the possibility of inflating values to demonstrate success, particularly if the data are being used for performance evaluation. Nor does asking the client to do the rating ensure objectivity. Clients may indicate a greater level of progress to please a worker they have grown to respect or may inflate scores to feel successful. Thus, to reduce the subjectivity of rating it is important to try to make the behaviours as concrete and measurable as possible and, if feasible, to employ an outside rater to complete the scale.

7. Responding to the Case

The BAB single-subject design does not employ a baseline or a pre-intervention data collection component; instead the treatment phase is the first study period, followed by the withdrawal of treatment and then its reapplication. This makes it a very practical research approach, as you may begin your study at the same time as you begin working with your client without requiring a lengthy period of time to delay intervention.

During your initial intervention little changed. However, talking increased dramatically during the baseline period, but then decreased when you began to work with N'dina again. Why, you may have asked? Does this indicate that the social work intervention was unsuccessful? To be an adept social work research practitioner, you should never stop being a social worker and staying closely attuned to the environment and to the person-in-environment. Even though N'dina's family was not Christian, this does not mean they did not celebrate the secular aspects of the religious-based event. Christmas was an extremely exciting time for N'dina just as it is for most seven-year-old girls, who are wrapped up in the mystery and spectacle of Saint Nicholas, his magic reindeer, and the host of gifts awaiting them on the morning of December 25. Thus, increased talking during the baseline period reflects "some external event or extraneous variable occurring during the course of the study that might interfere with the findings or be a confounding variable" (see Case Study 11).

Returning to vocalizations at home and factoring in the increase as being due to the events of Christmas, we see no change in response to the intervention, which was one goal of your work with N'dina. You do, however, observe a small change in classroom vocalizations in January. However, vocalizations at hockey have slowly but steadily decreased to the point where now, while N'dina is talking in class, she is talking much less to her friends Alex and Ben and less overall. The goal of talking in class is being met, but it conflicts with the goal of not affecting her overall vocalizations. What do you do next? You integrate your abilities as a social work practitioner and a social work researcher!

This is exactly the type of scenario that illustrates why it is imperative that you become both a social work practitioner and a social work research practitioner, and collect data and use evidence to inform your practice. In only five weeks you were able to facilitate N'dina's inaugural communications in school and empirically demonstrate her success. Her parents, her teacher, you, and most importantly N'dina all know that she is capable of talking in class, which was what brought her parents to you initially. However, your intervention is having some negative impact, and this too needs to be addressed. You and your social work intern will be meeting with N'dina and her parents and giving them a copy of your chart illustrating the changes, both positive and concerning. As you were aware that the literature was unclear about what intervention options would be best, this turn of events provides you the opportunity to revise the contract and move from a behaviour modification structure to one based on attachment theory, and to continue with your data collection as part of your ongoing work with N'dina and her family.

You have your social work knowledge base. You have your social work skills. You have your initial success. You have a client and support system engaged with you. You have a sound and thorough research process in place. You know you will not fail. What does this now allow you to do?

8. Research Insight

The other important aspect of this case study is that it has multiple data collection sites, which in single-subject design is referred to as a multiple-baseline approach. This research process is also part of a broader approach in research known as triangulation. Triangulation entails the collection of more than one set of data to assess if a relationship is occurring between the independent and dependent variable or between two variables of interest. In essence, single-subject multiple-baseline designs, both BA and AB, involve the same principles of comparison found in larger group designs, again illustrating that good research practice and good social work practice are the same thing.

9. Further Reflections

1a. *Enhance the single-subject study you designed in Case Study 13 by adding a goal attainment scale to it.*

1b. *Redesign your single-subject study from Case Study 13 to use a BAB approach.*

2. *What fears do you have about conducting research?*

3. *To begin to address those fears and your lack of experience in this practice area, begin your career as a social work practitioner researcher by incorporating a single-subject research design into your practicum learning contract as one of your goals.*

What would you do if you knew you couldn't fail?

10. Additional Reading

Cytrynbaum, S., Ginath, Y., Birdwell, J., & Brandt, L. (1979). Goal attainment scaling: A critical review. *Evaluation Review, 3*(1), 5–40.

Kazdin, A.E. (l982). *Single-case research designs: Methods for clinical and applied settings*. New York: Oxford University Press.

Kazi, M.A.F. (1996). Single-case evaluation in the public sector. *Evaluation, 2*, 85–97.

Kiresuk, T.J., Smith, A., & Cardillo, J.E. (Eds.). (1994). *Goal attainment scaling: Applications, theory, and measurement*. Hillsdale, NJ: Lawrence Erlbaum.

Murphy, K., & Weinstein, S. (1991). The application of single-system research in social work with addictions. *Employee Assistance Quarterly, 7*(2), 83–98.

Neuman, K. (2002). From practice evaluation to agency evaluation: Demonstrating outcomes to the United Way. *Social Work in Mental Health, 1*(2), 1–14.

Nugent, W.R. (1996). Integrating single case and group comparison designs for evaluation research. *Journal of Applied Behavioral Science, 32*(2), 209–26.

Soliman, H.H. (1999). Post-traumatic stress disorder: Treatment outcomes for a Kuwaiti child. *International Social Work, 42*(2), 163–75.

Tripodi, T. (1994). *A primer on single-subject design for clinical social workers*. Washington, DC: National Association of Social Workers.

Vonk, M.E., Tripodi, T., & Epstein, I. (2007). Single case designs. In *Research techniques for clinical social workers* (pp. 155–73). New York: Columbia University Press.

Woodward, C.A., Santa Barbara, J., Levin, S., & Epstein, N.B. (1978). The role of goal attainment scaling in evaluating family therapy outcome. *American Journal of Orthopsychiatry, 48*(3), 464–76.

11. Internet Resources

Education.com, "Single-Case Designs":
http://www.education.com/reference/article/single-case-designs/

S.L. Odom, W.H. Brown, T. Frey, N. Karasu, L.L. Smith-Canter, and P.S. Strain, "Evidence-based Practices for Young Children with Autism Contributions for Single-Subject Design Research":
http://citeseerx.ist.psu.edu/viewdoc/download?doi=10.1.1.459.9591&rep=rep1&type=pdf

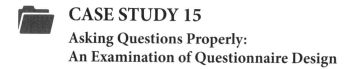

CASE STUDY 15

Asking Questions Properly:
An Examination of Questionnaire Design

1. Preamble

The most precious gift subjects involved in your research study can give you is their time, for it is a finite commodity that can never be replaced. Researchers need to be appreciative of all those who give of themselves so that we may become knowers. Thus all researchers, not only those from the discipline of social work, have the responsibility of being as well-prepared as possible in conducting their studies but also of making sure the format they use to gather information is intelligible to participants in the study.

2. The Problem

As part of the requirements for your MSW, you must participate in and successfully complete a research/integration seminar than runs parallel with your practicum. As part of your practicum, you must complete some type of research initiative. One of your classmates, being a clever master's student, determines that the easiest piece of research is to design and distribute a questionnaire.

3. The Process

You have learned in the research courses leading up to your research/integration seminar that response rate is always a key issue when using questionnaires to collect data and that questionnaire design affects response rates. Thus, prior to implementing the questionnaire, and to impress the course professor, your classmate asks to use the seminar group as a pre-test to provide feedback in enhancing the content and presentation of the questionnaire and how best to administer it.

4. The Research

Figure 2.15a reproduces the questionnaire presented to the seminar group to complete.

Figure 2.15a   A Questionnaire to Critique

EAP

CONTACT PERSON QUESTIONAIRE

Date of Interview: _____

Name: _____

Organization: _____

SECTION A: Organizational Background Information

1. Organization Name: _____

2. Organization

 Function   : _____

3. Workforce Size: _____

4. Male/Female Ratio: _____

5.   Unionized: () No

                                    () Yes

                                                        Union Afiliation:_____

                                                        Local: _____ Size: _____

                        Local: _____ Size: _____

                                                Local: _____ Size: _____

6. Medical Department: () No go to question 7.

                                    () Yes

                                                        Composition:_____

                                    _____

SECTION B: Employee Assistance Program Information

7. What year was the EAP began? _____

8. How many people used it last year? _____

9. Who initated the program:

              () Management   () Labour   () Medical

              () Joint Labour-Managment Initiative   () Don't now

              () Other(please specify)_____

10.   Did the person(s) initiating your organization's EAP have any affiliation to a self-help group

              () Yes () No () Don't Know

11.   What is your EAP's focus(check more than one if appropriate):

              () assessment and referral ()treatment

              () health promotion ()prevention

              () other (please specify) _____

              _____

12.   Within your Employee Assistance Program who assists troubled employes?

1. Volunteers Internal to the Workplace

 2. Professionals Internal to the Workplace

              3. Professionals External to the Workplace

4. Volunteers External to the Workplace

()   a. recovering individuals

()   b. self-help groups

13.   Reasons volunteer are (are not) used?

_____

_____

_____

_____

_____

_____

_____

PART C: SELF-HELP/MUTUAL AID GROUP IN THE WORKPLACE

14.   Are there any self-help groups being used to assist troubled employees in your EAP?

         () No,   end of interview.

         () Don't Know, end of interview.

         () Yes,   which ones?

         _____

_____

15.   Are meetings held at the worksite?

         () No   end of interview.

         () Don't Know end of interview.

         () Yes

16.   For any self-help groups that meet on-site please state, If you know when they meet and how often.

Group	Meeting Time	Meeting Frequency
_____	_____	_____
_____	_____	_____
_____	_____	_____
_____	_____	_____
_____	_____	_____
_____	_____	_____
_____	_____	_____
_____	_____	_____

5. Question

1. *If you were a member of the research/integration class who received this draft of the survey instrument, what recommendations would you have to improve it to increase the likelihood that respondents would actually complete and return it?*

6. Social Work Practice

Collecting Information Using a Questionnaire

Your first question to ask in conducting survey research is: How will I collect the information using a questionnaire? Will it be mailed out, conducted over the telephone, or done person to person, or will it be an electronic questionnaire completed online? While face-to-face and telephone surveys tend to provide the most representative samples, mail and electronic questionnaires are easier to obtain replies to. Anonymity is greater with mail and e-surveys, but the reliability of answers is lower. Electronic surveys also tend to have the lowest rate of return. Thus a balance between budget, accuracy, detail, and response rate must be considered when determining which survey design process you will select.

In designing the questionnaire itself the social work researcher needs to be clear on what type of data is desired:

- Attitudinal: what people want
- Beliefs: what people think is true
- Behaviours: what people actually do
- Attributes: demographic information describing respondent characteristics.

Next, you need to determine the type of question structure that will be used. Will the questionnaire employ open-ended questions that allow subjects to use their own words, which provides you with the broadest information possible but makes analysis more difficult; or fixed-alternative questions, where the respondent is asked to select an answer from a predetermined list constructed by the researcher; or some combination of the two? Finally, themes should be linked so that the respondent can easily follow what you are hoping to ask. Also, ensure that your opening questions are easy to answer and do not deter a client from spending his or her precious time helping you.

The goal of survey research is to get back the greatest number of fully completed questionnaires, each one containing valid and reliable information. A problem arises if you mail out 500 questionnaires to a randomly selected sample of individuals in a population and only 100 are returned, because the generalizability of your data can be questioned. There is a strong argument that respondents who return questionnaires are different in some way from those who do not; at the very least, they are more cooperative. In this case you would have received only a 20 per cent return rate (100/500). While a researcher strives to achieve as high a return rate (RR) as possible, it is not uncommon to read research that reports an RR of less than 50 per cent. When you are evaluating a piece of research, return rate is one of the key criteria for judging the generalizability of the results. If the return rate is low, you should be cautious about a study's external validity. In high-quality research, investigators present data that compare responders to non-responders to try to show that they are similar, but the best way to avoid this problem is to make every effort to maximize your return rate. One means of doing so is to provide potential respondents with a compelling reason why it is important for them to complete the questionnaire, or at least to communicate with them in a manner that makes them feel important for doing so. All correspondence should be personalized, which means directed to a specific person if at all possible. You don't want to send out questionnaires to "occupant" or, even worse, "head of the household." To increase responses, it is also a good idea to have the endorsement of a person or organization that respondents will trust and respect. Potential respondents are more likely to comply if the survey has legitimacy in their eyes. Keeping a questionnaire short and telling people how long it will take to complete it are also helpful measures, as is designing the questionnaire in a conversational mode with an introduction and a thank you statement at the end. Finally, some researchers have found it productive to include incentives, such as gifts of small value or an opportunity to participate in a draw or lottery if they return a completed questionnaire. Incentives can help, but they need to be small in value and acceptable from an ethical perspective. Even if you achieve a high percentage of returns, this does not necessarily mean that you have in your possession good data, that is, valid and reliable responses. People can rush through a survey, not take it seriously, or even purposely answer incorrectly. There is no way for you to determine this by just looking at the completed questionnaire. You have to accept the answers that respondents provide and consider them as data, but the results will reflect this error. As well, respondents may return the questionnaire but leave a question blank: they don't answer it at all. This reduces the return rate for that question, and in the worst case – when a number of questions are left unanswered – the questionnaire may have to be discarded.

While these problems cannot be entirely eliminated, there are practices related to questionnaire design that can help minimize them. That is why it is particularly important to spend time on and give attention to the questions, the questionnaire, and the way the questionnaire will be administered. These are key to attaining the goal of receiving a large number of fully completed questionnaires each containing valid and reliable information.

The Questionnaire Development Process

Crafting a good questionnaire requires time and attention to detail. The first thing to do when using a questionnaire for quantitative data collection is to identify a list of variables, called data elements, that you will need to measure. These variables are identified from your research questions or hypotheses. Make sure your list of variables is complete. The survey will provide the data you need to answer your research questions, but if you haven't identified all the relevant variables you might not get the information you require. As well, it is unethical to ask people for information when you do not plan to use it in your data analysis. It might be nice to know certain things about the people in your survey, but "nice to know" is not justification for asking. People voluntarily agree to participate in research, and what they are asked to do can be considered an intrusion. We need to make sure we don't waste their time, and because of this we only measure what we need to know.

Once you have a list of appropriate data elements, the next step is to design a question that will provide the data. Every question on your questionnaire should have a purpose related to the research activity. Some questions provide data needed to answer the research questions. Other questions supply information needed to address methodological concerns; for example, we may wish to collect demographic information to compare respondents to the population to enhance arguments for generalizability.

When the questions have been developed, the next step is to organize them into a questionnaire. Effective questionnaire design is an art and involves more than listing the questions as they are developed. The organization and appearance of the questionnaire can make a contribution to the goal of a high response rate. People may not feel like completing a messy questionnaire that appears unprofessional or confusing to them (as in Figure 2.15a).

Once the questionnaire has been developed, the next step is to proofread and pre-test it. You do not want to distribute a questionnaire containing spelling or grammatical errors. It is best if someone other than the author does the proofreading; it is more difficult to identify mistakes in your own work because you are too close to the product. Pre-testing is the process of having others complete a draft of the questionnaire and provide feedback about features such as clarity of instruction, comprehension, and attractiveness of the questionnaire. Pre-testers can also provide helpful feedback about questions that don't make sense or that are incomplete or ambiguous in some way. While you can ask colleagues to provide you with feedback at the start of designing a questionnaire, when you think it is ready for use it is best to ask people who are similar to intended respondents to pre-test the questionnaire, as they have insights from the perspective of those who will actually be completing it. The final step is to incorporate feedback from pre-testers into the questionnaire. If pre-testing results in a number of suggestions you may wish to pre-test a second time. Time spent in design and pre-testing is well worth it when issues of reliability, validity, and maximum response rate are at stake.

Designing Questions

Single-item questions come in two general forms, fixed-alternative and open-ended. In the fixed-alternative form a question is posed and a respondent is asked to select his or her answer from a list provided by the researcher (Figure 2.15b).

To create a fixed-alternative question the researcher has to be aware of all possible answers, and it is best if there are a reasonable number of alternatives. You wouldn't ask for age by listing a hundred numbers and asking the respondent to identify their age from the list. A fixed-alternative question must have answer categories that are mutually exclusive and exhaustive. "Mutually exclusive" means that the possible answers must be conceptually distinct; they cannot overlap in meaning. You can ask that a respondent check as many answers as apply, but again each answer must be distinct. "Exhaustive" means that all possible answers are provided, that each respondent can find an answer to match his or her response. For example, consider the question posed in Figure 2.15c.

The question illustrated in Figure 2.15c is neither mutually exclusive (where do you check if your income is $20,000?) nor exhaustive (where do you check if your income is under $15,000?). To keep the number of possible answers at a reasonable level, sometimes a researcher will list the five or six most likely answers and then include a final category labelled "Other." This also helps to make sure that the list of possible answers is exhaustive, since if a respondent's answer is not listed, the "Other" category would be appropriate. However, depending upon the situation, use of an "Other" category can also be problematic because it can hide information. If, for example, you fail to identify a popular answer category this could lead to a large number of

Figure 2.15b   Fixed-Alternative Question

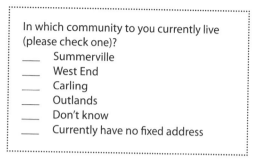

Figure 2.15c   A Problematic Question

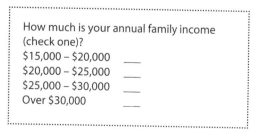

Figure 2.15d   Open-Ended Question

What did you like about the program?
_____
_____
_____
_____
_____
_____
_____
_____

respondents answering with "Other." To avoid losing information, sometimes a researcher will place a line after the "Other" answer and ask respondents to write in their answer. In general, pre-testing will help you identify if your fixed-alternative questions meet these important criteria.

Open-ended questions ask respondents to answer a question using their own words. The question is posed and space is provided for respondents to write their answer (Figure 2.15d).

Deciding which form of question to use is up to the researcher. Quantitative researchers usually prefer to use fixed-alternative questions whenever possible. They are easier for respondents to answer, since they only have to identify the correct answer, not think one up themselves. Some people are tempted to skip questions that require them to think: they can't be bothered or aren't sure that their answers are appropriate. Keeping the number of open-ended questions to a minimum also typically reduces the number of unanswered questions and decreases the amount of time it takes to complete the survey, thus increasing response rate as well. In addition, fixed-alternative questions are easier to code so there is no ambiguity. For example, compare the two approaches as applied to determining the sex of a respondent, illustrated in Figure 2.15e.

In this situation using an open-ended form could confuse a respondent. Using the fixed-alternative form makes it clear that concerning the variable *sex*, the researcher is looking for the biological designation of the respondent, not an opinion about the activity, frequency level, or attitude towards. And since open-ended questions produce text and not numbers or codes, there is concern that they are open to interpretation bias on the part of the researcher. This is why those interested in minimizing ambiguity find the fixed-alternative form of question more acceptable, while those wishing for the narrative responses of participants opt for the open-ended approach. Finally, using fixed-alternative questions has the advantage of avoiding the need to interpret a respondent's handwriting (assuming the traditional paper-and-pencil format). Data could be lost or incorrectly read if handwriting is illegible.

Figure 2.15e   Possible Ambiguity

The fixed-alternative approach:
Sex
____   Male
____   Female
____   Transgender
The open-ended approach:
Sex: _____

No matter which form a question takes, there are criteria that identify good questions. These fall into three areas: wording, bias, and answerability. The actual words chosen for the question are important. The question needs to be clear and the words used as precise as possible. For example, the question "How much do you drink on a daily basis?" is ambiguous. The researcher may have intended to measure a respondent's alcohol intake, but others could see this as a question about intake of all beverages. "What kind of a car do you drive?" could generate answers like "truck, van, SUV" or you could get "Ford, Toyota, Volvo." You also want to be careful that any jargon or acronyms you use are familiar to your intended respondents. "Is your PTSD causing any bizarre cognitions or physical distress such as TMJ?" may be meaningless to anyone else but you. As well, some words are simply too vague to be of use. For example, if you ask someone if they had a bad home life it will be difficult to compare across respondents, since "bad" is a vague and relative term. It is also good practice to try to avoid using negative terms in a statement. Even a single "not" can be missed by a reader. For example, in the question "When would you not intervene in your partner's use of physical punishment with your child?" it would be very easy to miss the word "not."

Figure 2.15f   The Good Agency

The service at this agency is (please check one):
Extremely good   _____
Very good   _____
Good   _____
Poor   _____

It is also very important to present and phrase questions in a manner that does not signal bias on the part of the researcher. A researcher who asks the question "Do you believe that English-speaking Canada should become a multicultural society of different ethnic groups, or would you prefer a system that will select immigrants who will integrate into a united English-speaking Canadian culture?" signals that he wants respondents to answer in a certain way, to agree with his opinion on the matter. Even something as subtle as the question contained in Figure 2.15f could be interpreted an intentional bias.

Given these choices, it is very likely that the agency will receive at least a "good" rating. Words chosen for possible response categories can bias responses towards a researcher's preferred conclusion. When posing a question, you want to be sure that you are asking people to consider only one thing, so they can clearly answer it. A question such as "Do you like the colour and décor of our waiting room?" can be confusing for people to answer if they don't like the shade of blue on the walls but do like the curtains. This type of question is referred to as a double-barrelled question, and can be very difficult to identify. For example, the question "Are your parents employed?" is doubled barrelled. You are asking about the employment status of two people in one question.

Even if you avoid the problem of double-barrelled questions, people may have difficulty answering. There are some questions people cannot answer accurately, such as "How many episodes of violence have you seen on television, at the movies, or on DVD in the past year?" When asked to remember past events, respondents will try to give you an answer, but it may not be very reliable. Questions that ask people to remember past experiences are in general subject to error; and the longer the time frame or less memorable the event, the larger the error is likely to be. Some questions are simply unanswerable. You can ask these types of questions, but either you won't get an answer or, if you do, it will clearly be influenced by a respondent's perception of what is socially acceptable. Consider "Did you cheat on your income tax last year?" or "Do you brush your teeth after every meal?" Questions that refer to sex, criminality, and socially unacceptable behaviour are difficult ones for people to answer totally truthfully.

Finally, there are questions that people may not be able to answer because they lack the relevant knowledge. For example, you can ask clients whether they agree or disagree with your new policy on missed appointments and assume they know what that policy is; but if they don't know what it is, their responses are not going to convey valuable data. The amazing thing is that people will often try to answer even if they don't know what they are talking about; they want to be helpful, they want to save face, or they confuse the question with something that they do know something about, and thus they provide you with inaccurate information, which is often worse than having no information. To be safe, the best way to ask this last type of question is to state the policy first and then ask the agree/disagree question.

Multi-Item Questions

While some variables can be measured by employing a single question, others require the use of multiple items. The most frequently used multi-item measures include checklists and scales. Checklists present the respondent with a list of items, and they are asked to check as many as apply to them. Their score is the sum of the items checked. For example, there are checklists to measure physical health that list a number of physical ailments. Respondents are asked to check all those they are currently experiencing. Those who check only a few problems are considered in better health than those who check many. While these scales are popular and easy to use, they do assume that each problem on the list carries equal weight. Thus it is important to make sure that, within reason, they do. You wouldn't consider someone who had lung cancer to be in better health than someone with a runny nose, sore feet, and an earache, but if these problems were listed separately on a checklist the second person, with a score of three, would be considered in poorer health than the first person, with a score of one.

There are different forms of multi-item scales, but the most commonly used type of scale for social work research is called a Likert Scale. When respondents are asked to complete a Likert Scale they are presented with a number of statements that address the construct being measured. They are asked to respond to each statement according to a scale that ranges on a continuum of extremes, such as disagree/agree or never/often. The steps along the continuum are assigned numbers. The nomenclature can be a bit confusing because the continuum presented with each statement is called a scale and the entire set of statements is also called a Scale. Here we use "Scale" with a capital "S" to designate the set of statements. Figure 2.15g presents a Likert Scale for measuring social isolation.

There are eight items on this Scale. For the first item a person who never felt as if there were people to talk would circle the number "1"; someone who felt

Figure 2.15g   Scale of Social Isolation

Below is list of common feelings. We would like to know how often you have felt each feeling in the past two weeks. For these questions your answer could range from "never" to "often." Read the question and then circle the number that best describes your feeling in response. For example, if you have felt "rarely" alone, circle number "2" next to the question. Remember that questions refer to the last two weeks.

Never	Rarely	Sometimes	Often
1	2	3	4

How often have you felt:

	Never	Rarely	Sometimes	Often
1. There are people to talk to	1	2	3	4
2. Alone	1	2	3	4
3. Part of a group of friends	1	2	3	4
4. Left out	1	2	3	4
5. Close to someone	1	2	3	4
6. People understand you	1	2	3	4
7. There are people to turn to	1	2	3	4
8. Isolated	1	2	3	4

that there sometimes were would circle "4." Respondents experiencing high levels of social isolation are likely to answer "Often" (4) for statements 2, 4, and 8. However, they would also likely answer "Never" (1) for statements 1, 3, 5, 6, and 7. The measure of a respondent's level of social isolation would be the sum of the score on each item included in the Scale. However, before this is done the positive items (1, 3, 5, 6, and 7) need to be recoded to reflect the direction for the Scale, which is negative. This is called reverse coding. For reverse-coded items such as the ones on this Scale a "1" becomes a "4"; a "2" becomes a "3"; a "3" becomes a "2"; and a "4" becomes a "1." The direction of the statements is varied to make sure that respondents don't get into what is called a response set bias. Sometimes when you are completing a Scale, after the first few statements you can tell that for most of the remaining statements you are likely to circle a certain number. Designers of the Scale do not want you to stop reading the statements and start to circle the expected number. To offset this tendency, they change the direction to slow respondents down and make them think about and respond accurately to each statement. After adjusting for reverse-coded items and summing the scores, the higher a respondent's composite score is, the higher their level of social isolation is. Someone with a score of 26 would be more isolated than someone with a score of 18.

The form of all Likert Scales is similar but the actual design details may vary. For example, the scale can have more than four points along the continuum. It is up to the researcher who develops the scale to determine how many points are used. If the scale has an even number of points, respondents cannot choose a neutral or middle-ground answer. The use of an even-numbered scale forces them to move in one direction or the other. In order to increase the ability of the scale to differentiate among respondents, it is best to use at least four points. But it is unlikely that you will encounter a Likert Scale with more than 10 choices. As the number of points increases, the ability of a respondent to differentiate between levels is greatly reduced. Not all Likert Scales provide word cues with the numbers either; however, at a minimum the extreme values need to be labelled. These extremes are called the anchors. Depending upon the statements and what the Scale measures, anchors can be opposites such as "agree/disagree," "like me/ not like me," "satisfied/unsatisfied," or "never/often."

Developing a scale requires advanced research knowledge, and it is very seldom that a social work researcher independently designs a multi-item scale. A great deal of research time and attention has been directed towards the development of useful rating scales for common psychosocial constructs. Appropriate measures can be identified when conducting a literature review by noting what Scales other researchers have used to measure the variables of interest to you. If they align with how you have conceptualized the constructs you are interested in, then you can consider using them in your research. Standardized rating scales are also published in compendiums of commonly used psychological tests, and many scales are now available on the Internet (e.g., http://www.walmyr.com). There is no need to reinvent the wheel, or the questionnaire in this case, if a suitable measure is already available. When you have identified a potential scale, make sure it has strong psychometric properties, that is, it has established reliability and validity (see Case Study 10). It is also important not to add or delete any of the items on the scale or to change the wording of items, or the order of the questions, as such changes could affect its reliability and validity; you would in essence be using a scale that is different from the one developed and tested. Even the completion instructions have to be presented exactly as developed.

When researchers want to measure complex psychosocial characteristics they usually select a multi-item scale. This approach results in a more valid measurement, since using a number of statements breaks down a complex construct into its various dimensions. In addition, using a multi-item scale introduces more variability into the measurement activity, enabling finer differentiation among respondents. If you asked a group of respondents to indicate on a scale of 1 to 5 how depressed they were, this single-item approach would only allow you to group respondents into five categories: the ones, the twos, the threes, the fours, and the fives. However, if you used a multi-item depression scale comprised of five statements each rated on a five-point scale, possible scores would range from 5 to 25, creating 21 categories.

Crafting a Questionnaire

Once you have determined which questions you wish to ask, you need to create the questionnaire. As with designing individual questions, designing questionnaires is somewhat of an art. The overall goal is to create a questionnaire that looks professional, clearly communicates how to complete the questions, and makes people want to complete and return it. The professional look of a questionnaire communicates to respondents that the people conducting the research are legitimate, serious, and competent at what they do. You want to make sure that the look of the questionnaire conveys these qualities. This means that the text must have no spelling mistakes or grammatical errors, the font and spacing must be aesthetically pleasing, and the questionnaire must be consistent and symmetrical throughout.

Try to keep the questionnaire as short as possible, but short in this case refers to the number of questions, not the physical size. Cramming questions onto one page to make a questionnaire appear short detracts from its appearance and may result in missed questions or inaccurate recording of answers. The order of the questions is also an important design feature. There should be a logical flow between questions. This means grouping questions on similar topics together and having topics flow logically from one to the next. You want to show that you have thought about what it will be like to answer the questionnaire and have built in ways to make it an efficient and enjoyable experience. Try to position questions of opinion near the beginning. Since nearly everyone likes to be asked their opinion, these questions engage people's interest and get them into "answering mode." Sensitive questions (sex, religion, money) should be placed further along so as not to alarm respondents just as they start answering the survey. They may refuse to answer any other questions if they are offended near the beginning. One

Figure 2.15h   Normalizing Questions

It is quite common for spouses or partners to have arguments from time to time.
We rarely agree with others on everything.
In the past seven (7) days (one week), how many arguments would you say you had with your partner or spouse? (please check one)

over 10 ____
8 – 10 ____
4 – 7 ____
1 – 3 ____
none ____

way to increase the likelihood that people will give more accurate answers when asked to self-disclose perceived deviant or socially awkward behaviours is to normalize the activity in the preamble to the question. Figure 2.15h provides an example of how such normalization can be phrased.

Also, the accepted advice for self-administered questionnaires is to position the demographic information at the end of the questionnaire. It is often the easiest for the respondent to answer and will encourage people to stick with it to the end. If a person encounters questions that require more thought near the end of the questionnaire, they may give up and stop answering, figuring that they have done most of the job. Remember, the goal is to get them to answer all the questions.

If a number of questions have a similar response set, they can be grouped together in a matrix format as illustrated in Figure 2.15i.

Also, if you are asking questions that do not apply to all respondents, guide people past the ones that don't apply to them by creating contingencies as illustrated in Figure 2.15j.

Finally, it is important to describe in detail how people are to answer the questions. Do you want them to circle, check, or write in an answer? If the questionnaire is to be self-administered it needs to include clear instructions so respondents know what is required of them. The instructions on how to complete the Social Isolation Scale in Figure 2.15g are a good illustration of how detailed you need to be. If you are at all

Figure 2.15i   Example of Matrix Format

We are interested in your opinion about the waiting room at our agency.
Please rate the features by circling the number that best describes your view.

Feature	Poor	Adequate	Good	Excellent
Temperature	1	2	3	4
Availability of seating	1	2	3	4
Cleanliness	1	2	3	4
Quality of toys for children	1	2	3	4

Figure 2.15j   Contingency Question

> 1. Do you have children living at home? Yes ___   No ___
>   (if no please go to question 4)
> 2. How many of your children are currently enrolled in elementary school? _____
> 3. How many of your children are currently enrolled in secondary school? _____
> 4. In the past week how many times have you eaten at a restaurant? _____

concerned about making sure respondents complete a question correctly, you can even give an example of what you would like them to do.

Administering a Questionnaire

Individuals can complete self-administered questionnaires on their own, but the questionnaires need to be distributed to them in some way. In situations where respondents are together at a certain time and place, a questionnaire can be handed out to the group and collected when they have completed it. Administering questionnaires in this way has the advantage of increasing response rates, as it is convenient for people to complete the questionnaires and the researcher is handy to collect the completed forms and answer any questions that arise. You also know who actually completed the questionnaire. If you mail it out or have it completed on a website you can never be certain that the person who answered the questions was the intended respondent.

Mail-out surveys have a long history in research practice. Respondents are mailed a package containing a letter of explanation, the questionnaire, and a return-addressed stamped envelope. They are asked to complete the survey and mail it back in the envelope provided. Once the package has been mailed out a researcher has no control over whether or when a respondent will choose to reply. A single mailing usually results in a low return rate, so most survey research includes two to three follow-up mailings. Any more than three becomes expensive and does not usually produce a significant increase in the number of responses returned. The follow-up mailing can be a postcard reminding people to complete the questionnaire or a full replacement package. There is no firm rule about when to send out a follow-up mailing, but it is usually time to do so when replies from a previous mailing begin to drop off significantly. If the returned surveys have identifying information on them, then subsequent mailings need only be sent to non-responders, though this will not be possible if the data are being collected anonymously. In this case subsequent mailings need to be sent to the entire sample; but receiving follow-up mailings can be quite annoying for people who have already responded and expensive if the sample is large. One way to avoid these problems is to include a self-addressed stamped postcard with the initial package. Respondents who complete the questionnaire are asked to write their name on the postcard and mail it back at the same time as the completed questionnaire but not in the questionnaire envelope. When the researcher gets the postcard he or she knows that the respondent named on the card completed the questionnaire, and the respondent's name can be taken off the list for future mailings.

Mail-out surveys have two advantages over interviewing: they cost significantly less and the characteristics of the interviewer cannot influence the respondent's answers. However, there are also disadvantages to mailing out surveys. As previously mentioned, when you receive a completed questionnaire you really do not know who actually completed it. You also do not know their state of mind at the time they completed it or whether or not they took the task seriously. Problems can also arise if respondents have questions, since there is no one there to provide clarification. And finally, it may also take a long time to get your data, especially if follow-up mailings are planned.

With advances in technology, more researchers have turned to the Internet to distribute their questionnaires. They contact potential respondents, usually by email, and ask them to access a website that contains the questionnaire. This approach does not address the problem of knowing who completed the questionnaire, but using the Internet does save money on postage and allows data to be directly added to a database, eliminating the possibility of data entry errors. An added advantage is that there are a number of web-based tools that can be used to help design professional-looking questionnaires with features that make it easy and efficient for people to complete them.

Several studies have looked at which approach will produce the best response rate. An early study found that electronic surveys solicited more complete answers, as people appeared willing to reveal more personal and truthful information through the anonymity of the computer (Carini, Hayek, Kuh, Kennedy, & Ouimet, 2003). Watt, Simpson, McKillop, and Nunn (2002) reported that typically response rates to online surveys are about 32 per cent while paper surveys averaged 33 per cent. However, a study of 134 employees who were asked to complete both a paper and an electronic survey found that while the electronic surveys were marginally easier complete and more enjoyable than paper surveys, paper-based questionnaires produced a higher response rate (Croteau, Dyer, & Miguel, 2010). A similar result was found by Csiernik and Csiernik (2012) in their study on occupational assistance. They sent 200 four-page surveys by mail and 200 electronically to a random sample of Canadian companies and had 45.5 per cent of the paper surveys retuned but only 25.5 per cent of the electronic ones.

7. Responding to the Case

The errors in the questionnaire presented for your critique ranged from simple things such as presentation, layout, and spelling to more substantive items such as not conceptualizing terms and not obtaining the consent of participants. Rather than provide a detailed listing of the numerous revisions necessary to make the questionnaire presentable, we present the actual final version in Figure 2.15l. The final questionnaire included a page of terminology explaining the various concepts, along with a consent form. Before the interview began subjects received two copies of the consent form. If they agreed to participate they would sign both, keep one, and return the other to the researcher, thereby indicating that they voluntarily agreed to be interviewed for the explicit purposes discussed in the consent form (Figure 2.15k).

Also, the research process did not actually entail subjects individually completing a questionnaire; rather, this was a survey instrument used to collect data on individuals about to participate in a focus group, and thus the questions were individually asked of each participant by the researcher in a face-to-face interview. The survey instrument was filled out by the researcher, not the subjects. How does this new information affect the way in which you would have assessed and critiqued the questionnaire presented for your review?

Figure 2.15k   Consent Form

CONSENT FORM

for a research study examining
THE DEVELOPMENT OF AN INTEGRATED MODEL OF
OCCUPATIONAL ASSISTANCE
EMPLOYEE ASSISTANCE FOCUS GROUP PHASE

Thank you for taking the time to assist in this research study that is examining the idea of how to make the work site a healthier place. This study is being conducted by Richard Csiernik, a doctoral candidate at the University of Toronto, as one component of a doctoral dissertation. You are under no obligation to participate in the session. However, by taking part in the research you can assist in shaping programs to improve the well-being of others.

Your responses to the questionnaire and during the focus group session will remain confidential. The data collected from six (6) focus groups will be presented only in aggregate form. The individual questionnaire that you will be asked to complete should take less than five minutes of your time, while your focus group meeting should take approximately one to one and one-half hours. Your answers to the questions will be totally anonymous, with the researcher being the only person who will know your actual replies. It will not be possible to identify your specific responses in any way. If you are unsure of a question please do not hesitate to ask. If you are uncomfortable about answering a question you are under no obligation to respond. You are also free to leave the session at any time.

I have read the above statement and have been informed of the purpose of this research. By signing this consent form I still understand that my taking part in the study remains entirely voluntary and I know that I may end my participation at any time. I may also choose not to answer any question with which I am not comfortable.

_____   _____
Signature   Date

Figure 2.15l   Formal Questionnaire

TERMS

Employee Assistance Programs (EAPs) are workplace-based programs that provide assistance to employees and their family members with a wide range of problems such as alcoholism, substance abuse, family concerns, budgeting, and other related health and social issues. EAPs attempt to assist employees by providing counselling or by referring employees to counsellors or self-help groups outside the workplace.

Self-help groups are informal, voluntary, small groups that provide mutual aid. They are usually formed by peers who have come together for shared assistance in satisfying a common need, overcoming a common problem or bringing about a desired social or personal change. Self-help groups emphasize face-to-face social interactions while having members assume personal responsibility for their problems. They can provide material assistance as well as emotional support.

Workplace health promotion programs are a combination of education and activities that support positive health practices. Most programs focus on improving health by encouraging participation in a range of programs such as fitness and exercise, nutrition and eating properly, blood pressure screens, and stop-smoking programs.

In the model I am examining I am looking at the next stage in the evolution of workplace-based assistance, wellness. My definition of wellness includes physical, emotional, and social well-being.

Physical well-being may be thought of in terms of fitness, nutrition, control of substance abuse, adequate rest and sleep, and both taking care of and actively attempting to prevent any health problems from occurring.
Psychological well-being is the ability to cope in a positive way with crises that occur and with the everyday stresses that affect all of us.
Social well-being is the ability to develop and maintain healthy relationships with others, including the development of appropriate connections with friends, families, and co-workers.

EMPLOYEE ASSISTANCE FOCUS GROUP
PARTICIPANT BACKGROUND QUESTIONNAIRE

1. Organization _____
2. Years with organization _____
3. Position _____

4. Role in EAP _____

5. Union/Association Member: ( ) Yes ( ) No

6. Gender: ( ) Male ( ) Female

7. Age: ( ) Under 25   ( ) 25–34   ( ) 35–44
              ( ) 45–54   ( ) 55–64   ( ) 65+

8. Have you taken any formal courses in EAP: ( ) Yes ( ) No

   If yes, please specify what course, from whom or what institution that you took the course, and when you completed it:

Course   Institution/Source   When

THANK YOU

EMPLOYEE ASSISTANCE PROGRAM
CONTACT PERSON QUESTIONNAIRE

Date of Interview: _____

Organization: _____

SECTION A: ORGANIZATIONAL BACKGROUND INFORMATION

1. Organization Name: _____

2. Organization Function: _____

3. Workforce Size: _____

4. Male/Female Ratio: _____

5. Unionized: ( ) No *go to question 6.*

   ( ) Yes

   Union Affiliation:_____

   Local: _____   Size: _____

   Local: _____   Size: _____

   Local: _____   Size: _____

6. Medical Department: ( ) No *go to question 7.*

   ( ) Yes

   Composition:_____

SECTION B: EMPLOYEE ASSISTANCE PROGRAM INFORMATION

7. What year was the EAP begun? _____

8. How many people used it last year? _____

9. Who initiated the program:

   ( ) Management   ( ) Labour   ( ) Medical

   ( ) Joint Labour–Management Initiative ( ) Don't Know

   ( ) Other(please specify)_____

10. Did the person(s) initiating your organization's EAP have any affiliation to a self-help group such as Alcoholics Anonymous, Parents Without Partners, Stroke Recovery Association.

    ( ) Yes ( ) No ( ) Don't Know

11. What is your EAP's focus (check more than one if appropriate):
   ( ) assessment and referral   ( )treatment
   ( ) health promotion   ( )prevention
   ( ) other (please specify) _____
   _____

12. Within your Employee Assistance Program who assists troubled employees?
   1. *Volunteers Internal to the Workplace*
      ( ) a. recovering individuals (A.A. or other self-help group members)
      ( ) b. union counsellors
      ( ) c. referral agents
      ( ) d. peer counsellors
      ( ) e. self-help groups in the workplace
   2. *Professionals Internal to the Workplace*
      ( ) a. social workers
      ( ) b. psychologists
      ( ) c. occupational health nurse
      ( ) d. occupational physician
      ( ) e. human resources staff (personnel department)
      ( ) f. other counselling professional (please specify)
      _____

   3. *Professionals External to the Workplace*
      ( ) a. private practice social workers
      ( ) b. private practice psychologist
      ( ) c. multidisciplinary EAP agency
      ( ) d. consortia
      ( ) e. other (please specify)
      _____

   4. *Volunteers External to the Workplace*
      ( ) a. recovering individuals
      ( ) b. self-help groups
13. Reasons volunteers are (are not) used?
   _____

SECTION C: SELF-HELP/MUTUAL AID GROUPS IN THE WORKPLACE

Self-help groups are informal, voluntary, small groups that provide mutual aid. They are usually formed by peers who have come together for shared assistance in satisfying a common need, overcoming a common problem, or bringing about a desired social or personal change. Self-help groups emphasize face-to-face social interactions while having members assume personal responsibility for their problems. Self-help groups can provide material assistance as well as emotional support.

14. Using the above definition as your guide are there any self-help groups being used to assist troubled employees in your EAP?
   ( ) No   *end of interview.*
   ( ) Don't Know   *end of interview.*
   ( ) Yes   *which ones?*
   _____
   _____

15. Are meetings held at the worksite?
   ( ) No   *end of interview.*
   ( ) Don't Know   *end of interview.*
   ( ) Yes
16. For any self-help groups that meet on-site please state, if you know, when they meet (before, dur-ing, or after work) and how often (daily, 2–3 times a week, weekly, bi-weekly, or monthly).

Group	Meeting Time	Meeting Frequency
_____	_____	_____
_____	_____	_____
_____	_____	_____
_____	_____	_____
_____	_____	_____
_____	_____	_____
_____	_____	_____

THANK YOU

8. Research Insight

Surveys (phone, email, web, computer interactive voice response or IVR) can be a use-ful and less costly way of a reaching large numbers of participants on any number of research questions. However, like any type of research endeavour there are strengths and limitations about the end product of each approach.

Mail   **Advantages:** easy to do and cost-efficient; the cost of responding is perceived to be much higher.

Disadvantages: response rates can be low if the survey is not well designed or followed up as outlined by Dillman (2000); can also be problematic for low-literacy participants, and less probing and follow-up by interviewer.

Phone   **Advantages:** can reach a large number of participants; anonymous and flexible; rapid data collection, particularly when using comput-er-assisted devices; good for short surveys on an issue; procedures are standardized.

Disadvantages: impersonal nature of phone contact; not obtaining enough complete responses to be able to generalize results; most phones have call screening so poor response rates can result; lack of attention by participant; lengthy survey can be tiring.

Online	**Advantages:** easy to develop and easy to respond to; relatively cost-effective; less time is needed if survey is well developed; convenient for participants; anonymity increases response rates; data collection is easier with tools such as Excel and the Statistical Package for the Social Sciences (SPSS).
	Disadvantages: missing data; participants cannot be followed up with or probed deeper about issues; can be viewed as phishing online and often deleted by participants; requires much more programming by researcher to get online survey running.
Face-to-face	**Advantages:** more social interaction and increase in response rate and follow-up questions, can allow for a longer interview, non-verbal communication (body language) can be also collected; higher response rates, especially if participant lacks written or verbal skills.
	Disadvantages: is much more expensive and requires much more training of research assistants than any other approach; time-consuming; may not be a representative sample; less control of interview and environment in which interview takes place (Grinnell & Unrau, 2011).

Disadvantages of Self-Constructed Questionnaires

Regardless of which format is used, any instrument that you construct yourself will not be a valid instrument in that you have not ascertained its content validity, criterion validity, or construct validity (see Case Study 10). While this should not dissuade you from undertaking this type of research, it is an issue you should be aware of when both conducting your own work and reviewing that of others. As well, as with any questionnaire, self-constructed ones are limited by:

- the recall of participants
- the thoughtfulness of participants
- the truthfulness of participants
- the amount of time spent in responding
- the interpretation of each question's intent by participants
- the inherent bias of those who created the instrument.

9. Further Reflections

If you do value those who participate in your research and give you some of their time, you should always conclude your questionnaires the way these were, by thanking your subjects for helping you gain knowledge.

1. *What can you offer other than a thank you to people who give of their time to participate in your research?*
2. *What can you do to maximize response rates to your questionnaires?*
3. *How many drafts of a questionnaire do you anticipate writing before it is ready for use? How many drafts of each question should be written?*

10. Additional Reading

Babbie, E. (1990). *Survey research methods.* Belmont, CA: Wadsworth.

Barribeau, P., Butler, B., Corney, J., Doney, M., Gault, J., Gordon, J., . . ., & Palmquist, M. (2005). *Survey Research.* Writing@CSU. Colorado State University Department of English. http://writing .colostate.edu/guides/research/survey/

Bruck, M., Ceci, S.J., & Hembrooke, H. (1998). Reliability and credibility of young children's reports. *American Psychologist, 53,* 136–51.

Carini, R.M., Hayek, J.C., Kuh, G.D., Kennedy, J.H., & Ouimet, J.A. (2003). College student responses to web and paper surveys: Does mode matter? *Research in Higher Education Journal, 44*(1), 1–19.

Couper, M.P. (1997). Survey introductions and data quality. *Public Opinion Quarterly, 61,* 317–38.

Croteau, A.M., Dyer, L., & Miguel, M. (2010). Employee reactions to paper and electronic surveys: An experimental comparison. *IEEE Transactions on Professional Communication, 53*(3), 249–59.

Csiernik, R., & Csiernik, A. (2012). Canadian Employee Assistance Programming: An overview. *Journal of Workforce Behavioural Health, 27*(2), 200–16.

Czaja, R., & Blair, J. (2004). *Designing surveys: A guide to decisions and procedures.* Thousand Oaks, CA: Pine Forge Press.

Dillman, D.A. (1978). *Mail and telephone surveys.* New York: Kai Chen Wiley.

Dillman, D.A. (2000). *Mail and Internet surveys: The tailored design method* (2nd ed.). New York: Wiley.

Eysenbach, G., & Wyatt, J. (2002). Using the Internet for surveys and health research. *Journal of Medical Internet Research, 4*(2), e13.

Fink, A. (2005). *How to conduct surveys: A step-by-step guide* (3rd ed.). Thousand Oaks, CA: Sage.

Grinnell, R.M., & Unrau, Y.A. (2011). *Social work research and evaluation: Foundations of evidence-based practice* (9th ed.). Oxford: Oxford University Press.

Hamby, S., Sugarman, D.B., & Boney-McCoy, S. (2006). Does questionnaire design impact reported partner violence? *Violence and Victims, 21,* 507–18.

Kenagy, G. (2005). Transgender health: Findings from two needs assessment studies in Philadelphia. *Health & Social Work, 30*(1), 19–26.

Murray, P. (1999). Fundamental issues in questionnaire design. *Accident and Emergency Nursing, 7,* 148–53.

Nulty, D.D. (2008). The adequacy of response rates to online and paper surveys: What can be done? *Assessment & Evaluation in Higher Education, 33*(3), 301–14.

Peterson, R.A. (2000). *Constructing effective questionnaires.* Thousand Oaks, CA: Sage.

Rattray, J., & Jones, M.C. (2007). Essential elements of questionnaire design and development. *Journal of Clinical Nursing, 16,* 234–43.

Rubin, A., & Parrish, D. (2007). Views of evidence-based practice among faculty in master of social work programs: A national survey. *Research on Social Work Practice, 17*(1), 110–22.

Shannon, D., Kai Chenson, T., Searcy, S., & Lott, A. (2002). Using electronic surveys: Advice from survey professionals. *Practical Assessment, Research & Evaluation, 8*(1). Retrieved from http://ericae.net/pare/getvn.asp?v=8&n=1

Sue, V., & Ritter, L. (2007). *Conducting online surveys.* Thousand Oaks, CA: Sage.

Van Selm, M., & Jankowski, N.W. (2006). Conducting online surveys. *Quality & Quantity, 40*(3), 435–56.

Watt, S., Simpson, C., McKillop, C., & Nunn, V. (2002). Electronic course surveys: Does automating feedback and reporting give better results? *Assessment & Evaluation in Higher Education, 27*(4), 325–37.

Witkin, B.R., & Altschauld, J.W. (1995). *Planning and conducting needs assessments: A practical guide.* Thousand Oaks, CA: Sage.

11. Internet Resources

Questionnaire Development

Southampton Education School, "What Is a Questionnaire?":
    https://www.youtube.com/watch?v=CfEga-dr_Ww
Graham R. Gibbs, "Questionnaire Layout & Question Wording. Part 2 of 3 on Questionnaire Design":
    https://www.youtube.com/watch?v=BZLVI5zae2E
Elon University Poll, "7 Tips for Good Survey Questions":
    https://www.youtube.com/watch?v=Iq_fhTuY1hw
Elon University Poll, "A Survey in 10 Steps":
    https://www.youtube.com/watch?v=U1MYM35qUr8
TuitionKit, "Questionnaire Design":
    https://www.youtube.com/watch?v=HfGyiRBwSec

Advantages and Disadvantages of Online Surveys

Explorable, "Online Surveys":
    https://explorable.com/online-surveys

Fluid Surveys University, "Is an Online Survey Right for You? Advantages and Disadvantages of Different Survey Formats":

https://fluidsurveys.com/university/is-an-online-survey-right-for-you-advantages-and-disadvantages-of-different-survey-formats/

Inquisium, "Advantages and Disadvantages of Online Surveys":

http://survey.cvent.com/blog/market-research-design-tips-2/advantages-and-disadvantages-of-online-surveys

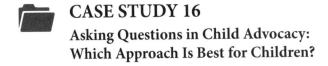

CASE STUDY 16

Asking Questions in Child Advocacy: Which Approach Is Best for Children?

1. Preamble

There has been much written in the literature about hearing the voices of children in child custody and access disputes. Yet very little has been documented about hearing the voices and practice experiences of child legal representatives and mental health professionals who may also be involved in the family justice process. One would expect that a lawyer or mental health professional for the child can provide an important independent voice about the "best interests" of the child that is not institutionally constrained, such as child welfare agencies are, or psychologically predisposed, as the parents may be. These questions need to be further explored given the serious implications for children's emotional and physical development before and after separation and/or divorce.

2. The Problem

Children who experience parental separation and divorce are a population at risk. Researchers and mental health professionals have consistently found that these children face an array of emotional, academic, physical, and behavioural difficulties. When parents cannot resolve their custody and access disputes amicably, they may request the court to order an assessment of each parent's parenting abilities and/or independent child legal representation for children. A recognized leading organization representing children in Ontario (the Office of the Children's Lawyer, Ministry of the Attorney General) has an intake process whereby they determine if a lawyer will be assigned to represent a child and the child's legal interests before the court or a clinical investigator will be assigned to evaluate the child and the family situation to make recommendations to the court about the custody of and access to the child.

Sensitivity is critical in working with any social work client population. Typically, client systems are not particularly interested in research outcomes or your need to know, which of course ultimately results in better practice. For clients, resolution of the presenting problem will almost always outweigh participating in a research project. High-conflict families are typically characterized by significant rates of litigation and re-litigation, anger and mistrust, and poor communication skills, and they also experience considerable difficulty in cooperating and negotiating child/parent issues with one another. Children of high-conflict separating and/or divorcing parents experience higher rates of psychological problems, and thus a balance between serving clients' needs and conducting appropriate and ethical research is essential.

3. The Process

Both the social science literature and research literature describe high-conflict families as multidimensional. Conflict is all but inevitable in the separation or divorce process. Many of the families experience difficulties such as poor communication, lack of trust of one another, alcohol and/or drug misuse, or abuse, and may have few problem-solving skills. When a child custody dispute comes before the court and the judge requires assistance in his or her decision making, either parent or the court can request a lawyer for the child or an investigation and report about the child and each parent's ability to meet the needs of the child. Typically, the older the child the more easily her or his views and wishes can be ascertained by legal representation, and a lawyer is assigned the case. In other cases when there are more clinical issues involved, a clinical investigator is assigned to conduct an investigation and report to the court. When a referral is made to the Office of the Children's Lawyer (OCL) it has discretion whether to assign a lawyer or a clinical investigator to the case. The OCL decisions are based primarily on the age of the child and the issues in dispute: custody and/or access.

You have been tasked with designing a qualitative questionnaire for interviewing family justice stakeholders including lawyers, clinicians, and administrators to help facilitate decision making at the intake level for the OCL, and specifically to develop clear criteria in the assignment of cases to lawyers and/or clinical investigators.

4. The Research

The organization has requested that you develop a questionnaire to assist in identifying which cases might be better assigned to a lawyer and which to a clinical investigator. Your knowledge of developmental theory and systems theory leads you to believe that the younger the child, the more difficult it would be for a lawyer to ascertain the child's wishes. In addition, children typically do not want to be caught in the middle and forced to choose between their parents. Thus, you need to examine what the literature says about these high-conflict families with a view to understanding the population and being able to assist in identifying which cases require a lawyer and which a clinical investigation. To facilitate this process, you may also want to interview lawyers and clinical investigators along with other pertinent stakeholders to understand how they do their work and what is involved in the areas of legal representation and clinical investigations of the family.

5. Questions

1. *How would you outline your research design?*
2. *How would you sample the mental health professionals, lawyers, and family justice stakeholders for this study?*
3. *What questions would you ask representatives of these three groups?*

6. Social Work Practice

Structured Interviews

A great deal of data comes from interviewing the stakeholders of a program. These interviews are sometimes referred to as key informant interviews, since the respondents usually have insider knowledge about the program and its implementation. Interviewing to collect qualitative research data can be approached in one of two broad ways. In a structured interview, the interviewer follows an interview schedule and asks questions exactly as they are worded and ordered on the schedule. In this way, interview schedules are similar to self-administered questionnaires. However, interview schedule questions are usually worded in a more conversational manner. For example, you are more likely to ask the question "How old are you?" than to say "Age." As well, the structure of an interview schedule is slightly different. Demographic information is placed at the beginning of the interview and more sensitive questions are placed near the end. This is done because asking straightforward questions that have easily retrieved answers at the beginning of the interview starts to develop rapport between interviewer and interviewee. By the time the more sensitive questions arrive there is an established relationship that will increase the likelihood that the interviewee will answer those more challenging or revealing questions. It can also be helpful to build in a sense of timing for the respondent with statements such as "I only have three more questions to ask" or "We are about halfway through the questionnaire." These statements actually appear on the questionnaire and are read out loud by the interviewer in every interview. As with self-administered questionnaires, it is also a good idea to use contingency questions to ensure respondents are not asked to answer questions that do not relate to them.

In structured interviewing the interviewer is directed not to alter the questions in any manner or to "help" a respondent answer in any way, although standardized non-directional probes such as "Can you tell me more about that?" or "Are there any other points you would like to make?" may be used to ensure a full answer to some questions. Most questions on the schedule are either in fixed-alternative form or are very brief open-ended questions to which the interviewer records the exact words of the respondent's answer. Data collected in this manner are typically intended for quantitative research designs because the approach is very standardized and objective and the data collected are often superficial and straightforward. Interviewers are trained to demonstrate a constrained level of affect because they don't want emotionality to interfere with the quality of the data. They are instructed to be professional, pleasant, and polite but not to engage the respondent in conversation concerning any of the answers they are given. Interviews replace self-administered questionnaires if respondents are illiterate or too young to read the questions or if the researchers believe they will get a higher response rate by interviewing respondents. For example, marketing surveys in shopping malls are often conducted as interviews. Think about your own reaction. Would you prefer to pick up a self-administered questionnaire at a booth at the mall or would you rather have a conversation with a live interviewer? The latter approach seems quicker, involves less hassle, and is generally more enjoyable to most, which is why it's the preferred approach in this situation.

As with self-administered questionnaires, interview schedules should be pre-tested and interviewers should have ample opportunity to practice before being sent out to collect the data. In general, researchers obtain a higher completion rate with interviews than with self-administered questionnaires, and there are typically fewer unanswered questions or "I don't know" responses. People being interviewed are engaged in a social interaction, and there are norms and expectations that come into play. When we are asked a question by another person we try to provide an answer. The tendency of interviewees to provide answers does, however, introduce a further concern: is the answer reliable? As the interview is a social situation, an answer may reflect social desirability, that is, the respondent provides the answer he or she believes to be socially acceptable to the interviewer. For example, if you are conducting research on preparedness for a possible flu epidemic, you ask the question "Do you always wash your hands after using the bathroom?" You are likely to get the answer "yes," but this answer may not reflect actual behaviour. There is no guarantee that if you asked the same question on a self-administered questionnaire you would get a more accurate answer, but when one is asked the question in person it is harder to reply with an answer that goes against social conventions. The interviewee will ascribe certain views to the interviewer based upon the latter's personal characteristics, and will provide answers that he or she perceives as acceptable to the interviewer. It is important to keep in mind, then, that the interview context may change your judgments about the reliability of the answers to your questions.

Interviewing places the interviewer in contact with the interviewee, and because of this there is the opportunity to collect additional information about respondents. Such things as the respondent's surroundings if the interview is conducted in the home, their emotional response to the questions, and their non-verbal communications can also be noted. However, there may be ethical concerns unless the respondent is told that the additional information is being gathered.

Increased response rates, a reduction in unanswered questions, and access to supplementary information are all advantages of interviewing respondents, but there are also a number of disadvantages to selecting this approach. For example, as mentioned above, the characteristics of the interviewer may influence the nature of the responses. What the interviewer is wearing, physical appearance, even features such as gender and tone of voice can all produce measurement error. This phenomenon has been well researched and is referred to as researcher reactivity.

Some questions are difficult to ask in an interview format, particularly questions that have a large number of alternative answers. By the time an interviewer has reached the end of the list of possible replies, the respondent has forgotten the options at the beginning of the list. If respondents can read, this problem can be overcome to some extent by providing respondents with a "show card" that lists the possible answers; the respondent selects an answer and then returns the card to the interviewer.

Another problem that can affect the quality of the information is that the data are filtered through the interviewer before being recorded. There is always the possibility that errors are made in recording data or interpreting answers, which is why training and supervising interviewers is a crucial component of using this approach to data collection. An additional disadvantage of interviewing is that it can be quite time-consuming and expensive. As well, when you interview a respondent you cannot offer him or her anonymity. You can assure the respondent that the information you collect will be kept confidential, but if you can connect persons to their answers then the data collection is no longer anonymous.

Naturalistic Interviewing

The second form of interviewing is referred to as naturalistic or unstructured. In this case the interviewer is attempting to conduct a natural conversation with the respondent. The interview schedule consists of a list of open-ended questions or topics that the interviewer would like to discuss with the respondent, but the order and wording of the questions are much less prescribed and rigid than in a structured interview. In some cases the interviewer has only the first or starting question identified ahead of time, and the flow of the interview is determined entirely by the respondent's answer to the first question. This approach to collecting data is more consistent with qualitative research designs. Naturalistic interviewing is also an art and requires a great deal of practice and skill to do well. It often requires that a certain level of trust develop between the participants to achieve the level of openness and comfort required to elicit a deeper level of information. As a function of their training in communications and interpersonal skills, social workers often make excellent qualitative interviewers.

In naturalistic interviewing, questions are answered by respondents using their own words, thus making the recording of answers an important consideration. An interviewer could take notes to record answers, but this makes it difficult to accurately reflect the full extent of an answer, and the act of recording may interfere with the natural conversational tone of the data collection process. Therefore, researchers employing naturalistic interviewing either audiotape or videotape interviews and then transcribe the tapes to obtain their data. The text of these conversations is then used for qualitative analysis. Respondents must be told that tape recordings are being made, for it is unethical to secretly tape research conversations. Since tapes and transcripts are artefacts of the research process, they must be treated ethically in terms of confidentiality and also in terms of retention, storage, and eventually destruction. Also, if outside transcribers are used they must agree to respect the confidentiality of the information.

As a major purpose of qualitative interviewing is to gain a deep understanding of the respondent's experience, it is not unusual for an interviewee to experience emotional reactions when answering questions. In structured interviews, used primarily in quantitative research, emotion is seen as interfering with data collection and is totally discouraged. In naturalistic interviewing the expression of emotions can provide important insight and is seen as acceptable when honestly experienced. However, the interviewer must be sensitive to the need to respond if appropriate. The interviewer may have to suspend an interview to allow the interviewee to deal with expressed emotions. In this case, the needs of the person supersede the needs of the research task.

Focus Groups

Another approach to collecting data is the group interview or focus group. This is a particularly useful approach for both needs assessment and formative evaluation projects because it brings together a number of stakeholders to discuss the topic of interest.

Focus groups are small groups of, ideally, six to eight people who are brought together to talk with the researchers. The conversation is facilitated, usually by one of the researchers, and the group's discussion is recorded for analysis through note taking and audiotape and/or videotape. Who facilitates the session is an important consideration because of the possibility that the relationship between facilitator and participants will bias the conversation. For example, it may be difficult for the director of a program to obtain objective feedback from his or her employees since the employer-employee relationship introduces a natural biasing effect.

A focus group session usually follows the format of a naturalistic interview in that the questions are open ended and the course of the discussion is often free flowing and determined by the discussants. The interviewer may have a list of topics or starting questions but is flexible as to when and how to use the questions. Focus groups are helpful in that they allow the researcher to bring together a group of stakeholders to share their thoughts, concerns, and perspectives on the issue. The group dynamic can yield information that may not come forward in an individual interview or even across a series of individual interviews. Participants in the group listen to and build upon each other's comments, providing much greater insights than would typically arise from merely conducting multiple individual interviews.

The purpose of the group discussion must be clear to participants, and attempts made to keep the group on task. Facilitators should take care not to interject their own opinions or direct the group's discussion in ways that could bias the outcome. Just as with an individual interviewer, focus group facilitators need to develop rapport and trust with the group members, and through active listening determine the best sequence of questioning. To provide useful information the focus group process needs to be well facilitated. There is a group dynamic occurring that needs to be understood and directed to obtain the best outcome. There may be domineering individuals who need to be controlled, quiet or unassertive individuals who need to be encouraged to speak up, or participants with a hidden agenda that needs to be balanced by other perspectives in the group. Facilitators must also beware of the possibility of "group think" developing during the discussion. This occurs when one perspective takes hold of the group so that participants seem to be in agreement but actually do not all share the same opinion. Some withhold their true feelings and only appear to be supportive of the predominant group opinion or dominant group members. Also, in a group setting it may be difficult to have individuals discuss sensitive issues in front of others. There are some topics that it is better to approach by interviewing individuals alone. It is also not possible for the researcher to guarantee that what is shared in the group will be kept confidential. The researcher can promise that what he or she hears in the group will not be shared with others outside the group, but cannot guarantee that other participants will hold to the same standard.

In designing your qualitative questionnaire you need to ensure trustworthiness, which is the qualitative equivalent of reliability and validity in quantitative research. To establish trustworthiness you need to address the issues of credibility, transferability, dependability, and confirmability. To confirm credibility your interviews should be substantive, one to two hours in length; be tape recorded; and then be fully transcribed. As well, similar questions could be asked in different ways to establish consistency on the part of respondents. Transferability entails keeping a journal of notes and detailed descriptions of responses, while dependability involves keeping an audit trail of all the research carried out. Finally, confirmability is the process of describing in great detail the issues and themes gathered and how this was done.

Once data collection is complete you would begin your analysis. A common approach for long interviews is to transcribe verbatim all audiotaped interviews and review for themes. Interviews can be transcribed into any word-processing software program such as WordPerfect or Microsoft Word and then be translated into text format and imported into NVivo, a software program for retrieving and sorting information. This specialized program aids in identifying text segments, attaches categories to segments, and sorts all text segments that relate to a specific category or theme.

Once analysis is complete you can interpret and present the results, which of course is an entire process in and of itself!

7. Responding to the Case

In your role of social work researcher your first step is again to conduct a thorough literature review regarding high-conflict families and the role of child legal representation and clinical investigations. You begin to construct your questionnaire based upon your findings in the literature. You know that in order to gather the most pertinent information you will also need to interview the most experienced lawyers and clinical investigators employed by the Office of the Children's Lawyer. You determine that there will be inclusion and exclusion criteria based on years of experience, gender, and geographic location.

A reasonable sample selection would be 10 lawyers and 10 clinical investigators from across the province of Ontario who have a minimum of five years of experience in this area, which allows for adequate practice experience. Along with these 20 interviews, 10 judges would be a good number to include.

Examples of pertinent questions to ask for this type of research are:

Lawyer/Clinical Investigator Questionnaire:

1. What can you tell me about your role in child legal representation? (*Prompt:* What steps and/or processes do you go through when representing children?)
2. What can you tell me about your role in clinical investigations? (*Prompt:* What steps and/or processes do you go through when gathering information for your investigation?)
3. What are the strengths and limitations of your role (independent child legal representation and/or clinical investigation)?

Stakeholder Questionnaire (Judges):

1. How helpful do you find independent child legal representation? (*Prompt:* Do you find it helpful in your decision making?)
2. How helpful do you find clinical investigations? (*Prompt:* Do you find it helpful in your decision making?)
3. In which types of cases do you find that you order one form over the other as most helpful to you in your decision making?

8. Research Insight

A significant distinguishing feature of qualitative research is that it employs an inductive reasoning process to interpret and structure the meanings that can be derived from information you collect. In qualitative research knowing is only possible through deconstructing the meanings of a phenomenon. The theoretical lens from which you approach your question, the strategies you use to conceptualize your ideas, the manner in which you collect your data, and the understanding you have regarding what is relevant all shape the process of qualitative research.

There are five fundamental approaches to qualitative research: grounded theory, ethnography, field research, phenomenology, and case study. Grounded theory is a broad-reaching approach that attempts to develop theories about the phenomena being examined based upon direct observation of the researchers and is grounded in the data collected from the field. It is inductively derived from the study of the phenomenon it represents. This leads to core theoretical concepts being identified while the data is gathered, as data collection, analysis, and theory have a reciprocal relationship. This allows linkages between the theoretical concepts and the data to occur during the actual data collection, making this a more dynamic and interactive process. As each new observation had the potential to create a new association, the process of grounded theory is an ongoing loop with new observations leading to new ideas; you do not begin with a theory and then prove it, but instead you begin with an area of study and allow what is relevant to that area of study to emerge.

Ethnography is a very time-consuming and detailed form of qualitative research. This approach entails immersing oneself in a particular social setting and observing the environment and individuals that the researcher is most interested in better understanding. It involves interpreting the processes and products of cultural behaviour. It is concerned with capturing, interpreting, and explaining the way in which people in a group, organization, community, or society as a whole live and make sense of their lives. Ethnographers document a broad array of human experiences, from belief patterns to social relationships, daily interactions and ways of living to the social and cultural understanding of health and wellness. This approach necessitates that the researcher immerse herself or himself into fieldwork via participant observation.

Critical ethnography is a variant form of ethnography with a value-laden orientation focus that challenges the status quo in order to empower individuals to have more authority, addressing unequal power relations and applying new understandings through a process of critical thinking. Having an explicitly stated value-laden orientation implies that when you conduct qualitative research from a critical ethnographic standpoint, you are imposing a value system that places any culture into a wider discourse of power relations and history, which serves an emancipatory interest. Conventional ethnography observes culture for the purpose of describing, whereas critical ethnography does so to support change. Critical ethnography takes a normative and political position as a means of invoking social consciousness and societal change.

Field research, like ethnography, was founded in the field of anthropology; however, field research offers a broader approach to qualitative research in that the researcher will literally go into the field – or in the case of social work into a community group, agency, or organization – to observe the group in its natural state. In this way, field research is akin to ethnography, since the field researchers will make extensive notes based on their direct observations. The major distinction is that field researchers will interact with research participants, becoming participant observers, rather than just observing as outsiders to the process. Field research is both a means of data collection and a theory-generating activity. As it is qualitative in nature it occurs without any type of hypothesis in place, but rather as an ongoing process.

The goal of phenomenological research is to understand how others view the world, and how this view may vary from commonly held views, by focusing on a person's subjective interpretations of what the individual experiences. Phenomenology is equal parts research philosophy and research practice. Its goal is to promote an understanding of the relationship between states of individual consciousness and social life. Phenomenological research is conducted through intensive direct interviewing of individuals to fully understand their standpoint and is more common in social work than is ethnography or field research. A goal is to become *verstehen*: which is an empathetic effort to move into the mind of another. As with all forms of qualitative research, gaining insights into the participant's subjective experiences is crucial.

The final form of qualitative research is the case study approach. Like the examples in this book, a case study presents a detailed analysis of one specific case, be it a person, group process, activity, or research dilemma.

9. Further Reflections

1. *What are the strengths and limits of each of the three data-gathering techniques described?*
2. *Which of your existing social work skills can you utilize with each of the three methods of data gathering?*
3. *What are the differences between assessing and interviewing a client and interviewing a research subject?*
4. *What are the differences between running a focus group and running a psycho-educational or support group?*

10. Additional Reading

Amato, P.R., & Keith, B. (1991b). Parental divorce and the well-being of children: A meta-analysis. *Psychological Bulletin, 110*(1), 26–46.

Bala, N. (1996). Mental health professionals in child-related proceedings: Understanding the ambivalence of the judiciary. *Canadian Family Law Quarterly, 13*, 261–312.

Bala, N., Birnbaum, R., & Bertrand, L. (2013). The role of the children's lawyers: Instructional advocate or best interests guardian? Comparing legal practice in Alberta & Ontario – Two provinces with different policies. *Family Court Review, 51*(4), 681–97.

Birnbaum, R. (2005). Hearing the voices of lawyers and clinical investigators who represent children in custody and access disputes. *Canadian Family Law Quarterly, 24*(3), 281–303.

Birnbaum, R., & Bala, N. (2010). Towards a differentiation of "high conflict" families: An analysis of social science and Canadian case law. *Family Court Review, 48*(3), 403–16.

Birnbaum, R., Bala, N., & Boyd, J.P. (2016). The Canadian experience with the Views of the Child Reports: A valuable addition to the toolbox? *International Journal of Law, Policy and the Family*. http://lawfam.oxfordjournals.org/cgi/content/full/ebw004?ijkey=AwgxmH23ZnQDLuS&keytype=ref

Birnbaum, R., & Saini, M. (2012). A scoping review of qualitative studies on the voice of the child in child custody disputes. *Childhood*, *20*(2), 260–82. http://dx.doi.org/10.1177/0907568212454148

Birnbaum, R., & Saini, M. (2012). A qualitative synthesis of children's participation in custody disputes. *Research on Social Work Practice*, *22*(4), 400–9. http://dx.doi.org/10.1177/1049731512442985

Birnbaum, R., Saini, M., McCleary, L., & Hurwitz, H. (2013). A community-based response to address the needs of high conflict separated families. *Ontario Association of Children's Aid Societies Journal, 58*(1), 15–23.

Cameron, K.A., Salazar, L.F., Bernhardt, J.M., Burgess-Whitman, N., Wingood, G.M., & DiClemente, R.J. (2005). Adolescents' experience with sex on the web: Results from online focus groups. *Journal of Adolescence*, *28*(4), 535–40.

Emery, R.E. (1999). *Marriage, divorce, and children's adjustment*. Newbury Park, CA: Sage.

Hare, F.G. (1999). Applications of Multidimensional Similarity Scaling (MDS) in evaluation research. *Children and Youth Services Review*, *21*(2), 147–66.

Ka'opua, L.S., Gotay, C.C., & Boehm, P.S. (2007). Spiritually based resources in adaptation to long-term prostate cancer survival: Perspectives of elderly wives. *Health & Social Work*, *32*(1), 29–39.

Krueger, R.A., & Casey, M.A. (2009). *Focus groups: A practical guide for applied research*. Thousand Oaks, CA: Sage.

Lewis, J.A. (2009). Redefining qualitative methods: Believability in the fifth moment. *International Journal of Qualitative Methods*, *8*(2), 1–14.

Luborsky, M. (1994). The identification and analysis of themes and patterns. In J. Gubrium & A. Snaker (Eds.), *Qualitative methods in aging research* (pp. 189–210). New York: Sage.

Madison, D.S. (2011). *Critical ethnography: Method, ethics, and performance*. Thousand Oaks, CA: Sage.

McCracken, G. (1988). *The long interview: Qualitative research methods* (Vol. 13). New York: Sage.

McDavid, J.C., & Hawthorn, L.R. (2005). *Program evaluation and performance measurement*. London: Sage.

McGuire, L.E. (2003). Using qualitative methods to evaluate a group: Does the survival skills for women program increase self-sufficiency? *Social Work with Groups*, *26*(4), 43–57.

Miles, M.B., & Huberman, A. (1994). *Qualitative data analysis*. New York: Sage.

Morgan, D. (1996). *Focus groups as qualitative research* (2nd ed.). London: Sage.

Padgett, D.K. (1998). *Qualitative methods in social work research: Challenges and rewards*. Thousand Oaks, CA: Sage.

Pecora, P.J., Dodson, A.R., Teather, E.C., & Whitteker, J.K. (1983). Assessing worker training needs: Use of staff surveys and key informant interviews. *Child Welfare*, *62*(5), 395–407.

Rutter, D., Tyrer, P., Emmanuel, J., Weaver, T., Byford, S., Hallam, A., . . ., & Ferguson, B. (2004). Internal versus external care management in severe mental illness: Randomized controlled trial and qualitative study. *Journal of Mental Health (Abingdon, England)*, *13*(5), 453–66.

Saini, M., & Shlonsky, A. (2012). *Systematic synthesis of qualitative research*. Oxford: Oxford University Press.

Sandelowski, M. (1995). Triangles and crystals: On the geometry of qualitative research. *Research in Nursing & Health, 18*, 569–74.

Sapsford, R., & Jupp, V. (2006). *Data collection and analysis* (2nd ed.). London: Sage.

Silverman, D. (2001). *Interpreting qualitative research: Methods for analysing talk, text and interaction*. Thousand Oaks, CA: Sage.

Stewart, D.W., Shamdasnai, P.N., & Rook, D.W. (2006). *Focus groups: Theory and practice*. London: Sage.

Velasquez, J.S., Kuechler, C.F., & White, M.S. (1986). Use of formative evaluation in a human services department. *Administration in Social Work, 10*(2), 67–77.

11. Internet Resources

Qualitative Research

Introduction to Qualitative Research, "Qualitative Design":
   https://www.youtube.com/watch?v=d9HgeqU8dSA
Yale, "Fundamentals of Qualitative Research Methods: What Is Qualitative Research":
   https://www.youtube.com/watch?v=wbdN_sLWl88
Danielle Giroux, "Qualitative Research Methods":
   https://www.youtube.com/watch?v=lSb9xG5f3F0

Focus Groups

Accionmutua, "Effective Focus Groups":
   http://www.sharedaction.org/contentOnly/images/httpdocs/accionmutua/pdf/AMFocusGroups.pdf
Yale, "Fundamentals of Qualitative Research Methods: Focus Groups":
   https://www.youtube.com/watch?v=cCAPz14yjd4

CASE STUDY 17
What Does It All Mean? Qualitative Interviews with Children about Their Views and Experiences of Family Justice Professionals

1. Preamble

> In serving the best interests of children, we serve the best interests of all humanity.
>
> – Carol Bellamy, former executive director of
> the United Nations Children's Fund (UNICEF)

2. The Problem

When parents separate, decisions have to be made that will have a significant impact on their children. Finding ways to include children's participation in making those decisions is often referred to as promoting "the voice of the child." There is a range of different approaches to include children in the decision making process, each with advantages and disadvantages. Consistent with the *Convention on the Rights of the Child*, the inclusion of children in the decision making process following parental separation or divorce process is emerging as a critical and controversial issue for practice, policy, and research. There is growing recognition that children have the right to participate and that their participation can result in decision making that better reflects their needs. Further, if children are authentically involved in the decision making process, their parents may be more likely to settle on a parenting plan that is not judicially determined; the benefits of a child-focused and cooperative settlement include a less expensive process, a reduction in conflict that harms children, and the promotion of a resolution that reflects the views and preferences of the children involved.

A range of different approaches that can be applied to include children in the decision making process, including child legal representation, child custody assessment, interviews by a judge, mediator, or parenting coordinator, and views of the child reports. While there is no empirical research that establishes a "best" way to engage children or how to obtain children's views and preferences, there is much advocacy by professionals acting as "gatekeepers" for children's participation. However, once you have heard, and recorded, their voices, how do you make sense of it all?

3. The Process

In Case Study 4, "Ethical Issues of Obtaining Consent to Interview Children in Post-Separation Disputes," you read about the process of obtaining ethics approval for interviewing children. However, once you have your data you have to translate the information the children provided by sorting, sifting, and organizing the data in a way that allows for interpretation and thus allows the relevant themes to emerge.

4. The Research

As stated in Case Study 4, "Ethical Issues of Obtaining Consent to Interview Children in Post-Separation Disputes," 30 children were recruited from closed family court files in three Toronto, Ontario, court locations. The sample size in qualitative research is determined by saturation of themes that emerge from the interviews (Denzin & Lincoln, 1994/2011; Mason, 2010; Saini & Shlonsky, 2012; Sandelowski, 1995). Saturation was reached as new codes/themes emerged. Journaling was also conducted by the researcher, which included observations and reflections of the interviews as suggested by an audit trail (Charmaz, 2006; Fossey, Harvey, McDermott, & Davidson, 2002). The interviews were audiotaped and transcribed verbatim.

5. Questions

A semi-structured interview guide was used and each child was asked to reflect on the following questions:

1. *What do you remember about your parents' separation? What was it like for you?* (Prompt: *emotionally/academically/behaviourally*)?
2. *How did you find out about the plans that were made for your care (i.e., did parents, your lawyer/social worker, the judge tell you)? What do you think would be best way for children to learn about the arrangements for their care?*
3. *How were you involved in decisions your parents made about living apart? What do you think would be the best way to be involved or not?*
4. *Did plans for your care change over time? How were you involved in decision making about the changes?*
5. *What can you tell me about your involvement/participation in the process? (Did you feel heard/understood, were your wishes put forward, who told you about the final decision?)*

6. *What did you find helpful about being involved in the process (legal, legal/social work, judicial interview, child custody assessment)? What was not helpful?*
7. *Is there anything else that you would like to say or ask me about?*

What would you do in order to make sense of the hundreds of pages of qualitative data collected over 40 hours of taped interviewing from the respondents?

6. Social Work Practice

A major challenge of qualitative research and analysis is that, given the amount of data available, there are no exact rules, formulas, or tests that can be generally or universally applied. Regardless of which approach you adopt the first step is data reduction. In order to begin to understand the meaning of qualitative data you need to develop codes and categories and sort all the transcribed text into categories. Coding is simply the process of organizing and sorting your data. Codes serve as a way to label, compile, and organize data. The codes you develop allow you to summarize and synthesize your data. In linking data collection and interpreting the data, coding becomes the basis for developing the analysis. An inductive approach is one standard manner in which to develop codes from the data, rather than using a pre-existing coding frame, which is the norm with grounded theory. This is done through open, axial, and selective coding (Corbin & Strauss, 1990; Grinnell & Unrau, 2011; Saini & Shlonsky, 2012). Open coding consists of developing the categories of information, axial coding refers to the interconnectedness of the categories, and selective coding is building the story that connects the categories. In open coding, documents or other field notes can be used to support the text.

For example, a 12-year-old child is talking about her parents' separation and the impact it had on her. She states, "I could not concentrate at school and always cried during the day." In another part of the interview, she says, "I felt scared as I did not know what would happen next."

The first step is to identify categories and meaning in both of those statements and explore the similarities and differences in their tone and texture. The two statements can be coded initially as loss of control or being scared. The court documents may also support these codes, as the child's teacher reported that she cried all day as she did not know what would happen next in her life. Constant comparative analysis arose from grounded theory methodology (see Case Study 16). It involves examining one piece of data – be it an interview, a statement, or a theme – and comparing it with all others that may be similar or different in order to develop conceptualizations of the possible relations between various pieces of data. Its purpose is to find patterns and commonalities in the data, typically using pre-existing or emergent theory against which to compare the new data. In contrast, phenomenological data analysis approaches look for the underlying structure or essence of the experience through intensive study of individual cases. For example, using the above statement from the 12-year-old, are the two statements similar or dissimilar? What is the storyline?

A phenomenological approach purposefully avoids comparisons and instead focuses on the detail of the lived experience of the participant(s) in order to generate new descriptions and conceptualizations. The process entails immersing yourself in the data to produce rich description of the deeper meaning of the phenomenon you are examining. For example, using the above statement from the 12-year-old would focus on how this child is experiencing her parents' separation and divorce. Her experience is feeling scared.

Ethnographic analysis uses an iterative process in which ideas arising from involvement with the research participants in their natural setting are transferred into a written format. The process involves sorting through all of the information you have collected in order to detect and interpret thematic categories, search for inconsistencies and contradictions, and generate conclusions about what is happening and why.

A final area of qualitative analysis is narrative and discourse analysis. Human experience is greatly shaped and transformed through linguistic representation. The primary tools of social work itself are verbal and written communication. Subjective life experiences take on distinct meaning once they are shared, whether verbally, in writing, through artistic imagery, or by text. Narrative analysis is a strategy that recognizes the extent to which the stories we tell provide insights about our lived experiences. In comparison, discourse analysis views speech not as a direct representation of human experience, but rather as an explicit linguistic tool constructed and shaped by numerous social or ideological influences. The focus of discourse analysis is to attempt to understand what is represented through the ways individuals communicate ideas.

Another applied example of qualitative analysis was presented by Maykut and Morehouse (1994), who built upon Glaser and Strauss's (1967) constant comparative method. They began by recording each interview they conducted and then transcribing each verbatim. Next they scanned the data several times using a line-by-line analysis, paying attention to recurrent and important keywords or phrases used by the participants. Each one of these ideas and concepts was coded as a unit of meaning. Each unit of meaning was then compared to all other units of meaning. Themes and concepts that overlapped were combined. A prominent idea, word, or phrase was selected and written on an index card. This word/phrase became the first provisional category. A second prominent idea, word, or phrase was then selected and written on another index card.

If the second data card looked or felt like the meaning of the first card, it was included under the first provisional category. If the second data card did not fit the first provisional category, it was placed under another provisional category. As new themes were identified they were matched to existing provisional categories, but if they did not fit, a new category was created and named as needed. After six to eight cards were accumulated in a category, a rule of inclusion was written to serve as the basis for including or excluding subsequent data cards in the category. Additional data cards that satisfied the rules were included and those that did not were categorized elsewhere. Data analysis continued until all data cards were categorized into a substantive category and overlap was reduced. The researchers then analysed the relationships and patterns across the provisional categories, identifying salient themes. This process was strengthened as there were multiple persons involved in the process working independently. The list of units can then be compared to determine which themes are prominent. This last step is valuable for all forms of qualitative data analysis as multiple perspectives enhance credibility, dependability, and confirmability of the data.

There are many different coding approaches. Zhang and Wildemuth (2009) provide an example of content analysis. Their process involves eight systemic and transparent procedures for processing data:

1. All interviews must be audio recorded and transcribed verbatim.
2. The unit of analysis is defined by identifying individual themes and expressions of ideas within each individual transcript.
3. Next, homogeneous categories are developed along with a coding theme.
4. The clarity and consistency of coding is tested by examining sample data. If required the coding will be revised using an iterative process until sufficient coding consistency is achieved.
5. At this point all transcriptions can be coded in an iterative fashion. New themes and concepts can be added as they emerge.
6. The data is then rechecked for coding consistency.
7. At this point conclusions can be drawn by identifying relationships between categories, uncovering patterns, and testing categories against the full range of data.
8. The final step is to present the method and analytic process used in analysing the data.

Yet another option is the interpretative phenomenological approach (IPA), which can be applied to both individual interviews and focus group data (Palmer, Larkin, de Visser, & Fadden, 2010). There is no one set method of working with data in IPA; rather it involves a set of common principles, moving from the specific views of one person reviewing the data to a shared perspective. IPA analysis is also iterative and inductive, beginning by reflecting on the preconceptions of those conducting the analysis. The analysis itself involves line-by-line coding of the experiential claims, concerns, and understanding of each participant focusing intently on the words used. Once this is complete, identification of emergent themes occurs followed by a dialogue among those examining the information about what the themes might mean for participants in the context of the research question, leading to the development of a more interpretative account of the information.

Palmer et al. (2010, pp. 104–5) offer this example to illustrate the specific steps involved in their protocol:

1. Objects of Concern and Experiential Claims
    a. pick out experiential claims and concerns as they appear in the transcript
    b. summarize these and sort into emergent patterns
2. Positionality
    a. explore the role played by facilitators, keeping track of questions, permissions, encouragements, redirections, and other verbal and non-verbal cues
    b. explore the function of statements made by respondents (What is their perspective/stance?)
3. Roles and Relationships
    a. examine references to other people. What roles and relationships are described? What sorts of meanings and expectations are attributed to these relationships?
    b. What are understood to be the consequences of these?
4. Organization and Systems
    a. examine references to organizations and systems. How are they described? What sorts of meanings and expectations are attributed to these?
    b. What are understood to be the consequences of these?
5. Stories
    a. examine the stories told by participants: look at the structure, genre, imagery, and tone
    b. What does each story achieve? How do participants support or impede each other to share their experiences?
6. Language

Throughout stages 1–5, monitor language use, paying particular attention to use of metaphor, euphemism, and idioms. Consider:

    a. Patterns (repetition, jargon, stand-out words and phrases)

    b. Context (impact on language used, descriptions of feelings/emotive language, jargon and explanation of technical terms, impact of facilitator)

    c. Function (How/why is certain language used? Is it employed to emphasize a point, to shock, to provoke agreement or disagreement, to amuse/lighten the tone?)

7. Adaptation of Emergent Themes (for Focus Group Analysis)

Return to the emergent themes from step 1b and adapt them according to the work done subsequently. Answering the following questions will help with this process:

    a. What experiences are being shared?

    b. What are individuals doing by sharing their experiences?

    c. How are they making those comments/stories meaningful to one another?

    d. What are they going as a group?

    e. What are the consensus issues?

    f. Where is there conflict? How is this managed/resolved?

8. Integration of Multiple Cases (for Focus Group Analysis)

Where more than one focus group has taken place, integrate the work done with each to build up an overall analysis of the topic you are investigating. Data should be checked to ensure sufficient homogeneity between focus groups to allow for successful integration.

To draw the analysis to completion:

a. Pick out commonalities and distinct differences between groups, drawing out superordinate themes.

b. Frequently revisit the transcripts to check themes in relation to original claims to assist in ensuring accuracy.

c. Consider the analysis in the wider context of existing relevant theories, models, and explanations.

7. Responding to the Case

In the case discussed, three child custody assessments were reviewed that described the children's experiences during the dispute. Interrelationships (axial coding, such as looking at new ways after the open coding) examine the context, causal conditions that were present and helped develop a visual portrayal from the overarching themes (see Figure 2.17a). From this diagram, you can see higher-order themes (protectionist views, liberationist views, equal voice) and continue to unpack these themes to uncover more meanings.

Figure 2.17a   Children's Experiences with Family Justice Professionals

Within qualitative research, knowledge, assumptions, and interpretations of the data can have very different meanings for the researcher as well as the children. One way of maintaining awareness of this potential challenge is to keep the codes as close as possible to the data. For example, one child who responded to the question about what she remembered about her parents' separation stated, "I knew she [mother] could not look after us and as much as I wanted to stay with her, it is better with my father" (Birnbaum, Bala, & Cyr, 2011, p. 409). That statement was coded as "children's views and preferences can provide important contributions towards a parenting plan" (Code 001, see Table 2.17a).

Another way of capturing the themes and coding is through a visual representation (see Figure 2.17b; Birnbaum & Saini, 2012).

The raw data from the transcripts is further organized into the codes using specially designed software for qualitative analysis such as NVivo, Ethnograph, Ask.Sam, NUD*IST, and ATLIS. Once the data is entered into a program it is critical that checking and re-checking of the codes is done to allow more familiarity with the data and with the tightness of fit of raw data to codes. While the whole process is very detailed and refined over and over again as the researcher becomes immersed in the different meanings, patterns begin to emerge as children's lived experiences are categorized as both risks and benefits (see Table 2.17b; Birnbaum & Saini, 2012).

8. Research Insight

What can occur in qualitative data analysis – from the words spoken during the interview or focus group process to the actual sorting, coding, and analysing of the data – is that participant's voices (children's in this case study) can be heard in a very powerful way that can provide important practice, policy, and research implications. Common themes emerged during this process that reflected the strength and resiliency of children during times of parental separation, which tend to be lost or at the very least minimized by family justice professionals and their parents.

Table 2.17a   Codes Developed with Each Transcript

Participant	Number of Codes
001	100
002	25
003	10
004	20
005	8
006	2
007	5
008	2
009	2
010	2
011	4
012	1
013	1

Figure 2.17b   Visual Representation of Coding

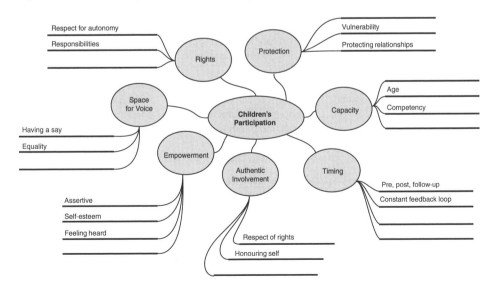

Table 2.17b   Risks, Benefits, and Considerations for Children's Participation

Theme	Risks	Benefits	Considerations
Democratic	Children's views are considered but not given equal weight in the decision making process. Attempts to include children's views can further marginalize them from the process when these views are not given due weight in accordance with their views and preferences.	Children's views and preferences can provide important contribution to the applicability and relevance of parenting plans. Providing space for equal voice during and after separation and divorce has the benefit of keeping children informed about the process of the separation and helps them to look towards the future.	Children should have equal voice about issues that concern them, including parenting arrangements, routines, and relationships with both parents. Children want to be included in decisions that impact their lives; therefore, space should be created to foster this participation.
Rights	Children generally want the right to have contact with both parents, but this may not be in their interest if there are situations of family violence. Children's rights can be compromised if they are coerced and unable to express their rights independent from their parents.	Children benefit from knowing that they have rights within a context where so much control has been taken away by the separation. Exercising rights provide children with the sense of empowerment, self-esteem, and autonomy.	Children should be heard in all cases of separation and divorce. There should be a distinction between the right to be heard and the right to make a choice.
Protection	A protectionist stance can smother their ability to express their views and preferences. Not paying enough attention to safety issues can place children in a difficult situation.	Protecting children from harm can help them better adjust to the separation process. Protecting children from loyalty conflicts can help protect important relationships and minimize the vulnerabilities caused by the exposure to these conflicts.	By mitigating protection concerns, children are better able to freely express their views and preferences while protecting their relationships with their parents.
Capacity	Children may not have the maturity and capacity to state views and preferences that are in their best interests.	Children can express their views in age- and development-relevant ways so that they are included in the decision making process.	Including children's views and preferences should be consistent with children's ages and stages of development.

Table 2.17b   (*continued*)

Theme	Risks	Benefits	Considerations
Authentic Involvement	Providing superficial credence to children's views can further marginalize them from the decision making process.	Children benefit when they feel that their views and preferences are genuinely considered by adults.	Children should be co-creators of parenting plans, and they should share responsibility in making these decisions.
Timing	Involving children too late in the separation process can impact their right to have a say in all aspects of the parenting plan.	When children are told about the separation earlier rather than later, they generally feel more a part of the decision making process.	Children should be provided with constant feedback about the separation process and should be informed about the process so they can make informed views about the situation.
Methods	Children's views by third parties can distort the translation of these views. Children are sometimes unaware of what happens when they share their views with professionals who do not provide follow-up.	Methods of representing children's views and preferences can help to ensure children's views are considered within adult-focused models for decision making within family court procedures.	Children should be informed about the court process, the limits of confidentiality, the purpose of providing their views, and the weight these views will have on the overall outcomes.

There is no question that researchers need to be sensitive to children's experiences while the children report on the most intimate, emotionally laden aspects of their lived experiences. This of course is the case with any marginalized or oppressed population you interact with during the course of your qualitative research. Equally important is that the researcher must adhere to the highest ethical concerns of (1) consent and assent; (2) the obligation to protect children/vulnerable clients from harm while also respecting their rights; and (3) meeting the challenge of ensuring that children/vulnerable clients have equal access to research initiatives and the potential benefits that accrue. Finally, it is important to remember that not everyone wants or need to be interviewed about their experiences and that respect for the individual's right to be heard or not must come before all else in conducting any type of research.

9. Further Reflections

What emerged from this study was that children want and need to be heard. There is no one method (child legal representation, judicial interviews, views of the child reports, or child custody assessments) that is superior. In fact, what we learn is that children need different methods at different times throughout the process – an important message when working with any group. Choice, opportunity, and availability of resources are fundamental to the process.

10. Additional Reading

Birnbaum, R., Bala, N., & Cyr, F. (2011). Children's experiences with family justice professionals and judges in Ontario and Ohio. *International Journal of Law, Policy and the Family*, *25*(3), 398–422.

Birnbaum, R., & Saini, M. (2012). A qualitative synthesis of children's participation in custody disputes. *Research on Social Work Practice*, *22*(4), 400–9. http://dx.doi.org/10.1177/1049731512442985

Charmaz, K. (2006). *Constructing grounded theory: A practical guide through qualitative analysis. Introducing Qualitative Methods series* (1st ed.). Oxford: Blackwell Publishers.

Corbin, J., & Strauss, A. (1990). Grounded theory research: Procedures, canons, and evaluative criteria. *Qualitative Sociology*, *13*(1), 3–21.

Creswell, J.W. (2014). Qualitative methods. In *Research design: Qualitative, quantitative, and mixed methods approaches* (4th ed.) (pp. 183–214). Thousand Oaks, CA: Sage.

Cutcliffe, J.R. (2005). Adapt or adopt: Developing and transgressing the methodological boundaries of grounded theory. *Journal of Advanced Nursing*, *51*, 421–8. http://dx.doi.org/10.1111/j.1365-2648.2005.03514.x

Denzin, N., & Lincoln, Y. (2011). *The Sage handbook of qualitative research*. Thousand Oaks, CA: Sage. (Original work published 1994).

Fossey, E., Harvey, C., McDermott, F., & Davidson, L. (2002). Understanding and evaluating qualitative research. *Australian and New Zealand Journal of Psychiatry*, *36*(6), 717–32.

Glaser, B.G., & Strauss, A.L. (1967). *The discovery of grounded theory*. Hawthorne, NY: Aldine Publishing.

Grinnell, R.M., & Unrau, Y.A. (2011). *Social work research and evaluation: Foundations of evidence-based practice* (9th ed.). Oxford: Oxford University Press.

Mason, M. (2010). Sample size and saturation in PhD studies using qualitative interviews. *Forum Qualitative Sozialforschung/Forum: Qualitative. Social Research*, *11*(3), 8. Retrieved from http://nbn-resolving.de/urn:nbn:de:0114-fqs100387

Palmer, M., Larkin, M., de Visser, R., & Fadden, G. (2010). Developing an interpretative phenomenological approach to focus group data. *Qualitative Research in Psychology*, *7*(2), 99–121.

Saini, M., & Shlonsky, A. (2012). *Systematic synthesis of qualitative research*. Oxford: Oxford University Press.

Sandelowski, M. (1995). Focus on qualitative methods: Sample size in qualitative research. *Research in Nursing & Health*, *18*, 179–83.

Zhang, Y., & Wildemuth, B.M. (2009). Qualitative analysis of content. In B.M. Wildemuth (Ed.), *Applications of social research methods to questions in information and library science* (pp. 308–19). Westport, CT: Libraries Unlimited.

11. Internet Sources

Canada, Department of Justice, Publications:
   http://www.justice.gc.ca/eng/fl-df/pub.html
CAFCASS, "Research at CAFCASS":
   https://www.cafcass.gov.uk/contact-us/research.aspx
UNICEF Canada, "About the Convention on the Rights of the Child":
   http://www.unicef.ca/en/policy-advocacy-for-children/about-the-convention-on-the-rights-of-the-child
British Colombia, "Parent Guide to Separation and Divorce":
   http://parents.familieschange.ca/dealing-with-change/childrens-rights-and-responsibilities
Library of Congress, "Children's Rights: International and National Laws and Practices":
   http://www.loc.gov/law/help/child-rights/
Better Evaluation, "Coding Part 2: Thematic Coding":
   http://betterevaluation.org/resources/guides/coding_part_2

CASE STUDY 18
Q & Q: Employing Both a Qualitative and a Quantitative Approach

1. Preamble

The debate between quantitative and qualitative researchers as to which is the superior methodological approach has gone on for years, and more than likely will continue to be argued. Historically the debate has revolved around the competing paradigms or world views of positivists (rationalist position) versus constructionists (naturalist position). More recently, the debate has shifted to investigating the different stances on the nature of reality and ways of knowing that distinguish these two paradigms. Each contains distinctive traditions and theories of knowing that underwrite different research designs, data collection techniques, and approaches to ensuring data quality.

2. The Problem

Your local child welfare agency is yet again attempting to evaluate the impact of changing service technologies on their social work staff. Specifically, the provincial government, which funds the agency, wishes to know how effective the mandated risk assessment tool is in helping or hindering social workers working with children and families.

3. The Process

The agency has undergone many different evaluation processes in the last few years. Most of the early studies used a quantitative approach, while the more recent ones have tended to use an exclusively qualitative process. However, in none of the evaluations have the workers themselves been given much opportunity to present their stories or discuss their direct observations. The agency has just spent nearly $1 million on improving its computers so that its social workers have state-of-the-art technology, and has begun yet another evaluation process to assess the impact of technology on practice efficiency.

4. The Research

As neither an exclusively quantitative approach nor an exclusively qualitative approach has led to any definitive answers in the previous evaluations, the latest set of evaluators, led by you, decides to incorporate both into the research design. The two questions that the agency needs answered so that they can prepare a report for their provincial funding body are:

i. What is the impact of information technology on social workers and their ability to complete their duties? Consider both people and computers and how the two interact.
ii. Does the use of technology facilitate or hinder social workers' abilities to work with children and families?

5. Questions

1. *How will you design the research study incorporating both quantitative and qualitative approaches so that a more comprehensive answer to the two questions posed can be provided?*
2. *What types of research designs will you consider as possibilities to answer the two distinct questions?*

6. Social Work Practice

Post-Positivism versus Interpretivism

Research can most broadly be grouped into one of two methodological approaches: quantitative and qualitative. Quantitative methodology is based in what philosophers refer to as post-positivism. People who accept this interpretation believe that there is an external reality, and while we cannot comprehend all of it, within certain methodological constraints a researcher can objectively stand outside a phenomenon of interest and objectively measure it. Quantitative methodology includes techniques associated with scientists: research involving experiments and surveys. Most of the physical sciences and their methods were developed from this philosophical perspective.

The alternative perspective, interpretivism or constructivism, suggests reality is socially constructed and experientially based. People who accept this interpretation believe that scientists can never totally separate themselves from a phenomenon of interest since their observations of a phenomenon are influenced by their personal construction of it. People who hold this view of reality reject positivistic methods and have developed a research approach more in line with their philosophical perspective. This is the qualitative approach and is built upon the assumption that is it impossible for a researcher to be totally objective. Research is acknowledged as a social process between an inquirer and another person of interest to the inquirer. The methodology of this approach has been developing over the past 40 years and includes such techniques as ethnography, social history, and grounded theory. Qualitative research contains very little measurement and often none, but instead depends upon a deep engagement with the topic of interest, frequently through extended observation and conversation.

Comparing Qualitative and Quantitative Research Approaches

At first, traditional science did not endorse qualitative research, but after years of extended dialogue and debate there has been a coming together of perspectives. It has generally been agreed, at least in social work, that one approach is not necessarily better than the other, and that both have a role to play in developing our understanding of a very complex world. Both approaches have standards of quality and rigour and have preferred methodological techniques. As a postmodern social worker, you appreciate the fact that there is no one absolute way in which to contextualize the world. As a postmodern social work researcher, you must therefore equally appreciate that there is no one best way of doing research. Thus, there really is no debate about which is superior, qualitative or quantitative research – both are not only equally valid but offer richness and depth to the many social work research questions that need to be posed. As outlined in Tables 2.18a and 2.18b, both approaches provide information that allows us to interpret reality, and together they provide a much richer evidence-based foundation from which to practise social work.

Table 2.18a   Comparing Quantitative and Qualitative Research

Criterion	Quantitative Term	Qualitative Term
Role of theory	Deductive; testing of theory	Inductive, generating theory
Ontological orientation	Objectivism	Constructionism
Epistemological orientation	Natural science model	Interpretivism
Goal of investigation	Prediction, confirmation	Understanding, description, discovery

Table 2.18b   Quantitative and Qualitative Research Equivalents

Criterion	Quantitative Term	Qualitative Term	Qualitative Techniques Used
Truth value	Internal validity	Credibility	Prolonged engagement Persistent observation Triangulation Peer debriefing Negative case analysis Referential adequacy Member checks
Applicability	External validity	Transferability	Thick description Reflexive journal
Consistency	Reliability	Dependability – how clear is the research process?	Audit trail Reader knows the process that the researcher followed Reflexive journal
Neutrality	Objectivity	Confirmability – are the themes supported?	Quotes, case descriptions, and examples support the themes, ideas, and concepts Reader matches the themes with the quotes

Qualitative Techniques

As qualitative research relies heavily upon narratives with limited use of numbers, additional rigour has been devoted to techniques used to establish the trustworthiness, applicability, and consistency of the data collected. There are 10 particular processes employed to ensure the credibility, transferability, dependability, and confirmability of the data collected through qualitative research.

Prolonged Engagement. In qualitative data collection, intensive involvement is expected to occur with participants. The researcher is expected to develop an in-depth knowledge of the culture – spending an extended period of time in the setting getting to know and understand the participants and their standpoints – in order to manage the threats to trustworthiness. Prolonged engagement provides scope to the qualitative research process.

Persistent Observation. Qualitative interviewing should be a lengthy process, with persistent observation relating to the depth of the data collection. Interviews generally take one to two hours in establishing the parameters and thoroughly discussing the themes of the study. There can also be more than one interview conducted if needed.

Triangulation. While not exclusive to qualitative research, triangulation is a process that qualitative researchers should include in their research protocol. Triangulation is simply ensuring that there are multiple data sources used to explore the same issue, be they interviews, focus groups, journal notes, transcripts, historic documents, or case notes. Triangulation is an approach to data analysis that synthesizes data from multiple sources, in so doing enhancing the credibility of the findings.

Peer Debriefing. Peer debriefing is a process used to enhance the credibility of qualitative research. It is the interaction of co-investigators, research assistants, and other team members to review the ideas emerging from the research and to seek feedback from each other on the findings in order to obtain a more accurate interpretation of the data.

Negative Case Analysis. When conducting qualitative research, the researcher and entire research team also need to look for exceptions to the emerging themes both in the data and in the literature. This is done to determine if the negative cases can provide an equally if not more credible explanation for the phenomenon being studied. Negative case analysis can also aid in revising, broadening, and confirming the patterns emerging from the data analysis.

Referential Adequacy. This relates to the fact that the themes and ideas emerging from the data can be found in different or multiple sources, including but not limited to the audiotapes and transcripts of the interviews or focus groups held.

Member Checks. This is either a formal or informal process where findings are presented to a lay audience, for example the parents of children in a study, to determine if the themes make sense to them and resonate with their experience.

Thick Description. In qualitative research all aspects of the process need to be described in detail. Thick description entails the detailed discussion of both the phenomenon being examined and the context within which the phenomenon occurs. Thus, the sample is well described, as are the time, location, and other pertinent features of the research process, and not only the information directly obtained from study participants.

Reflexive Journal. In qualitative research there needs to be continuous formal and informal checking of the data. Qualitative researchers should make extensive notes during the course of their work. These notes should be added to upon reading and re-reading each transcript, with additional memos and notes set down during the analysis phase to outline and document decisions made during this stage of the research. A qualitative researcher should always have access to this reflexive journal, adding to it and reflecting upon it through the entire research process.

Audit Trail. A social worker engaged in qualitative research should make extensive research field notes, have a detailed interview guide, tape all interviews or interactions with study participants, and have transcripts available to illustrate the process in which he or she engaged. As well, there should be notes indicating the process of analysis, the process used to reduce the data, and how categories were constructed. An audit trail should be able to highlight the rationale of the entire qualitative research process from the development of the first questions to the final analysis of the data and writing of the report.

7. Responding to the Case

After considerable discussion with fellow students and your professor, you decide to use a survey design incorporating both qualitative and quantitative data collection techniques to capture the social workers' thoughts on their satisfaction with the present technology. In addition, you want to ask the social workers whether they believe technology helps or hinders their work with families. Using Table 2.18b, you begin the process of organizing your methodology to ensure you have captured criteria for both reliability and validity in your design.

You send out your requests for participation to all child welfare agencies in the province. From those that respond, you select three social workers in each office to interview. The quantitative component of the survey contains structured questions such as:

Please answer the following questions by rating them on the following five-point Likert scale:

1. Not at all helpful
2. Somewhat helpful
3. Helpful
4. Very helpful
5. Extremely helpful

1. Do you believe that the use of the risk assessment tool helps you in your decision making?
2. Do you find that the new technologies have helped you in your work with families?
3. Do you find that case consultation helps you in your work with families?

The qualitative questions posed are more open ended, seeking to obtain more detailed information:

4. What can you tell me about the use of the risk assessment tool?
5. Have you found that the tool facilitates or hinders your work?
6. What would you find to be the most useful to you in your work with these families?

Combining results from both qualitative and quantitative questions makes possible a broader interpretation of this and any other issue.

8. Research Insight

Mixed methods research entails, by definition, mixed method data analysis. While quantitative data analysis, which will be examined in greater depth in Case Studies 21–23, can be more intimidating, qualitative data analysis is typically far more time-consuming, as examined in Case Study 17.

9. Further Reflections

1a. Which approach to research are you more drawn to, qualitative or quantitative? Why?
1b. How does this relate to your ontological stance (Case Study 1)?
2a. What are the advantages and limitations of using a mixed methods approach to answering your research question?
2b. Can the two approaches ever be equally balanced, or is it more likely that one approach will be dominant?
3.   Why is triangulation such a critical concept for social work research?

10. Additional Reading

Campbell, D., & Stanley, J. (1963). *Experimental and quasi-experimental designs.* Chicago: Rand McNally.

Casebeer, A.L., & Verhoef, M.J. (1997). Combining qualitative and quantitative research methods. *Chronic Diseases in Canada, 18*(3), 130–5.

Creswell, J.W. (2012). *Qualitative inquiry and research design: Choosing among five approaches.* Thousand Oaks, CA: Sage.

Deren, S., Oliver-Velez, D., Finlinson, A., Robles, R., Andia, J., Colon, H.M., . . ., & Shedlin, M. (2003). Integrating qualitative and quantitative methods: Comparing HIV-related risk behaviours among Puerto Rican drug users in Puerto Rico and New York. *Substance Use & Misuse, 38*(1), 1–24. http://dx.doi.org/10.1081/JA-120016563.

Johnson, R.B., Onwuegbuzie, A.J., & Turner, L.A. (2007). Towards a definition of mixed methods research. *Journal of Mixed Methods Research, 1*(2), 112–33. http://dx.doi.org/10.1177/1558689806298224.

Kuhn, T.S. (1970). *The structure of scientific revolutions* (2nd ed.). Chicago: University of Chicago Press.

Kushner, K., & Morrow, R. (2003). Grounded theory, feminist theory, critical theory: Towards theoretical triangulation. *Advances in Nursing Science, 26*(1), 30–43. http://dx.doi.org/10.1097/00012272-200301000-00006.

Leech, N.L., Dellinger, A.B., Brannagan, K.B., & Tanaka, H. (2010). Evaluating mixed research studies: A mixed methods approach. *Journal of Mixed Methods Research, 4*(1), 17–31. http://dx.doi.org/10.1177/1558689809345262.

Mason, M. (2010). Sample size and saturation in PhD studies using qualitative interviews. *Forum Qualitative Sozialforschung/Forum: Qualitative. Social Research, 11*(3), 8. Retrieved from http://nbn-resolving.de/urn:nbn:de:0114-fqs100387

Maykut, P., & Morehouse, R. (1994). *Beginning qualitative research: A philosophic and practice guide.* London: Routledge.

Miles, M.B., & Huberman, A.M. (1984). *Qualitative data analysis: A sourcebook of new methods.* Newbury Park, CA: Sage.

Morgan, D.L. (2007). Paradigms lost and pragmatism regained: Methodological implications of combining qualitative and quantitative methods. *Journal of Mixed Methods Research, 1*(1), 48–76. http://dx.doi.org/10.1177/2345678906292462.

Padgett, D.K. (1998). *Qualitative methods in social work research: Challenges and rewards.* Thousand Oaks, CA: Sage.

Silverman, D. (2005). *Doing qualitative research.* Thousand Oaks, CA: Sage.

Stricker, G. (1992). The relationship of research to clinical practice. *American Psychologist, 47*(4), 543–549. http://dx.doi.org/10.1037/0003-066X.47.4.543.

Stricker, G. (1997). Are science and practice commensurable? *American Psychologist, 52*(4), 442–448. http://dx.doi.org/10.1037/0003-066X.52.4.442.

Stricker, G., & Trierweiler, S.J. (1995). The local clinical scientist: A bridge between science and practice. *American Psychologist, 50*(12), 995–1002. http://dx.doi.org/10.1037/0003-066X.50.12.995.

Thorne, S. (2000). Data analysis in qualitative research. *Evidence-Based Nursing, 3*(3), 68–70. http://dx.doi.org/10.1136/ebn.3.3.68.

11. Internet Resources

Qualitative Data Analysis

Eductech Wiki, "Methodology Tutorial – Qualitative Data Analysis":
http://edutechwiki.unige.ch/en/Methodology_tutorial_-_qualitative_data_analysis

PR Post, "An Example of How to Perform Open Coding, Axial Coding and Selective Coding":
https://prpost.wordpress.com/2013/07/22/an-example-of-how-to-perform-open-coding-axial-coding-and-selective-coding/

C. Taylor and G.R. Gibbs, "How and What to Code":
http://onlineqda.hud.ac.uk/Intro_QDA/how_what_to_code.php

Triangulation

Danny G., "Triangulation in Qualitative Research Podcast – Short Version":
https://www.youtube.com/watch?v=aTEbA2LZaIg

B2B whiteboard, "What Is Triangulation (Qualitative Research)?":
https://www.youtube.com/watch?v=DPOhrdBGsLc

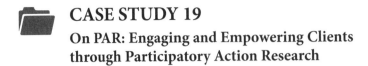

CASE STUDY 19
On PAR: Engaging and Empowering Clients through Participatory Action Research

1. Preamble

Social work research can be a valuable component of your practice as an agent of change. It can be a means of empowerment for your clients, and the products of research can be effective instruments for social justice. The process of research and the outcomes produced have the capacity to become the tools you purposefully select to achieve community change and improve social conditions, especially when you value your clients as much as you do your expert knowledge.

2. The Problem

Homelessness is an increasingly pressing social, economic, and political concern. While there is much diversity among those who are homeless, and the factors that lead to homelessness are becoming clearer, particularly the role of poverty, there remain those who are still blamed for their homelessness and who wear the label "hard to house." Many of those who wear this brand also have mental health issues. Julia was given a psychiatric diagnosis as a teenager and has had ongoing contact with the mental health system for over 40 years. She has been street engaged most of her adult life and has experienced the risks that come with that, including unstable relationships, sexual assault, incarceration, hunger, and more than one case of hypothermia. However, she was not one of the invisible homeless that exist in all communities; she was loud, she was flamboyant, and she made people uncomfortable, partly because she displayed her "homelessness" in such a prominent way and on a regular basis. Julia would also not accept the traditional resources offered those with mental health issues, including existing shelter options as her primary housing choice. Instead, she opted not to follow the prescribed rules and to sleep where she could when she could, despite the associated risks. Somewhat serendipitously, however, she did begin to visit Neighbourhood House, a grassroots community agency, and slowly began to regularly attend drop-in sessions, though more often she would just drop in for conversation and support. Over many months Julia developed a trusting relationship with several of the social workers. The question raised at one monthly staff meeting by several of the social workers was:

Could the agency push beyond its mandate and its daily routine of support to provide more permanent help for Julia and other women like her in the community? Did the agency have the capacity to challenge itself and the community to develop an alternative housing option unlike anything else that currently existed? Could the knowledge of Julia and other street-engaged women like her be used to design a client-centred low-cost supported-housing alternative based upon their lived experiences rather than solely upon the expert opinion of housing professionals?

3. The Process

In 1999 the Canadian Social Sciences and Humanities Research Council (SSHRC) introduced a new funding opportunity to encourage and support the collaboration of university-based researchers with community-based partners, the Community-University Research Alliance (CURA). CURAs were based on equal partnerships to provide coordination and support for planning and carrying out of community-based and university-supported research activities of mutual importance to all partners.

The housing challenge that Julia brought to Neighbourhood House became the catalyst that brought together for the first time in such large numbers a contingent of community agencies and activists in collaboration with an interdisciplinary group of academics from the local university. An advisory group was created that included membership from homeless shelters, hospitals, community mental health agencies, existing social housing program providers, consumer-survivors, and researchers from different disciplines as well as governmental policy analysts. While Julia acted as an advisor to members of the group, she did not regularly participate on the advisory committee, as the schedule she kept was not sufficiently consistent to allow her to attend scheduled meetings.

4. The Research

The advisory committee began to explore the potential for creating a housing project using community economic development (CED)[4] strategies and tools. Many of the staff Julia had come into contact with believed that community development was not just

---

4 Community economic development involves activities undertaken locally by a specific defined community to provide economic opportunities and improve social conditions in a sustainable manner.

about project development alone, but rather envisioned a movement towards a broader sustainable, long-term solution to issues of poverty, mental health, and homelessness. For this reason, advocacy and education for structural and policy change were seen as fundamental principles of the process and an integral part of the initiative. Neighbourhood House staff had previously been involved in other CED initiatives, including research, development, and implementation of peer lending circles for entrepreneurs and provision of small-business supports as well as assisting in the implementation of a community forum for the Affordable Housing Task Force. One of the goals of this project was to encourage mental health consumer-survivors in the community to actively contribute to the determination of the desired characteristics for the proposed housing, and allow them to serve not just as sources of information but as equal partners in the process. Critical to the initiative, because of its traditional funding source, was the need not only to demonstrate this involvement but also to provide data-supported outcomes for the endeavour.

5. Questions

1a. *As the social work leader of the group, how would you outline the process you would undertake in planning the research component of the project?*

1b. *How would you introduce the research to the stakeholder groups in the community?*

1c. *What steps would you take to involve community members in the project?*

1d. *What would you need participants to understand before you began the process?*

1e. *What are your distinct short-term and long-term goals?*

2a. *As a mental health consumer-survivor, how would you outline the process you would want undertaken in the planning and implementation of this research?*

2b. *What are the primary concerns that you would want addressed?*

2c. *What are your distinct short-term and long-term goals?*

2d. *What are your ultimate desired outcomes?*

2e. *What are your initial thoughts on being asked to be part of a research process to determine what type of housing you require?*

3. *What barriers are there in making the traditional objects of research active participants and equal members of the research process?*

4. *What are the signs that the stakeholders are ready to engage in a Participatory Action Research process?*

6. Social Work Practice

Participatory Action Research

Participatory action research (PAR) has emerged as a significant methodology for intervention, development, and change within communities and groups. It is a research process in which the community participates in the analysis of its own reality in order to promote a social transformation for the benefit of participants who are oppressed. It involves research, education, and action and is an outgrowth and integration of community development and research. The creation of new knowledge is an essential component of PAR, as its goal is the emancipation from oppressive and exploitative relationships of the clients, who in this process are not merely clients or consumers of service but equal participants in the process.

Participatory action research is one form of action research that traces its origins to the theory and practice of prominent Latin American activist scholars, such as Paulo Freire and Orlando Fals-Borda, who initially drew from neo-Marxist and critical theory. Freire's classic book *Pedagogy of the Oppressed* (1993) offered a detailed Marxist class analysis in his exploration of the relationship between the colonizer and the colonized. He examined the struggle for justice and equity within the educational system of Brazil and proposed a new pedagogy as a response to the traditional formal models of adult education, where the teacher stood at the front and instructed students who were passive recipients of the information. This theoretical foundation has melded with feminist, queer, and race theories to promote an approach that challenges patterns of domination and supports social resistance.

The inaugural proponent of action research was German social psychologist Kurt Lewin, one of the founders of the Gestalt school, who first used the term in 1946 to describe a new approach to knowledge gathering. Lewin saw action research as a comparative research process that examined the conditions and effects of various forms of social action and research leading to social change. He envisioned the process as a series of spiral steps, each of which is composed of a repeating circle of planning, action, and fact-finding about the result of the action. He emphasized that this form of research should focus on participative group processes in order to address conflicts, crises, and structural changes within groups and organizations. While action research is based upon a group of people involved in a cyclical iterative process of action and learning, PAR involves more than a group of researchers working through the cycles together. PAR implies and necessitates the involvement of community members who are the direct stakeholders in the outcome, and allows those who are typically the subjects of research to become the researchers themselves.

Participatory action research's methodological stance is rooted in the belief that valid knowledge is produced only in collaboration and in action. Along with its Marxist roots, PAR draws from phenomenology to challenge established academic routines, though without discarding the need to accumulate and systematize knowledge. The function of participation is to create not only new knowledge but also new skills in a community, and thus the role of social work researcher involves the dual functions of educator and activist, with the research process coming to be viewed as an overtly political one.

Nonetheless, the most prominent research paradigm across the majority of academic disciplines still remains logical positivism. The close of the twentieth century did witness the emergence and growth of the interpretive paradigm in the social sciences, with its greater emphasis upon the relationship between socially engendered concept formation and language. This paradigm is highlighted by qualitative methodological approaches that include phenomenology, ethnography, and hermeneutics and is distinguished by its belief in a socially constructed, subjectively based reality that is influenced by culture and history. However, even in its use of qualitative approaches the researcher typically remains the expert and interpreter of data. Practitioners of participatory action research work in yet another paradigm, that of *praxis*. Praxis is the process of acting upon the conditions one faces in order to change them. It deals with the disciplines and activities predominant in the ethical and political lives of people. In a praxis approach, knowledge is derived from practice and practice is informed by knowledge in a continuous process. In PAR, researchers do not view themselves as neutral observers but rather as themselves active stakeholders in the research-driven change process.

Participatory action research integrates scientific investigation with education and political action. Researchers work with members of a community to understand and resolve community problems, to empower community members, and to democratize research. Methods employed include: (1) group discussions of personal experience, (2) interviews, (3) surveys, (4) focus groups both composed of and led by community members, and (5) analysis of public documents. PAR has become an alternative model for social scientists who question the traditions of detached and value-free research and seek an approach that is less hierarchical and serves the interests of those with little power.

McTaggart (1989) offered a summary of the key attributes of participatory action research:

Figure 2.19   The Process of Participatory Action Research

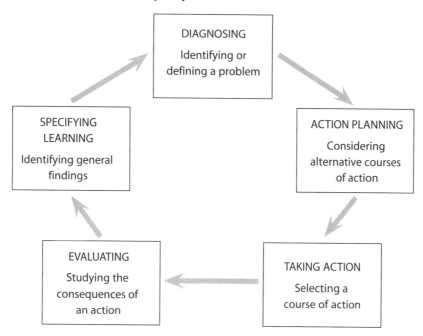

1. Participatory action research is an approach to improving social practice by changing it and learning from the consequences of the changes.

2. PAR is contingent upon authentic participation that involves a continuing spiral of action planning, taking action in order to implement plans, systematic observing and evaluating, reflecting and learning, and then diagnosing and beginning the planning again (Figure 2.19). The process can be initiated either through the initial collection of data in an area of interest and reflection upon this information, which then leads to the creation of a plan for action, or by first making an initial change, collecting data upon what has occurred as a result of the intervention, reflecting upon the change, and then building more refined plans of action.

3. PAR is collaborative, as those responsible for producing action are also involved in improving the community based upon the action. The collaborating group is widened over the research process in order to directly involve as many individuals as possible who are affected by the practices being researched.

4. PAR establishes self-critical communities of people participating and collaborating in the research processes of planning, acting, observing, and reflecting. It aims to build communities of people committed to enlightening themselves about the relation-

ship between circumstance, action, and consequence and to emancipating themselves from the institutional and personal constraints that limit their power to live by their legitimate and freely chosen social values.

5. PAR is a systematic learning process in which people act deliberately through remaining open to surprise and responsive to opportunities. It is a process of using critical intelligence to inform action and developing it so that social action becomes praxis, critically informed committed action.

6. PAR involves people in theorizing about their practices. This engages them in being inquisitive about and coming to understand the relationship between circumstances, action, and consequences in their own lives. The theories that PAR develops may be expressed initially in the form of rationales for practice. These initial rationales are then subjected to critical scrutiny through the process of engaging in participatory action research.

7. PAR requires that people put their practices, ideas, and assumptions about institutions to the test by gathering compelling evidence for substantiation.

8. PAR involves not only keeping records that describe what is happening as accurately as possible but also collecting and analysing the group's judgments, reactions, and impressions about what is occurring.

9. PAR involves participants in objectifying their own experiences. This can be done by keeping a personal journal in which participants record their progress and their reflections about two parallel sets of learnings: (a) about the practices themselves, how the individual and collective practices are developing, and (b) about the process of studying the practices, how the action research project is going.

10. PAR is a political process because it involves people in making changes that will affect others. For this reason it sometimes creates resistance to change, both in the participants themselves and in others directly and indirectly affected by the changes.

11. PAR involves making critical analyses of the institutionally structured situations, such as projects, programs, and systems, in which people work. The resistance to change encountered by a researcher is often due to conflicts between the proposed new practices and the accepted practices around processes such as communication, decision making, and educational work of the institution being studied. This critical analysis aids the researcher to act politically by (a) involving others collaboratively in the research process and inviting them to explore their own practices, and (b) working in the wider institutional context towards more rational understandings, more just processes of decision making, and more fulfilling forms of work for all involved.

12. PAR starts small by working on minor changes that individuals can manage and control and working towards more extensive patterns of change. These might include

critiques of institutions, which might lead to ideas for the general reform of projects, programs, or system-wide policies and practices. Participants should be able to present evidence on how they articulated the thematic concern that holds their group together and on how they established authentically shared agreements in the group.

13. PAR starts with small cycles of planning, acting, observing, and reflecting, which can help to define issues, ideas, and assumptions more clearly so that those involved can generate more powerful questions for themselves as their work progresses.

14. PAR starts with small groups of collaborators but widens the community of participating action researchers so that it gradually includes more and more of those involved in and affected by the practices in question.

15. PAR allows and requires participants to build records of their improvements through recording:

- their changing activities and practices;
- changes in the language and discourse they use to describe, explain, and justify their practices;
- change in the social relationships and forms of organization that characterize and constrain their practice; and
- development of their expertise in the conducting of action research.

Participants must be able to demonstrate evidence of a group climate where people expect and give evidence to support each other's claims. They must show respect for the value of rigorously gathered and analysed evidence and be able to provide and defend evidence to convince others.

16. PAR allows and requires participants to give a reasoned justification of their social and educational work to others, because they can show how the evidence they have gathered and the critical reflection they have engaged in have helped them to create a developed, tested, and critically examined rationale for what they are doing. Having developed such a rationale, they may legitimately ask others to justify their own practices in terms of their own theories and the evidence of their own critical self-reflection.

Participatory research fulfils the social justice criterion of relationship equality, but to fully infuse social work research with an ethic of social justice requires an action orientation as well. PAR is the research approach that most clearly supports these criteria. Morris (2002) describes PAR as "research in which research participants are ideally involved and in control at every stage of research and in which the goal is to take action on research findings for positive social change" (p. 10). PAR has five key features:

1. Participation of the people being studied
2. Inclusion of popular knowledge
3. A focus on power and empowerment
4. Consciousness raising and education of participants
5. Political action

Participation in the research process of the people being studied is best viewed as a continuum. An example of a low level of participation would be asking those who were interviewed to read and comment upon the transcripts of their interviews. Other, more involved forms of stakeholder participation in participatory action research include:

- Ownership and identification of the research issue
- Participation in data collection
- Participation in the process of evaluating actions and planning action cycles
- Participating in managing the research process, including the action and learning cycles
- Working as co-researchers and authors

The principle of collaborative resource presupposes that each person's ideas are equally significant as potential resources for creating interpretive categories of analysis, negotiated among the participants. It also strives to avoid the skewing of credibility stemming from the prior status of idea holders.

The social work researcher engaged in a PAR process can play a variety of roles, among them planner, leader, catalyser, facilitator, teacher, designer, listener, observer, synthesizer, and reporter. The main role, however, is to nurture local leaders to the point where they can take responsibility for the process. This point is reached when those who were once exclusively the objects of research understand the methods and are able to carry on when the initiating researcher leaves.

Feminist Research

Feminist research is related to participatory action research in that both use primarily qualitative methodologies and both have action orientations. Feminist research is designed to bring about change in women's lives by confronting sexism and attempting to alter social institutions that promote or perpetuate sexism. The feminist critique of quantitative research approaches was a reaction against existing sexist bias within the social sciences, with the emphasis upon exposing male-dominated disciplines and research structures.

The epistemological criteria for feminist research are built upon four pillars:

1. all knowledge is socially constructed;
2. the dominant ideology is that of the ruling group;
3. there is no such thing as value-free science; and
4. as people's perspectives vary systemically with their position in society, the perspectives of men and women vary likewise.

A unique standpoint exists not only as a result of gender but as a result of women being a dominated class.

Qualitative research is central to feminist research, which provides a postmodernist perspective to knowledge creation, as it allows women to tell their own stories in their own voices. In this form of research the investigator encourages the silenced to speak. Feminist research is used for the ongoing construction of complex realities and as a means to empower women. Participants and researchers come to a common understanding of what they are creating through empathetic connections. Like PAR, feminist research seeks to facilitate personal and societal change through research. However, in this process research is the mechanism for advocacy of a feminist value system and perspective. As with all forms of feminism, feminist research is sensitive to how relations of gender and power permeate all spheres of life. As well, it incorporates the researcher's own stated bias and perspective into the research process. Beyond being women centred, feminist research strives to understand the subjective experiences of the women involved in the research process. Safety is of paramount concern given many of the sensitive issues examined by social work researchers. The underlying rationale for feminist research is that members of the most and least powerful groups have distinct understandings of the world and that the perspective of those outside the dominant group develops from their daily activities, and thus those activities are important to study and understand. Women are seen as outsiders from within; they are absent and invisible.

Questions arising from a feminist research standpoint include:

- Whose interests are being served by the research?
- Who is defining the question and how has it been defined?
- Who is defining the outcome and how is it being defined?
- Does the intersection of gender, sex, race, age, socioeconomic status, geographic location, sexual orientation, ability, and disability obscure or magnify aspects of the research?
- How does the research empower women, and which women are empowered?

- Does the research change the context that contributed to the disempowerment?
- What practical implications does the research have?

Feminist research also forces us to ask the most critical question of all: Who can be a knower?

7. Responding to the Case

The Participatory Action Research Process

The first step in any research process requires that the group find a focus. The advisory committee had a purpose, and a general idea of what it wanted to do and how to do it, but what was still missing was in-depth knowledge of what had been tried and succeeded or failed: of the literature. The advisory committee called upon its academic partners, led by researchers from the fields of social work and nursing, to form a subgroup to conduct the literature review on behalf of the committee. Shortly thereafter, the academic subgroup discovered that there was literally no literature on the needs or status of or even any type of demographic data on community-based mental health consumer-survivors in Canada, let alone significant information on their housing status and needs.

With this lack of information, the advisory committee completed the funding proposal, placing emphasis equally upon the need for further information in this practice area and the unique structure of the advisory committee, with the intent of conducting the project using a participatory action research focus. Among the budget items requested was funding for meals and public transportation costs for the advisory committee members. While this was among the smaller budgetary items, it was not without significance. Without this funding, several of the consumer-survivors would not have been able to fully participate in the process, especially as the PAR grew in breadth over its lifespan. A lack of opportunity for equal involvement in the process might have resulted in some reverting to being merely objects of the research rather than equal partners.

Another small item that was unanticipated but also became an issue was meeting space. Some consumer-survivors would not attend meetings or events held within the confines of some of the institutional members of the advisory group because of what they saw as previous oppressive practice towards those with mental health issues. Thus, all meetings were held on neutral ground as defined by the advisory committee collectively.

Data Collection

Beginning with the initial input from the consumer-survivor members of the committee, the quantitative data collection was greatly supplemented with focus groups held in a range of community locations, including shelters, group homes, community agencies, and drop-in centres. Over five years a total of 1,500 interviews of community-based mental health consumer-survivors were conducted, along with 63 focus groups held in both urban and rural settings that involved 550 individuals. As well, 11 additional focus group sessions were held and attended by 75 family members of mental health consumer-survivors. Input into the questions posed, the analysis, and the final documents came from all committee members. However, there was still concern regarding sufficient balance on the committee and in the process between academics, community practitioners, and the mental health consumer-survivors, and worry that the consumer-survivor perspective was not being adequately incorporated. This led to a series of "search conferences" that ran parallel to the annual data collection cycle.

The Search Conference: A Participatory Action Research Tool

Search conferences are a PAR strategy used to obtain feedback from a broader range of stakeholders than those who are immediately charged with managing the initiative and who are involved in its day-to-day evolution. Developed by the Tavistock Institute in England in the 1960s, it is a mechanism for data collection, to enhance participant and community involvement and to help confirm the process or to offer new ideas and directions for research based upon what has been learned and what still needs to be discovered. Search conferences are attended by stakeholder group members, particularly those whose community is being studied, along with researchers, policy makers, and, when possible and appropriate, decision makers, including bureaucrats and politicians. Typically, content is contributed entirely by the members of the community affected, with staff serving only as facilitators. Information may be presented or items simply listed during the opening plenary attended by all, without any critique offered. After the presentation of information the material is discussed in greater depth in small groups, with these groups then reporting back to the entire conference after their deliberations. From this a composite picture is created of how all those in attendance interpret the findings, the meaning of them, and what needs to be acted upon now and what additional research is required. The process typically concludes with an examination of the environmental context within which the plan is being created and/or against a broader social and political background, and then the group proceeds to construct an outline for the next set of initiatives.

During the life of this project five search conferences were held. Each provided an opportunity for the advisory group to obtain feedback from the group the PAR process was intended to serve and also to obtain direction from the entire spectrum of stakeholder groups from the community. There were presentations from community groups as well as from researchers and students, along with performances dramatizing the life of those with mental health issues and addresses by politicians indicating their support for the project, particularly in election years. Group discussions and consensus exercises were conducted to establish priorities for the following year, with each search conference concluding by examining the environmental context and what needed to be prioritized for the forthcoming year.

Average attendance was over 100 persons, with a range of 80 to 150, and again this included a mix of stakeholders: academics, community professionals, members of the local mental health consumer-survivor group, as well as a few unaffiliated community members who had either been interviewed or participated in one of the focus groups. One of the additional PAR-driven initiatives was that at the end of each interview conducted or focus group held, participants were informed of the next planned search conference and told that their input was welcome at that point as well. Those contributing information to the process were informed that there was no cost to attend a search conference, meals and refreshments would be provided throughout the day, and public transportation costs would be covered.

Intended and Unintended Outcomes

The initial motive for this entire process was to develop an alternative housing option for Julia, and this did occur, but it did not last. For three years Julia and nearly two dozen other women with unique yet related life stories had their own apartments that were developed, planned, and implemented as part of the PAR process. However, because of financing issues, ownership concerns, the location of the housing development, and the ongoing need for mental health and social supports beyond what had been initially anticipated, the doors were ultimately closed and the women who had been housed were relocated to more traditional supportive housing.

In the exit interviews conducted prior to relocation the women offered some very specific critiques of the failed housing development, yet they also overwhelmingly reported that the housing had provided them a structure that supported a feeling of security. They viewed the most positive features as having people available to talk to and who could help with day-to-day problem solving, and having their own garden. Several women mentioned that this was the first time they had an opportunity to garden since they were children. The inclusion of the garden had been a wonderful addition to their lives and indicated that the project was not just about the provision of basic housing but about what they wanted and needed. In the spirit of Lewin's initial conceptualization of action research, the resulting gestalt that was unleashed by this PAR process could never have been anticipated or written into a funding proposal.

By the third year of the project the position of advisory committee co-chair had been filled by one of the leaders of the local mental health consumer-survivor association. With the dissolution of the housing project that was the foundation of the entire initiative, her organization stepped up and applied for funding for an alternative housing option for those living in the community with mental health issues, and was awarded the funding. However, rather than having professionals oversee the project, the proposal that was accepted, and continues to operate today housing both men and women, was and is peer supervised and managed.

The research generated also led to changes in policies, specifically in how social assistance payments are made to those with chronic disabilities in the province of Ontario. The research was used in the development of a new shelter complex that incorporated on-site medical and social work services along with a mix of temporary and permanent housing with separate floors for women and men. That process, while not based in PAR, did directly ask former shelter residents what they wanted in the new development.

The data were also used to change hospital policy so that no person admitted to a local hospital with a mental health issue was discharged to "no fixed address." As well, the process led to organizing of all-candidates debates at both the provincial and federal levels, where members of the consumer-survivor community who had participated in the PAR were prominent in organizing the events and asking questions related to mental health issues and policies. Multiple articles were written and many presentations made, some co-authored by consumer-survivors. This began to fill the void of knowledge on this social issue that had existed at the commencement of the project. The PAR also led to the development of many new relationships and the breaking down of some unspoken barriers between some government and not-for-profit agencies. As well, a sense of competence and efficacy arose in some participants, who prior to the project had merely been objects of research processes but who had now become knowers.

8. Research Insight

The fundamental core value of social work lies in its ability to contribute to empowerment of individuals in society and to social change. Participatory action, feminist, and feminist participatory action research can all contribute towards empowerment and social change, a concept not adequately acknowledged as part of either social work research practice or social work practice in general. As a profession we are committed to the achievement of social justice; thus our actions should reflect and flow from the values of equity and action. If we assume a social justice approach to social work research then it should affect the focus of what we study, how we approach the conduct of research, and what we choose to do with the findings.

Social work research must reflect the same values with which social work has historically been associated, that is, the pursuit of social change and social justice and the role of researcher as change agent. Social work researchers have an obligation to subscribe to the basic values and ethical practice of the profession of social work. As a social work student, it is important that you appreciate research as a legitimate field of practice, particularly empowerment practice, and understand that research is not a field populated by specialized social workers, but rather that all social work practitioners have a professional and ethical obligation to be practitioner researchers, particularly when this contributes to social change.

9. Further Reflections

1. *What ethical issues arise for a social worker participating in participatory action research?*
2. *What limits might an agency place on your engagement in this type of research?*
3. *In what ways can social work researchers be change agents and social activists outside of using a participatory action or feminist research approach?*

10. Additional Reading

Allen, D., & Hutchinson, T. (2009). Using PAR or "abusing its good name"? The challenges and surprises of photovoice and film in a study of chronic illness. *International Journal of Qualitative Methods*, 8(2), 115–28.

Antle, B., & Regehr, C. (2003). Beyond individual rights and freedoms: Metaethics in social work. *Social Work*, 48(1), 135–44. http://dx.doi.org/10.1093/sw/48.1.135.

Arieli, D., Friedman, V., & Agbaria, K. (2009). The paradox of participation in action research. *Action Research*, 7(3), 263–90. http://dx.doi.org/10.1177/1476750309336718.

Arnstein, S. (1969). A ladder of citizen participation. *Journal of the American Institute of Planners*, *35*(4), 216–24. http://dx.doi.org/10.1080/01944366908977225.

Cawson, P., Mercer, S., & Barbour, R. (2007). Involving deprived communities in improving the quality of primary care services: Does participatory action research work? *Health Services Research*, *7*(88). Retrieved from http://www.biomedcentral.com/1472-6963/7/88. http://dx.doi.org/10.1186/14726963-7-88

Dankoski, M.E. (2000). What makes research feminist? *Journal of Feminist Family Therapy*, *12*(1), 3–19. http://dx.doi.org/10.1300/J086v12n01_02.

Eckhardt, E., & Anatas, J. (2007). Research methods with disabled populations. *Journal of Social Work in Disability & Rehabilitation*, *6*(1/2), 1–22.

Fals-Borda, O. (1987). The application of participatory action-research in Latin America. *International Sociology*, *2*(4), 329–47. http://dx.doi.org/10.1177/026858098700200401.

Fine, M., & Torre, M. (2006). Intimate details: Participatory action research in prison. *Action Research*, *4*(3), 253–69. http://dx.doi.org/10.1177/1476750306066801.

Forchuk, C., Csiernik, R., & Jensen, E. (Eds.). (2011). *Homelessness, housing, and mental health: Finding truths – creating change*. Toronto: Canadian Scholars' Press.

Freire, P. (1993). *Pedagogy of the oppressed*. New York: Continuum.

Harding, S. (Ed.). (1987). *Feminism and methodology: Social science issues*. Bloomington: Indiana University Press.

Harding, S. (1993). *Whose science? Whose knowledge? Thinking from women's lives*. New York: Cornell University Press.

Hesse-Biber, S. & Leavy, P. (Eds.). (2007). *Feminist research practice: A primer*. Thousand Oaks, CA: Sage. http://dx.doi.org/10.4135/9781412984270.

Kemmis, S., & McTaggart, R. (1988). *The action research planner* (3rd ed.). Victoria, Australia: Deakin University.

Knightbridge, S., King, R., & Rolfe, T. (2006). Using participatory action research in a community-based initiative addressing complex mental health needs. *Australian and New Zealand Journal of Psychiatry*, *40*(4), 325–32. http://dx.doi.org/10.1080/j.1440-1614.2006.01798.x.

Lewin, K. (1946). Action research and minority problems. *Journal of Social Issues*, *2*(4), 34–46. http://dx.doi.org/10.1111/j.1540-4560.1946.tb02295.x.

Longres, J., & Scanlon, E. (2001). Social justice and the research curriculum. *Journal of Social Work Education*, *37*, 433–63.

Maiter, S., Simich, L., Jacobson, N., & Wise, J. (2008). Reciprocity: An ethic for community-based participatory action research. *Action Research*, *6*(3), 305–25. http://dx.doi.org/10.1177/1476750307083720.

McNicoll, P. (1999). Issues in teaching participatory action research. *Journal of Social Work Education*, *35*, 51–62.

McTaggart, R. (1989). Sixteen tenets of participatory action research. Presented at 3er Encuentro Mundial Investigacion Participatva (Third World Encounter on Participatory Research), Managua, Nicaragua, 3–9 September 1989. http://www.caledonia.org.uk/par.htm

Morris, M. (2002). *Participatory research and action*. Ottawa: Canadian Research Institute for the Advancement of Women.

Nelson, J., Janzen, R., Trainor, J., & Ochocka, J. (2008). Putting values into practice: Public policy and the future of mental health consumer-run organizations. *American Journal of Community Psychology, 42*(1/2), 192–201. http://dx.doi.org/10.1007/s10464-008-9191-y.

Reid, C., Tom, A., & Frisby, W. (2006). Finding the "action" in feminist participatory action research. *Action Research, 4*(3), 315–32. http://dx.doi.org/10.1177/1476750306066804.

Sprague, J. (2005). *Feminist methodologies for critical researchers*. Toronto: Altamira Press.

Stewart, R., & Bhagwanjee, A. (1999). Promoting group empowerment and self-reliance through participatory research: A case study of people with physical disability. *Disability and Rehabilitation, 21*(7), 338–45. http://dx.doi.org/10.1080/096382899297585.

Susman, G. (1983). Action research: A sociotechnical systems perspective. In G. Morgan (Ed.), *Beyond method: Strategies for social science research* (pp. 95–113). London: Sage.

Swigonski, M. (1994). The logic of feminist standpoint theory for social work research. *Social Worker, 39*(4), 387–93.

Tzavaras-Catsambas, T., & Preskill, H.S. (2006). *Reframing evaluation through appreciative inquiry*. Thousand Oaks, CA: Sage.

Wang, C. (2006). Youth participation in photovoice as a strategy for community change. *Journal of Community Practice, 14*(1/2), 147–61. http://dx.doi.org/10.1300/J125v14n01_09.

11. Internet Resources

Participatory Action Research

Center for Instructional Innovation and Assessment, "Using the PAR Approach":
https://www.youtube.com/watch?v=jo9OKzBKb5A

Ken Long, "Participatory Action Research: An Example Research Proposal Framework":
https://www.youtube.com/watch?v=wtIEL-gn0l4

Abe Oudshoorn, "Participatory Action Research":
https://www.youtube.com/watch?v=yrF7cVESMzg

E. Alana James, "Participatory Action Research + Complexity":
https://www.youtube.com/watch?v=s-SAJPF5xiA

F. Baum, C. MacDougall, and D. Smith, "Glossary: Participatory Action Research":
http://www.ncbi.nlm.nih.gov/pmc/articles/PMC2566051/

J. Bergold and S. Thomas, "Participatory Research Methods: A Methodological Approach in Motion":
http://www.qualitative-research.net/index.php/fqs/article/view/1801/3334

Feminist Research

PAR-L, "Introduction to Feminist Research":
http://www2.unb.ca/parl/research.htm

khanacademymedicine, "Feminist Theory":
https://www.youtube.com/watch?v=LHPOLSywdi0

bmyersable's channel, "Standpoint Thoery":

    https://www.youtube.com/watch?v=hsZ1ZxcKvmg

Sharlene Nagy Hesse-Biber, "Feminist Research":

    http://www.sagepub.com/sites/default/files/upm-binaries/43563_1.pdf

Dr. Jane Wambui, "An Introduction to Feminist Research":

    https://www.researchgate.net/file.PostFileLoader.html?id=54946308d5a3f2e0038b4698&assetKey
=AS%3A273655202811911%401442255892660

CASE STUDY 20
Measuring Client Satisfaction: Do They Like Me?

1. Preamble

One of the most common approaches to program evaluation is gathering client satisfaction data. As social workers we are concerned that the service experience be a positive one for our clients, and we should be responsive to any suggestions that clients have about how to deliver the service more effectively. It is also assumed that there is an association between client satisfaction and service effectiveness. The most common approach to measuring client satisfaction is to survey clients and collate their responses across a number of program dimensions.

2. The Problem

Martha was the newest social worker hired by the Greater St. Albert School Board. She was assigned to work with students in an urban elementary school setting. The role of a social worker in the education system is to work with students whose psychosocial problems interfere with learning in the classroom. She surveyed the teachers to identify the most common and problematic student behaviours, and on the basis of the data decided to offer an eight-session educational group program for boys aged 8 to 10 lacking impulse control. The program she selected was one recommended by another social worker who had graduated from the University of British Columbia–Okanagan the year Martha began her undergraduate studies and who now worked for an adjacent school board but at a rural school. He had used the program a number of times and was sure it worked well.

3. The Process

Martha knew that as part of the program she would need to conduct a survey to see if the boys liked the group and if they had any suggestions on how to improve it for future groups. The information would also be forwarded to the principal of the school and to her supervisor, Abby, a graduate of the University of Regina School of Social Work. Abby was anxious to receive any information that could be incorporated into the roll-up reports she was required to prepare as part of department accountability and to demonstrate the value of social work within the education system. These reports would be reviewed by the Board of Education, the body responsible for overseeing education in the district. Being new, Martha wanted to make a good impression on her supervisor and on the principal of the school, and of course she also wanted to ensure that the students liked participating in the program.

4. The Research

The program protocol had already been well established outside of the St. Albert area. However, it had never been conducted in Martha's school board, nor had the eight-session group been evaluated before or the participants' views on the programming been considered. Before starting the group Martha knew that she should begin collecting data, but what and when?

5. Questions

1. *What are three uses for client satisfaction information?*
2. *What factors should Martha take into consideration in the preparation of the client satisfaction survey?*
3. *How would you draft your version of the client satisfaction survey for the program?*
4. *What are the steps in the process that Martha should follow to finalize and administer her survey?*

6. Social Work Practice

Issues with Collecting Client Satisfaction Data

Measuring client satisfaction can provide social workers with valuable information to improve their programs and services, but like all measurement tasks, it is important that our design decisions be methodologically sound and the approach we take to data collection be reasonably rigorous. Our objective is to determine what people actually think about their experience with the service, not what they are willing to say they think – and there can be a difference. It is interesting that efforts to gauge the client experience consistently indicate high levels of satisfaction regardless of whether the assessment is global, of the service as a whole, or is a more detailed assessment of specific aspects of the program.

There are a number of reasons for this. First, people usually select a program they believe will meet their needs, so they are predisposed to like it; disgruntled people quit a program before the evaluation takes place. Second, women and children, prime users of social work services, consistently rate more favourably. Added to this is the possibility, especially in long-term programs, that people are rating a service highly so as not to alienate their caregivers and helpers. And finally, some people are so appreciative that anyone is willing to help them that this is reflected in high ratings. Social workers need to be cautious when they review the results of client satisfaction.

Developing Good Data Collection Instruments

What can we do to improve the information content of client satisfaction efforts? To begin with, we can use more than the usual quantitative questionnaire data to generate satisfaction feedback. We can supplement our understanding with qualitative comments and suggestions from clients. This, as we have seen, is referred to as triangulation: measuring a construct by using more than one approach. We can add sections on our questionnaires for open-ended questions to generate comments, or we can conduct interviews or focus groups with program participants. In taking this approach, it is important to try to ensure that you are receiving balanced feedback, that is, you are not just talking with people who are satisfied with the program. It is important to make the effort to engage those who are dissatisfied as well. This is called negative case analysis, and it enhances the trustworthiness of qualitative research. Also, it is best if those conducting the interviews or focus groups are not directly involved in the provision of services. Participants may be hesitant to directly pass along negative comments to those who were involved in the delivery of their service. Finally, to increase objectivity it is best if the comments are reviewed and summarized by a person not directly involved in the program. Having a third party analyse the data reduces the likelihood that others will consider the analysis to be biased in favour of the program or service.

If you plan to use a quantitative questionnaire to measure satisfaction, it is important that you follow recommendations on how to design a high-quality questionnaire. Client satisfaction questionnaires typically consist of multi-item scales to measure various dimensions of the program and open-ended questions to allow respondents to add their own narrative comments. Scales can be custom designed by those involved in the program (see Figure 2.20a), or you can use already existing professionally developed scales such as the CSQ-8 (see Figure 2.20b). If you design your own scales they can be customized to correspond to specific program components. As well, the process of developing scales may be helpful in deepening your understanding of your clients and their concerns, particularly if clients are involved in designing the questionnaire. Existing scales, on the other hand, have the advantage of rigorously developed psychometrics; that is, they have demonstrated reliability and validity. If you develop your own scales, at least pre-test the questionnaire with people similar to your clients before using it in your program. Also, ask others outside your group to comment on your scales' face and content validity – do they look like they measure all dimensions of client satisfaction?

Administering the Data Collection Tool

Once you have your questionnaire designed or chosen, the next set of decisions has to do with how you plan to administer it. As previously discussed, mail-out questionnaires commonly have a very high "non-return" rate. Once a service is completed people are not keen on completing questionnaires; usually the only ones you get back are from "happy customers." If you do use mail-out questionnaires make sure they are short, easy to complete, and have a return-addressed envelope with sufficient postage. You should also consider offering respondents some form of incentive to return the questionnaire and plan to make personal or telephone contact to increase the return rate.

While mail-out questionnaires have their drawbacks, supervised administration of the questionnaires has its problems as well. Many programs ask participants to complete a satisfaction questionnaire at the end of the service. If this happens when people are anxious to leave, have other appointments, or are emotionally distressed you are not likely to get reliable information. Specific time should be set aside to complete the questionnaire when respondents are not rushed or overly emotionally. As with qualitative methods of collecting satisfaction data, it is best if the person supervising the administration of the questionnaire is not the person who provided the service. Again, having the social worker who worked with the person enquire as to their satisfaction, even in the form of a self-administered questionnaire, may influence the respondent's answers.

Finally, some consideration should be given to the best time to ask clients to comment on their experience. You need to be cautious about the influence of a recall bias. People tend to make their judgments based on recent events, and if a program was delivered over eight weeks, for example, it is likely that respondents' opinions will be focused on the last few weeks. It is easier to remember recent events, so they can carry a disproportionate weight in making judgments. If a program ends with a celebration

Figure 2.20a   Example of a Custom-Designed Questionnaire

Below are some sentences. Read each one and then circle the answer that best describes how you feel. If you agree with the sentence circle "YES." If you don't agree with the sentence circle "NO," and if you can't make up your mind circle "NOT SURE."

	☺	☹	😐
The program helped me	YES	NO	NOT SURE
I liked the group leader	YES	NO	NOT SURE
The group was fun	YES	NO	NOT SURE
I would come again	YES	NO	NOT SURE
I would tell my friends to come	YES	NO	NOT SURE

event, or if termination is focused on positive outcomes, these may colour the person's assessment of the entire program. Also, if you wait until the end of a program to gauge satisfaction there is nothing you can do to make mid-course corrections. Information received after the program has terminated may be helpful to make adjustment for future programs but will not allow you to adjust the program as it unfolds. Some social workers therefore conduct periodic evaluations of client satisfaction to allow for program enhancements during program delivery.

Figure 2.20b   CSQ – 8

Please help us improve our program by answering some questions about the service you have received. We are interested in your honest opinions, whether positive or negative. Please answer all the questions. We also welcome your comments and suggestions. Thank you very much; we really appreciate your help.

How would you rate the quality of service you received?
☐ Excellent
☐ Good
☐ Fair
☐ Poor

Did you get the kind of service you wanted?
☐ Definitely not
☐ No
☐ Not really
☐ Yes, generally
☐ Yes, definitely

To what extent has our program met your needs?
☐ Almost all of my needs have been met
☐ Most of my needs have been met
☐ Only a few of my needs have been met
☐ None of my needs have been met

If a friend were in need of similar help, would you recommend our program to him or her?
☐ No, definitely not
☐ No, not really
☐ Yes, generally
☐ Yes, definitely

How satisfied were you with the amount of help you received?
☐ Quite dissatisfied
☐ Indifferent or mildly satisfied
☐ Mostly satisfied
☐ Very satisfied

Have the services you received helped you to deal more effectively with your problems?
☐ Yes, they helped a great deal
☐ Yes, they helped somewhat
☐ No, they really didn't help
☐ No, they seemed to make things worse

In an overall, general sense, how satisfied are you with the service you have received?
☐ Very satisfied
☐ Mostly satisfied
☐ Indifferent or mildly satisfied
☐ Quite dissatisfied

If you were to seek help again, would you come back to our program?
☐ No, definitely not
☐ No, not really
☐ Yes, generally
☐ Yes, definitely

7. Responding to the Case

Martha needs information about how her students experience the program. Her approach should include both qualitative and quantitative components. Given that it is the first time she has offered the program, she may want to collect information during the program as well as when it has ended. After the midpoint of the program she may want to consider conducting a short focus group session. The actual facilitation of the group should be handled by another social worker who is not involved with the program. This could happen at the beginning of the fifth meeting of the group. The facilitator could have a few open-ended questions such as: What have you liked about the program so far? What would you like to see changed? Questions should be constructed to encourage discussion, so questions such as "Do you like the program?" or "Do you think we should offer it again?" would not be appropriate. After conducting the session, the facilitator can give Martha a summary of the discussion and indicate how satisfied the students are at this point in time. This will allow Martha to make adjustments based upon the student feedback.

In the last session of the program Martha can again ask her facilitator to come in and administer a short pen-and-paper questionnaire. The questionnaire should probably be limited to a few fixed-alternative questions, since elementary school–aged boys are not usually responsive to tasks that require written work. The questionnaire should have age-appropriate language and be simple to complete. Martha should send the proposed questionnaire to her supervisor, to the facilitator, and to any other person she thinks could give her constructive feedback. She may want to ask a non-participating student or small group of students to give her feedback about the clarity of the instructions and the understandability of the questions. There should be time set aside in the last session specifically to complete the questionnaire, and it should not be administered after the pizza party that celebrates the end of the program, unless of course Martha is smart enough to have read this entire book prior to beginning the research process and wants to bias the results in her favour.

8. Further Reflections

1a. *What is it about being liked that is important to social workers as professionals?*

1b. *What is it about being liked that is important to you personally in your role as a beginning social worker?*

2. *Why is it that often social work researchers are not liked, particularly those conducting evaluations?*

3. *How much more confidence do you now have about conducting research compared with when you began studying research?*

4. *What has changed? How can you extrapolate that to other facets of your social work practice?*

9. Additional Reading

Attkisson, C.C., & Zwick, R. (1982). The client satisfaction questionnaire: Psychometric properties and correlations with service utilization and psychotherapy outcome. *Evaluation and Program Planning, 6*(3), 229–314.

Brooks, F., & Brown, E. (2005). A program evaluation of Los Angeles ACORN's welfare case advocacy. *Journal of Human Behavior in the Social Environment, 12*(2/3), 185–203. http://dx.doi.org/10.1300/J137v12n02_10.

Fischer, R., & Valley, C. (2000). Monitoring the benefits of family counseling: Using satisfaction surveys to assess the clients' perspective. *Smith College Studies in Social Work, 70*(2), 271–86. http://dx.doi.org/10.1080/00377310009517592.

Gaston, L., & Sabourin, S. (1992). Client satisfaction and social desirability in psychotherapy. *Evaluation and Program Planning, 15*(3), 227–31. http://dx.doi.org/10.1016/0149-7189(92)90085-9.

Kapp, S., & Propp, J. (2002). Client satisfaction methods: Input from parents with children in foster care. *Child & Adolescent Social Work Journal, 19*(3), 227–45. http://dx.doi.org/10.1023/A:1015580015223.

Kapp, S., & Vela, R. (2004). The unheard client: Assessing the satisfaction of parents of children in foster care. *Child & Family Social Work, 9*(2), 197–206. http://dx.doi.org/10.1111/j.1365-2206.2004.00323.x.

Larsen, D.L., Attkisson, C.C., Hargreaves, W.A., & Nguyen, T.D. (1979). Assessment of client/patient satisfaction: Development of a general scale. *Evaluation and Program Planning, 2*(3), 197–207. http://dx.doi.org/10.1016/0149-7189(79)90094-6.

LaSala, M.C. (1997). Client satisfaction: Consideration of correlates and response bias. *Families in Society, 78*(1), 54–64. http://dx.doi.org/10.1606/1044-3894.737.

McMurtry, S.L., & Hudson, W.W. (2000). The Client Satisfaction Inventory: Results of an initial validation study. *Research on Social Work Practice, 10*(5), 644–63.

Rush, B., & Harris, J. (2000). *Client satisfaction and outcomes within Ontario's withdrawal management centres.* Toronto: Centre for Addiction and Mental Health.

Shapiro, J.P., Welker, C.J., & Jacobson, B.J. (1997). The youth client satisfaction questionnaire: Development, construct validation, and factor structure. *Journal of Clinical Child Psychology, 26*(1), 87–98. http://dx.doi.org/10.1207/s15374424jccp2601_9.

Soliman, H.H., & Poulin, J. (1997). Client satisfaction with crisis outreach services: The development of an index. *Journal of Social Service Research, 23*(2), 55–76. http://dx.doi.org/10.1300/J079v23n02_04.

Taylor, K., Gorey, K., Hansen, F., Ierullo, B., & Chacko, J. (1999). Adequacy of the shelter allowance: A comparison of social assistance recipients in Windsor, Ontario, before and after provincial budget cuts. *Canadian Social Work, 1*(1), 64–70.

Walsh, T., & Lord, B. (2004). Client satisfaction and empowerment through social work intervention. *Social Work in Health Care, 38*(4), 37–56. http://dx.doi.org/10.1300/J010v38n04_03.

World Health Organization. (2000). *Client satisfaction evaluations.* New York: WHO.

10. Internet Resources

B2B International, "Customer Satisfaction Surveys & Research":
  https://www.b2binternational.com/publications/customer-satisfaction-survey/

R. Al-Abri and A. Al-Balushi, "Patient Satisfaction Survey as a Tool towards Quality Improvement":
  http://www.ncbi.nlm.nih.gov/pmc/articles/PMC3910415/

B. White, "Measuring Patient Satisfaction: how to Do It and Why to Bother":
  http://www.aafp.org/fpm/1999/0100/p40.html

CASE STUDY 21
Statistics: Adding Some Numbers

1. Preamble

There are three kinds of lies: lies, damn lies and statistics.

– Benjamin Disraeli

He uses statistics as a drunken man uses lamp posts …
For support rather than illumination.

– Andrew Lang

Up to this point the case studies have for the most part avoided anything statistical, knowing many social workers' natural aversion to all things numeric. However, at some time you will have to face the fact that some forms of research do entail mathematical calculation, even if it is only to evaluate the truth of what others are telling you. Remember that statistics are your friends; like all friends sometimes you like them and they are easy to get along with and understand, and sometimes they are more difficult to deal with but in the long run worth the effort.

2. The Problem

During elections, polls are frequently used to provide insights into how political parties and individual candidates are doing. Initially they were used for information, but as technology and the sway of the media has changed they can often seem to be making news rather than reporting news. In one Canadian provincial election, the Environics Research Group and Angus Reid Research Group both conducted polls during the same week to gauge the popularity of the Conservative government that was the ruling party. However, one poll stated that the Conservatives were leading while the other claimed that the Liberals were in the lead. Both polls agreed that the New Democratic Party (NDP) was third in voter popularity.

3. The Process

Environics conducted its poll for a newspaper with a known Liberal editorial bias. The Angus Reid poll conducted the following day was prepared for *Southam News*, which at that time was owned by Conrad Black, before he was imprisoned, whose politics were to the right of the political spectrum. The New Democratic Party does not have a major media champion with a social democratic bias and thus that party did not come first in any poll that week.

4. The Research

Both polling firms used standard and acceptable sampling sizes and appropriate sampling methods. Environics showed the Conservatives trailing the Liberals 37 per cent to 42 per cent while the Angus Reid poll showed the Conservatives ahead with 41 per cent of popular sentiment while the Liberals had the support of 34 per cent. Both groups had the NDP with approximately 20 per cent of popular support. With the number of people sampled the polls had a 95 per cent confidence rating and a margin of error of + or − 2.5 per cent.

5. Questions

1. *What does all this mean?*
2. *Based on the polls who is going to win the election?*
3. *What is the limitation of this type of data?*

6. Social Work Practice

Statistics is simply a way of organizing, summarizing, or manipulating sets of data such that we can draw some sort of conclusion from what you have observed. You certainly do not have to become a statistician to understand research or be able to assess basic findings. You do however need to understand some basic language that flows from the previous case studies. There are two types of statistics, descriptive and inferential, and they correspond to certain forms of data sources and sampling formats.

Descriptive statistics are a way to present quantitative data in a manageable form. They simplify samples of information and describe a set of numbers in a summarized manner highlighted by averages and dispersion, or ranges. Descriptive statistics is most commonly associated with central tendencies or summary averages. Central tendency consists of three variables: the arithmetic mean, or average; the mode, the single response given most frequently; and the median, the score or result that falls in the middle of all of the replies. The median will have just as many observations below it as above it.

Inferential statistics is concerned with inductive reasoning and the drawing of conclusions from data rather than merely summarizing the information. When looking for causation or drawing inferences from our research findings we use inferential statistics. Inference is the degree of confidence we have when we say that an apparent relationship between two variables observed within a given research sample is a real one that probably exists among cases and the population of interest outside of the sample.

The theory and rules of statistics are concerned with the reliability of drawing such conclusions and the probability of error of that conclusion. Probability sampling is based upon, not surprisingly, probability theory, which relates to the mathematical likelihood of an event occurring. In probability sampling we are trying to obtain a representative sample of what would occur if we were able to ask everyone in the population of interest, though we know this is virtually impossible; thus we must always consider two additional factors any time we see a number: sampling error and confidence levels.

The premise of polling and all other forms of large data collection is that if we select enough people randomly from a population, this smaller number of persons or cases from that population will provide us with a relatively accurate interpretation of an outcome that would arise if we could ask everyone. This is based upon the premise of the normal curve, also referred to as the normal distribution or bell curve, as illustrated in Figure 2.21.

Figure 2.21   Normal Distribution

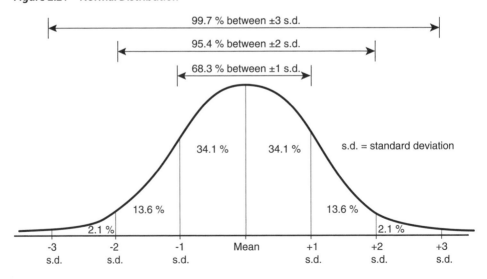

There are several important facets of a normal distribution:

- The normal curve is balanced and equal such that the range between 0 and +1 is identical to the space between 0 and −1. Likewise the number of people or cases that would fall between 0 and +2 is identical to that between 0 and −2, and −1 to −3 is equal to +1 to +3.
- Fifty per cent of cases fall between 0 and the negative end of the scale and 50 per cent fall between 0 and the positive end of the scale.
- The numbers across the bottom of the curve are standard deviation gradients, which is a measurement of range. They are also called z score readings. If the curve in Figure 2.21 represented a math test and your z score was 0 it would mean that 50 per cent of your classmates scored worse than you and 50 per cent scored better. If your z score was −1 it would mean you scored better than 16 per cent of your classmates $(0.5 + 2.0 + 13.5)$ while 84 per cent $(34 + 34 + 13.5 + 2 + 0.5)$ scored better than you did.

Sampling error is simply the margin of error to be expected given the size of the population and the number of persons in your sample who were selected from the total population to provide the data required for the study. Confidence interval (CI) reflects the accuracy of our sample statistic. The standard level used is 95 per cent, though others can be used, such as 90 or 99 per cent. When you state that you have a 95 per cent CI it means that if the same number of people are sampled repeatedly from the entire population of interest, the range of numbers you would come up with would be between the lower and upper limit of what the actual value would be if you could count everyone 95 times out of 100. What this also means is that in every random sample, in every poll, in every study, there is a small chance (5 per cent with a 95 per cent CI and 1 per cent with a 99 per cent CI) that the value presented does not actually represent the true result if you had the ability to ask everyone in your population of interest.

In probability sampling we select a standard number of people from the population based on three factors:

- how large the population is (10,000; 100,000; 1,000,000);
- the margin of error we can accept (+ or − 2.5 per cent; + or − 3.5 per cent; + or − 5 per cent);
- the confidence level we require (90 per cent; 95 per cent; 99 per cent).

Table 2.21a Reported Poll Results:
Percentage

	Environics	Angus Reid
Liberals	42	34
Conservatives	37	41
NDP	20	21

7. Responding to the Case

Before being able to say what this all means we need to understand what the numbers represent. The case study indicated that the confidence level was 95 per cent, which is a very high standard of measurement. It means that if we were to sample eligible voters in Ontario 100 times, 95 times the people we asked would provide a value representative of the entire population. However, this does mean that of those 100 samples, there is a likelihood that five times the results would in fact *not* represent the attitudes, beliefs, behaviours, or attributes of the entire population. The second fact is margin of error. In both polls the margin of error used was + or − 2.5 per cent, which is a very acceptable level. However, it does have some interesting implications, as highlighted in Tables 2.21a and 2.21b. Finally, what the case study did not indicate was how many people were actually asked for whom they were going to vote. In 1996 the adult population of Ontario was approximately 8.5 million people. Using a sample size calculator (http://www.surveysystem.com/sscalc.htm) and based upon a CI of 95 per cent and a margin of error of + or − 2.5, this means that 1,536 people of voting age were polled in both the Environics and Angus Reid polls. However, based on probability they were two entirely different groups of 1,536 people, which explains why there is a difference in the outcome … or is there?

Table 2.21a represents what the newspapers reported; however, Table 2.21b provides you the range of possible values of the entire population given the limitations of only asking 1,536 people to predict how 8.5 million people would vote (though in reality less than 50 per cent of the eligible electorate typically votes in Canadian elections). The economic and time savings of this procedure are quite evident, but this expedience does come with some limits. When you examine the ranges in Table 2.21b you will note the degree of overlap between the scores of the Liberals and Conservatives. You will also note the overlap in the two surveys of the NDP totals. Considering that the Conservatives actually won that election, it appears that if you have money to spend on a pollster you are better off going with Angus Reid, doesn't it?

Table 2.21b Actual Poll Results: Considering
Standard Error

	Environics	Angus Reid
Liberals	39.5–44.5	31.5–36.5
Conservatives	34.5–39.5	38.5–43.5
NDP	17.5–22.5	18.5–23.5

8. Research Insight

Following are some important definitions to help you better understand the statistical aspects of research.

Statistics – the science of learning from data and of measuring, controlling, and communicating uncertainty; it entails the collection, analysis, interpretation, presentation, and organization of data.

Statistic – a number that represents a piece of information; a fact or piece of data from a study of a large quantity of numerical data.

Frequency – the absolute number of times a value appears.

Frequency Distribution – a table or graph that lists a set of scores and how often they occurred within a set of data. The categories must always be mutually exclusive and exhaustive.

Probability – the measure of the likelihood that an event will occur. The greater the probability of an event, the more likely the event is to occur.

Dispersion – indicates how spread out a data set is. It is most commonly represented through range or standard deviation.

Normal Distribution (normal curve, bell curve) – the graphic representation of the distribution of a large symmetrical population that follows a set bell pattern. The curve on the top is shorter and wider than the curve on the bottom because the curve on the top has a bigger standard deviation.

Standard Deviation (SD, σ, s) – a calculation used to measure the amount of difference or dispersion of a set of data. It can also be represented as *SD*, by the Greek letter sigma (σ) for the *population* standard deviation, or by the letter "s" for the *sample* standard deviation.

Margin of Error – the maximum expected difference between the true population score if all members of the population were to be sampled and the value obtained from an actual sample of the population. For the margin of error to have value it needs to be accompanied by a probability statement indicating the likelihood that the value truly reflects the actual population. This is its CI.

CI – used in inferential statistics to indicate a value that measures the likelihood (probability) that a population attribute will fall between the numbers specified, typically 95 or 99 per cent.

The z score (standard score) – indicates how many standard deviations an individual case/subject is from the average or midpoint. A *z* score of 0 indicates the individual's result is the same as the mean or average score of the group. A negative *z* score indicates a reading that is below the average score, while a positive *z* score is an above-average outcome. Thus a +1 score is one standard deviation above the mean and a −2 is two standard deviations below the average score of the group. A *z* score allows you to determine how each individual person or element ranked compared to the entire group.

9. Further Reflections

You earn bonus points if during your discussion you considered how the questions were asked or what questions were asked. The Angus Reid poll began by asking each respondent for which party they were most likely to vote. However, the Environics Poll, polling for a Liberal-supporting newspaper at a time when the Liberals were the Opposition party, began by asking those sampled what their thoughts were on workfare, government cutbacks, privatization of public firms, the forthcoming tax cut, hospital closures, and an impending civil servants strike. They then asked if the person would be voting for the current government or another party.

Keep in mind when dealing with research that you can typically never prove that you are right, only that you are probably not wrong and that there really are lies, damn lies, and statistics. Make sure you know the difference!

10. Additional Reading

Adams, M. (1999). The dead grandmother/exam syndrome and the potential downfall of American society. *Annals of Improbable Research*, *5*, 3–6. Retrieved from https://www.improbable.com /airchives/paperair/volume5/v5i6/GrandmotherEffect%205-6.pdf and http://www.ct.edu/files /csus-resolutions/93-059.pdf

Aron, A., Coups, E., & Aron, E. (2010). *Quick references for determining the power of tests. Statistics for the behavioral and social sciences: A brief course* (5th ed.). Upper Saddle River, NJ: Prentice Hall.

Greenhalgh, T. (1997). How to read a paper: Statistics for the non-statistician. 1: Different types of data need different statistical tests. *British Medical Journal*, *315*(7104), 364–6. http://dx.doi .org/10.1136/bmj.315.7104.364.

Kanzler, G. (2010). *Statistics for the terrified* (5th ed.). London: Prentice Hall.

Kraemer, H.C., & Blasey, C. (2015). *How many subjects? Statistical power analysis in research*. Thousand Oaks, CA: Sage.

Leik, R.K. (1997). *Experimental design and the analysis of variance*. Thousand Oaks, CA: Pine Forge Press. http://dx.doi.org/10.4135/9781483348940.

Rowntree, D. (2000). *Statistics without tears*. Boston, MA: Allyn and Bacon.

Vogt, W.P. (2011). *Dictionary of statistics and methodology: A nontechnical guide for the social sciences* (4th ed.). Thousand Oaks, CA: Sage.

Weinbach, R., & Grinnell, R., Jr. (2014). *Statistics for social workers* (9th ed.). New York: Longman.

11. Internet Resources

Introduction to Statistics

Sage, "Introduction to Statistics":
   http://www.sagepub.com/sites/default/files/upm-binaries/40006_Chapter1.pdf

Normal Distribution

Math Is Fun, "Normal Distribution":
   https://www.mathsisfun.com/data/standard-normal-distribution.html
Khan Academy, "Introduction to the Normal Distribution":
   https://www.khanacademy.org/math/probability/statistics-inferential/normal_distribution/v
   /introduction-to-the-normal-distribution
David W. Stockburger, "Introductory Statistics: Concepts, Models, and Applications":
   http://www.psychstat.missouristate.edu/introbook/sbk11.htm
how2stats, "Normal Distribution – Explained Simply":
   https://www.youtube.com/watch?v=xgQhefFOXrM

Margin of Error

Khan Academy, "Margin of Error":
   https://www.khanacademy.org/math/probability/statistics-inferential/margin-of-error/v
   /margin-of-error-1
Pamela Hunter, "Margin of Error and Confidence Levels Made Simple":
   http://www.isixsigma.com/tools-templates/sampling-data/margin-error-and-confidence-levels
   -made-simple/
American Research Group, "Margin of Error Calculator":
   http://americanresearchgroup.com/moe.html

CIs

Graph Pad, "Interpreting a Confidence Interval of a Mean":
   http://www.graphpad.com/guides/prism/6/statistics/index.htm?stat_more_about_
   confidence_interval.htm
Khan Academy, "Confidence Interval":
   https://www.khanacademy.org/math/probability/statistics-inferential/confidence-intervals/v
   /confidence-interval-1
Stat Trek, "What Is a Confidence Interval?":
   http://stattrek.com/estimation/confidence-interval.aspx
Mr. Nystrom, "What Is a Confidence Interval?":
   https://www.youtube.com/watch?v=vWFdiGg7f6k

Brandon Foltz, "Confidence Intervals":
    https://www.youtube.com/watch?v=9GtaIHFuEZU

z score

pspollard1's channel, "Normal Distribution and z-scores":
    https://www.youtube.com/watch?v=mai23vW8uFM
statisticsfun, "How to Calculate z Scores Used in Statistics Class":
    https://www.youtube.com/watch?v=fXOS4Q3nJQY&feature=iv&src_vid=1xhCL5m4nI0&
    annotation_id=annotation_202153
Math Meeting, "Z Scores – Statistics":
    https://www.youtube.com/watch?v=NY2zWGBXBhU

Sample Size Calculator

Creative Research Systems, "Sample Size Calculator":
    http://www.surveysystem.com/sscalc.htm
Raosoft, "Sample Size Calculator":
    http://www.raosoft.com/samplesize.html

CASE STUDY 22
Descriptive Statistics: The First Step from Guessing to Knowing

1. Preamble

When social workers work with clients we observe them as part of the assessment process to obtain therapeutic insights. After we have worked in a field for an extended period of time we tend to be able to see trends or anticipate outcomes based on our client interactions, which enhances our practice. However, we typically tend not to formalize this process in any manner, so clinical judgment is sometimes dismissed due to our inability to numerically substantiate our beliefs and move them into a more objective format. Fortunately it does not take much data, much mathematical knowledge, or much time to change a guess into a fact, to move from belief to knowledge.

2. The Problem

Despite foundations in Judeo-Christian principles, spirituality is not a theme universally associated with social work education and some have even claimed that social work was anti-Christian in its orientation (Santandrea, 1998). This is partially because, as a client-centred profession, social work (philosophically and theoretically) supports each client's right and entitlement to self-determination. This then mandates ethical social workers to support clients in their decisions concerning extremely controversial topics such as the right to die, termination of a pregnancy, and the rights of gay, lesbian, or transgendered persons that can create conflict with those of strong faith. Combining this mandated orientation with feminist, structuralist, postmodernist, and anti-oppressive theoretical teachings at the post-secondary level has led to a belief expressed by many, both outside and within the profession, that social workers do not have strong faith or that spiritual matters are unimportant.

3. The Process

A small study compared 25 randomly selected third-year bachelor of social work students with 25 randomly selected third-year liberal arts honours students attending a Canadian Catholic university. The intent was to compare the spirituality of the two groups to ascertain if spirituality was as important to those studying social work as to their liberal arts honours counterparts.

4. The Research

Participation in the study was voluntary. Subjects provided basic demographic information along with completing the JAREL Spiritual Well-Being Scale (Hungelmann, Kenkel-Rossi, Klassen, & Stollenwerk, 1987). The JAREL consists of 21 statements scored on a six-point Likert scale, thus allowing a maximum score of 126. The results are presented in Table 2.22a.

5. Questions

1. *What similarities are there between the two groups?*
2. *What differences are there between the two groups?*
3. *Were the social workers in the group as spiritual as their liberal arts honours counterparts?*

6. Social Work Practice

Descriptive statistics are used to describe the core features of a data set with the goal of finding some pattern among the outcomes of the research. They assist in bringing understanding to large amounts of data in simple ways. While very useful and valuable, descriptive statistics do not allow us to make conclusions beyond the data we have analysed or reach conclusions regarding any hypotheses. There are two key aspects of descriptive statistics: measures of central tendency (mean, median, and mode) and measures of dispersion (range, standard deviation).

Central tendency represents the middle values of your data. There are three distinct measures:

Mean – the average score, which is determined by adding all the individual scores and then dividing by the total number of subjects, cases, or elements in the sample. In calculating the mean the precision of your presentation should be to one decimal point past the value of the data. In the following examples, as the data is presented in whole numbers, you are allowed to present your answer to one decimal point.

data 2, 4, 6, 8, 10	mean: 30 / 5 = 6	presentation 6.0
data 2, 3, 4, 4, 6, 7	mean: 26 / 6 = 4.3333333	presentation 4.3
data 2, 2, 4, 5, 6, 6	mean: 25 / 6 = 4.1666666	presentation 4.2

Median – the midpoint of your data set. To calculate the median begin by ordering all the individual scores from low to high. The median will be the midpoint of the ranking. If there is an even set of numbers the median is the value that falls between the two.

Table 2.22a   Raw Data

| Participant | Social Work Participants | | | | Liberal Arts Honours Participants | | | |
	Sex	Age	Monthly Religious Service Attendance	JAREL	Sex	Age	Monthly Religious Service Attendance	JAREL
1	Female	39	0	100	Male	19	0	87
2	Female	38	4	116	Male	21	0	91
3	Female	34	0	101	Female	21	0	85
4	Female	20	0	102	Female	20	4	108
5	Female	33	2	102	Female	33	4	110
6	Male	40	1	101	Female	19	0	91
7	Female	25	1	97	Female	20	2	100
8	Male	25	0	84	Male	21	2	92
9	Female	40	0	95	Male	21	1	94
10	Female	25	4	111	Female	21	1	92
11	Female	29	0	105	Male	21	0	81
12	Male	22	2	120	Female	21	1	88
13	Female	22	1	106	Male	21	1	102
14	Female	29	1	107	Male	20	0	102
15	Female	28	3	106	Male	21	1	88
16	Female	29	1	106	Female	21	1	87
17	Female	27	1	115	Female	21	4	114
18	Female	21	1	100	Female	19	0	89
19	Female	20	1	98	Female	21	4	122
20	Male	41	1	88	Female	21	1	90
21	Female	21	3	100	Female	21	3	112
22	Female	22	0	88	Female	20	1	102
23	Female	29	1	100	Female	21	1	100
24	Female	40	0	102	Female	21	4	105
25	Female	26	0	102	Female	44	2	102

data 2, 4, 6, 8, 10 median = 6.0
data 2, 3, 4, 4, 6, 7 median = 4.0
data 2, 2, 4, 5, 6, 6 median = 4.5

Mode – the most common score in the data set. It is determined by frequency.

data 2, 4, 6, 8, 10 no mode as each item appears only once
data 2, 3, 4, 4, 6, 7 mode = 4.0
data 2, 2, 4, 5, 6, 6 bimodal = 2.0 and 6.0, as each appears twice

Measures of dispersion (measures of spread) describes the variability in a sample or population. This is used in conjunction with measures of central tendency to provide a broader overview of the data. Measure of dispersion provide additional insight into how meaningful the measures of central tendency are. The greater the dispersion, the more variability there is in the data; the less the dispersion, the less the variability.

Range – the difference between the highest and lowest scores in a data set. This is the simplest measure of spread and is calculated as: maximum value – minimum value.

data 2, 4, 6, 8, 10 10 – 2 = 8 range is 8.0
data 2, 3, 4, 4, 6, 7 7 – 2 = 5 range is 5.0
data 2, 2, 4, 5, 6, 6 6 – 2 = 4 range is 4.0

Standard deviation – a calculation used to measure the amount of difference or dispersion of a set of data. It can also be represented as *SD*, by the Greek letter sigma (σ) for the *population* standard deviation, or by the letter "s" for the *sample* standard deviation.

The **sample standard deviation formula** is:

$$s = \sqrt{\frac{\Sigma (X - \overline{X})^2}{n-1}}$$

where
s = sample standard deviation
Σ = sum of ...
X = each individual score
$\overline{X}$ = mean (average) of the sample
n = number of scores in sample.

The process of calculating standard deviation consists of seven steps:

Step 1: Calculate the mean (average).
Step 2: Subtract each individual score (X) from the sample's mean (average).
Step 3: Square each individual value you obtain in step 2.
Step 4: Add all of the individual values you obtained in step 3 together.
Step 5: Take the total number of cases or subjects (n) and subtract 1.
Step 6: Divide your total from step 4 by your value from step 5.
Step 7: Take the square root of your answer from step 6. This is your standard
   deviation.

Data set: 2, 4, 6, 8, 10 = 30   there are five cases (elements)

Step 1:   mean: 30 / 5 = 6
Step 2:   2 − 6 = −4   4 − 6 = −2   6 − 6 = 0   8 − 6 = 2   10 − 6 = 4
Step 3: $-4^2 = 16$ $-2^2 = 4$ $0^2 = 0$ $2^2 = 4$ $4^2 = 16$
Step 4:   16 + 4 + 0 + 4 + 16 = 40
Step 5   2, 4, 6, 8, 10 = 5 cases   5 − 1 = 4
Step 6   40 / 4 = 10
Step 7 $\sqrt{10}$ = 3.1622776   presentation = 3.2

Data Set: 2, 3, 4, 4, 6, 7 = 26   there are six cases (elements)

Step 1:   mean: 26 / 6 = 4.3
Step 2:   2 − 4.3 = −2.3   3 − 4.3 = −1.3   4 − 4.3 = −0.3   4 − 4.3 = −0.3
          6 − 4.3 = 1.7   7 − 4.3 = 2.7
Step 3: $-2.3^2 = 5.29$ $-1.3^2 = 1.69$ $-0.3^2 = 0.09$
          $-0.3^2 = 0.091.7^2 = 2.89$ $2.7^2 = 7.29$
Step 4:   5.29 + 1.69 + 0.09 + 0.09 + 2.89 + 7.29 = 17.34
Step 5   2, 3, 4, 4, 6, 7 = 6 cases   6 − 1 = 5
Step 6   17.34 / 5 = 3.468
Step 7 $\sqrt{3.468}$ = 1.8622566   presentation = 1.9

Data Set: 2, 2, 4, 5, 6, 6 = 25   there are six cases (elements)

Step 1:   mean: 25 / 6 = 4.2
Step 2:   2 − 4.2 = −2.2   2 − 4.2 = −2.2   4 − 4.2 = −0.2   5 − 4.2 = 0.8
          6 − 4.2 = 1.8   6 − 4.2 = 1.8

Step 3: $-2.2^2 = 4.84$ $-2.2^2 = 4.84$ $-0.2^2 = 0.04$ $0.8^2 = 0.64$

$1.8^2 = 3.24$ $1.8^2 = 3.24$

Step 4: $4.84 + 4.84 + 0.04 + 0.64 + 3.24 + 3.24 = 16.84$

Step 5 2, 2, 4, 5, 6, 6 = 6 cases $6 - 1 = 5$

Step 6 $16.84 / 5 = 3.468$

Step 7 $\sqrt{3.368} = 1.8352111$ presentation = 1.8

Summary Table

	data set 1	data set 2	data set 3
mean	6.0	4.3	4.2
median	6.0	4.0	4.5
mode	none	4.0	2.0; 6.0
range	8.0	5.0	4.0
standard deviation	3.2	1.9	1.8

7. Responding to the Case

The first step in describing your data is to tabulate the numbers you have obtained. In this study there were four variables: sex, age, monthly religious service attendance, and the JAREL score. Sex is nominal data (see Case Study 5) so all you are able to calculate is frequency. Age and monthly religious service attendance are ratio data (see Case Study 5) as there is an absolute zero. In examining age, social work participant 24 is 40 years old. She has lived twice as long as social work participant 4, who is 20. Likewise, social work participant 12 on average attends a religious service twice as often as social work participant 19. Mean, median, and mode can be calculated for these two variables. The JAREL scale is a more interesting calculation because of mathematical assumption. Although the JAREL scale presents like ratio data, it is actually ordinal (see Case Study 6). While we treat most Likert data that is numeric as if it were ratio, having a score of 120 as social work participant 12 did does not mean that he is 20 per cent more spiritual than social work participant 1, who scored 100. What you can correctly state, however, is that participant 12, who scored 120, has a greater sense of spirituality or that spirituality is more important to him than to participant 1, but it is not a direct mathematical relationship as you find with interval or ratio data.

Table 2.22b provides a summary of the raw data from Table 2.22a. It indicates that both groups had more female than male respondents. This is not atypical as social work is a female-dominated program of study and likewise more women than men are currently attending university in general. The social work participants were older, which is an important difference worth noting and discussing. While the liberal arts honours participants attended religious services slightly more than did their social work colleagues, the social work participants scored higher on the JAREL with a smaller range

Table 2.22b Descriptive Statistics Summary

data type	Social Work Participants				Liberal Arts Honours Participants			
	Sex	Age	Monthly Religious Service Attendance	JAREL	Sex	Age	Monthly Religious Service Attendance	JAREL
	nominal	ratio	ratio	ordinal	nominal	ratio	ratio	ordinal
mean	none	29.0	1.1	102.1	none	22.0	1.5	97.4
median	none	28.0	1.0	102.0	none	21.0	1.0	94.0
mode	female	29.0	1.0	100.0 and 102.0	female	21.0	1.0	102.0
range	none	20.0	4.0	37.0	none	25.0	4.0	41.0
standard deviation	none	7.2	1.2	8.4	none	5.3	1.5	10.4

and standard deviation, even though the single highest score belonged to a member of the liberal arts group. This leads to some interesting thoughts regarding the relationship between the two variables, but before discussion of those, the three questions posed can be answered.

1. What similarities are there between the two groups?

   Both groups are predominantly female.
2. What differences are there between the two groups?

   Social work students are an older group. Liberal arts undergraduates on average attend more religious services but social work students scored higher on spirituality. There is more dispersion among the liberal arts sample than the social workers in religious service attendance and the JAREL but less with regard to age.
3. Were the social workers in the group as spiritual as their liberal arts honours counterparts?

   No; based on this sample, they are more spiritual.

While these findings do not allow you to draw conclusions, they do allow you to describe the situation and move from beyond believing or thinking to knowing and thus to understanding the situation better, which is the goal of descriptive statistics.

8. Research Insight

If you wish to take the next step and begin to draw conclusions regarding whether social work students are actually more spiritual than their liberal arts honours peers, rather than just describing the differences, you need to take the next step and move into the realm of inferential statistics, as discussed in Case Study 23.

9. Further Reflections

What do you believe? What do you know? What is the value in terms of producing change, in advocating for clients, and in new policy development of knowing rather than just believing?

10. Additional Reading

Csiernik, R., & Adams, D. (2002). The impact of social work education on students' spirituality. *Currents: New Scholarship in the Human Services*, *1*(1), 1–17.

Csiernik, R., & Adams, D. (2003). Social work students and spirituality: An initial exploration. *Canadian Social Work*, *5*(1), 65–79.

Hungelmann, J., Kenkel-Rossi, E., Klassen, L., & Stollenwerk, R. (1987). *JAREL Spiritual Well-Being Scale*. Milwaukee, WI: Marquette University College of Nursing.

Kanzler, G. (2010). *Statistics for the terrified* (5th ed.). London: Prentice Hall.

Rowntree, D. (2000). *Statistics without tears*. Boston, MA: Allyn and Bacon.

Santandrea, M. (1998). How Catholic are we? *King's Herald*, September, 16–17.

Weinbach, R., & Grinnell, R., Jr. (2014). *Statistics for social workers* (9th ed.). New York: Longman.

11. Internet Resources

Descriptive Statistics

Khan Academy, "Displaying and Describing Data":
https://www.khanacademy.org/math/probability/descriptive-statistics

Teresa Johnson, "Introduction to Descriptive Statistics":
https://www.youtube.com/watch?v=QoQbR4lVLrs

Central Tendency

MathHelp.com, "Central Tendency | Mean Median Mode Range":
https://www.youtube.com/watch?annotation_id=annotation_1736036691&feature=iv&src_vid=81zcjULlh58&v=hX-BsyXGyb8

Laerd Statistics, "Measures of Central Tendency":

    https://statistics.laerd.com/statistical-guides/measures-central-tendency-mean-mode-median.php

David M. Lane and Heidi Ziemer, "What Is Central Tendency?":

    http://onlinestatbook.com/2/summarizing_distributions/what_is_ct.html

Standard Deviation and Variance

Bozeman Science, "Standard Deviation":

    https://www.youtube.com/watch?v=09kiX3p5Vek

Math Is Fun, "Standard Deviation and Variance":

    https://www.mathsisfun.com/data/standard-deviation.html

Wikihow, "How to Calculate Standard Deviation":

    http://www.wikihow.com/Calculate-Standard-Deviation

Easycalculation.com, "Standard Deviation Calculator":

    https://www.easycalculation.com/statistics/standard-deviation.php

CASE STUDY 23

Inferring What You Know: Selecting an Appropriate Statistical Test

1. Preamble

The stereotype and unfortunately somewhat of a reality is that social workers, in particular social work students, fear math. The issue in research, however, is that when you are in fear of numbers *False Evidence Appears Real*, and that can lead us to break the first rule of the profession: to do no harm.

2. The Problem

In recent decades, the trend in mental health has been towards not only deinstitutionalization but also dehospitalization, which has led to hospital bed closures and poorly planned discharge of individuals into a community with support services that lack funding. It is well accepted that people with mental illness are over-represented in the homeless population; however, this has not generally been linked to discharge from hospital. People living on the streets or in shelters are at an increased risk of contracting medical illnesses, such as tuberculosis or HIV infection, or becoming a victim of physical or sexual assault. Individuals who had no stable housing before admission, had low clinical improvement during hospital stay, received less therapeutic measures, were discharged early, and received no care after discharge have the greatest risk (Forchuk et al., 2008). To respond to this, health care teams should be addressing individuals who are identified as being without stable housing by immediately initiating the discharge plan on the day of the person's admission. While the issue of discharge from the psychiatric ward to shelters, or the street, is difficult to track, a targeted mental health study was able to collect data on this phenomenon for one community.

3. The Process

The average length of stay in hospitals has shortened and the available housing market has greatly diminished across Canada. Sometimes the only way to admit the next patient who is in crisis is to discharge one who is psychiatrically stable, even if appropriate housing has not been obtained. Hospital staff have to immediately assess the housing situation upon admission to even have a chance of making appropriate arrangements if a change is required. Even if this occurs, the process for obtaining public income support may be longer than the hospitalization, and there are policy and practice restrictions on the ability to access community start-up costs that would cover the first and last months' rent. Affordability has been recognized as one of the three main housing needs in Canada. With a shortage of affordable housing, the client may need help finding suitable accommodation and will need to move quickly with the rental fees when an appropriate place is found. Often individuals are forced to live with others, go to a shelter, or if no other options exist, go out on the streets. Tragically, these persons are at risk of falling victim to the sex and/or drug trade and other unsafe occupations to establish and maintain housing. These individual and systemic issues are relevant to mental health professionals, as they illustrate the complexities and hardships of clients that may not be so clearly presented upon hospital admission but are crucial at time of discharge. When mental health care professionals are aware of system issues impacting vulnerable populations, they must act as advocates for change to practices within the health care system and so assist in reducing negative outcomes with consumers.

4. The Research

A pilot study was undertaken to test a direct intervention to prevent homelessness following a psychiatric admission. The study employed a randomized control design to evaluate the effectiveness of the new, yet extremely simple, approach. Participants who were at risk of being discharged to "no fixed address" were enrolled in the study and completed an initial interview while hospitalized. At the end of the interview, they chose an envelope which determined whether they were in the intervention or control group. All participants were randomly selected using this envelope method to avoid selection bias. Those in the intervention group received specialized assistance from a housing advocate to find housing including fast-tracking their income support. Those in the control group received the usual care individuals have received for years. While the usual care did not include direct and immediate assistance with housing, referral to the hospital social worker for housing support if requested by the health care team during inpatient stay was encouraged, though not mandatory.

Participants were recruited from an acute care psychiatric ward within a general hospital ($n = 12$) and a tertiary care psychiatric hospital ($n = 2$). These sites provide all the psychiatric inpatient services for the broader community. Nine men and five women were selected and all 14 completed all phases of the study with regard to the primary outcome of current housing. Participants were equally divided, with seven in the intervention group and seven in the control group. Participant characteristics including

Table 2.23 Participant Characteristics

Characteristics	Control (n = 7)	Intervention (n = 7)
Female	2	3
Male	5	4
Age – mean years (SD)	31 (13.4)	35 (15.2)
Age – range	18–52	21–63
Length of admission (weeks)		
Mean (SD)	1.7 (0.7)	3.4 (5.6)
Marital status		
Single/never married	4	5
Separated/divorced	2	2
Married/common-law	1	0
Primary diagnosis (self-reported)		
Schizophrenia	2	3
Mood disorder	2	4
Anxiety disorder	2	0
Other	1	0
Average length of time to be housed (days)	180	2

SD, standard deviation

age, primary diagnoses, marital status, and length of hospital stay are summarized in Table 2.23. The control and intervention group participants were similar at the period of enrolment; thus additional variables were not controlled for during the analysis.

It was hypothesized that participants in the intervention group, those receiving assistance to obtain housing, would be more likely to obtain and maintain housing than those in the control group. It was further hypothesized that the intervention group would have less utilization of hospital services after discharge, and would maintain a higher level of functioning and quality of life compared with the control group.

5. Questions

1. *What statistical test do you need to conduct to determine what the findings mean?*
2. *Based on your results what action do you take?*

6. Social Work Practice

The purpose of inferential statistics is to allow researchers to make informed decisions about the populations they are interested in based upon samples taken from that population. However, even with randomization, errors can occur that make the results less accurate and decrease the validity of the findings. In other cases randomization is not possible and instead groups need to be matched, which is often the case in social work research. Inferential statistics are used to make predictions (inferences) about a population based upon observations drawn from a sample of that population. Inferential statistics are simply the techniques that allow us to use these samples to make generalizations about the populations from which the samples were drawn. However, it is essential that the sample accurately represent the population (see Case Study 7). Inferential statistics arise because regardless of how good the sample, unless everyone is asked, there will be a degree of sampling error (Case Study 21) in any study conducted and thus a sample will never perfectly represent the population.

To get to the point in the research process where the use of inferential statistics is actually required takes a long time. The first step is the development of the *research hypothesis* (Case Study 9), the statement created by researchers when they speculate upon the outcome of their study. However, in research we never prove our hypothesis because of the limitations of sampling; rather we try to demonstrate that the results could not occur simply by chance. This is the *null hypothesis* (H_0). When we disprove the null hypothesis using inferential statistics it means that the result of our study is probably the result of our intervention, but only probably.

How likely the outcome observed occurs by chance is denoted by the letter p and relates to the concept of statistical significance. *P value* is how strong the likelihood is that you can reject the null hypothesis and how likely (probable) the result you have observed was caused by your independent variable. A p value of 0.05 means 95 times out of 100 the outcome did not occur by chance while a p value of 0.01 means that the outcome occurred by chance 1 out of 100 times. A research outcome is deemed to be *statistically significant* based on the p value. This signifies that you are certain the inferential statistic you calculated is reliable, which leads you to reject the null hypothesis. When you reject the null hypothesis by definition you accept your hypothesis and the likelihood ($p = 0.05$ or $p = 0.01$) that the independent variable caused a change in the dependent variable.

Once you have your hypothesis and null hypothesis you need to select which type of statistical test to employ. This is totally reliant upon the nature of your data. Data can only fall into one of four categories (see also Case Study 6):

nominal	descriptive data with no numeric value
ordinal	rank order data from high to low which can be categorical (lowest, low, high, highest) or numeric as in Likert scales, where it is opinion and not actual numeric differences that create the ranking
interval	numbers with a mathematical relationship (4 is twice as large as 2, 5 is half as large as 10) but with no 0 point on the scale
ratio	numbers with a mathematical relationship (2 is half as large as 4, 10 is twice as large as 5) with an absolute 0 point on the scale

Once you know the type of data you have, determining the type of statistical test to apply becomes much easier. The five most commonly used inferential statistics in social work are described below.

Chi-square is used when you have nominal or categorical (non-numeric) ordinal data. Its common use is to compare observed data with data we would expect to obtain according to a specific hypothesis. For example, if, you expected 10 of 20 children brought into foster care to be placed for adoption and the actual observed number was 6, you would want to know if your practice model and adoption matching process are meeting expectations. Statistically what you are looking for is the "goodness to fit" between the observed and expected outcomes. You want to ask if the deviation (the difference between the observed and the expected outcome) was the result of chance or the result of other factors. The chi-square test is always testing the null hypothesis, which states that there is no significant difference between the expected and observed result.

The t test is a statistical examination of the average (mean) of two distinct populations that you wish to compare. It is used when the sample size is small and also when the variance (dispersion) of the two groups is unknown. A *t* test allows you to compare whether two groups have different average values and how unlikely it is that this difference occurred as a result of random chance in sample selection. A *t* value is obtained that indicates the *p* value. The *p* value of course tells you how likely it is that the result occurred due to your intervention (the independent variable) or if the difference is just due to chance. The *t* test can be used with any data for which you can calculate a mean.

ANOVA stands for analysis of variance and its principle is similar to a *t* test, only it is used when you are comparing more than two unrelated groups and rather than a *t* value you obtain an *F* score. As with the *t* value, each *F* score is associated with a *p* value that indicates if your outcome is due to your intervention or due to chance.

Correlation is a statistical technique used to measure and describe the strength and direction of the relationship between two variables. Correlation requires two scores

Figure 2.23   Correlation

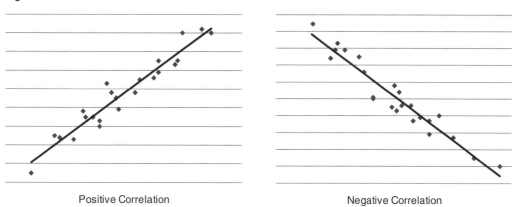

Positive Correlation   Negative Correlation

from the *same* individual. A positive correlation indicates the extent to which the two variables increase in relation to each other; a negative correlation indicates the extent to which one variable increases as the other decreases (Figure 2.23). It is important to keep in mind that correlation does not mean causation; it simply reflects the relationship between two variables. The most common method to calculate correlation is Pearson's *r*. The range of Pearson's *r* is +1 to −1. The closer to +1 or −1 the stronger the relationship is between the two variables you are examining, and the closer to 0 the less likely there is any type of relationship between the two.

Linear regression is a method for predicting the value of a dependent variable *y*, based on the value of an independent variable *x*. It is the process of discovering the straight line that best fits the relationship between your independent (explanatory) and dependent variables. If there is a best-fit line for the data, the line can be used for estimating other values. This allows you to predict a value of the dependent variable (*y*) based upon the knowledge of the value of the independent variable (*x*). A linear regression line is calculated as $y = a + bx$, where *x* is the independent (explanatory) variable and *y* is the dependent variable. The slope of the line is *b*, and *a* is the intercept (the value of *y* when $x = 0$).

One final concept to be aware of for better understanding inferential statistics relates to *statistical power* (probability levels): *type I and type II errors*. A type I error occurs when you reject the null hypothesis when the null hypothesis is actually true. This is equivalent to a false positive. You state that an outcome occurred not by chance but from the effect of the independent variable on the dependent variable when in fact it did occur by chance. Type II errors are the opposite of type I errors. In this case the null hypothesis is not rejected, implying that the outcome occurred by chance rather than as a result of your intervention, when in fact your intervention did produce the change in client outcome. This is equivalent to a false negative: you indicate your counselling or policy change was not responsible for improved client functioning when in fact it was.

There are three methods to combat type I and type II errors. The first is to maximize sample size, for as sample size increases, sampling error decreases. The second is to have a high p value such as 0.05, which allows for an error on average only one out of every 20 trials, though of course moving p to 0.01 would decrease the risk even further. The third is to alter effect size which is the most difficult to achieve. Effect size is the quantitative measure of the strength of a reported relationship. To increase effect size you need to either increase the difference between the average of the treatment group and the average of the control group or decrease the population variance, neither of which can be done once a study is complete.

7. Responding to the Case

Differences between the mean scores of the intervention and control groups were determined using t tests on ratio data (e.g., age) and chi-square for nominal data (e.g., housed/homeless). There were no statistically significant differences at baseline between the two groups on any variable examined.

With regard to the primary outcome measure, the pilot revealed that all individuals in the intervention group attained independent housing within two days of discharge and maintained housing when interviewed at the three- and six-month intervals. In contrast, all but one individual in the control group failed to attain housing and remained homeless at the three- and six-month intervals. The one exception was engaged in the sex trade to earn an adequate income to avoid homelessness. While in this case there really is no need to conduct a statistical analysis as the data is so obvious, the result was (χ^2, $p < 0.001$). This meant that there was less than a 1 in 1000 chance this outcome occurred by chance.

The results of this pilot investigation were so dramatic that randomizing to the control group stopped and plans were begun to routinely implement the intervention. Ultimately, hospital recidivism and homelessness were prevented in this participant group by helping these individuals at a crucial transition period from hospital into the community. The study statistically indicated that a simple policy change that would be relatively inexpensive to make would virtually eliminate homelessness among mental health consumer-survivors being discharged from hospital back into the community.

8. Research Insight

Despite how intimidating statistics may appear at first, and it certainly is daunting, if you approach the use of numbers in research as you would any other problem it is much easier to deconstruct the process and slowly and methodically address the problem. Technology has been of great assistance; no longer are extensive math calculations necessary to obtain your p value and ascertain if your intervention led to the change in a client or not. However, it remains vital you understand what you are doing and why, if not the exact math. To this end in section 11, "Internet Resources," along with videos describing each statistical test in greater detail, a test calculator is provided. For each of these, all you have to do in input your data and the calculation will be conducted for you. However, you still have to know what you are asking or the outcome will remain meaningless.

While much was learned in Case Study 22 by applying descriptive statistics, more even can be determined by applying a t test to compare the means on the JAREL scale of the social work group (102.1) and the honours liberal arts group (97.4). The t value (difference between the scores) is 1.765262. This was calculated by inputting the JAREL scores of the two groups into a simple t test calculator (http://www.socscistatistics.com/tests/studenttest/Default2.aspx). The p value generated by a t value of 1.765262 is 0.04194 (a value also determined by the t test calculator), which means the result is significant at $p < 0.05$. You now have all the knowledge and skills necessary in order to conduct research and to draw conclusions, such as social work students have a greater sense of spirituality than do their honours liberal arts counterparts, with a 95 per cent degree of confidence.

9. Further Reflections

How much more comfortable are you now with the concepts of research and statistics than you were when you first read and completed Case Study 1? You were asked earlier, "What would you do if you knew you couldn't fail?" so …

10. Additional Reading

Aron, A., Coups, E., & Aron, E. (2010). *Quick references for determining the power of tests. Statistics for the behavioral and social sciences: A brief course* (5th ed.). Upper Saddle River, NJ: Prentice Hall.

Forchuk, C., Csiernik, R., & Jensen, E. (Eds.). (2011). *Homelessness, housing and the experiences of mental health consumer-survivors: Finding truths – creating change.* Toronto: Canadian Scholars' Press.

Forchuk, C., MacClure, S.K., Van Beers, M., Smith, C., Csiernik, R., Hoch, J., & Jensen, E. (2008). Developing and testing an intervention to prevent homelessness among individuals discharged from psychiatric wards to shelters and "no fixed address." *Journal of Psychiatric and Mental Health Nursing, 15*(7), 569–75. http://dx.doi.org/10.1111/j.1365-2850.2008.01266.x.

Randolph, K.A., & Myers, L.L. (2013). *Basic statistics in multivariate analysis*. Oxford: Oxford University Press. http://dx.doi.org/10.1093/acprof:oso/9780199764044.001.0001.

Rosenthal, J.A. (2011). *Statistics and data interpretation for social work*. New York: Springer.

Thompson, B. (2002). "Statistical," "practical," and "clinical": How many kinds of significance do counselors need to consider? *Journal of Counseling and Development, 80*(1), 64–71. http://dx.doi.org/10.1002/j.1556-6678.2002.tb00167.x.

Thompson, B. (2006). Role of effect sizes in contemporary research in counseling. *Counseling and Values, 50*(3), 176–86. http://dx.doi.org/10.1002/j.2161-007X.2006.tb00054.x.

Urdan, T. (2010). *Statistics in plain English* (3rd ed.). New York: Taylor and Francis.

Vacha-Haase, T., & Thompson, B. (2004). How to estimate and interpret various effect sizes. *Journal of Counseling Psychology, 51*(4), 473–81. http://dx.doi.org/10.1037/0022-0167.51.4.473.

Weinback, R., & Grinnell, R., Jr. (2014). *Statistics for social workers* (9th ed.). New York: Longman.

11. Internet Resources

Introduction to Inferential Statistics

The Doctoral Journey, "Introduction to Statistics: What Are They? And, How Do I Know Which One to Choose?":
   https://www.youtube.com/watch?v=HpyRybBEDQ0
Brian Caffo, "Introduction to Statistical Inference":
   https://www.youtube.com/watch?v=WkOinijQmPU

Hypothesis Testing

Public Resources Organization, "Science Pirates Songs – Hypothesis Song":
   https://www.youtube.com/watch?v=giC6ZYBIeFY
Mr. Nystrom, "Null and Alternative Hypotheses":
   https://www.youtube.com/watch?v=spwEHuHOMuk
Stomp on Step 1, "Null Hypothesis, p-Value, Statistical Significance, Type 1 Error and Type 2 Error":
   https://www.youtube.com/watch?annotation_id=annotation_368732233&feature=iv&index=16&list=PLnxX3HMtI5fkzNdLpA-0qCSUYLXxLJQH6&src_vid=6_xBpWoUIRg&v=YSwmpAmLV2s
Math Holt, "Null and Alternative Hypotheses":
   https://www.youtube.com/watch?v=702c5GA7HZ4

p value

Mr. Nystrom, "What Is a P Value? What Does It Tell Us?":
  https://www.youtube.com/watch?v=-MKT3yLDkqk
jbstatistics, "What Is a p-value?":
  https://www.youtube.com/watch?v=HTZ8YKgD0MI
FredDoreyStatistics's channel, "The p value – What Does It Mean?":
  https://www.youtube.com/watch?v=02HiygxmWk4

How to Choose a Statistical Test

sparkling psychology star, "How to Choose a Statistical Test":
  https://www.youtube.com/watch?v=fv5SW5-_u2M
Statistics Learning Centre, "Choosing which Statistical Test to Use – Statistics Help":
  https://www.youtube.com/watch?v=rulIUAN0U3w
Nikos Ntoumanis, "Choosing a Statistical Test":
  https://www.youtube.com/watch?v=tNXOTbXarH4

Chi-square

Brandon Foltz, "Introduction to the Chi-square Test":
  https://www.youtube.com/watch?v=SvKv375sacA
Social Science Statistics, "Chi-square Calculator":
  http://www.socscistatistics.com/tests/chisquare/default2.aspx
Bozeman Science, "Chi-squared Test":
  https://www.youtube.com/watch?v=WXPBoFDqNVk
Khan Academy, "Chi-square Distribution Introduction":
  https://www.khanacademy.org/math/probability/statistics-inferential/chi-square/v
  /chi-square-distribution-introduction

Covariance

Brandon Foltz, "Understanding Covariance":
  https://www.youtube.com/watch?v=xGbpuFNR1ME

t test

Brandon Foltz, "Two Populations, t-test with Hypothesis":
  https://www.youtube.com/watch?v=oJjkjkY6mmA
Social Science Statistics, "*T*-Test Calculator for 2 Independent Means":
  http://www.socscistatistics.com/tests/studenttest/Default2.aspx

ANOVA (Analysis of Variance)

J. David Eisenbeg, "Analysis of Variance (ANOVA)":
 https://www.youtube.com/watch?v=ITf4vHhyGpc
College of Saint Benedict & Saint John's University:
 http://www.physics.csbsju.edu/stats/anova.html, ANOVA

Pearson Correlation

Brandon Foltz, "Understanding Correlation":
 https://www.youtube.com/watch?v=4EXNedimDMs
Social Science Statistics, "Pearson Correlation Coefficient Calculator":
 http://www.socscistatistics.com/tests/pearson/
David M. Lane, "Computing Pearson's r":
 http://onlinestatbook.com/2/describing_bivariate_data/calculation.html

Simple Regression

Quant Concepts, "The Easiest Introduction to Regression Analysis! – Statistics Help":
 https://www.youtube.com/watch?v=k_OB1tWX9PM
Brandon Foltz, "Simple Linear Regression (Part 1), The Very Basics":
 https://www.youtube.com/watch?v=ZkjP5RJLQF4
Ncula, "Statistics Calculator: Linear Regression":
 http://www.alcula.com/calculators/statistics/linear-regression/

Type I and Type II Errors

Prof RobBob, "Type 1 Error Type 2 Error Power 1 Sample Mean Hypothesis z-Test":
 https://www.youtube.com/watch?v=WZwheNGwb9w
Berkley, "Type I and Type II Errors":
 http://www.stat.berkeley.edu/~hhuang/STAT141/Lecture-FDR.pdf
Khan Academy, "Type 1 Errors":
 https://www.khanacademy.org/math/probability/statistics-inferential/hypothesis-testing/v/type-1-errors

Effect Size

Villanova University, "The Concepts of Statistical Power and Effect Size":
 http://www83.homepage.villanova.edu/richard.jacobs/EDU%208603/lessons/stastical%20power.html
Robert Coe, "It's the Effect Size, Stupid: What Effect Size Is and Why It Is Important":
 http://www.leeds.ac.uk/educol/documents/00002182.htm

CHAPTER THREE

Critiquing Research

Introduction

In a perfect world each research project attempted would be carefully designed and flawlessly executed; each scientific paper published would be comprehensive and engaging. However, as we all know, the real world is less than perfect. Research practice is often messy and problematic, particularly for social workers, since we conduct most of our inquiry outside the highly controlled and sterile environment of a scientific laboratory. The realities of field investigation and the compromises required to complete a research project often combine to create a less than perfect product. This is not an apology for poor research, nor is it reason to consider scientific inquiry a futile endeavour. Rather, it is an honest assessment of the existing situation and, more importantly, justification for the need to engage in critical reflection on what we read and to thoughtfully determine what information to incorporate into our knowledge of the world. One of the main reasons you are taking a research course and have been "actively encouraged" to read this book is to acquire the knowledge and skills that will enable you to become a critical consumer of social work research.

This has become even more important with the increasing use of electronic resources and searching. Historically it was simple to assess if a source was of the highest quality: it would appear in a peer-reviewed journal and you would know it was peer-reviewed as it would be sitting in a stack in the basement of the campus library. This remains the surest first evaluative criterion; however, given the cost of journals to libraries there are very few stacks remaining and virtually all resources, regardless of quality, are online. This century has seen the consolidation of control of the majority of journals into the hands of just a few international publishing conglomerates. With this has come increasing costs to access peer-reviewed materials, even by authors once they have published their own work. This in turn led to the development of a second type of journal and publishing platform: open access. Open-access journals are readily available not only through traditional university library databases but also online without having to use any search engine beyond Google Scholar or often even just Google. With the emergence of open-access journals, the large publishing companies countered by offering their authors the option of open-access publishing. If you do not have access to a post-secondary library and want this research, you can pay for it with an average cost of approximately $40 per article. Open-access articles have the author pay the publisher up front so that there are no restrictions on access; anyone can access it at any time from any electronic source and download it onto their own computer. These articles are still peer-reviewed and thus are of the highest quality, though this does not mean there are not methodological and interpretative limits, simply that other experts have reviewed the work and deemed it has methodological rigour and is not (overly) flawed in its premise or presentation.

However, another class of publications has arisen in parallel: predatory journals. Predatory journals charge authors money to have their work published but only provide an editing service rather than any type of peer-review system using expert colleagues who critically assess the article, determining its strength, limits, and overall contribution to the literature. In some cases these predatory journals do not even provide an editing service. It is rare in peer review to have an article accepted without any changes. Typically feedback from peers recommends major revisions, and it is also quite common to have an article rejected outright for publication because of its inadequacies. The lack of any type of quality control of predatory journals was wonderfully exposed by engineer Alex Smolyanitsky, who submitted a paper entitled "Fuzzy, Homogeneous Configurations" to a series of journals under the names Maggie Simpson, Edna Krabappel, and Kim Jong Fun. The fabricated article written by fictitious authors was accepted by two journals, which, if Maggie, Edna, and Kim had paid enough money, would have published it. However, the article, being open access, is available in its entirety for anyone to read and cite through a simple Google Scholar search. This experiment was repeated by *Ottawa Citizen* reporter Tom Spears, who sat down and with no knowledge in this area wrote "Acidity and Aridity: Soil Inorganic Carbon Storage Exhibits Complex Relationship with Low-pH Soils and Myeloablation Followed by Autologous PBSC Infusion." It was accepted by eight different journals who offered to publish it for a fee ranging from $1,000 to $5,000. It too can be found via Google and Google Scholar.

Another instance demonstrating the total lack of any type of screening or academic integrity that occurs within the field of predatory publications is computer scientists David Mazières and Eddie Kohler's infamous "Get Me Off Your Fucking Mailing List" paper, which included the grievous error of labelling both Figure 1 and Figure 2 "get me off your fucking mailing list," along with repeating this phrase over and over again in the body of the article. This paper was actually published in the *International Journal of*

Advanced Computer Technology. Perhaps what is even more worrisome is that not only can you find the article on Google (http://www.scs.stanford.edu/~dm/home/papers/remove.pdf), you can also find it on Google Scholar, which might legitimize the journal in unintended ways if the intent of the article is not understood. Further, the *International Journal of Advanced Computer Technology*'s website states that articles published with them will be indexed in six different sources, including Google. They also state that while they are a trademark journal, which means they charge a fee for publishing work, they do not compromise quality of research and the review process will take one to two weeks. A highly efficient peer-reviewed social work journal that is considered to have a quick review process will take as long as four months to review an article, though six to eight months is not atypical for the first phase of the social work peer-review process. It takes this long in part because reviewers are providing extensive feedback on the article's adequacy for publication and those changes, typically extensive, that are needed for it to be published. Once the article is revised it must be resubmitted to the editors, and sometimes to the original reviewers, to ascertain if the limits with the article have been sufficiently addressed to ready it for publication.

While the second edition of the book was under revision, an email was received by one of the authors indicating that journal X, an "internationally-recognized" open-access publisher, welcomed submissions to its journal. The bonus is that the author could "impress the world" by being published in this journal, and if the article was submitted between August 21 and September 20 it would be half the regular cost.

Unfortunately, this is not a totally new trend; before there were predatory journals, whose sole purpose is profit rather than the dissemination of high-quality research findings to further knowledge, there were vanity presses. A vanity press is one that will publish your book and print as many copies as you like, as long as you personally pay for it.

Thus, the function of this final section of the book is to give you some practice in critical evaluation of published research. It provides you with two research papers based on real-world research projects, one qualitative and one quantitative. You will be asked to carry out an evaluation of the quality of each of the two study designs and implementations and to consider the applicability of its findings for social work practice. Working with an entire article will provide you with the opportunity to examine and critique the entire research activity and to practise drawing conclusions about the quality and usefulness of research findings.

The first step is to carefully read the paper to identify any problems in the design or implementation of the project. To help you do this in a comprehensive and efficient manner, we have provided two critical evaluation templates, one for quantitative research and one for qualitative. By approaching the task in a systemic fashion, you increase the likelihood that you will consider the most important features of the research and identify important issues and problematic outcomes. As well as addressing the quality of the design and implementation, the template will allow you to evaluate the quality of the written paper presentation. All three aspects are important in coming to your overall assessment of the research.

The next step is to consider each of the problems that you have identified and determine the extent to which these undermine your confidence in the findings of the research. Obviously there are certain "fatal flaws" that in themselves suggest that the research is not trustworthy and the findings should not be considered as useable knowledge. For example, a clearly non-representative sample or measures with poor psychometric properties would put in question a quantitative study. Qualitative research that does not establish prolonged engagement or employs a decidedly biased analytical frame would also be suspect. It is more likely that you will identify a number of minor difficulties, the type of problems that reflect necessary compromises or the impact of unexpected events. A word of caution at this point: it is easy to become overly critical and even smug when purposefully seeking faults. Don't. Those taking this approach are in danger of disregarding potentially important and helpful findings. Recall that science is a provisional activity. Nothing is "proven," and as social scientists we always need to be open to new findings or to the refinement of existing theory. Each person has to reach a reasonable balance between nitpicking, fault finding, and naive acceptance. The good research studies as well as the bad ones are relatively easy to identify; it's the in-between efforts that need careful consideration. Unfortunately, there are no easy rules, such as "Three errors and it's rubbish!" Every situation needs to be thought through in light of what the project attempted and what it accomplished. The onus is on each research consumer to conduct a thoughtful evaluation before deciding what to do. As well, you need to reflect on the difficulty in creating new knowledge and the relative ease in finding imperfections with a process and a product that may have taken years to complete.

Following each research paper is a critical analysis that is provided to illustrate the process or research evaluation and to allow you to compare the issues you identified with those of more experienced evaluators. Your individual analysis will more than likely have fewer issues, though you may have identified many of the same issues and may even have raised additional concerns. The key to this activity is that you give careful consideration to a wide variety of factors and make reasonable judgments based upon your work. Practice makes perfect, and here is an opportunity to practice in a setting with few truly negative outcomes. When you are done you should feel more confident in attempting this important task. The templates are a suggestion; in using them you will identify needed modifications and make personal adjustments. The process you eventually adopt will develop over time as you practise this important skill. All social work practitioners need to develop a set of standards and criteria for reviewing and evaluating claims of new knowledge in order to responsibly develop their professional expertise.

Critical Analysis of Qualitative Research

Part A – Purpose

1. What is the research problem? What is (are) the research question(s)?
2. What is your opinion of the quality of the literature review section of the report? Is there a solid conceptual framework to guide the research?
3. Has the researcher provided a clear statement of reflexivity?
4. In your estimation did the study commit any ethical violations? If so, do you feel that the benefits justify the ethical violations?

Part B – Measurement

1. What are the concepts under investigation?
2. How were these concepts defined at the start of the research? Are these definitions clear and acceptable?

Part C – Participants

1. How were participants and sites selected? Did the researcher consider creating maximum variation in participant selection?
2. Did the researcher seek out negative cases and include data from such sources?
3. Did the researcher provide enough information on the characteristics and circumstances of participants so that readers can assess transferability of findings?

Part D – Design

1. How were questions/topics developed? How were the data collected? Were interviews transcribed for analysis?
2. Did data collection occur over a long enough period of time to reduce possible reactivity or lack of openness?
3. Was triangulation used in data collection or were all data collected using a single collection approach?

Part E – Data Analysis and Reporting

1. Is it clear what data analytical techniques were used? Are these techniques appropriate for the type of data collected?
2. Was data analysed by more than one researcher? How were multiple interpretations integrated into study results?
3. Did the researcher provide examples of how interpretations emerged, i.e., from codes to categories or from subthemes to themes?
4. Is the interpretive framework integrated, i.e., are results presented as a logically connected whole, not as a series of unrelated categories?
5. Did the researcher employ member checking to generate feedback on researchers' interpretation of the data?
6. Did the report include sufficient illustrative examples using participants' own words?
7. Have the researchers documented any limitations? What are they, if any? Did you note any limitations not mentioned by researchers?
8. What ideas did the authors have about further research? Do these extend the current project in reasonable ways?

Part F – Overall Evaluation

What is your overall opinion of the quality of this research? As a social worker, would you be interested in these findings? How might you incorporate them into your practice, if at all?

Critical Analysis of Quantitative Research

Part A – Purpose

1. What is the research problem? What are the research questions and/or hypotheses?
2. What is the general purpose of the inquiry? (e.g., exploratory, descriptive, or explanatory)
3. What is your opinion of the quality of the literature review section of the report?
4. In your estimation did the study commit any ethical violations? If so, do you feel that the benefits justify the ethical violations?

Part B – Measurement

1. What are the concepts (variables) under investigation?
2. How were the variables nominally defined?
3. For each measure:
    - How was it measured? (e.g., single item, scale, index, checklist, rater observation)
    - What is the level of measurement?
    - For each measure that is a scale or an index:
        (a) Did the authors address the validity of the measure? If so, what was reported?
        (b) Did the authors test the reliability of the measure? If so, what was reported?
4. From the evidence provided by the authors would you conclude that these are valid and reliable measures?

Part C – Participants

1. Describe how the sample was selected. Is it a probability or non-probability sample? What sampling method was employed by the authors? (e.g., snowball, simple random, convenience)
2. What population was the sample intended to represent? Do you have any concerns about the extent to which the sample represents the population? If so, what are they?
3. Did the authors address the generalizability of their findings? If so, what did they conclude?

Part D – Design

1. Was the research experimental, cross-sectional, or longitudinal in nature?
2. How were data collected? (e.g., interview, questionnaire, observation, secondary data)
3. If data are secondary, did the researcher address reliability of original data collection?
4. If data were primary, were instruments pre-tested on persons similar to participants?
5. What is your evaluation of the quality of the data collection process? Do you have any concerns?

Part E – Data Analysis and Reporting

1. What statistical analysis was applied to the data? Was the analysis appropriate for the level of measurement?
2. Did the researchers address the meaningfulness of statistically significant results?
3. Are the key findings of the statistical analysis addressed in the discussion section?
4. Have the researchers documented any limitations? What are they, if any? Did you note any limitations not mentioned by researchers?
5. What ideas did the authors have about further research? Do these extend the current project in reasonable ways?

Part F – Overall Evaluation

What is your overall opinion of the quality of this research? As a social worker, would you be interested in these findings? How might you incorporate them into your practice, if at all?

Additional Reading

Barbour, R.S., & Barbour, M. (2003). Evaluating and synthesizing qualitative research: The need to develop a distinctive approach. *Journal of Evaluation in Clinical Practice, 9*(2), 179–86. http://dx.doi.org/10.1046/j.1365-2753.2003.00371.x.

Barker, C., & Pistrang, N. (2005). Quality criteria under methodological pluralism: Implications for conducting and evaluating research. *American Journal of Community Psychology, 35*(3–4), 201–12. http://dx.doi.org/10.1007/s10464-005-3398-y.

Beall, J. (2015). Criteria for determining predatory open-access publishers. *Scholarly open access.* https://scholarlyoa.files.wordpress.com/2015/01/criteria-2015.pdf.

Berger, M., & Cirasella, J. (2015). Beyond Beall's List: Better understanding predatory publishers. *College & Research Libraries News, 76*(3), 132–5.

Bernard, H.R., & Bernard, H.R. (2012). *Social research methods: Qualitative and quantitative approaches.* Thousand Oaks, CA: Sage.

Creswell, J.W. (2012). *Qualitative inquiry and research design: Choosing among five approaches.* Thousand Oaks, CA: Sage.

Creswell, J.W. (2013). *Research design: Qualitative, quantitative, and mixed methods approaches.* Thousand Oaks, CA: Sage.

Davies, D., & Dodd, J. (2002). Qualitative research and the question of rigor. *Qualitative Health Research, 12*(2), 279–89. http://dx.doi.org/10.1177/104973230201200211.

Denzin, N.K., & Lincoln, Y.S. (2011). *The Sage handbook of qualitative research.* Thousand Oaks, CA: Sage.

Eakin, J.M., & Mykhalovskiy, E. (2003). Reframing the evaluation of qualitative health research: Reflections on a review of appraisal guidelines in the health sciences. *Journal of Evaluation in Clinical Practice, 9*(2), 187–94. http://dx.doi.org/10.1046/j.1365-2753.2003.00392.x.

Gersten, R., Fuchs, L.S., Compton, D., Coyne, M., Greenwood, C., & Innocenti, M.S. (2005). Quality indicators for group experimental and quasi-experimental research in special education. *Exceptional Children, 71*(2), 149–64. http://dx.doi.org/10.1177/001440290507100202.

Grinnell, R.M., Jr., & Unrau, Y. (2005). *Social work research and evaluation: Quantitative and qualitative approaches*. Boston: Cengage Learning.

Haug, C. (2013). The downside of open-access publishing. *New England Journal of Medicine, 368*(9), 791–3. http://dx.doi.org/10.1056/NEJMp1214750.

Holosko, M.J. (2006). *Primer for critiquing social research*. Belmont, CA: Thomson Brooks/Cole.

Morse, J.M. (2003). A review committee's guide for evaluating qualitative proposals. *Qualitative Health Research, 13*(6), 833–51. http://dx.doi.org/10.1177/1049732303013006005.

Morse, J.M., Barrett, M., Mayan, M., Olson, K., & Spiers, J. (2002). Verification strategies for establishing reliability and validity in qualitative research. *International Journal of Qualitative Methods, 1*(2), 1–19.

Rubin, A., & Babbie, E. (2015). *Empowerment series: Essential research methods for social work*. Boston: Cengage Learning.

Thompson, B., Diamond, K.E., McWilliam, R., Snyder, P., & Snyder, S.W. (2005). Evaluating the quality of evidence from correlational research for evidence-based practice. *Exceptional Children, 71*(2), 181–94. http://dx.doi.org/10.1177/001440290507100204.

Winter, G. (2000). A comparative discussion of the notion of "validity" in qualitative and quantitative research. *Qualitative Report, 4*(3/4). Retrieved from www.nova.edu/ssss/QR/QR4-3/winter.html.

A QUALITATIVE DESIGN[1]
Surviving the Tornado: Psychiatric Survivor Experiences of Getting, Losing, and Keeping Housing

Cheryl Forchuk, RN, PhD, School of Nursing, University of Western Ontario

Catherine Ward-Griffin, RN, PhD, School of Nursing, University of Western Ontario

Rick Csiernik, PhD, RSW, School of Social Work, King's University College

Katherine Turner, BA, LLB, CED (dip.), Director, Margaret's Haven Non-Profit Housing

The recent trend in de-institutionalization from hospital to community for psychiatric consumer-survivors has frequently led to housing concerns. Psychiatric survivors have been consistently found to be overrepresented in homelessness populations (1, 2, 3, 4, 5, 6, 7). The issue of housing stability has become an important concern for this population.

The Canadian Mortgage and Housing Corporation (8) examined the issue of housing stability for consumer-survivors and emphasized the importance of preference in determining an individual's ability to stabilize in housing. They note that the process of making a house a home is based on interactions between three key dimensions: person factors, support factors, and housing factors. For a housing situation to be stable, individuals should receive appropriate support within a physical and social housing environment suited to individual characteristics, goals, preferences, strengths, and needs. CMHC notes that housing stability is often defined as duration of stay. They suggest that an appropriate measure of stability should include consideration of quality of housing mobility rather than simply the quantity of moves.

Research from New Zealand expands upon the concept of designing housing for consumer-survivors to facilitate housing stability (9). This work focuses on the issue of sustainability in the context of mental health and housing as an attribute of the wider environment rather than of a particular house. A "sustainability framework" was developed that details the array of supports and resources necessary to maintain independent living. Access to each of the following four categories of resources is necessary for true

---

1 The text is taken directly from the published article. This journal did not use APA referencing style.

sustainability: (1) a supportive regulatory environment implying well-enforced statutory government frameworks that apply to safeguarding human rights, combating discrimination, labour market regulation and land use, building codes, and housing standards; (2) material resources that include adequate, suitable housing to choose from, income to pay for it, and access to basic necessities; (3) service resources that include clinical services, housing facilitation services, and personal support services tailored to individual need; and (4) social resources that include community supports, groups, families, and cultural and social networks.

The issue of housing preference has been explored in the literature, as a means of addressing the housing needs of persons with mental illnesses. This research has consistently found that independent living is preferred (10, 11, 12, 13, 14). Unfortunately, psychiatric consumer-survivors often face many obstacles in obtaining and keeping independent housing. As well, a review of existing research on supported and supportive housing undertaken by the *Cochrane Review* (15) found a lack of conclusive evidence regarding the effectiveness of supportive housing as opposed to supported housing options. They suggest that further research is required in this area. A cautionary note was injected by O'Malley and Croucher (16), who indicate that the assumption that patients will progress from higher to lower levels of supported accommodation over time may be marginalizing the needs of individuals with particularly challenging behaviour who require long-term, permanent accommodation with higher levels of support.

In summary, although housing issues are known to be of concern for psychiatric survivors, there are many gaps in the literature. Studies have focused on issues such as housing preference, homelessness, and housing stability. The subjective experiences related to housing remain largely unexplored. The purpose of this investigation was to explore experiences of psychiatric consumer-survivors in relation to housing and to identify potential solutions to difficulties encountered by this population. The study design was descriptive-qualitative and used a focus group method for data collection. Ethics approval was granted through the University of Western Ontario (08396E), and data were compiled July through August 2002.

Method

Participants were recruited through posters and word of mouth. Posters advertising groups were placed in locations intended to recruit individuals living in a range of housing types. This included shelters, group homes, transitional housing programs, and public housing units. Posters were also sent to community mental health agencies, a consumer-survivor self-help organization, and the public library. Posters indicated we were interested in recruiting people with a history of mental illness to discuss issues related to housing and mental health and gave the time and location of the next group. Letters of Information, which outlined the project in more detail, were available below the poster and were also distributed and reviewed prior to beginning each group. Groups were held in a spectrum of community locations including shelters, group homes, community agencies, and drop-in centres. Staff at the group locations were also helpful in using word of mouth to encourage people to attend. Food, usually pizza, was available at each of the group discussions to encourage and acknowledge attendance.

Nine focus groups averaging seventy-five minutes in length were conducted in both urban and rural areas in southwestern Ontario over a two-month time period, with five to thirteen participants per group; five groups include both men and women. Two groups had only women and two groups had only men. Group attendance or numbers were not known in advance of the group. Research team members led the groups. A common set of open-ended research questions and prompts were used as guides for all groups. This guide included questions such as: What is your current housing like? What kind of housing would you prefer? What was the best place you ever lived? What made it so good? What stops you from being in that ideal place now? These questions were used to stimulate conversation. Issues raised in each individual group were explored in more detail.

Ninety psychiatric survivors who lived in shelters, group homes, supported apartments, and independent living participated in the study. There were fifty-one female and thirty-nine male participants. No demographic items were asked, but field notes included a description of participants. Participants appeared to range in age from late teens to late sixties, but the majority appeared to be in their forties and fifties. The groups appeared to be predominantly Caucasian with some representation from visible minorities including Asian and African Canadian and First Nations.

Group discussions were audiotaped and transcribed verbatim. Two note-takers were present during each group to record field notes. Field notes were completed during and immediately following each group. These included a description of the setting and participants, as well as general impressions. These were added to the transcripts and included in the analysis.

This descriptive qualitative study used an ethnographic method of analysis (17, 18). A full ethnography would require a longer period of observation. A broad approach was wanted to assist in understanding the patterns related to housing and mental health in the social and cultural contexts of the participants across multiple settings. The ethnographic analysis method suggested by Leininger (17, 18) included first identifying and listing descriptors and then developing these into patterns. Patterns were then synthesized to obtain broad themes, and themes were tested by reviewing them against raw data. Data were initially analysed independently by each team member. Following this, team members met on three different occasions to compare and further develop the identified themes. A matrix was used to assist in developing the identified patterns (e.g., living with fear, losing control) into larger themes. Team members who made slight revisions to the interpretation of themes and patterns then reviewed the matrix and transcripts. The initial analysis was presented to a group of seventy-five key stake-holders (e.g., consumer-survivors, researchers, members of community agencies) in November 2003. The audience was explicitly asked for oral or written feedback about the analysis and metaphor used. Feedback was received from six consumers (four oral, two written), all supporting the analysis and metaphor. Supportive written feedback was also received from two community mental health service providers. Written feedback tended to be brief, e.g., "Tornado: a great metaphor."

Results

Based on the analysis of the focus group data, findings of this qualitative study reflect the shared experiences of psychiatric survivors related to housing. As depicted in Figure 3, the metaphor of a tornado was used to describe the upheaval and loss encountered by the study participants. Few phenomena can form as quickly as a tornado

Figure 3   Three Overlapping Phases of Destruction within the Tornado of Mental Illness

Phase 3

Gaining Stability

Phase 2

Struggling to
Survive

Phase 1

Losing Ground

– Rebuilding Relationships

– Securing Personal Space

– Receiving Professional Services

– Accessing Social Supports

– Losing Control of Basic
  Human Rights
– Living in Fear

and create such devastation in such a short time and such a random way. While the probability of being actually caught up in a tornado is quite small and survival is likely, it is nonetheless a substantive force that cannot be ignored (19). Tornadoes do not just enter lives unexpectedly – they rip them apart and scatter the accumulated possessions of a lifetime haphazardly, often across vast distances and usually without warning (19, 20, 21, 22).

Analysis revealed three overlapping phases of destruction within the tornado of mental illness: (1) *Losing Ground*, (2) *Struggling to Survive*, and (3) *Gaining Stability* (see Figure 3). Depending on certain environmental forces, psychiatric survivors moved between and among the three phases of the tornado. Five major themes were also identified within each level of destruction. "Living in fear" and "losing control of basic human rights" were dominant themes within Losing Ground, while "accessing social supports" and "receiving professional services" illuminated the most common themes within Struggling to Survive. Finally, the themes "securing personal space" and "rebuilding relationships" are best illustrated within Gaining Stability. In describing their experiences related to housing, participants saw this as related to broader experiences related to supports. In other words, obtaining and maintaining housing was related to obtaining and maintaining a broad base of supports ranging from assistance with their psychiatric symptoms to income supports. Beginning with the most devastating phase of the tornado, the following section describes each of these themes, accompanied by illustrative quotes.

Phase 1: Losing Ground

Losing ground was the first and most destructive phase of the tornado identified within the study findings. Metaphorically speaking, this is when the tornado is at its greatest strength, uprooting people as well as causing the most damage, perhaps even death. Indeed, some individuals with mental illness may not survive these "killer" tornadoes, especially if they had experienced consistent loss and destruction as a result of poor housing conditions. As described by two participants:

> Some of the homes have been condemned ... four of them, I had to leave because they burnt right down. I lost everything.
>
> So I had to leave everything, and that isn't the first time. I had lost a lot of belongings, seven times to fire, and five times to just up and leaving, and carrying whatever I could. So I am getting pretty tired of it.

Loss of current living arrangements also frequently occurred when individuals needed to be hospitalized due to their mental illness. As one woman explained:

They made me give up my apartment … I left everything behind – my couch, my TV, everything, my fish tank, everything. I left it all behind because they said I wasn't well enough to go back, I wasn't able to look after myself.

The first theme, living in fear, dominated within this phase. Participants were fearful of many things, among them of being hurt and of losing their lives and/or their possessions. One young man remarked:

There has been a lot of violence in my building … one guy here tells me he is going to kill me daily.

Another commented that she did not want to live in a house where there may be people who will harm her or her family, in spite of the low rent:

Even if I were to get housing and they said, "Oh, you could pay $97 a month for a one bedroom," I wouldn't take it – considering what is out there. I mean the guy next door may be a pyromaniac, and the other one might be a pedophile for all I know.

Women who lived in shelters and other living arrangements that housed both men and women shared additional concerns:

Him and me were in [ ] together. He attempted to rape me on the ground … went back there this year, after finally a year and a half, only to find out that this guy's been let off.

Others agreed that women and men living together constituted a risk to women's safety. One man stated:

If there is female … 3 rooms over, hey you're going to have like ten dogs [males] over, right! So to put it more plainly, it would just be a festival. It wouldn't work … it would be trouble.

Losing control of basic human rights was the second predominant theme within Losing Ground. It was apparent that persons with mental illnesses felt deprived of adequate income, which led to inadequate food and housing. One woman explained:

The comfort allowance [personal needs allowance] is the same today as it was ten, twelve years ago in 1990. It is like the government has something against people with mental illness. We are being punished and held down financially. If you have a mental illness, they say, "Here's this," and shove you into a corner … I have nothing.

Housing conditions are deplorable at times where many people with mental illness are expected to live in cramped conditions, frequently sharing limited toileting facilities. A man living in a shelter shared the following description:

You are living with and sleeping with twenty-five other guys, and you gotta deal with their noise when they come in and out of the room. And as far as the rest goes, I mean we're all men and we all do what men do, so if you gotta do it, you do it.

Other participants reported that they were treated "like children" who had no choice but to comply with the rules. One man explained:

You have to beg for a drink when you want one. I find I get thirsty a lot. You're not supposed to be around the kitchen, you get yelled at.

Phase 2: Struggling to Survive

Struggling to survive was the second phase of the tornado identified within the study findings. As people started to pick up the pieces from the destruction caused by the tornado, they still struggled with meeting their basic needs. As one woman explained:

I was in an apartment of my own and I was trying to cope with it, but I didn't have any support. They just dumped me here.

For others, energy was expended on accessing social supports. Such supports were seen as critical to maintaining more independence in housing. One man explained how he needed to use a variety of supports in order to survive, and yet at times these social programs were inadequate to meet his basic needs:

I am sorry, but a can of beans and a little bit like that once a month is not going to go anywhere … and the food bank is here but it is only going to feed you for two days, and when you have no money, what do you do for the other twenty-eight days?

Other participants attended church programs to obtain adequate food and shelter:

In the wintertime, they have suppers at the church over there. I go for a free meal. Meals are usually on at some of these churches all around the city.

In addition to providing meals, some of the churches and housing providers offered professional counselling services. Many participants also relied heavily on health professional services in order to survive this phase of the tornado. However, the quotes in the following section illustrate the difficulty that individuals with mental illness have in accessing and receiving professional services in a timely fashion. If their symptoms are not treated they fear losing their housing.

Phase 3: Gaining Stability

Gaining stability is the final phase of the tornado. Participants within this phase reported that they were beginning to rebuild their lives. Since most of their basic physical and medical needs were met, they were free to concentrate on securing personal space and rebuilding relationships. Some of the participants spoke about the importance of having their own place, of setting down roots again:

> I am in my fifth home … But this one I know that I can stay for two years and I can finally go to a permanent home after that. So I know I'll finally be able to have a home that I can call home for quite awhile.

Others commented on the differences between their current living arrangements and their previous types of housing. Most notably, people mentioned that they appreciated living in a "nice" neighbourhood, being "allowed" to have pets, and having their own bathroom and kitchen appliances. As one female participant aptly described it:

> In this house I used to live in, there were twenty people in the same house. So, now there is eight, and there's a huge difference … there is more space to yourself.

The final theme, building relationships, was most evident within this last phase of the tornado. In the early phases of the tornado, relationships were usually tenuous or destructive. Those who were gaining stability spoke about the importance of relationships and how strong relationships with friends or family were key to their health and well-being. One participant described how sharing meals with someone led to a strong friendship:

> I was on the main floor and I had a lady friend on the other floor and we switched back and forth for meals. One night I would cook, the next night she would cook, and she'd supply the vegetables or if she was coming to my place I'd supply the meat … we are still good buddies even though I have been out of there all these years. And she is out of there too, and we still communicate.

Discussion

A question to consider is: "What is the tornado?" Is the tornado the experience of mental illness or the experience of society's response to mental illness? The participants' descriptions would suggest the latter. The loss and destruction experienced was not linked to the experience of symptoms, such as depression or hallucinations. Rather, it was related to the loss of home, possessions, relationships, and human dignity. The consequence of such loss after experiencing a mental illness would seem to have more to do with the societal response to the illness rather than the illness per se.

When an actual tornado strikes, there is usually immediate disaster relief. Government aid is available and community organizations from near and far move quickly to provide tangible supports. What happens when psychiatric survivors experience their more personal tornadoes? It may be that the tornado is only perceptible to family and close friends who, with their proximity, feel the strong winds of disaster. Perhaps these forces are invisible to those more distant. Or perhaps the disaster is visible from a distance but simply does not provoke in others a need to respond.

Certainly government aid is not quick to arrive, particularly in Ontario, Canada. There has been no increase in community mental health funding or disability income support for over a decade despite inflation and continued policies of "deinstitutionalization." Individuals receiving assistance from the Ontario Disability Support Program actually risk having the housing portion of this cut during a hospitalization on the assumption that since they are hospitalized payment of rent would not be required. But few landlords cease to charge rent during a hospitalization, so individuals, as some of our participants described, can lose not only their apartment but also their furniture and the family album. Others lost their belongings when the treatment team believed they could not live independently due to their illness. They were discharged to a group living situation that could not accommodate many of their possessions, including furniture and pets.

Some strategies would seem to flow from the issues described by participants. As participants initially *lost ground*, the issues of living in fear and losing control over their basic human rights surfaced. Much of this was related to being forced into unsafe or otherwise inappropriate housing. Participants *struggled to survive* by accessing social supports and receiving professional services. The timely availability of such supports and services might assist consumer-survivors to move more quickly to *gaining stability*. The stability was maintained through securing personal space and rebuilding relationships. Accommodation, which includes personal space and control, was described as critical to these consumers in rebuilding their lives. Relationships can be facilitated through consistent professional relationships. As well, support can be provided by peer-support and consumer-survivor organizations, which can give back a sense of belonging. Many participants described the role of churches in facilitating their recovery through tangible supports that went beyond traditional spiritual support.

Conclusion

The metaphor of a tornado was used to capture the experience that consumer-survivors of psychiatric illness described in relation to housing and their illness. Many described a devastating experience of losing much of what was important to them, and going through a long arduous process to rebuild their lives after the devastation. Health care providers and policy decision makers need to be aware of the losses that are not simply a result of the symptoms of mental illness, but rather of the response to the illness. A caring community response, including adequate housing, adequate income support, and available community care, may have the potential to assist people in rebuilding their lives.

Works Cited

1. Cohen, C.I., & Thompson, K.S. Homeless mentally ill or mentally ill homeless? *American Journal of Psychiatry*, 169 (1992): 816–823.
2. Draine, J., Salzer, M., Culhane, D., et al. Role of social disadvantage in crime, joblessness and homelessness among persons with serious mental illness. *Psychiatric Services*, 53 (2002): 565–573.
3. Drake, R.E., & Wallach, M.A. Homelessness and mental illness: A story of failure. *Psychiatric Services*, 40 (1999): 589.
4. Goering, P., Tolomiczenko, G., Sheldon, T., et al. Characteristics of persons who are homeless for the first time. *Psychiatric Services*, 53 (2002): 1472–1474.
5. Koegel, P., Burnam, M.A., & Baumohl, J. The causes of homelessness, in *Homelessness in America*, ed. J. Baumohl. Phoenix: Oryx, 1996.
6. Lamb, H., & Lamb, D. Factors contributing to homelessness among the chronically and severely mentally ill. *Hospital and Community Psychiatry*, 41 (1990): 301–305.
7. Robertson, M. The prevalence of mental disorder among homeless people, in *Homelessness: A prevention-oriented approach*, ed. R. Jahiel. Baltimore: Johns Hopkins University Press, 1992.
8. *Evaluating housing stability for people with serious mental illness at risk for homelessness*. Final Report, prepared for CMHC by Community Support and Research Unit, Centre for Addiction and Mental Health: 2001.
9. Peace, R., & Kell, S. Mental health and housing research: Housing needs and sustainable independent living. *Social Policy Journal*, 17 (2001).
10. Carling, P.J. Housing and supports for persons with mental illness: Emerging approaches to research and practice. *Hospital and Community Psychiatry*, 44 (1993): 439–449.

11. Carling, P.J. (ed.). *Return to community: Building support systems for people with psychiatric disabilities*. New York: Guilford, 1995.

12. Ridgway, P., & Zipple, A.M. The paradigm shift in residential services: From the linear continuum to supported housing approaches. *Psychosocial Rehabilitation Journal*, 13 (1990): 20–31.

13. Tsemberis, S., & Eisenberg, R.F. Pathways to housing: Supported housing for street-dwelling homeless individuals with psychiatric disabilities. *Psychiatric Services*, 51, no. 4 (2000): 487–493.

14. Nelson, G., Walsh-Bowers, R., Hall, G. et al. A comparative evaluation of supportive apartments, group homes, and board-and-care homes for psychiatric consumer-survivors. *Journal of Community Psychology*, 25, no. 2 (1998): 167–188.

15. Chilvers, R., Macdonald, G.M., & Hayes, A.A. Supported housing for people with severe mental disorders. *Cochrane Review*, 2 (2004).

16. O'Malley, L., & Croucher, K. *Supported housing services for people with mental health problems: Evidence of good practice?* Toronto: York University, Centre for Housing Policy, 2003.

17. Leininger, M.M. Transcultural care diversity and universality: A theory of nursing. *Nursing and Health Care*, 6, no. 4 (1985): 208–212.

18. Leininger, M.M. Importance and uses of ethnomethods: Ethnography and ethno-nursing research. *Recent Advances in Nursing*, 17 (1987): 12–36.

19. Grazulis, T. *The tornado: Nature's ultimate windstorm*. Norman: University of Oklahoma Press, 2001.

20. Barnes-Svarney, P., & Svarney, T. *Skies of fury*. New York: Simon & Schuster, 1999.

21. Simon, S. *Tornadoes*. New York: Morrow, 1999.

22. Galiano, D. *Tornadoes*. New York: Rosen, 2000.

CRITIQUE

by Rachel Birnbaum

Part A – Purpose

1. Research Problem/Question

The research problem was to explore experiences of psychiatric consumer-survivors in relation to housing and identify potential solutions to difficulties encountered by this population. There were five research questions:

- What is your current housing like?
- What kind of housing would you prefer?
- What was the best place you lived?
- What made it so good?
- What stops you from being in that ideal place now?

2. Literature Review and Conceptual Framework

There is a lack of a conceptual/theoretical framework. While some studies were cited that explored the gaps in the literature, there were no studies that explored the barriers for psychiatric survivors from a structural point of view (i.e., psychiatric diagnosis/medical model approach).

3. Reflexivity

Reflexivity involved filed notes and observations. Participants were asked for written and oral feedback on the analysis and metaphor used.

4. Ethics

No ethical violations were committed.

Part B – Measurement

1. Concepts and Variables

Concepts included: losing ground (living in fear, losing basic human rights); struggling to survive (accessing social supports, receiving professional services); and gaining stability (securing personal space, rebuilding relationships). These were described using the metaphor of a tornado.

2. Definitions

The concepts were defined well.

Part C – Participants

1. Selection

Participants were recruited through posters and word of mouth. Posters advertising groups were also placed in locations where the authors hoped to recruit individuals living in a range of housing types, and were sent to community mental health agencies, a consumer-survivor self-help organization, and the public library. There were no limits placed upon the numbers who could participate, and a broad range of sampling was conducted.

2. Negative Cases

No negative case analysis was presented.

3. Transferability

There is sufficient information on participants' characteristics and circumstances to assist in transferability of findings.

Part D – Design

1. Question/Topic Development – Data Collection – Interview Transcription

Topics and questions were developed from the literature review. Data were gathered from focus groups, with group discussions audiotaped and transcribed verbatim. An ethnographic method of analysis was used.

2. Reactivity

Data were not gathered over a long period of time.

3. Triangulation

Triangulation of data gathering was not used. However, analysis did involve triangulation of data.

Part E – Data Analysis and Reporting

1. Data Analytical Techniques Used

The ethnographic analysis conducted was appropriate for this type of data.

2. Data Analysis by More than One Researcher

More than one researcher analysed the data and multiple interpretations were integrated into the study. Key stakeholders' and consumers' feedback, both oral and written, formed parts of the analysis.

3. Examples of How Interpretations Emerged

Interpretations emerged from codes to overlapping themes.

4. Interpretive Framework Integrated

Results flow from the data obtained.

5. Member Checking Used to Generate Feedback on Researchers' Interpretation of Data

Member checks were done.

6. Sufficient Illustrative Examples Provided

Sufficient illustrative comments were made to support codes and themes.

7. Limitations Documented

The researchers did not document any limitations to the study. For example, they note that they needed a longer period of time to carry out a full ethnography. Questions remain about what other findings could have been made and not included.

8. Ideas for Further Research

The researchers noted that there are still problems in the system. They suggested strategies on how to combat issues raised in the themes presented.

Part F – Overall Evaluation

Overall, this is a good study that raises practical issues in working with these survivors. As a practising social worker, I believe that many suggestions are made from a practice point of view that resonates in the clinical work with this population.

A QUANTITATIVE DESIGN

An Examination of Two Different Approaches to Visitation-Based Disputes in Child Custody Matters

Rachel Birnbaum

Approximately 20 per cent of divorced families in North America seek the intervention of court-related professionals to negotiate suitable custody or access arrangements after separation or divorce (Johnston & Roseby, 1997; Maccoby & Mnookin, 1992). As these family situations are already fraught with conflict, judges seek assistance from mental health professionals for information about child–parent interactions and relationships that will guide the decision making process in custody and access disputes (Gould, 1998; Stahl, 1994). In addition, the use of mental health professionals is appealing because they can help separating or divorcing families to manage the additional tension and animosity that is often generated during court proceedings (Kruk, 1992).

Child custody assessments are conducted by social workers, psychologists, and psychiatrists. These mental health professionals interview children and families and obtain independent information from teachers, doctors, and others associated with the family to make recommendations to the court about where children should live, with whom, and how often they will visit the other parent. Yet little is known about the processes involved in the assessment and what the outcomes are. In other words, there is no conclusive empirical information on whether one particular child custody arrangement is better than another or whether one particular visitation[2] arrangement is preferable to another. In addition, there are few studies that examine the impact of these assessments on children and families after separation or divorce. That is, how do children and families experience the assessment process?

The following study is meant to explore this gap in the literature. Specifically, the study examined two approaches to visitation-based disputes before the court: a problem-solving assessment approach and a traditional assessment approach. Process and outcomes variables will be compared in order to evaluate whether one approach yields a differential response over the other. Traditional child custody and visitation-based

---

2 The words "visitation" and "access" are here used interchangeably.

assessments have involved the assessment of each parent's personal and marital history, the quality of the parent-child dyad, and the child's functioning and perceptions (Birnbaum & Radovanovic, 1999). A report is written to the court recommending a custodial and/or access arrangement that best meets the emotional, physical, and financial needs of the child. Historically, the evaluations have followed the traditional adversarial approach that pits one parent against the other under the legal umbrella of the "best interests test." Courts, lawyers, and assessors are beginning to appreciate how the traditional child custody assessment has been time-consuming and costly, both financially and emotionally (Birnbaum & Radovanovic, 1999). An alternative to the traditional evaluation is one that is based on a focused solution-oriented approach. This alternative differs from the former in four ways: (1) the amount of personal and relationship history that is taken; (2) the extent to which allegations about the other parent are explored; (3) the extent to which the present and future are emphasized; and (4) the amount of time it takes to implement the evaluation: up to 20 hours in the case of the focused approach and 35 hours for the traditional approach. The former is based on a problem-solving solution-oriented process, the aim of which is to facilitate resolution among parents disputing visitation-based matters before the court (Birnbaum & Radovanovic, 1999).

Several factors contributed to the development of the solution-oriented approach. These were: to reduce court delays in cases involving visitation-based disputes, to reduce the stress of the conflict on the child, to respond in a timely and cost-effective manner, and to reduce protracted and unnecessary litigation that compromises the emotional well-being of children.

Research Questions and Hypotheses

The questions in the study addressed the association between two different types of child custody assessment interventions (focused versus traditional) and the following outcomes: children's behavioural/emotional adjustment and parental satisfaction. Satisfaction refers to parents' satisfaction with a number of aspects of the assessment process: the social worker's attitude towards the dispute, how their concerns were listened to, thoroughness of the evaluation, the length of time the evaluation took, and the report's recommendations. It is measured by taking the sum of these five items, each of which is rated on a five-point Likert scale ranging from very unsatisfied to very satisfied (Austin & Jaffe, 1990; Birnbaum & Radovanovic, 1999; Radovanovic et al., 1994).

The research hypotheses to be examined are listed below. All hypotheses generated are based on a two-tailed test.

H_1 = There will be differences found between the focused and traditional child custody evaluation interventions with respect to children's adjustment post-separation mean scores at baseline.

H_2 = There will be differences found between the focused and traditional child custody evaluation interventions with respect to children's adjustment post-separation mean scores after the evaluation intervention.

H_3 = There will be differences found between the focused and traditional child custody evaluation interventions with respect to mothers' satisfaction mean scores.

H_4 = There will be differences found between the focused and traditional child custody evaluation interventions with respect to fathers' satisfaction mean scores.

Research Setting

The sample for the study was recruited from the Office of the Children's Lawyer (OCL), an independent law office within the Ministry of the Attorney General, in Ontario, Canada. The OCL represents the interests of children before the court in custody and access matters and child welfare proceedings as well as civil litigation and estate matters. All custody and access investigations are court ordered, pursuant to Section 112 of the Courts of Justice Act.

Sample Selection

The sample comprised biological parents who were disputing visitation problems before the court. Criteria for inclusion in this study included the following: (a) biological parents only, (b) one child had to be between the ages of 5 and 16 years of age, (c) the parents had to be able to understand English to complete the questionnaires, and (d) each parent had to provide both oral and written informed consent. All families were court-ordered to undergo an investigation and report pursuant to Section 112 of the Courts of Justice Act by the Children's Lawyer social worker. Specifically, the families were recruited from Metropolitan Toronto, the Regional Municipalities of Peel and Durham, Simcoe County, and Ottawa, Ontario. A randomized sample of 115 biological pairs of mothers and fathers who met the inclusion/exclusion criteria between 15 January 1999 and 31 August 2000 and who had at least one child between 5 and 16 years of age were eligible for participation in the study. In families who had more than one child, only the eldest child was chosen so that the criterion of independence of observations could be met. Of the 115 biological pairs of mothers and fathers who agreed to participate in this study before baseline data were gathered, 20 pairs withdrew from the study, leaving a sample size of $N = 95$ biological pairs of mothers and fathers.

The 20 pairs of parents withdrew for the following reasons. Three pairs of parents settled the dispute before the investigation began; seven pairs of parents had issues that required further evaluation and/or investigation by child welfare authorities and were therefore in violation of the inclusion criteria; three pairs of parents withdrew their dispute before the court; the father in one pair moved to another province; in two pairs of parents the fathers were illiterate; in two others the mothers could not understand the questionnaires; in one pair the mother's lawyer refused to have her client participate in the study; and in the last pair the father, who was self-represented, agreed with his ex-partner not to participate. Of the 95 pairs of biological parents who participated in the study, 36 per cent of mothers and 44 per cent of fathers withdrew by Time 2.

Consent Procedures

Due to the legal nature of the proceedings and the fact that any materials filed with the Office of the Children's Lawyer could be potentially subpoenaed for litigation purposes, the consent process had to be carefully reviewed with the parents and the OCL staff. Therefore, the researcher consulted with the Children's Lawyer of Ontario about freedom of information and privacy issues and was assisted in the wording of the final version of the Parent Information and Consent Form.

All families who were referred by the court between 15 January 1999 and 31 August 2000 for a custody and/or access investigation by the OCL received a Parent Information Letter and Consent Form in the mail. These forms explained the study and requested their participation. The Parent Information Letter outlined the voluntary nature of the study and clarified that the parents could withdraw at any time during the investigation and still expect to receive service from the OCL. The Consent Form established that they understood the purpose of the study, and requested their authorization to proceed. Two research assistants, trained to explain the process, were available to parents during their first and last interviews, to assist with filling out the questionnaires and to answer any questions that might arise.

Data Collection

Instruments

The relationship between parental satisfaction and children's adjustment post-separation were investigated using a number of instruments, both standardized and exploratory. Since information obtained from different informants is not likely to converge (Johnston, 1994; Offord et al., 1996; Twaite, Silitsky, & Luchow, 1998), information was obtained from both mothers and fathers regarding the child's psychosocial adjustment. The following section describes the instruments used at baseline and follow-up (pre- and post-measures).

Children's Lawyer Intake Questionnaire

Demographic information was collected from the Children's Lawyer Intake Form that was used to determine whether the OCL should become involved in the matter before the court. In the majority of cases, both parents completed the intake form requesting information about each parent's age, income, and ethnicity, the age and gender of the child, the length of time since the separation, the length of the relationship, and concerns that each parent had about the other with respect to child-rearing and child-care responsibilities.

The Hollingshead Four Factor Index of Social Status was used to calculate the socio-economic status of each parent (Hollingshead, 1975). This index uses each individual's educational background, occupational background, gender, and marital status to establish their social status. The education factor is ranked on a seven-point scale (e.g., 1 = less than grade 1; 7 = graduate professional training). The occupational factor is ranked on a nine-point scale (1 = farm labourers/menial service workers/welfare recipients; 9 = higher executives/professionals). Each of these factors is weighted and a computed total score ranging from 8 to 66 is arrived at. The higher the score of an individual or family unit, the higher the status accorded by other members in society. This index has been validated through census data gathered in the United States in 1970 and is widely used for research purposes (Hollingshead, 1975).

Child Behaviour Checklist, Parent and Teacher Rating Form

Child adjustment was measured by using the Child Behaviour Checklist (CBCL) (Achenbach, 1979; Achenbach & Edelbrock, 1983) for ages 4 to 16 years. The CBCL is a widely used instrument that inquires about the frequency and severity of symptoms that children have exhibited over the past six months. This scale provides established norms by age group and gender of the child. The questionnaire consists of 113 items that yield scores that reflect how problematic the child's overall behaviour is, the extent to which their behaviour is more internalizing (withdrawn, somatic complaints, anxiety, and depression) and externalizing (aggressive behaviour, delinquent behaviour such as fire setting, lying), and how socially competent (activities, social and school subscales) they are.

The Teacher Report Form of the CBCL (Achenbach & Edelbrock, 1983) was also used to measure child adjustment. This is also a 113-item behaviour checklist similar in form to the parents' version. The child's teacher completed the form based on the child's behaviour in the classroom during the previous two months. Over the summer months a different teacher sometimes filled out the Time 2 form, usually with the assistance of the child's previous teacher. If the child changed schools, the school principal was instructed to have the new teacher complete the form based on the child's behaviour that he/she observed for at least two months.

Since both the mother and father were asked to complete the forms in this study, the average of their individual scores was used as a single score. Johnston, Kline, and Tschann (1989) argue that when there is a discrepancy between the mothers' and fathers' scores, an average can be used for the purpose of analysis. In addition, two analyses of covariance were conducted. The first Ancova model involved only custodial parent ratings, excluding gender, on all three behaviour problems by type of evaluation intervention, controlling for Time 1 score as rated by the custodial parent. To increase the sample size and control for sampling bias, the second Ancova model involved obtaining data from non-custodial parents when there were no data available from the custodial parent. Correlations were also conducted with mothers, fathers, and teachers to assess for any agreement between the three respondents on the same child.

Procedure for Data Collection

Parents who met the inclusion/exclusion criteria were randomly assigned to either the traditional evaluation intervention or the focused evaluation intervention. Each parent then received a package of information that included a letter of acceptance of their case by the Office of the Children's Lawyer, a Parent Information Letter that outlined the voluntary nature of the research, and a consent form. The study was introduced to the parents as one that was seeking information about how to assist children caught in the midst of separation and/or divorce and about how to improve the services of the Children's Lawyer. The Parent Information Letter emphasized that the research study was separate from the assessment process and that the social worker would not have access to any of the information. The parents were given the name and contact information for both the Clinical Coordinator of Social Work and the principal investigator in case they had any questions regarding the nature of the study.

When the administrative assistant in the OCL telephoned the parents to arrange the interview with the social worker, the assistant ascertained their willingness to participate in the study. If they agreed, the parents were requested to arrive approximately 35 minutes earlier to complete the forms. If they could not meet at the OCL, the forms were mailed out to each parent in a return envelope addressed to the principle investigator. The research assistant then conducted telephone follow-ups to ensure that the forms were mailed in. The majority of the parent interviews took place at the OCL. Parents were greeted by one of two research assistants and were requested to complete the forms that were in an envelope marked "Confidential Research." When the parent completed them, they were then placed back in the same marked envelope. Each parent also completed the consent form and received a copy. Due to the number of different forms, some parents who arrived at the OCL for their interview took the forms home and mailed them back. A school questionnaire (CBCL Teacher Rating Form) and a return addressed envelope were sent out the following day for the child's teacher to complete, along with a copy of the parent's consent form. If the teacher did not return the form within three weeks, the research assistant telephoned the school to remind the principal to return the completed form.

The social worker would notify the researcher when the case was completed so that each parent could fill out the Time 2 forms. The same procedure as previously outlined occurred at Time 2 with respect to completing and returning the forms. This was done before the social worker met with the parents. A different research assistant conducted a telephone interview with each parent to obtain information about the parent's satisfaction with the service and to ask questions contained in the fidelity checklist, both focused and traditional, to confirm that the intervention each parent believed they received was the intervention they actually received. The same research assistant conducted a telephone interview with each social worker to collect information on the fidelity checklist, both focused and traditional, to determine whether the intervention the parents received matched the intervention the social worker was supposed to provide.

The researcher conducted a court record review when the case was completed to determine the court's disposition and a file review to obtain information about the number of hours for each intervention and to calculate the cost of the evaluation intervention.

Data Analysis

The quantitative data collected were entered into a microcomputer using the Social Sciences – SPSS 10.0 for Windows Version (Nie et al., 1975). An alpha level of $p < 0.10$ was established as a test of the research hypotheses. This less conservative alpha level was also chosen because the potential outcome of these research questions may influence public policy, and there is a need to avoid any harm to either children or their parents. Therefore, if there are any real differences between the focused evaluation intervention and the traditional evaluation intervention with respect to these outcomes, it is important that every effort be made to ensure that they are found. All other analysis conducted that did not directly involve the research hypotheses used the traditional alpha level of $p < 0.05$.

Comparative analysis of nominal or ordinal level data involved the use of the chi-square test and the Mann-Whitney U test. Analysis of variables measured at the interval and/or ratio level involved the use of independent t tests for differences between means. Paired t tests comparing pre- and post-scores were conducted, as were correlations between parent scores and parent/teacher scores. In addition, an Ancova was conducted that examined for differences in post-intervention effects while controlling for baseline scores.

The assumptions underlying each statistical test were met. For all parametric tests of means, the homogeneity of variance was examined using Levene's test found in the t test and General Linear Model procedures in SPSS 10.0 for Windows Version (Nie et al., 1975). In general, all measures were examined for normality of distribution in the explore procedure in SPSS 10.0. Assumptions of chi-square are independence, that each respondent provides only one observation, and that there is a minimum expected value of at least 5 in each cell. Assumptions for the Mann-Whitney U test are also independence by design.

Results

Descriptive Analysis of the Parent and Child Questionnaire

The sample consisted of 95 biological mothers and 95 biological fathers. The age distribution of this sample was between 21 and 56 years of age. The mean age of mothers was 32.64 (SD = 6.62) and the mean age of fathers was 35.51 (SD = 7.27). The age difference between mothers and fathers was statistically significant, paired t test,

t (86) = −4.65, p < 0.000. The majority of parents were born in Canada (65 per cent) and 35 per cent came from outside Canada (Asia, West Indies, and Europe).

The mean income level of mothers was \$21,038.86 (SD = \$16,362.50) and did not differ significantly from that of fathers at \$26,028.75 (SD = \$18,232.61), paired t test, t (42) = −1.65, p > 0.11. There was only a 44 per cent response rate to this question. The mean income figures are similar to the Canadian national average of \$22,493.00 for females with single children under the age of 18 years but were less than that for males with single children under the age of 18 years, \$31,670.00 (Statistics Canada, 1997).

There were a total of 95 children in the sample. The age distribution was between 5 and 16 years of age. The overall mean age of the child was 7.36 (SD = 2.50). There were 50 boys with a mean age of 7.28 (SD = 2.86) and 45 girls with a mean age of 7.44 (SD = 2.06). The age difference between boys and girls was not statistically significant, independent t test, t (93) = −0.33, p > 0.75.

Summary of Results

The sample is composed of a majority of custodial mothers (84 per cent) who have on average been cohabiting for six years and have been separated for four years. In terms of socio-economic status, the majority of mothers and fathers can be described as semi-skilled workers with an average of a high school education. They have been involved with the legal system for an average of three years. The average age of the child was seven years. The most common visitation arrangement for the non-custodial parent, usually the father, was every other weekend and day access during the week.

Both mothers and fathers, regardless of intervention type, reported that access was much more regular after the involvement of the social worker. There was no association found between types of evaluation interventions and the clinician's recommendation in access arrangements.

With respect to the two research hypotheses, there was a statistically significant difference found between mothers' mean satisfaction scores in the focused evaluation intervention and those in the traditional evaluation intervention, t (68) = −2.55, p < 0.01. Mothers' mean satisfaction scores were lower in the traditional evaluation intervention, X = 16.64 (SD = 5.77), than in the focused evaluation intervention, X = 19.86 (SD = 4.79).

There was no statistically significant difference found at either Time 1 or Time 2 between the child's behaviour problems. However, the fathers' mean satisfaction score with the amount of sharing of information with the ex-partner at Time 1 by type of evaluation intervention was statistically significant, t (67) = 1.86, p < 0.07. At Time 1, fathers in the traditional evaluation intervention believed that they were sharing more information with their ex-partner (X = 1.97, SD = 1.40) than fathers in the focused evaluation intervention (X = 1.44, SD = 0.91). There was also a statistically significant difference found for fathers' assessment of their child's total behavioural problems at Time 1 by type of evaluation intervention. Fathers evaluated their child as having more total behavioural problems in the focused evaluation intervention, t (65) = −2.29, p < 0.03 (X = 53.37, SD = 10.23), than in the traditional evaluation intervention (X = 47.00, SD = 12.50). There was also a statistically significant difference found for fathers' assessment of their child's externalizing behaviour problems at Time 1 by type of evaluation intervention. Fathers evaluated their child as having more externalizing behavioural problems in the focused evaluation intervention, t (65) = −1.85, p < 0.07 (X = 49.74, SD = 9.20), than in the traditional evaluation intervention (X = 45.19, SD = 10.93). It should be noted that while fathers rated their child as having more behavioural problems in these two subscales, the children did not present in the clinically significant range. However, a statistically significant difference was found for teachers' assessment of the child's internalizing behaviour problems at Time 2 by type of evaluation intervention.

Teachers evaluated these children as having more internalizing behaviour problems in the traditional evaluation intervention, t (67) = −1.81, p < 0.08 (X = 50.97, SD = 10.83), than in the focused evaluation intervention (X = 46.75, SD = 8.11).

With respect to analysing the child's behaviour problems at Time 2 as reported only by custodial parents (N = 49), controlling for baseline behaviour problems, there were no statistically significant differences found between intervention types in the Ancova model and problem behaviours. When the sample size increased (N = 62) to include non-custodial parents when there were no data available from custodial parents, again no statistically significant difference was found. In addition, there were no statistically significant differences found between intervention types on the child behaviour measures based on the gender of the child.

Attrition

Analyses were conducted on baseline data to determine if the research hypotheses of child adjustment scores differed from those who had dropped out at Time 2. Tables 3a and 3b illustrate the results.

Tables 3a and 3b illustrate that there were no statistically significant differences found for the research hypothesis; that is, there were no differences found between those who completed Time 2 questionnaires and those who did not complete them with respect to baseline child adjustment. Demographic differences between both parents were also

Table 3a   Attrition in Child Behaviour Problems and Non-Responders and Responders by Type of Evaluation Intervention

Measure	N	M	SD	t	p
Child Behaviour Problems					
Mother Reports					
Total Behaviour Problems					
Non-responders	23	48.78	12.75	−.80	.42
Responders	58	51.12	11.42		
Mother Reports					
Internal Behaviour Problems					
Non-responders	23	50.89	11.71	−.50	.62
Responders	58	52.21	10.65		
Mother Reports					
External Behaviour Problems					
Non-responders	23	49.79	10.64	−.60	.55
Responders	58	49.43	11.33		

analysed to determine if there were any differences between those who completed Time 2 interview schedule and those who did not.

Mothers: There was a statistically significant difference between those who completed the interview schedule at Time 2 and those who did not, independent *t* test, *t* (89) = −3.22, p < 0.002. The mean age of mothers who did not complete the questionnaire was X = 29.88 (SD = 6.15), while the mean age of those who did complete the questionnaire was X = 34.28 (SD = 6.38). This suggests that younger mothers were less likely to respond to the interview schedule that was administered at Time 2 than were older mothers. There was no statistically significant difference between responders and non-responders for either mothers or fathers on demographic characteristics such as income, length of time between separation and the evaluation intervention, and the number of months separated.

Table 3b   Attrition in Child Behaviour Problems by Type of Evaluation Intervention

Measure	N	M	SD	t	p
Child Behaviour Problems					
Father Reports					
Total Behaviour Problems					
Non-responders	21	.29	.46	1.21	.23
Responders	39	.15	.37		
Father Reports					
Internal Behaviour Problems					
Non-responders	21	.38	.50	1.47	.47
Responders	39	.21	.41		
Father Reports					
External Behaviour Problems					
Non-responders	21	.05	.22	–.72	15
Responders	39	.10	.31		

Parents' Comments about Each Evaluation Intervention

Themes raised by parents and children are summarized in Tables 3c–3e with each type of evaluation intervention.

Research Context

The context of the research activity is often not reported, as the assumption has been that they are two different processes. In this study the context was important because it not only affected the response rate of the parents and teachers but also highlights their thoughts and feelings regarding the standardized forms they completed. The following comments illustrate this issue.

Some teachers telephoned the researcher advising that they had serious reservations about the 113-item Teacher Report Form. For example, they stated, "I do not have the authority to judge this child on the items as stated in the form," "Under the present provincial guidelines, I am not allowed to use these judgments [unclean personal

Table 3c   Positive Parent Comments Related to Each Evaluation Intervention

	Parents' Comments (Questions 1–3) Positive	
	Focused	Traditional
Mothers' Comments	"social worker was great, helped work out issues quickly," "social worker was very good, put the children above all, did not leave any loose ends, was very thorough," "service was amazing, supportive and understanding" "didn't blame either individual"	"very happy with the services," "great improvement in children," "happy with the way things went," "social worker was a keen observer, report was accurate in terms of what was addressed," "because of 3rd party involvement things went well"
Fathers' Comments	"service was excellent, social worker was very good," "social worker did thorough job, nice to have an organization that looks at both sides of story," "social worker was great, she really helped and made us able to understand child," "happy social worker disagreed with judge who wanted to give child decision-making powers"	"very happy with the service," "very impressed with the service received and the thoroughness of evaluation," "social worker treated both parents with respect, attention given to details"

Table 3d   Negative Parent Comments Related to Each Evaluation Intervention

	Parents' Comments (Questions 1–3) Negative	
	Focused	Traditional
Mothers' Comments	"report was very weak on the factual side, but it did not impede the process," "not happy with the recommendations for overnight visits and number of visits," "glossed over the issues, never asked the kids what they wanted," "don't think kids should be pulled out of school for interviews," "not enough time spent on evaluation but report was excellent," "should dig deeper into problems"	"process took much longer than it should have," "system should follow-up on progress of children," "judge prolongs things," "mistakes in the file, report should be approved by parents," "felt manipulated," "wasn't enough time spent investigating other party," "handled very well but not thrilled with the outcome"
Fathers' Comments	"complete utter waste of time," "cultural/educational differences may have impacted on interaction between social work and self," "feels access was determined without proper investigation, believed mother's lies," "overemphasized spanking issues with kids and underemphasized mother's drug problems"	"feel isolated from the process," "social worker didn't listen to audiotapes," "feels this service was not really needed," "feels social worker did not do report properly, should be longer observation and more detailed enquiries," "too many decisions were allowed by nine year old," "forms were negative (CBCL)," "too much focus on me"

Table 3e   Children's Themes Related to Each Evaluation Intervention

Focused	*Traditional*
"social worker really listened to what I had to say," "would have liked to speak to judge but understood why not," "would not have liked to tell my parents this without help," "children need this kind of help"	"social worker spent a lot of time listening to me but I did not get what I wanted," "questions seemed to focus a lot on me which I liked"

appearance, doesn't seem to feel guilty after misbehaving, overweight]," "I [principal] am not going to instruct my teacher to complete this form as s/he has no time," and "These items are not valid for this child."

Parents raised the following issues. Some fathers who had less visitation time with their child would often become quite tearful and upset when requested to complete their child's behavioural adjustment rating on the CBCL scale. For example, one father stated, "she [mother] does not allow me to see school reports so how can I know?" Another stated, "I do not know how s/he is doing in school because s/he will not allow me to visit the school." A third complained, "This form is very negative about children."

On the other hand, although fathers focused on how the forms made them feel and their ambivalence about not knowing how to answer some of the questions, they also became more reflective about their relationship with their child and were less concerned about the shortcomings of the other parent.

Discussion

The principal purpose of this study was to examine whether a solution-oriented approach to access-based disputes before the court is as effective as the more comprehensive, traditional evaluation intervention that has existed to date. A pilot study by Birnbaum and Radovanovic (1999) provided an opportunity for this quasi-experimental design. The pilot study also helped to ascertain whether the research questions were measurable, piloted the interview schedule, determined the feasibility of conducting the research at the Office of the Children's Lawyer, and provided preliminary data about the focused evaluation intervention. The results of that pilot study provided support for implementing a comparison design that had never before been done in this area.

The study had specific inclusion/exclusion criteria for access-based disputes before the court. It was exploratory in nature, as there are presently no studies in the literature that investigate these different evaluation interventions – focused versus traditional child custody and/or access evaluations – before the court (Birnbaum & Radovanovic, 1999). Methodological weaknesses have been described in the literature when exclusively mothers' reports are used (Lee, 1997), but this study gathered information from both mothers and fathers and the child's teacher on multiple outcomes.

The theoretical framework that formed the basis for this study is the developmental/ecological approach. This type of approach to access-based problems assumes that there is a period of rapid change in the family structure when there is a separation and/or divorce that is followed by a period of equilibrium. This change is also responsive to the child's developmental age and stage. A developmental/ecological approach also assumes that the child's developmental needs are influenced by multiple factors that are both internal and external to the child.

The discussion will also explore the narratives offered by parents and teachers about the research process. Many studies do not explore how the process of the research activity affects respondents. I would argue that the research process is inextricably linked to social work practice. It is important to integrate the research process into the research design, as it is the respondents/clients (e.g., parents and teachers) who are the ones who are being "investigated" and are asked to complete forms. Their involvement in the research process had a direct impact not only on their level of cooperation and participation in the study but also on the outcome of the evaluation process. More importantly, it is the respondents themselves who contribute the most information to both practitioners and policy makers when it comes to further work in this area.

Child's Behaviour Adjustment

Kinard (1998) and Radovanovic (1993) have suggested that children's ratings on the CBCL may be influenced by the rater's relationship to the child and by the different contexts in which the child is observed. The results of the present study, for the most part, are consistent with this observation. There was no association found between mothers' and fathers' reports of their child's behavioural functioning by types of evaluation interventions. Fathers rated their child with significantly more total behavioural problems and externalizing behaviour problems in the focused evaluation than in the traditional evaluation intervention at Time 1 (pre-evaluation intervention). Teachers rated the child as having significantly more internalizing behaviour problems in the traditional evaluation than in the focused evaluation intervention at Time 2.

When correlations of teachers' and parents' reports of child adjustment were considered, there were some correlations found. Mothers and teachers reported statistically significant agreement on total behaviour problems and externalizing behaviour problems at both Time 1 and Time 2. This suggests that both mothers and teachers agree on the child's behavioural functioning. On the other hand, there was no significant agreement between fathers' and teachers' reports on any of the behavioural problems.

Both mothers and fathers report statistically significant agreement on all three sub-scales (total behaviour problems and internalizing and externalizing behaviour problems) at Time 1. Irrespective of the low percentage of agreement (approximately 12 per cent), the congruence of parent ratings is significant in several ways. First, fathers are important informants in the process, and every effort was made to elicit their response. Many studies fail to report fathers' findings due to poor response rates from them (Kline et al., 1989; Lee, 1997). Second, the majority of the children (84 per cent) were in the sole custody of their mother and visited with their father on average every other weekend. While the amount of time the child spends with his/her father is considerably less than the time spent with the mother, this does suggest that fathers are important observers of their child's behaviour irrespective of the parental conflict and the different contexts in which the child is observed. Therefore, every effort must be made to include fathers' reports of their child in any future studies.

The mean adjustment scores of the children all fell within the normal range. These findings are consistent with other studies (Kline et al., 1989; Johnston, 1994; Radovanovic et al., 1994). At Time 2 less than 20 per cent of the children were found to be in the clinically significant range as rated by mothers and fathers. Even when one controls for custodial parent rating at Time 1, children still scored well within the normal range. Irrespective of the biased nature of this sample, it is surprising and distressing to see some of these children continuing to experience emotional and behavioural problems many years after their parents' separation and/or divorce.

As noted earlier, caution must be exercised when interpreting results of no difference. The average age of the child at the time of the study was seven years, and they had already experienced four years of their parents' separation. This study excluded parents who were at the more serious end of the conflict continuum, that is, those who had serious ongoing verbal and physical disputes between each other, sometimes in front of their child. Therefore, the children in this research, while caught up in their parents' dispute, were not exposed to the more serious ongoing acrimony between their parents.

Satisfaction

There was a significant difference found between mothers and fathers. Mothers were significantly more satisfied in the focused evaluation than in the traditional evaluation intervention; but there was no significant difference found in evaluation interventions with respect to fathers. These findings are important in several ways. First, this is the first study to evaluate satisfaction with the process and outcomes immediately following the evaluation intervention. Other studies have evaluated satisfaction one to two years later, and it is difficult if not impossible to discern the extent to which intervening events have influenced ratings of satisfaction (Austin & Jaffe, 1990). Second, the majority of the children were in the sole custodial care of mothers who reported such concerns as the child often hearing their parents fight and violence directed towards the child by the non-custodial parent, usually the father. Nonetheless, mothers' mean satisfaction scores were significantly higher in the focused evaluation intervention than in the traditional evaluation intervention. What is surprising about this finding is that the focused intervention did not give mothers as much time to address these serious concerns as did the traditional evaluation intervention. Third, access to the non-custodial parent, usually the father, increased and was described by both parents as regular following the involvement of the Children's Lawyer's Office. This suggests that the focused intervention evaluation facilitated problem solving between mothers and fathers that, in terms of visitation, decreased the discrepancy between what was expected and what actually occurred.

There was also a significant finding with respect to fathers' mean change scores regarding their satisfaction with the amount of sharing with their ex-spouse. Fathers' satisfaction scores went down slightly in the traditional evaluation intervention, while fathers in the focused evaluation intervention had higher satisfaction scores. However, this finding needs to be interpreted with caution, as attrition, as noted in the method section, was very high for fathers at Time 2.

Limitations of the Study

The following discussion highlights the two major research hypotheses that were tested in this study. A number of caveats must be voiced before proceeding with the limitations to the study. First, caution must be exercised when interpreting the results of "no difference" between the two different types of evaluation interventions. In this particular study, it is important to note the unique characteristics of the parents who qualified and chose to participate. The entry criteria excluded those parents with more serious problems and issues before the court (e.g., custody issues; a child who refuses to visit the other parent; sexual, physical, or emotional abuse between the parents and/or child), thereby creating a homogenous population of relatively mild to moderate levels of conflict as defined by Garrity and Baris (1994) and Johnston (1994). Furthermore, in this particular sample, mothers had the majority of sole care and custody of the child and fathers' visitation ranged from having no specific access schedule, to every other weekend, to supervised access. In addition, the parents had already been separated for an average of more than four years, and many of them had already established new relationships. Therefore, the degree of turmoil and unsettledness that often accompanies early separations was not present in this particular sample (Johnston, 1994). This may have a bearing on the level of communication and cooperation regarding how much information each parent shared with the other as well as how each parent resolved conflict with the other.

Sampling Issues

This study, as mentioned, was exploratory in nature, and the generalizability of the findings to other settings is limited in several ways. First, this sample represents parents who had been litigating for over three years prior to receiving service from the Office of the Children's Lawyer. They may well have settled their dispute because their experience with the court system was less than helpful. Second, the services were provided in a publicly funded office that enjoys high credibility within the courts of Ontario, and the parents may well have felt that they had little choice but to accept the recommendations made. Third, the sample was selected on the basis of parents who used the services of a public office versus those provided by a private practitioner. Therefore, the findings may not generalize to other samples, particularly those that include parents of higher socio-economic status. Fourth, the sample selected involved access-based disputes that met specific criteria for entry and therefore introduced a sampling bias. Fifth, the intake criteria of the OCL recommends that older children be legally represented and younger children have a social work investigation appointed, with ensuing report. The average age in this sample was seven years and therefore introduced a sampling bias towards older children. Sixth, mothers were more likely to complete all of the outcome measures in this sample, thereby creating a sampling bias. Finally, while this study had sufficient power to detect a medium to large effect size in many of the analyses, the results can only be generalized to the population represented by the sample, e.g., the inclusion/exclusion criteria.

Design Issues

In conducting outcome research it is important to have a randomized, controlled trial to evaluate the effectiveness of different interventions. The randomized quasi-experimental design in this study was deemed to be appropriate for a number of reasons. First, this is the first time a research study had ever been undertaken at the OCL. Therefore, there was concern that the questionnaires would be challenged by some lawyers and potentially subpoenaed for court purposes, creating further conflict and exacerbating the dispute before the court. Owing to these concerns, children could not be interviewed or observed (by anyone other than the social worker conducting the evaluation) or requested to complete a child questionnaire. Second, it is unethical to randomize parents and children into a purely randomized clinical control trial as found in "treatment" or "no treatment" groups. Moreover, the Office of the Children's Lawyer, having once accepted a case from the court, must provide a service. Third, while randomized trials attempt to minimize threats to internal validity, controlling for all aspects of the methodology is unmanageable if not impossible in the real world (Rubin & Babbie, 2013).

Interventions

While there was a statistically significant difference found between assessment interventions, caution must be exercised in interpreting this with respect to the clinical significance. First, both interventions were of short duration: 20 hours versus 35 hours. The average number of hours for the focused evaluation was 15.60 and the mean number of hours for the traditional evaluation intervention was 28.34. Both interventions spanned a two-and-a-half-month period (the Children's Lawyer is legally obligated to produce a report within 90 days). Second, while the social workers attended the research meetings and engaged in role-plays regarding each intervention, not all social workers fully participated or may have been interested in learning a new approach, the focused evaluation intervention. Waltz, Addis, Koerner, and Jacobson (1993) suggest that neither therapist training nor amount of therapist experience is correlated with treatment outcome. In other words, inferences cannot be drawn regarding the amount of training that the social workers received or their experience level. Third, some social workers were trained after they had already conducted the evaluation interventions. Kazdin (1986) argues that to conduct effective comparative outcome studies, more rigour needs to be applied at the initial stages to differentiate treatment conditions than is presently reported in the literature. Future research needs to incorporate training and evaluation of different interventions and worker compliance before the research is actually carried out. In addition, many social workers expressed a desire to understand the family history and each parents' allegations concerning each other to establish a rapport with the parents. This may also have influenced social worker compliance with the protocol in the focused evaluation intervention, since this approach does not encourage a parent to linger over his/her concerns about the other. Fourth, not every social worker carried out an equal number of cases in each evaluation intervention. Some social workers only did one or two cases, while others did more cases using both interventions. A Time 3 follow-up would have allowed for the collection of more data to test the research hypotheses and the validity of the interventions. Fifth, attrition is always a factor when conducting research. This study was no exception. Kazdin (1996) advises that there can be as much as 40 to 60 per cent loss of the sample at Time 2. In addition, trying to locate parents to obtain their satisfaction results with either evaluation intervention proved to be a challenging task, as many had moved since the completion of Time 2 data. While there were no significant differences found in attrition rates examining baseline data to determine differences in drop-out at Time 2 in this particular sample, there was 36 per cent sample loss for mothers and 44 per cent sample loss for fathers at Time 2.

Implications of the Theoretical Framework

Four theoretical frameworks contributed to our understanding of the process of separation and divorce. These same frameworks (family systems theory, life model approach, developmental theory, and conflict theory) guide the mental health professional in conducting child custody and access evaluations. Within each framework are risk and protective factors that affect children's development.

The developmental/ecological framework was selected as the major theoretical framework, as it incorporates both an integrative model and a practice approach that mental health professionals use in their work. More important, this framework allows for an exploration of both strength and resiliency factors in children and their parents, thereby allowing an integration of micro and macro perspectives. Future research needs to continue to incorporate this important theoretical perspective to guide different approaches that can be used in child custody decision making as demonstrated by this thesis.

Implications for Social Work Practice and Policy

From a resource point of view, the inclusion/exclusion criteria facilitated the identification of children and families who might benefit from a shorter, solution-oriented approach in a timely and cost-effective manner. This has significant policy implications for future directions with respect to advocating on behalf of children's interests. More training and more rigorous fidelity assessment tools are required to help differentiate the two clinical approaches. Furthermore, it will be important to provide clients with access to this alternative intervention, which represents a more active intervention by mental health professionals and a stronger, child-focused approach to family law, as well as the recognition that "one size does not fit all."

Implications for Future Research

Basic research continues to focus on outcomes that inevitably lead to developmental deficit factors (e.g., inter-parental conflict and child adjustment). Consequently, little is known about outcomes for children that promote and enhance resiliency (e.g., What individual child characteristics such as self-esteem and coping strategies are important? Why do some children appear less affected by their parents' separation and/or divorce than others?) Focusing on adaptive outcomes may lead to greater understanding of the transaction between the child and the child's environment (Grych & Fincham, 1992).

I would argue that more research is required regarding outcomes related to children involved in custody or access assessments. Since recommendations for children are predicated on the future, follow-up studies need to be carried out to evaluate whether or not the recommendations were of assistance to these children and their parents (emotionally and behaviourally). In this study, parents often stated that more follow-up should occur. I would also argue for better ways to develop interdisciplinary partnerships so that children can continue their relationships with each parent after separation or divorce.

Finally, further research should involve multiple methods, which are based on different epistemological positions that incorporate the child's life experience as well as each parent's life experience. Standardized questionnaires that presently exist (CTS, CBCL) may not fully capture the constructs that require investigation. There is a need to learn from children, their parents, mental health professionals, and researchers working collaboratively in the research process.

Works Cited

Achenbach, T. (1979). The child behaviour profile: An empirically based system for assessing children's behaviour and competence. *International Journal of Mental Health*, 7(3-4), 24–42. http://dx.doi.org/10.1080/00207411.1978.11448806.

Achenbach, T., & Edelbrock, C. (1978). The classification of child psychopathology: A review and analysis of empirical efforts. *Psychological Bulletin*, 85(6), 1275–1301. http://dx.doi.org/10.1037/0033-2909.85.6.1275.

Achenbach, T., & Edelbrock, C. (1983). *The manual for the child behaviour checklist and revised child behaviour profile*. New York: Queen City Printers.

Achenbach, T., McConaughy, S., & Howell, C.T. (1987). Child/adolescent behavioural and emotional problems: Implications of cross-informant correlations from situational specificity. *Psychological Bulletin, 101*(2), 213–232. http://dx.doi.org/10.1037/0033-2909.101.2.213.

Austin, G., & Jaffe, P. (1990). Follow-up study of parents in custody and access disputes. *Canadian Psychology, 31*(2), 172–179. http://dx.doi.org/10.1037/h0078889.

Birnbaum, R., & Radovanovic, H. (1999). Brief intervention model for access based post-separation disputes: Family and court outcomes. *Journal of Family and Conciliation Courts Review, 37*(4), 504–513. http://dx.doi.org/10.1111/j.174-1617.1999.tb00549.x.

Garrity, C.B., & Baris, M.A. (1994). *Caught in the middle: Protecting the children of high-conflict divorce*. Toronto: Maxwell Macmillan.

Gould, J.W. (1998). *Conducting scientifically crafted child custody evaluations*. Thousand Oaks, CA: Sage.

Grych, J., & Fincham, F. (1992). Interventions for children of divorce: Toward greater integration of research and action. *Psychological Bulletin, 110*(3), 434–454. http://dx.doi.org/10.1037/0033-2909.111.3.434.

Hollingshead, A.B. (1975). *Four factor index of social status*. New Haven: Yale University, Department of Sociology.

Johnston, J. (1994). High conflict divorce. In David and Lucille Packard Foundation (Ed.), *The future of children: Children and divorce*, pp. 165–82. Los Altos, CA: Packard Foundation.

Johnston, J., Kline, M., & Tschann, J. (1989). Ongoing post-divorce conflict: Effects on children of joint custody and frequent access. *American Journal of Orthopsychiatry, 59*(4), 576–592. http://dx.doi.org/10.1111/j.1939-0025.1989.tb02748.x.

Johnston, J., & Roseby, V. (1997). *In the name of the child: A developmental approach to understanding and helping children in highly conflicted and violent divorced families*. New York: Free Press.

Kazdin, A.E. (1986). Comparative outcome studies of psychotherapy: Methodological issues and strategies. *Journal of Consulting and Clinical Psychology, 54*(1), 95–105. http://dx.doi.org/10.1037/0022-006X.54.1.95.

Kazdin, A.E. (1996). Dropping out of child psychotherapy: Issues for research and implications for practice. *Clinical Child Psychiatry, 1*(1), 133–156. http://dx.doi.org/10.1177/1359104596011012.

Kinard, E.M. (1998). Methodological issues in assessing resilience in maltreated children. *Child Abuse & Neglect, 22*(3), 669–680. http://dx.doi.org/10.1016/S0145-2134(98)00048-9.

Kline, M., Tschann, J., Johnston, J., & Wallerstein, J. (1989). Children's adjustment in joint and sole physical custody families. *Developmental Psychology, 25*(3), 430–438. http://dx.doi.org/10.1037/0012-1649.25.3.430.

Kruk, E. (1992). Psychological and structural factors contributing to the disengagement of non-custodial fathers after divorce. *Family and Conciliation Courts Review, 30*(1), 82–101.

Lee, M. (1997). Post-divorce interparental conflict, children's contact with both parents, children's emotional processes, and children's behavioral adjustment. *Journal of Divorce & Remarriage, 27*(3/4), 61–82. http://dx.doi.org/10.1300/J087v27n03_05.

Maccoby, E., & Mnookin, R. (1992). Custody settlements in a California sample. Paper presented at the annual meeting of the American Association for Advancement of Science, Philadelphia.

McCracken, G. (1988). *The long interview: Qualitative research methods* (Vol. 13). Thousand Oaks, CA: Sage. http://dx.doi.org/10.4135/9781412986229.

Nie, H.H., Hull, C.H., Jenkins, J.G., Steinbrenner, K., & Bent, D.H.N. (1975). *SPSS: Statistical package for the social sciences*. New York: McGraw-Hill.

Offord, D.R., Boyle, M.H., Racine, Y., Szatmari, P., Fleming, J.E., Sanford, M., & Lipman, E.L. (1996). Integrating assessment data from multiple informants. *Journal of the American Academy of Child and Adolescent Psychiatry*, *35*(8), 1078–1085. http://dx.doi.org/10.1097/00004583-199608000-00019.

Radovanovic, H. (1993). Parental conflict and children's coping styles in litigating separated families: Relationships with children's adjustment. *Journal of Abnormal Child Psychology*, *21*(6), 697–713. http://dx.doi.org/10.1007/BF00916451.

Radovanovic, H., Bartha, C., Magnatta, M., Hood, E., Sagar, A., & McDonough, H. (1994). A follow-up of families disputing child custody/access: Assessment, settlement and family relationship outcomes. *Behavioral Sciences & the Law*, *12*(4), 427–435. http://dx.doi.org/10.1002/bsl.2370120411.

Rubin, A., & Babbie, E. (2013). *Research methods in social work* (8th ed.). Pacific Grove, CA: Brooks/Cole.

Stahl, P.M. (1994). *Conducting child custody evaluations: A comprehensive guide*. Thousand Oaks, CA: Sage.

Statistics Canada. (1997). Average annual income for lone-parent families. Catalogue no. 13-210-XPB.

Twaite, J.A., Silitsky, D., & Luchow, A.K. (1998). *Children of divorce: Adjustment, parental conflict, custody, remarriage and recommendations for clinicians*. Northvale, NJ: Jason Aronson.

Waltz, J., Addis, M.E., Koerner, K., & Jacobson, N.S. (1993). Testing the integrity of a psychotherapy protocol: Assessment of adherence and competence. *Journal of Consulting and Clinical Psychology*, *61*(4), 620–630. http://dx.doi.org/10.1037/0022-006X.61.4.620.

Critique

by Barbara Decker Pierce and Rick Csiernik

Part A – Purpose

1. Research Problem/Hypotheses

The purpose of the study was to examine alternative approaches to conducting social work assessments in parental child visitation–based disputes before the court, the traditional child custody/visitation–based approach and a problem-solving evaluative approach. The researcher does a good job of establishing the importance of social work assessments in these types of disputes. These assessments have a significant impact on the lives of families and children. The research is well focused upon one particular type of court-ordered assessment, those prepared for the resolution of visitation-based disputes. Four competing hypotheses regarding differences generated by the two approaches being studied were clearly labelled in their own section of the article. However, given the atheoretical nature of the investigation and its exploratory intent, hypotheses were not expected. Research questions would have been more suitable for this type of inquiry.

2. General Purpose of Inquiry

While the author maintains that this is an exploratory study, predicated by the lack of empirical research in the area of child custody assessments, the actual research appears much more focused that that. It is probably more appropriate to consider this a comparative evaluation. The purpose is to compare an alternative to the traditional approach to court-ordered assessments. Since the alternative appears to require less time, the purpose of the research is to determine if there are comparable levels of client satisfaction and if there is any difference in the level of child adjustment between the two approaches.

3. Literature Review

There was a rudimentary description provided of the traditional child custody/visitation process and the focused solution-oriented approach, along with how the latter evolved.

There was no discussion of how the activities of these two approaches are influenced by theory. Reference is made to the developmental/ecological approach as well as to family systems theory, the life model approach, developmental theory, and conflict theories in the article's closing section on implications of the theoretical framework. However, these are not connected in a meaningful way to the development of the alternative intervention. There is reference to another article by the same author, Birnbaum & Radovanovic (1999), that might contain more detail, but if this is the case it should be made clear.

4. Ethical Issues

A detailed discussion was presented on consent procedures. All participation was voluntary, and participants were allowed to withdraw from the study and did so for a variety of reasons, all of which were addressed in the article. The author also mentions that it was ethical concerns that restricted the random assignment of participants into the two assessment groups.

Part B – Measurement

1. Concepts and Variables

The traditional assessment approach, the solution-focused assessment approach, children's behavioural and emotional adjustment, and mothers' and fathers' satisfaction were the key variables investigated. Pertinent demographic information was also collected.

2. Nominal Definitions

As noted above, only minimal descriptions of the assessment approaches were provided. Child adjustment was not nominally defined. Satisfaction was defined as parents' satisfaction with a number of aspects of the assessment process.

3. Measures

Each family experienced one of two assessment approaches: either the traditional approach or the solution-focused approach.

Child adjustment was measured by using a well-established standardized measure commonly used in research in this area, the 113-item Child Behaviour Checklist (CBCL). There is not enough detail in the description of the checklist to determine the level of measurement, but it is likely ratio level. The instrument was completed by both parents, independent of each other. While the author states that the two independent ratings were combined and averaged, no results are presented concerning this combined measure. Results are reported for mother measures and father measures and for custodial parents. Each child's teacher was asked to complete a teacher's version of the CBCL.

Satisfaction was measured using a researcher-developed multi-item composite scale consisting of five aspects of satisfaction. Each item was rated on a five-point Likert scale with the anchors of "very unsatisfied" to "very satisfied." A satisfaction score was then derived by taking the sum of the items. This type of instrument provides ordinal data. The instrument description occurs in the introduction to the article, not in the measurement section.

Socio-economic status was determined using the Hollingshead Four Factor Index of Social Status, which uses nominal (gender and marital status) and ordinal (education on a seven-point scale, occupational level on a nine-point scale) data to determine status. Demographic data collected were both nominal (child's sex, ethnicity) and ratio (age, income, length of time of the relationship and of the separation).

4. Validity and Reliability

A fidelity checklist was employed, with both the social worker conducting the assessment and the parents to confirm the type of assessment actually delivered. However, results of this are not reported.

The Child Behaviour Checklist's validity and reliability were documented by the author, as were its limitations. The CBCL is not a culturally diverse and sensitive instrument, though this is not a unique limitation, as many traditional instruments commonly used in social work and other fields of research share this problem. Likert scales, despite their routine use, are rarely standardized or tested for reliability and validity, as they capture subjective impressions of participants on research-question-specific themes. Reliability data were not provided for this administration of the instrument. The validity and reliability of the satisfaction instrument were not supported.

The Hollingshead Four Factor Index of Social Status is a widely used instrument; however, it was validated against the 1970 U.S. census and so may have some historic and cultural limitations. While demographic data collection instruments typically provide valid and reliable data by virtue of the information they collect, they are rarely if ever tested for these qualities.

Part C – Participants

1. Sample Selection

The author states that a "randomized sample of 115 biological pairs of mothers and fathers … were eligible for participation." It is not clear what this means because the sampling frame is not described. Later in the paper the author states that all families referred to the court for custody and/or access investigation between specified dates received a recruitment letter. Were these 115 families all those who agreed to participate? If so, what is random about their selection? As well, at the start of the article the author states that the research focused on those who needed visitation assessments only. A much clearer description of the sample selection is required. There is no mention of how clients were divided into the two assessment groups; the author says in the limitations section that it was not by random assignment, but there should be some statement at this point as to how the decision was made.

2. Population

The population was intended to represent families undergoing child visitation assessments. An extensive discussion of the limits of the sample is provided at the conclusion of the article, including potential sampling bias around who used this service, age of children, completion of data forms, and socio-economic status.

3. Generalizability

Limits of generalizability are explicitly stated in the sampling issues subsection of the larger section entitled "Limitations of the Study," based upon issues with the sample and with ethical practice, recognizing that it is unethical to randomize parents and children into treatment and no-treatment groups.

Part D – Design

1. Type

While the author maintains that this was a quasi-experimental design, the alternative assessments do not meet the criteria of being interventions; that is, assessment type is not an independent variable. There is no intent to use the assessment to influence child adjustment. The measurement of child adjustment prior to the assessment experience allowed the researcher to control for possible differences between the two groups prior to assessment. There is no hypothesis suggesting that the assessment process would have an influence on child adjustment. What the researcher wants to confirm is that there is no difference in the level of child adjustment between the two groups. The assessment should not be referred to as an intervention. It is probably more accurate to consider this a descriptive study assessing the similarities and differences of two groups.

2. Data Collection

There was a clear separation between those providing the assessments and those collecting the research data. Good efforts were made to ensure that all participants, both parents and teachers, completed all the required questionnaires. However, there still appeared to be considerable missing data.

3. Reliability of Secondary Data

Demographic data were collected from the Children's Lawyer Intake Form. The author did not discuss the reliability of this data.

4. Instrument Pre-test

Pre-testing of the instrument was not described; however, the author does refer to an earlier pilot study. It is possible the instruments were pre-tested as part of that process.

5. Data Collection Process

The quality of the approach to data collection was high.

Part E – Data Analysis and Reporting

1. Statistical Analysis

Extensive and appropriate statistical analysis was applied to the data. However, the reporting of the data was inconsistent and incomplete. Readers of this article are interested in knowing (1) a description of the sample, (2) comparability of the groups, (3) impact of sample attrition on the measurement of child adjustment, (4) differences in satisfaction, and (5) differences in child adjustment. While the author addressed many of these topics, the presentation of results was confusing and would have benefited from tables containing all the results of the analyses. There were likely a number of analyses that resulted in the identification of no relationships or no differences between the groups, but this should be clearly stated. The author's choice of addressing mostly significant relationships in the results section makes it difficult for readers to appreciate the full scope of analyses conducted. Also, certain analyses appeared in the results section that had not been discussed previously. For example, the concept of "custodial parent" was not introduced prior to the presentation of the analysis. Given the way in which the measure was described in the methods section, an Ancova should have been conducted using the joint parent assessment of the child's adjustment.

Reporting of the sample size is inconsistent. Given the amount of missing data, there should be a clear indication for each analysis reported what the *n* was.

2. Meaningfulness of Statistically Significant Results

Meaningfulness was not discussed.

3. Key Findings

Key statistically significant findings and their limitations were addressed in the discussion section. The author states that "the discussion will also explore the narratives offered by parents and teachers about the research process"; however, there is no indication in the methodology about how such narratives were collected and nothing in the results section that reports on such matters.

4. Limitations

An extensive discussion of the limitations of the study was presented, in much greater detail than is typically found in a journal article.

5. Future Research

It is recommended that additional research be conducted pertaining to outcomes relating to children involved in custody and/or access evaluations.

Part F – Overall Evaluation

This is a substantially longer example than is typically found in peer-reviewed journals. Thus, there is greater detail in many sections than one would typically find, as multiple hypotheses are presented and there is extensive statistical analysis. Although this report is exploratory in nature, its findings are encouraging. It would appear that the focused approach to visitation assessments does not adversely affect child adjustment and that mothers find the process more satisfying. Certainly there is justification for further study of the focused approach.

Key learning points from this article follow.

Strengths:

- Important problem
- Good example of relevant evaluation work … support for decision making
- Good data collection
- Nice features such as examining attrition
- Variety of analysis well justified based on analysis of assumptions and relevant level of measurement
- Good discussion of limitations

Problem Areas:

- Hypothesis testing in a theoretical study
- Poor measure of satisfaction
- Poor tracking of sample size
- Incorrect design
- Concerns over cultural sensitivity of CBCL

Index

Note: Page numbers in italics followed by *f* or *t* denote figures and tables, respectively.

A B1 A B2 study design, 161–2
A BC study design, 159
AB study design, 155–7, *157f*
ABA study design, 157–9, *158f*, 161
ABAB study design, 159
ABAC study design, 159–60
ABC study design, 159
accidental (convenience) sampling, 103, *103t*
action research, 233
Affect Balance Scale (Bradburn, 1969), *83t*
analysis: constant comparative, 211–13; content, 213; discourse, 212; ethnographic, 212, 296–7; frameworks for critiquing, 289–92; interpretative phenomenological approach (IPA), 213–15; mixed methods, 228; narrative, 212; units of, 89–90
analysis of variance (ANOVA), 278
analysis, qualitative. *See* qualitative analysis
analysis, quantitative. *See* quantitative analysis
analysis, statistical. *See* statistics
anchors (in Likert scales), 182, 334
anonymity: about, 51, 174, 186, 191, 192, 200; information about, on forms, 42, 62, 64. *See also* confidentiality
ANOVA (analysis of variance), 278
answerability (of questions), 179–80
Armed Forces Epidemiological Board (US), 34
attrition. *See* mortality (attrition)
audit trail, 203, *225t*, 226–7
axial coding, 211

B-Only study design, 157–8
BAB study design, 168
baseline phases: about, 156, 157–8, 159, 161, 164, 168, 169; case study examples of, 153, *153f, 154f, 156t, 157f, 158f, 161t, 166f*
baselines, multiple, 169
BASIS-32, 133
Beck depression scale, 133
bell curve (normal distribution curve, normal curve), in statistics, *258f*, 261
Bellamy, Carol: on children, 209
bias: avoiding, 167, 178, 179, 181–2, 202, 250, 275; editorial, 256–7; examples of, 105; in feminist research, 239; in focus groups, 202; intentional, 91–2; in questions, 179, *179f*, 262; recall, 251–2; response set, 181–2; sampling, 91–2, 94–5, 314, 326; selection, *135t*, 136, 139, 140, 149; unintentional, 92
black community: case study example involving, 21–30

Canadian Institutes of Health Research (CIHR) guidelines, 36, 71–2
case-based learning, 3–7
cases (as units of analysis), 90
causal time order (time-order ambiguity), *134t*, 135
causality: experiment designs to establish, 146–7; in single-case study, 155; three criteria of, 115; case study example of, 108–17

central tendencies, 257, 266–8

Centre for Epidemiologic Studies Depression Scale (Radloff, 1977), *83t*

checklists: Child Behaviour Checklist (CBCL), 313–14, 334; ethics protocol submissions, 36–8; on questionnaires, 180–1; Teacher Report Form (CBCL), 314

chi-square test (in statistics): about, 278; examples of, 280, 316

Child Behaviour Checklist (CBCL), 313–14, 334

children and youth: considerations when researching, 57, 59, 196–8, 209, 219–20 (*see also* ethics; guidelines); informed consent of, 57–66; case study examples involving, 33–45, 57–66, 88–99, 144–50, 152–62, 164–70, 196–206, 209–20, 248–54, 309–29

Client Satisfaction Questionnaire (CSQ-8), 250–1, *252–3f*

client satisfaction, measuring, 249–53

cluster sampling, 94, *97–8t*

co-variation (of variables), 115

coding, 211–15; case study examples of, 215–17, *216f, 217f, 217t*

coercion, 44, 49–50

collaborative research. *See* participatory action research (PAR)

Committee on Human Experimentation, New York University (US), 34

community-based research. *See* participatory action research (PAR)

Community-University Research Alliance (CURA), 231

comparison group pre-test-post-test designs (non-equivalent comparison group designs): about, 147–8; case study example of, 148

comparison groups: about, 137–8, 146; case study example of, 89

concentration camp experiments (Nazi), 44

conceptualization: about, 81–2, *82t*; in qualitative analysis, 211, 212; in qualitative research, 204; case study example of, 79–85

concurrent validity, 125, *126t*

confidence interval (CI), in statistics, 259

confidentiality: about, 35, 51, 201; information about, on forms, 36, 42, 61, 63. *See also* anonymity

confirmability, in qualitative research, 203, 213, *225t*

conflicts of interest, 35, 36, 54. *See also* ethics

confounding variables, 113, *113f,* 115, 135; case study examples of, 44, 168. *See also* variable relationships

consent forms: about, 51; samples, 62, 64, *187–8f;* usage examples, 58–9, 187, 312, 314, 315

consent, informed: about, 44, 50–1; of children and youth, 57–66; failure to obtain, examples of, 44–5, 68; information about, on forms, 37–8, 39, 42; case study examples of, 33–46, 57–66, 75, 312

consistency, internal (of data), 123

constant comparative analysis, 211–13

construct validity, 125–6, *126t*

constructivism, 5, 223–4

content analysis, 213

content validity, 124–5, *126t*

contingency questions, 184, *185f,* 198

continua (on scales), 181

control groups: about, 137–8, 140, 146; ethical concerns and, 137–8; validity and, 135–8; case study examples of, 89, 94–5, 109, 116–17, 133, 147, 274–81

convenience (accidental) sampling, 103, *103t*

convergent validity, 126, *126t*

correlation, 278–9, *279f. See also* reliability (of data); validity (of data)

correlation coefficient, 123

credibility, in qualitative research, 203, 213, *225t,* 226, 238

criminal justice: case study example involving, 108–17

criterion-related validity, 125–6, *126t*

critical ethnography, 205

Cronbach alpha, 123–4

data: four types of, *278t*; levels of (*see* measurement: levels of); processing (*see* coding; statistics); quality of, 119, 123; raw (example of), 267; reliability, 121–4 (*see also* errors, types of); saturation, 104; secondary, 157

data analysis. *See* analysis; qualitative analysis; quantitative analysis

data collection: by clients, 160, 165; goal attainment scaling, 166–8; issues in, 121–2; mixed methods, 250–3; qualitative, 121–2, 200–3, 241–2; quantitative, 176–86. *See also* analysis; measurement; questionnaires; scales; scales, specific types

data elements (variables), 176

database searches: in literature review process, 10–12, 285–6

deception, 44–5. *See also* research ethics, guidelines

decision making, ethical, 52–3

deduction (theory testing), 111

delayed positive reaction, 158–9

demographic information: in comparison groups, 138; on questionnaires, 148, 174, 176, 184, 198

deontological ethics, 52, *53t*

dependability, in qualitative research, 203, 213, *225t*

dependent variables, 113–14, *113f*, 115. *See also* variable relationships

descriptive research: about, 29; case study examples of, 294–303, 309–29

descriptive statistics, 265–72; about, 257, 266; central tendency (mean, median, and mode), 266–7; measures of dispersion (range and standard deviation), 268–9; case study example of use, 267–71

designs. *See* experimental designs; longitudinal designs; quasi-experimental designs; single-case study designs

diffusion of treatment: about, *134t*, 137; case study examples of, 132–42, 140, 149

discourse analysis, 212

discriminant validity, 126, *126t*

discussion, guided: in case-based learning, 6

dispersion, in statistics, 261

Disraeli, Benjamin: on statistics, 256

divergent construct validity, 126

double-barrelled questions, 179–80

drug users: case study examples involving, 47–55, 132–42

effect size, 280, 326

electronic surveys, 185–6

empirical validity testing, 125–6

epistemology, 24, 27, 239

error, margin of. *See* margin of error

errors, examples of, 28, 94–5, 105

errors, types of: attribution, 25; measurement, 200; questionnaire-related, 175, 176, 180, 183, 186, 187; random, 121–4; sampling, 90–1, 259; systemic, 124–6; type I and type II, 279–80

ethical considerations, case study examples of, 33–45, 47–55, 57–66, 68–76, 128, 137, 219, 327

ethics: about, 35, 51, 144, 145–6; guidelines, 35–6, 38–9, 71–2, 73 (*see also* children and youth); social workers and, 14, 244; in decision making, teleological versus deontological, 52–3, *53t*. *See also* research ethics review committees (RERCs)

ethics submission forms: about, 36; examples of, 36–8, 39–43

ethnography, 205, 212, 296–7

evaluation (of programs), 141–2

exhaustiveness: of categories, 112, 261; in questions, 177

experimental designs, 146–7

experimental groups: about, 138; case study examples of, 94–5, 109, 116–17, 132–42, 147, 274–81

exploratory research: about, 29; Cronbach alpha in, 123; case study examples of, 68–76, 309–29 external validity: about, 139, *225t*. *See also* generalizability

external validity, threats to: about, *134t*, 139; case study example of, 149

extraneous variables, 113, 135; case study examples of, 44, 168. *See also* variable relationships

extrasensory perception (ESP) experiments, 68

face validity, 124, *126t*

Fals-Borda, Orlando, 233

Family Environmental Scale (Moos & Moos, 1994), *83t*

feminist research, 238–40, 244

field notes, 211, 226, 296

field research, 205

First Nations, about, 68–70, 76

fixed-alternative (single-item) questions, 177–8, 199; case study example of, 254

focus groups: about, 201–3; IPA analysis and, 215, 217; to measure client satisfaction, 250; case study examples of, 75, 88, 187–9, 296

formative evaluation, 202

forms: language usage in, 38, 50

Freire, Paulo, 233

frequency, behavioural, 155, 270–1, 313–14

frequency, in statistics, 261, 268

frequency distribution, in statistics, 261

Garvin's model, 13–14

General Health Questionnaire (Goldberg, 1978), *83t*

generalizability, 90–2, 103, 104, 134, 139, 155, 166, 174–5, 176, 191

generalizations, 111, 277

Glaser and Strauss, 212

goal attainment scaling (GAS), 166–8, *167t*

grounded theory, 204–5

group dynamics, 202–3

groups. *See* comparison groups; control groups; experimental groups; focus groups; participatory action research (PAR)

guidelines: for research ethics, 35–6, 38–9, 71–2, 73

Hamilton Anxiety Rating Scale, 121

harm: avoidance and reduction, 50, 128, 209, 219, 274; case study example of, 33–44; client comments on, 47; other examples of, 44–5, 68, 73–4. *See also* ethics

health care: case study example involving, 119–29

Hippocrates: on science, 33

history (as confounding variable): about, *134t*, 135; case study examples of, 140, 149

history-treatment interaction: about, *134t*, 139; case study example of, 149

Hollingshead Four Factor Index of Social Status, 313, 334

homelessness: case study examples involving, 230–44, 274–81

honeymoon effect, 158

hypotheses, 111–15, 277, 278, 311, 332

ideographic research, 155, 166

incentives (for participation), 49, 59–60, 175, 251

independent variables, 113–14, *113f*, 115. *See also* variable relationships

Indigenous peoples: about, 68–70, 76; harmful research involving, 44; case study examples involving, 47–55, 68–76

Indigenous Peoples' Health Research Centre guidelines, 71–2

induction (theory development), 111

inferential statistics, 274–81; about, 258, 277; chi-square test, 278, 316; linear regression, 279; null hypothesis, 277, 279–80; *p* value, 277, 280; Pearson's *r*, 279; research hypothesis, 277; *t* test, 278, 281, 316–17, 319; type I and type II errors, 279–80; case study examples of, 275–6, 280

informed consent. *See* consent, informed

institutional review boards (IRBs), 36, 45, 145

instrumentation (measurement tools): about, 135–6

Interagency Advisory Panel on Research Ethics, 72

internal validity: about, 134, *225t*; case study example of, 132–42

internal validity, threats to, *134t*, 135–8, 327; case study examples of, 139–41, 149, 156, 158

interpretative phenomenological approach (IPA), 213–15

interpretivism, 223–4

interval data, *278t*

interval-level data: about, *83t*, 84, *278t*; case study example of, 316

intervention phases: about, 156, 157–60; case study examples of, *153f, 154f, 156t, 158f, 166f*

interviewers, 186, 198–202

interviews: to measure client satisfaction, 250; naturalistic, 200–1 (*see also* focus groups); semi-structured, examples of, 59, 210–11; structured, 198–200

IPA (interpretative phenomenological approach), 213–15

JAREL Spiritual Well-Being Scale (Hungelmann et al., 1987): about, 266; examples of use, *83t, 267t*, 270–1, *271t*, 281

journal keeping, 203, 210, *225t*, 226, 236

journals, open-access, 285–6. *See also* literature review

journals, peer-reviewed, 285

journals, predatory, 286–7

judgment sampling, 103

knowledge: about, 23–8

known-groups validity, 125–6, *126t*

Krugman, Dr. Saul, 33–4

Lang, Andrew: on statistics, 256

language usage: about, 75–6, 79; in forms and questionnaires, 38, 50, 122, 179, 254; in IPA analysis, 214–15; in PAR, 237; in rating scales, 127, 128

Lewin, Kurt, 233

Likert scales: about, 181–2, *278t*, 334; examples of use, *83t*, 227, 266, *267t*, 270, 310, 334

linear regression (in statistics), 279

literature review: about, 10–12, 121, 127, 182, 226, 285–92; case study examples of, 71–2, 80, 88, 101–2, 119–20, 145, 165, 169, 197–8, 203, 240, 295, 309, 322–3, 333–4

logic models, 120n3, 127

logical positivism, 234

longitudinal designs, 34, 44–5, 48

mail-out surveys, 185–6

malnourishment experiments (Manitoba), 44

Mann-Whitney U test, 316

margin of error, 259, 260, 261. *See also* errors, types of: sampling

maturation effect: about, *134t*, 136; case study example of, 149

maximum variation (in sampling), 104

Maykut and Morehouse, 212

mean (in statistics), 266

measurement: instruments of, *83t*, 135–6 (*see also* scales); levels of, 83–5, *83t*, 89–90

median (in statistics), 266–8

member checks, *225t*, 226

mental health, case study examples involving, 101–6, 119–29, 274–81

mixed methods research and analysis, 222–8

mode (in statistics), 268

mortality (attrition): about, *134t*, 137; case study examples of, 140, 149, 318–20

multi-item questions, 180–3

multi-item scales, 84, 121, 123, 183, 250–1, 334

multiple-baseline approach, 169

mutual exclusivity: in questions, 177; of categories, 112, 261

narrative analysis, 212

Natural Sciences and Engineering Research Council (NSERC) guidelines, 36, 71–2

needs assessments, 29, 201

negative case analysis, *225t*, 250

negative correlation, 279, *279f*

New York State Department of Mental Hygiene (US), 34

Newton, Sir Isaac: on work of precursors, 11
nominal data, *278t*; about, 83–4, *83t,* 278, *278t*;
    case study examples of, 270, 280, 316, 334
nominal definition, 81, 82
non-empirical validity testing, 124–5
non-equivalent comparison group designs
    (comparison group pre-test-post-test
    designs): about, 147–8; case study example
    of, 148
non-equivalent control group designs, 138
non-probability sampling: about, 103–4, *103t*;
    convenience (accidental), 103, *103t*; purpo-
    sive, 103, *103t*; quota, *103t,* 104; snowball,
    103t, 104
non-proportional stratified random sampling,
    93–4, *97t*
normal distribution curve (normal curve, bell
    curve), in statistics, 258–9, *258f,* 261
normalizing questions, 183–4, *184f*
null hypothesis (in statistics), 277, 279–80

observation, persistent, 225, *225t*
observation, selective, 25
observation phases. *See* baseline phases
Office for Human Research Protection (US),
    45
Olivieri, Dr. Nancy, 54–5
ontology, 24, 27
open coding, 211
open-ended (single-item) questions, 178, *178f,*
    199, 201–2, 250; case study examples of,
    227, 254–5, 296
operationalization: about, 81, *82t,* 83, 119;
    case study example of, 79–85
ordinal data, *278t*; about, *83t,* 84, 270, 278,
    278t; case study examples of, 316, 334
overgeneralization, 25

p value (in statistics), 277, 280
PAR (participatory action research). *See*
    participatory action research (PAR)
paradigms: about, 22–3

participation, voluntary, 49–50. *See also*
    consent, informed
participatory action research (PAR): about,
    233–8, 244; process of, *235f,* 240–1; case
    study examples of, 68–76, 230–44
Pearson's *r* (in statistics), 279
Pedagogy of the Oppressed (Freire), 233
peer debriefing, *225t,* 226
persistent observation, 225, *225t*
phenomenology, 206
pilot projects: case study examples of, 88–99,
    108–17
politics: case study example involving, 256–62
population parameters, 91, 105
positive correlation, 279, *279f*
positivism, logical, 234
post-positivism, 223
praxis, 234
pre-test–post-test control group designs,
    135–6, 138, 146–7
pre-testing: interview schedules, 199; question-
    naires, 176–7, 251; scales, 128
precision. *See* measurement: levels of
predatory journals, 286–7
predictive validity, 125, *126t*
probability, in statistics, 261, 279–80
probability sampling: about, 92–4, *96–8t,*
    258; cluster, 94, *97–8t*; non-proportional
    stratified, 93–4, *97t*; proportional strati-
    fied random, 93, *97t*; simple random, 92–3,
    96t; systematic random, 93, *96t*; case study
    example of, 88–99
problem, defining. *See* research questions,
    establishing
program evaluation, 141–2
prolonged engagement, 225, *225t*
proportional stratified random sampling, 93,
    97t
psychometrics: rating scales for, 121–8, 182–3;
    case study example of, 119–29
psychosocial variables, 84, 126
purposive sampling, 103, *103t*

qualitative analysis, 211–19; framework for critiquing, 289–90

qualitative research: challenges of, 211; compared with quantitative research, 223–5, *224t, 225t*; data collection in, 121–2, 200–3; in feminist research, 239; five approaches to, 204–6; focus groups (*see* focus groups); naturalistic interviewing in, 200–1; questionnaires in, 203, 227, 250; sample sizes in, 104–5, 210; sampling in, 102–5; techniques of, 225–7; case study examples of, 101–6, 209–20, *218–19t*, 294–303

qualitative sampling, 102–5

quantitative analysis: framework for critiquing, 290–2; case study example of, 316–17

quantitative research: compared with qualitative research, 223–5, *224t, 225t*; data collection in, 176–86, 250–3, 313–15; data presentation in, 257–62; questionnaires in, 176–86, 227, 250–3; sample sizes in, 91, 104; sampling in, 90–7; structured interviewing in, 198–200; validity issues in, 134–5; case study examples of, 79–85, 88–99, 108–17, 119–29, 132–42, 309–29

quantitative sampling, 90–7

quasi-experimental designs: about, 138, 147–8; case study examples of, 144–9, 309–29

questionnaires, 171–93; administering, 185–6, 251–2; client satisfaction, 250–3; completion instructions, 184–5; designing, 122, 183–5; language usage in, 122, 179, 254; mixed methods, 250–3; multi-item questions in, 180–3; qualitative, 203, 227, 250; quantitative, 176–86, 227; question development for, 122, 176, 177–80; return rates (RRs) of, 174–5, 185, 251; self-constructed, 192; steps in developing, 176–7; surveys, 185–6, 191–2; case study examples of, *172–3f, 187–8f, 188–91f*, 204, *252f, 252–3f*. *See also* interviews

questions: ambiguous, 178, *178f*, 179; answerability of, 179–80; bias in, 179, *179f*, 262; contingency, 184, *185f*, 198; double-barrelled, 179–80; fixed-alternative (single-item), 177–8, *177f*; matrix format, 184, *184f*, 297; multi-item, 180–3, *181f*; normalizing, 183–4, *184f*; open-ended (single-item), 178, *178f*; for research (*see* research questions, establishing); sequence of, 183–4

quota sampling, *103t,* 104

racism: case study example involving, 21–30

randomized control trials (RCTs): about, 147; case study examples of, 147, 275, 280

range (in statistics), 268

rating scales, 121–8

ratio-level data: about, *83t*, 84, *278t*, 334; examples of, 280, 316

RCTs (randomized control trials), 147

recall bias, 251–2

referential adequacy, *225t,* 226

reflection: in case-based learning, 6–7

reflexive journal, *225t,* 226

regression, statistical. *See* statistical regression

Relaxation and Prevention (RAP) scale, 133

reliability (of data), 121–4, 199–200. *See also* validity (of data)

replication (of outcomes), 155, 157

representativeness (of samples): about, 90–2, 139, 174, 192, 258, 288; case study examples of, 95, 260

RERCs (research ethics review committees). *See* research ethics review committees (RERCs)

research: abuses of, 27; categories of, 29–30; feminist, 238–40; harmful (*see* harm); identifying purpose of, 8–9; ideographic, 166; literature review in, 10–12, 285–92; social workers and, 13–14, *14t*

research, collaborative. *See* participatory action research (PAR)

research, descriptive. *See* descriptive research

research, evaluation of: about, 285–7; steps in, 287–9; frameworks for, 289–92; case study examples of, 305–8, 332–8 research, explanatory, 29

research, exploratory. *See* exploratory research

research, feminist. *See* feminist research

research, mixed methods, 224–5, 228

research, qualitative. *See* qualitative research

research, qualitative and quantitative compared, 223–5, *224t, 225t*

research, quantitative. *See* quantitative research

research analysis. *See* analysis

research design. *See* experimental designs; longitudinal designs; quasi-experimental designs; single-case study designs

research ethics. *See* ethics

research ethics review committees (RERCs): about, 45; case study examples of, 48–9, 54, 59–60, 295

research ethics submissions. *See* ethics submission forms

research hypothesis (in statistics), 277

research paradigms: logical positivism, 234; praxis, 234

research process: about, 7–8, 12; steps in, 8–13, *8t, 17–18t,* 17–20

research questions, establishing, 9, 12–13; case study examples of, 28, 174, 223

researcher reactivity, 200

response rates, 171, 174–5, 185, 191–2, 199, 251

response set bias, 181–2

reverse coding, 181–2

Rosenberg Self-Esteem Scale (Rosenberg, 1965), *83t*

sample selection: case study examples of, 65–6, 311–12

sample size: about, 91, 104–5, 210, 278, 280; calculator, 105, 260; case study examples of, 274–81, 314, 318, 337, 338. *See also* representativeness (of samples); single-case study designs

sample standard deviation formula, 268

sample statistic, 90–1

samples (as units of analysis), 90

sampling: bias, 91–2, 94–5, 314, 326; errors, 90–1, 93, 258, 259, 280; frames, 92–4, *96–8t,* 105, 335; non-probability, 102–4, *103t;* probability, 92–4, *96–8t,* 258–9; qualitative, 102–5; quantitative, 90–2

Scale of Social Isolation, *181t*

scales: about, 84, 121–8, 270; multi-item, 84, 121, 123, 182–3, 250–1, 334; pre-testing, 128. *See also* measurement: instruments of

scales, specific types: Affect Balance Scale (Bradburn, 1969), *83t;* BASIS-32, 133; Beck depression scale, 133; Centre for Epidemiologic Studies Depression Scale (Radloff, 1977), *83t;* Child Behaviour Checklist (CBCL), 313–14, 334; Client Satisfaction Questionnaire (CSQ-8), 251, *252–3f;* Family Environmental Scale (Moos & Moos, 1994), *83t;* General Health Questionnaire (Goldberg, 1978), *83t;* Goal Attainment Scale (GAS), 167–8, *167t;* Hamilton Anxiety Rating Scale, 121; Hollingshead Four Factor Index of Social Status, 313, 334; JAREL Spiritual Well-Being Scale (*see* JAREL Spiritual Well-Being Scale); Likert scales (*see* Likert scales); Relaxation and Prevention (RAP), 133; Rosenberg Self-Esteem Scale (Rosenberg, 1965), *83t;* Scale of Social Isolation, *181t;* Social Stability Scale (Skinner, 1981), *83t*

scientific knowledge, 26

screening process (sample), 65–6

search conferences: about, 241; case study example of, 242–3

selection bias: about, *134t,* 135, 139, 275; case study examples of, 140, 149

selection-treatment interaction: about, *134t;* case study examples of, 140, 149

selective coding, 211

selective observation, 25

self-reporting Likert scale, 83, *83t*

setting-treatment interaction: about, *134t,* 139; case study examples of, 140, 149 sexism. *See* feminist research

simple random sampling, 92–3, *96t*

single-case study designs: AB, 155–7; ABA, 157–9, *158f,* 161; about, 155, 160; additional, 159–60; B-Only, 157–8; BAB, 168; case study examples of, 152–62, 164–9

single-subject research designs. *See* single-case study designs

snowball sampling, *103t,* 104

Social Sciences and Humanities Research Council (SSHRC), 36, 71–2, 231

Social Stability Scale (Skinner, 1981), *83t*

social work: in today's context, 7–8, 224, 244

social work students: case study example involving, 265–72

social workers: ethical obligations of, *14t,* 265; research-related roles of, 13, 14, *14t.* case study example involving, 222–8

sources, original, 105

standard deviation (in statistics): about, 261, 268; calculating, 268–70; sample formula, 268

standard score (*z* score), in statistics, 261–2

statistical power (probability levels), 279–80

statistical regression: about, *134t,* 136; case study example of, 149

statistics: about, 256–62; probability sampling in, 258–9; terminology of, 261–2; types of, 257–8; case study example of use, 260, 267–70

statistics, descriptive. *See* descriptive statistics

statistics, inferential. *See* inferential statistics

stratified random sampling, 93–4, *97t*

students: case study examples involving, 171–93, 265–72

surveys: about, 191–2; electronic, 186; mail-out, 185–6. *See also* questionnaires

systematic random sampling, 93, *96t*

systemic distortion, 124–6

t test (in statistics), 278, 281, 316–17, 319

target behaviour, 155–6, 158, 159, 160, 167

teleological ethics, 52–3, *53t*

temporal ordering (of variables), 115, 135

terminology, 76, 79

test-retest reliability, 123

testing (or initial measurement) effect: about, *134t,* 136; case study examples of, 140, 149

theory development (induction), 110–11

theory testing (deduction), 111

thick description, *225t,* 226

time series designs, 148, 155–6

time-order ambiguity (causal time order): about, *134t,* 135; case study example of, 149

transferability, in qualitative research, 203, *225t*

Tri-Council Policy Statement on Ethical Conduct for Research Involving Humans, 38–9

triangulation, 169, *225t,* 226, 250

Tuskegee syphilis experiment, 44–5

type I and type II errors (in statistics), 279–80

UN Convention on the Rights of the Child, 57, 209

United Nations Centre for Human Rights: on social work, 33

units of analysis, 89–90

universe (of elements), 90

validity (of data), 124–6; concurrent, 125, *126t;* construct, 125–6, *126t,* 192; content, 124–5, *126t,* 192; convergent, 126, *126t;* criterion-related, 125–6, *126t,* 192; discriminant, 126, *126t;* divergent construct, 126; face, 124, *126t;* known-groups, 125–6, *126t;* predictive, 125, *126t;* of self-constructed questionnaires, 192; threats to, *134t,* 135–8, 139, 149

validity (of data), external. *See* external validity

validity (of data), internal. *See* internal validity

validity, establishing: empirical approach, 125–6; non-empirical approach, 124–5

Vancouver Injection Drug Use Study, 48, 54

vanity presses, 287
variable relationships, 113–15, 135; causation in, 115; curvilinear, 114–15, *116f*; negative (inverse), 114, *115f*; positive, *114f*
variables: in experimental designs, 146–7, 156; in questionnaire design, 178, 180–3; in statistics, 257, 258, 278–9; types of, 112–13

Willowbrook hepatitis A experiments, 33–4, 43–4
withdrawal (reversal) study designs, 159
workplaces: case study example involving, 79–85

z score (standard score), in statistics, 261–2
Zhang and Wildemuth, 213